HOW POPULAR CULTURE DESTROYS OUR POLITICAL IMAGINATION

How Popular Culture Destroys Our Political Imagination: Capitalism and Its Alternatives in Film and Television explores the representations of capitalism, the state, and their alternatives in popular screen media texts.

Acknowledging the problems that stem systemically from capitalism and the state, this book investigates an often-overlooked reason why society struggles to imagine alternative economic and political systems in our neoliberal age: popular culture. The book analyzes 455 screen media texts in search of critiques and alternative representations of these systems and demonstrates the ways in which film and television shape the way we collectively see the world and imagine our political futures. It suggests that popular culture is the answer to the question of why it is easier to imagine the end of the world than the end of capitalism.

Contributing to the areas of sociology, media studies, and utopian studies, this book provides insights into the topic of popular culture and politics in a theoretically informed and entertaining manner. The book will be useful to both students and scholars interested in these topics, as well as activists and organizers seeking to make the world a better place.

Eugene Nulman is Associate Professor of Sociology at the Università degli Studi di Firenze in Florence, Italy. He has previously worked at the Scuola Normale Superiore in Florence, Italy and at Birmingham City University in Birmingham, UK. He has written on the subject of popular culture and society and social movements, with a focus on climate activism. He is the author of the books *Coronavirus Capitalism Goes to the Cinema* (2021) and *Climate Change and Social Movements: Civil Society and the Development of National Climate Change Policy* (2015). He has published academic work in journals such as *Third World Quarterly, Media, Culture and Society, Journal of Youth Studies,* and *Environmental Politics*.

HOW POPULAR CULTURE DESTROYS OUR POLITICAL IMAGINATION

Capitalism and Its Alternatives in Film and Television

Eugene Nulman

LONDON AND NEW YORK

Designed cover image: Shutterstock

First published 2025
by Routledge
4 Park Square, Milton Park, Abingdon, Oxon OX14 4RN

and by Routledge
605 Third Avenue, New York, NY 10158

Routledge is an imprint of the Taylor & Francis Group, an informa business

© 2025 Eugene Nulman

The right of Eugene Nulman to be identified as author of this work has been asserted in accordance with sections 77 and 78 of the Copyright, Designs and Patents Act 1988.

All rights reserved. No part of this book may be reprinted or reproduced or utilised in any form or by any electronic, mechanical, or other means, now known or hereafter invented, including photocopying and recording, or in any information storage or retrieval system, without permission in writing from the publishers.

Trademark notice: Product or corporate names may be trademarks or registered trademarks, and are used only for identification and explanation without intent to infringe.

British Library Cataloguing-in-Publication Data
A catalogue record for this book is available from the British Library

ISBN: 978-1-032-84772-6 (hbk)
ISBN: 978-1-032-84770-2 (pbk)
ISBN: 978-1-003-51491-6 (ebk)

DOI: 10.4324/9781003514916

Typeset in Sabon
by Newgen Publishing UK

To my wife, Francesca

CONTENTS

Lists of Figures	ix
List of Tables	x
Acknowledgments	xii
Introduction	1
1 Neoliberalism, TINA, and the *Titanic* Effects	11
2 Research Methods	38
3 Eight Limited Critiques of Capitalism and the State: Mapping the Terrain	52
4 Representations of Evil: A Cinematic Anthropology of Villains	74
5 Structural Critiques of Capitalism in Film and Television: Mr. Moneybags and the Hidden Abode	102
6 Representations of Crises, Colonialism, and Consumerism: Fat Cats, Starving Dogs, and Tulip Bulbs	123
7 Transferable Radicalness: Alternative Lifestyles in Film and Television	148

viii Contents

8   Radical Resistance in *The Lego Movie*: The Building
     Blocks of Utopia   172

9   Utopian Conclusions: Yesterday, Today, and
     Tomorrowland   196

Appendix: Films/Television Programs Analyzed   226
Index   242

FIGURES

0.1	Illustration by Gaily Ezer	xi
2.1	Film and Television Releases (2010–2022)	39
2.2	Number of Screen Media Texts Analyzed Organized by Year and Type	45
4.1	Indeed.com job Searches for "Stockbroker" Before and After the Release of *The Wolf of Wall Street* in the United States and United Kingdom	91

TABLES

2.1	Types of Political Films Suggested by Dimensions of Content and Intent	40
3.1	Examples of The Good, The Bad, and The Ugly Critique	56
3.2	Examples of The Counterbalanced Critique	58
3.3	Examples of The Reformable Critique	59
3.4	Examples of The Least-Worst System Critique	60
3.5	Examples of The Obscured Critique	61
3.6	Examples of The Overlooked Critique	63
3.7	Examples of The Historicized Critique	64
3.8	Examples of The Overreaching Critique	66

FIGURE 0.1 Illustration by Gaily Ezer

ACKNOWLEDGMENTS

This book was a product of fusion. Two of my passions, politics and film, came together in an attempt to understand the lack of radical vision and utopian desires in contemporary society. The question is an important one that has been discussed by many radical scholars and activists who seek to understand why challenges to our systems have been so few and far between. Personally, this question became meaningful after some years of political activism as an undergraduate student. I realized that my interest in positive social change was not shared by many even when they were introduced to the arguments and despite the fact that they could not really provide a counterargument. It was not merely that people were not exposed to the idea that there are systemic flaws in the structures under which we live, such as capitalism and the state – the systems this book focuses on; it was not merely that people could be convinced that such problems existed and could be solved through a change in the systems. Instead, it seemed that social idleness was related to a lack of collective political imagination.

Despite this, as activists (and activist scholars) we continue to try our best and do what we can to stimulate critical social dialogue, activate others, push for non-reformist reforms, and the like. But the deeper problem remains (and showed up in my previous academic work). During my years of activism, a large number of people helped me think through these questions in a wide range of ways. There are too many to name them all, but I want to give a shoutout to some people who I believe to be particularly important in this process: Gaily Ezer, Rudy, Joaquin Cienfuegos, Ellen Frieboes, Jake Myrie, Anita Sarkeesian, Jake Gelender, and all the folks who made up SCAF, Progressive Alliance, Anti-War on the World, and Berkeley Copwatch.

While I was interested in the question of why it is easier to imagine the end of the world than the end of capitalism as we know it – and beyond that of the state, white supremacy, patriarchy, etc. – I did not come across a compelling argument until I had the opportunity to teach Sociology of the Media over a number of years at Birmingham City University. The course, taught to second year undergraduate students, enabled me to engage in questions of popular culture and their interaction with society. With the students I explored the role of film, television, music, and social media in a neoliberal age. I am indebted to the university and my colleagues for my time there, but I am also indebted to those students who raised questions and prompted further discussion about the topic. The preparation for the module and the discussions that occurred during it eventually led to the idea of this book.

Once I took on the task of writing the book, it goes without saying that the most important source of support in the process was my wife. Not only did she have to endure my media consumption which was an absolute requirement for the book (she was often also forced to watch things she had no interest in because "I need it for the book"), but she sustained me throughout the process. I was assisted in early drafts of the book by a number of people through discussions on the topic, suggestions for films and television shows, and reading through draft chapters. These included (in alphabetical order) Alex Murray, Alex Norman, Andy Brogan, Bekah Everett, Charles Devellennes, Chris Chang, Edward Martin, Ina Freisen, Kehinde Andrews, Kirsten Forkert, Loraine Bussard, Nas, Peter, Phil Cattani, Tom Corbett, and Yana Bezirganova. I also had additional suggestions for screen media texts, even if I was unable to chase up every lead (sorry), from Ajay Parasram, Alan Bolwell, Alexandre Christoyannopoulos, Andrew Salerno-Garthwaite, Barbara Franchi, Brandon D. Eisenberg, Fahid Qurashi, Heather Alberro, Jess Windsor, Jodie Satterley, Kristina Krause, Michael A. McCarthy, Nathan Murthy, Nitasha Kaul, Rhiannon Lockley, Rob Turner, Rosie Narayan, Sarah Mills, Silvia Mattaliano, Toby Pengelly, and Vince Miller. My sincerest apologies if I've left anyone out.

Some of the most important help I received was from an undergraduate student at Birmingham City University, Anna-Symone Bateman. Anna-Symone was a fantastic student in the Department of Psychology. Her excellent performance made her eligible for the Volunteer Research Assistantship program that was offered in the School of Social Sciences which enabled undergraduates to gain research experience and insight into the research process by participating in a project. I am not sure how this is a reward for good performance, but I certainly hope that she got something of value from the experience. I may be wrong, but I believe Anna-Symone chose to work on my project. She must have had very limited options or there was a clerical error, but I am very thankful she ended up being assigned to my

xiv Acknowledgments

project. She read each of the draft chapters I had at the time and provided useful feedback on the clarity and content of the work. She saved me from a number of embarrassing spelling errors (any that do appear are my fault) and she really ensured that the writing was clear (or at least much clearer than it had been). Later drafts were read through by Phil Cattani who also was hugely helpful in copyediting my book proposal. Without his help you may not be reading this now.

Of course, none of this would be possible without my parents and grandparents. Regardless of which of the two passions prevailed they were always there to support me. Finally, I would like to thank my editor, Simon Bates, the staff at Routledge, especially Lakshita Joshi, Sue Cope, and Francesca Tohill, and the peer reviewers for all their encouragement and helpful comments.

INTRODUCTION

But most important, congratulations to all the [Screen Actors Guild (SAG)] members, both here today and everywhere .... You survived the longest strike in our union's history with courage and conviction ... [which] resulted in an historic billion-dollar deal. Your solidarity ignited workers around the world, triggering what forever will be remembered as the Hot Labor Summer. You took the hero's journey and stood at the front lines, strike captains led the march on the picket lines, and we all showed up to the rallies because you understood what our massive contribution means .... AI will entrap us in a matrix where none of us know what's real .... Dystopia stories can also become self-fulfilling prophecy. We should tell stories that spark the human spirit ... Collectively, the paradigm will shift towards peace and harmony.

(Fran Drescher, SAG President Speech
at the 30th Screen Actors Guild Awards,
February 25, 2024)

What if I told you that the problems of war, poverty, and exploitation continue to plague us because of the films and television shows we have watched? It is not about the violence or lack of family values that we find in popular culture. Instead, I want to argue that it is the (almost) complete lack of radical alternatives that we are presented with that enables the systems of power to continue to cause great harm. Many, from Greta Thunberg to Noam Chomsky, have argued that our economic and political systems must be radically changed in order to stop the systematic oppression that devastates the globe. Increasingly, more and more scholars, activists, and public intellections are connecting the problems of our times with structural

DOI: 10.4324/9781003514916-1

2 Introduction

aspects of the world we live in, particularly the systems of capitalism and the state. We are seeing rising economic inequalities, risks of pandemics, problems from climate change, threats in the form of artificial intelligence (AI), etc. Some of these problems run extinction level risks and each of these are increasingly being understood as problems that cannot be easily solved in isolation because they are parts of the wider consequences of capitalism and the state.[1] Organizing the production and distribution of goods through capitalism and organizing decision-making and control through states structurally produces a myriad of problems including exploitation, poverty, and world wars. These systems have also weaponized and even helped to construct differences around race, gender, sex, sexuality, and ability as an integral part of their structures. They have constructed formal and informal hierarchies of various forms, amassing power and wealth for a select few.

Many books explain the key problems of these systems and why simple reforms cannot be applied to solve them.[2] As critiques of these systems continue to expand, one major problem keeps arising: we cannot really imagine the world without capitalism or the state. If we cannot imagine the world without these, why would we replace them? This book argues that these oppressive systems persist because our political imaginations are hampered, and that our imaginations are hampered primarily because of our popular culture.

In many ways, the epigraph – taken from Fran Drescher's speech at the 2024 SAG Awards – speaks to this thesis. In 2023, Hollywood was at the center of grassroots political action and workers' struggle. Their efforts sparked a flame across workers in the United States. That summer, hotel workers, United Parcel Service (UPS) Teamsters, and United Auto Workers joined screen actors and the Writers Guild of America in holding major strike actions. This was paralleled by worker confrontations with employers and union organizing at Starbucks, Amazon, and Uber. Hollywood was at the heart of a fight against a heartless urge to extract more and more profit from workers, going so far as to effectively steal their identity and let AI work in their place. It is no accident that Drescher described AI as entrapping us "in a matrix where none of us knows what's real". "Matrix" only really makes sense in this context if we think about the widespread cultural imprint left by the film *The Matrix* (1999) in which the protagonist finds out that AI has taken over society and reproduced humans as an energy source. To sustain this energy source, however, the machines needed to plug humans into a virtual reality – the world as we know it. In her speech, Drescher is warning of a future AI that was built only through the imagination birthed out of these cinematic representations. In her role as a union president she is not only talking about the importance of the material struggle of strikes, pay, and exploitation; she is also speaking to the symbolic struggle in which their labor as actors is used. She is effectively arguing that the *messages* in popular culture have political consequences.

The messages in popular culture and its political consequences are what this book is about, and it reflects on similar ideas posed by the SAG President. This book attempts to answer the question of why it is easier to imagine the end of the world than the end of capitalism in a simple way, although in a manner that leads to more questions, as almost every answer does. It is easy to imagine the end of the world because we have seen it in film and television many times and we find it hard to imagine the end of capitalism because we almost never see it in popular culture. This book is about politics and popular culture. It interrogates films and television programs that have political content to see the ways in which capitalism and the state are critiqued and the alternatives that are presented.

A substantial amount has been written on the subject of politics and culture generally and on film and television – or what I will refer to as 'screen media texts' – in particular. However, most other discussions on this topic fit different kinds of analysis from the one I will present. One set of research explores radical artistic work that both challenges viewers with its content and its form and usually does not include a lot of mainstream *popular* culture.[3] Analysis of art cinema's political content fits this set but, as Alex Lykidis writes, art cinema "tends to ask different questions of its audience; not the straightforward narrative questions of Hollywood genre films".[4] Though still marginal, we can expect to find more content critical of capitalism and the state to come out of screen media texts that are more independent, but at the same time they will often have less of a reach in terms of audience and thus less of a wider cultural impact.[5] (Why these texts don't go viral is a worthy research question in itself as our current media systems enable the consumption of a range of texts from inside or outside the Hollywood production and distribution system.) Because of their layers of complexity, analysis of the politics of art films tends to be examined allegorically, requiring a complex method of analysis which likely does not capture the more surface-level perspective with which most audiences approach screen media content. Such allegorical readings can also be applied to mainstream films. For example, in *Reelpolitik Ideologies in American Political Film*, Beverly Merrill Kelley is interested in exploring a wide variety of ideologies as presented through (usually older) film, often requiring allegorical analysis of the content rather than a more surface-level reading[6] such as her interpretation of *The Godfather* (1972) as a fascist film. Although fascism is never discussed in the film, the author argues that the film romanticizes the Mafia and a particular moral structure which she interprets as fascist. Others have more complex readings, such as those that rely on psychoanalytic theory.[7]

4 Introduction

Another area of research on the subject of politics and popular culture interprets films and television programs within contemporary or historical political situations and contexts in a wide variety of ways. One example is the way that Milo Sweedler brilliantly allegorizes the film *Children of Men* (2006) as a mirror of contemporary globalization in his book *Rumble and Crash*.[8] Jameson's dialectical approach, which places the historical location of a text as a central element of analysis, is another example.[9] Other texts use film and/or television primarily to explain other subjects to its audience. For example, Ronnie D. Lipschutz's book *Political Economy, Capitalism, & Popular Culture* critically explores the political economy – everything from junk bonds to alienation – using the content of films as examples.[10] Some of the literature explores how the particularities of the politics and economics of Hollywood or other major systems of popular cultural production affect the popular culture we consume, including their political messages, such as *The Political Economy of Hollywood: Capitalist Power and Cultural Production*.[11] In such research, the questions focus on how politics and economics shape popular culture, rather than how popular culture shapes politics and economics. Where research does ask some questions about popular culture's political implications, they are usually more interested in looking at specific policy areas or impacts – such as looking at the representations of a particular war or the effects of media exposure on views of environmentalism – than in the radical questions of systemic critique.[12]

The approach taken in this book is somewhat different from the literature discussed above because it looks at mainstream American popular screen media texts and explores their explicit political content (broadly defined to include questions of economics) with a look toward structural critiques of political and economic systems as well as representations of their alternatives. The book is focused on seeing to what extent critical representations and their alternatives exist and to reflect on what this means for our collective political imaginations. One may rightfully ask why we would expect to find radical political content in mainstream films produced by capitalists for the purpose of profit-making. There are several important things to mention regarding this critical point. First, previous research has shown the ways in which *some* screen media texts challenge capitalist and state ideologies. Some have argued that popular culture contains a lot of political and even left-leaning content, and that capitalists and businessmen are more likely to be portrayed negatively than positively whereas 'liberals' are presented as good, intelligent, and friendly.[13] Hollywood itself is often labelled as being on the left. Second, while explicit radical political content may be less prominent, there is nothing inherently radical about presenting alternative societies or ways of living. From a purely surface-level perspective, these representations would not be a critique of our systems but simply an exploration of something

Introduction **5**

else. Such representations of the 'other' are often found in science fiction and fantasy screen media texts. Third, Lenin is said to have written "the capitalists will sell us the rope with which we will hang them" because it is argued that capitalism simply responds to market demands and that it even enables market interactions to occur that ultimately undermine capitalism.[14] In the case of popular culture, we could argue that capitalists want money from their investments more than they care about the ideological content of the works they invest in. If it has an audience, they will produce it. If a director, actor, or screenwriter has a following, they may be given relatively free rein, and it is possible that these artists do have something critical to say. Finally, as discussed in Chapters 5 and 6 – spoiler alert! – there are a number of screen media texts that include radical political content. What is interesting to note, however, is that far fewer texts present positive alternatives. Rather than radical critiques of capitalism or the state, representing positive alternatives appears to be the line in the sand that mainstream media will rarely let artists cross. This is despite Mazierska noting that cinema – and we can extend this to television – has become increasingly diverse and, referencing Rancière, that screen media is "a site where it is possible to imagine alternatives to the dominant economic and political model".[15]

To make the case that the lack of radical alternative representations plays a large part in reinforcing an ideology that sustains the status quo, this book presents an analysis that cites over 500 film and television programs (including content from streaming services such as Netflix and Prime), most of which present a critique of our current society at some level. I situate my analysis utilizing a wide array of theoretical arguments from diverse academic disciplines. My argument requires me to convince you of several key points:

1) ideology is central to why systems that cause economic, social, and environmental harms continue to exist;
2) part of that ideology is that we don't have to like the system we have, as long as we don't believe that a better system is possible;
3) popular culture plays an important role in constructing our ideology and, therefore, it is important to understand how popular cultural texts represent capitalism, the state, and their alternatives;
4) although a substantial subset of films and television series present critiques of our current economic and political systems, most are *limited critiques* and few actually develop a radical critique that calls for the system to be replaced;
5) although there are a number of screen media texts that do present a radical critique, rarely are any alternatives offered;
6) even alternative lifestyles are rarely represented in a positive way in popular culture;

6 Introduction

7) when there are positive representations of lifestyle they fail to translate into alternative *politics*;
8) in the few cases where radical critiques and alternative systems are present in a film or television show, a more mainstream and less critical reading of the text will be made readily available. That is, there may be censorship, both overt and self-censorship, when it comes to the popular culture industry to prevent truly radical critiques and alternative representations.

This book hopes to solidify the argument that popular culture's failure to provide us with alternative visions of economic and political systems is perpetuating an ideology that prevents us from realizing a better world. Moreover, the book also wants to highlight the positive examples of film and television texts that do present us with such representations of alternatives and explain why they are so few and far between. But the book would perpetuate this lack of alternative representations if it did not try to provide a solution to the problem at hand, accompanied by its own kind of alternative vision. I hope to accomplish all of this in the following chapters.

To Be Continued ...

Chapter 1, Neoliberalism, TINA, and the *Titanic* Effects, looks at the relationship between popular culture and ideology by tracing some of the thoughts on the subject from Philip Sidney's ideas in the sixteenth century to contemporary scholars, including Fredrik Jameson and Slavoj Žižek, and others in-between, such as György Lukács, Theodor Adorno, and Stuart Hall. The chapter argues that popular culture is politically important but also that it is currently situated in and reproduces the idea that 'There Is No Alternative' – or TINA, for short. This phrase became fundamental to the ideology of neoliberalism which solidified itself as a mainstream political project that reached hegemony through Margaret Thatcher, the prime minister of the United Kingdom from 1979 to 1990. Although the book mostly examines screen media texts made in the United States, the importance of her role in advancing neoliberal ideology is why we start our journey with Thatcher.

Chapter 2 provides details about the research methods undertaken for this book. It looks at which screen media texts were selected to analyze, why, and how that analysis took place. The data obtained in the process serves as the basis for the examples and theorizing in subsequent chapters. The central objective of Chapter 3 is to acknowledge that there are a substantial number of media texts that are critical of the state or capitalism while simultaneously pointing out that the overwhelming majority of these texts present rather limited critiques of these systems. The critiques are limited in several ways and a given text can depict multiple limited critiques. The chapter identifies eight different ways in which the critiques are limited:

1) the good, the bad, and the ugly critique;
2) the counterbalanced critique;
3) the reformable critique;
4) the least-worst system critique;
5) the obscured critique;
6) the overlooked critique;
7) the historicized critique;
8) the overreaching critique.

Each of these critiques is explained in detail and film and television programs that contain these limited critiques are noted, along with examples.

Chapter 4 explores how villains that represent capitalist and state systems are portrayed in screen media texts in order to demonstrate how our culture of encoding and decoding texts may prevent us from reading them in a critical or radical way. In particular, Chapter 4 argues that the representation of the villain often creates a space in which they embody evil. That is, rather than representing the problem as being systemic, the problem is individualized. Similarly, when screen media texts attempt a critique using an anti-hero who represents the problem with an existing institution, our culture of consuming media often pressures us to sympathize with and take the perspective of that anti-hero which ultimately undermines the critique.

While politically neutral or conservative texts heavily outnumber texts that are critical, and the texts with limited critiques outnumber texts with *radical* critiques, Chapters 5 and 6 want to shine a light on the positive examples. Chapter 5 puts the focus on films and television shows that represent some of the problems with capitalism as identified in Karl Marx's *Capital: Volume I*. Primarily, the chapter looks at the problems of surplus-value, alienation, and the profit motive. Chapter 6 looks at examples of radical representations that concern capitalism's cyclical nature of boom and bust that inevitably impoverishes many people. The state is also complicit in this problem as capitalism relies on the state to do its bidding. Examples of screen media texts that demonstrate neocolonialism are also identified, along with texts that point out the problems of commodity fetishism. Looking across screen media texts that contain radical critiques, the end of Chapter 6 shows that only a few actually present a positive vision and, when they do, those positive visions are themselves rather limited.

Chapter 7 contends that rather than looking at screen media texts that directly address questions of capitalism and the state, we could look at films and television shows that depict any kind of positive alternative such as alternative family structures and lifestyles. Perhaps if people consume

8 Introduction

such texts, they will be able to transpose these alternatives onto other systems, such as the state and capitalism, and ideologically be open to radical possibilities within those spheres of life. This leads to the concept of *transferable re-transcoding* which will be fully explained in the chapter. While the concept is useful, the data from the texts concerning alternative relationships and lifestyles leads to an unfortunate conclusion: there are few texts that depict such alternatives positively and even those that do do not often align politically when directly addressing questions concerning the state or capitalism, thus undermining their transferability. More generally, we should be aware that counternormative representations that do not directly tackle the fundamental political and economic institutions can become incorporated into the capitalist ideological structures, removing anything that may be directly damaging to itself and thus undermining the potential of radical transferable re-transcoding.

Chapter 8 finds a positive example of both a radical critique and a representation of an alternative in the unlikely form of *The Lego Movie* (2014). Not only does the chapter explore the various radical arguments made in the film but it also seeks to understand the ways in which the film masks its own ideology and prevents it from being explicitly radical. It is possible that only through such camouflage could radical representations be offered on the big or small screen. The book concludes with Chapter 9, Utopian Conclusions: Yesterday, Today, and Tomorrowland, which points to a film that in its narrative makes a very similar argument to this book. *Tomorrowland* (2015) blames the media for creating its own feedback loop of negativity that would eventually lead to global destruction if it were not for the heroes of the film, which, like *The Lego Movie*, identify the community as the vehicle for radical change. Other representations of such 'utopian' communities are discussed and critiqued, arguing that such representations can either be radical urban 'multitudes' or a form of conservative communalism. In the end, the book provides a potential solution to this problem by suggesting a radical form of screen media creation which not only enables the possibility of radical content but is also in itself an act of prefiguring utopia.

Notes

1 For economic inequalities see e.g., Gottiniaux et al. 2015; for pandemics, see e.g., Davis 2020 and Nulman 2021; for climate change, see e.g., Saito 2023; for AI see e.g., Walton and Nayak 2021.
2 See e.g., Chomsky 2013; Graeber 2011; Wright 2020.
3 For example, Hes 1979; Newton 2019; Mazierska and Kristensen 2022
4 Lykidis 2020, 12.
5 See e.g., Wayne 2001.
6 Kelley 2012, also see Biskind 2018.
7 McGowan 2003.

8 Sweedler 2019; also see Lykidis 2020.
9 E.g. Jameson 2005, also see Burnham 2016.
10 Lipschutz 2010.
11 McMahon 2022.
12 See, e.g., Bryant and Oliver 2009, Biskind 2018.
13 E.g., Groseclose 2011; Mcintosh et al., 2003; Lamer and O'Steen 1997; also see examples in Giglio 2005.
14 See Chapter 8, endnote 50 for greater detail about the origins of this quotation.
15 Mazierska 2018, 10.

References

Biskind, Peter (2018) *The Sky is Falling: How Vampires, Zombies, Androids and Superheroes Made America Great for Extremism*, New York: The New Press.
Bryant, Jennings and Oliver, Mary Beth (eds.) (2009) *Media Effects: Advances in Theory and Research*, 3rd Edition, New York: Routledge.
Burnham, Clint (2016) *Fredric Jameson and The Wolf of Wall Street*, New York: Bloomsbury.
Chomsky, Noam (2013) *On Anarchism*, New York: New Press.
Davis, Mike (2020) 'The Coronavirus Crisis Is a Monster Fueled by Capitalism', in *These Times*, https://inthesetimes.com/article/coronavirus-crisis-capitalism-covid-19-monster-mike-davis.
Giglio, Ernest (2005). *Here's Looking at You: Hollywood Film and Politics*, New York: Peter Lang.
Gottiniaux, Pierre, Munevar, Daniel, Sanabria, Antonio, and Toussaint, Eric (2015) *World Debt Figures 2015*, CADTM.
Graeber, David (2011) *Debt: The First 5,000 Years*, Brooklyn: Melville House.
Groseclose, Tim (2011) *Left Turn: How Liberal Media Bias Distorts the American Mind*, New York: St. Martin's Press.
Hes, John (1979) 'Notes on U.S. Radical Film, 1967–80', *Jump Cut: A Review of Contemporary Media*, 21: 31–35.
Jameson, Fredric (2005) *Archaeologies of the Future: The Desire Called Utopia and Other Science Fictions*, London: Verso.
Kelley, Beverly Merrill (2012) *Reelpolitik Ideologies in American Political Film*, Lanham, MD: Lexington Books.
Lamer, Timothy and O'Steen, Alice Lynn (1997) 'Businessmen Behaving Badly: Prime Time's World of Commerce', *Media Research Center*. http://archive.mrc.org/spe cialreports/1997/sum/sum19970616.asp. Accessed Oct. 10, 2018.
Lipschutz, Ronnie D. (2010) *Political Economy, Capitalism, and Popular Culture*, Lanham, MD: Rowman & Littlefield Publishers.
Lykidis, Alex (2020) *Art Cinema and Neoliberalism*, Cham, Switzerland: Palgrave Macmillan.
Mazierska, Ewa (2018) 'Introduction', in Ewa Mazierska, and Lars Kristensen (eds.) *Contemporary Cinema and Neoliberal Ideology*, New York: Routledge.
Mazierska, Ewa and Kirstensen, Lars (eds.) (2022) *Third Cinema, World Cinema and Marxism*, New York: Bloomsbury Academic.
McGowan, Todd. (2003). 'Looking for the Gaze: Lacanian Film Theory and Its Vicissitudes', *Cinema Journal*, 42(3), 27–47.

McIntosh, William D., Murray, Rebecca M., Murray, John D. and Sabia, Debra (2003) 'Are the Liberal Good in Hollywood? Characteristics of Political Figures in Popular Films from 1945 to 1998, *Communication Reports*, 16(1): 57–67.

McMahon, James (2022) *The Political Economy of Hollywood: Capitalist Power and Cultural Production*, London: Routledge.

Newton, James (2019) *The Anarchist Cinema*, Bristol: Intellect.

Nulman, Eugene (2021) *Coronavirus Capitalism Goes to the Cinema*, Abingdon: Routledge.

Saito, Kohei (2023) *Marx in the Anthropocene: Towards the Idea of Degrowth Communism*, Cambridge: Cambridge University Press.

Sweedler, Milo (2019) *Rumble and Crash: Crises of Capitalism in Contemporary Film*, Albany, NY: State University of New York Press.

Walton, Nigel and Nayak, Bhabani Shankar (2021).' Rethinking of Marxist Perspectives on Big Data, Artificial Intelligence (AI) and Capitalist Economic Development', *Technological Forecasting & Social Change/Technological Forecasting and Social Change*, 166 (May): 120576.

Wayne, Mike (2001) *Political Film: The Dialectics of Third Cinema*, London: Pluto Press.

Wright, Erik Olin (2020) *Envisioning Real Utopias*, London: Verso.

1
NEOLIBERALISM, TINA, AND THE *TITANIC* EFFECTS

On September 15, 1976, 700 businessmen gathered for lunch at the Wentworth Hotel in Sydney, Australia.[1] There was an air of awe and anticipation among the capitalists who awaited the arrival of the guest of honor to the five-star hotel. Speaking to a journalist from the *Daily Telegraph*, one businessman said the honoree was "world class" while another called her "a very great lady". The star of the evening walked in, joining her guests in the lavish mirrored ballroom. It was Mrs. Margaret Thatcher. She had recently been appointed head of the Conservative Party and Leader of the Opposition, and she was three years away from becoming the prime minister of the United Kingdom. With all eyes on her, Thatcher made her way to the podium to deliver a speech which would make history.

Upon arriving at the podium she cleared her throat, perhaps self-conscious of her voice. At that time in her career her speech was considered by critics to be shrill. Her own biographer later described her voice as "the hectoring tones of the housewife".[2] Later, with the help of Laurence Olivier who introduced her to a speech coach at the Royal National Theatre, she would solve this problem and make herself more palatable to a patriarchal society. She didn't need any help making herself more palatable to the capitalist class, however. "I am always very pleased to have the opportunity to talk to businessmen …", she said, going on to spell out the neoliberal position that she became notorious for. Businesses are the creators of wealth and "the politician's role is to set the circumstances in which the wealth-creators—you—can use all your talents to play your chosen role in society".[3] She may as well have said, "The executive of the modern state is but a committee for managing the common affairs of the whole bourgeoisie". This was the succinct description

DOI: 10.4324/9781003514916-2

of the state's role in capitalism written in *The Manifesto of the Communist Party*.[4]

Between the time of Marx and Engels' *Manifesto* and Thatcher's neoliberal government came a type of governance that merged capitalism with state planning. This welfare state, in which the government invested in state-owned housing, transport, and other key industries, was Thatcher's great villain. And in this speech at the Wentworth Hotel, she argued that this type of market interventionism by the state was untenable for capitalism. While the economists advocated Keynesian positions of state intervention in the marketplace in order to limit the damage done by profit-seeking and competition, Thatcher disagreed. She argued that while these policies' observable effects appear to be good, their unseen consequences equate to problems in the long run. She referred to this as the "iceberg effect" where the invisible, larger portion of the iceberg is the long-term problem caused by state interference that was missed by the Keynesian economists.

For Thatcher, there was only one option: we must adopt a neoliberal model of government that would enable the "natural laws" of capitalism to flourish unfettered. Otherwise, we would experience economic decline that would invariably have the same result but with graver consequences.

> It is obvious that if policies are formulated only on the basis of what can be seen immediately and ignore what should be foreseen in the future, the 'iceberg effect' will become the Titanic effect! And who suffers? We all do if we refuse to face reality until it comes face to face with us. Then there is no alternative.[5]

These final four words, "there is no alternative" were to ring out with every electoral success Thatcher's party would go on to experience in 1979 and with every policy Thatcher would go on to pass. These four simple words were to scatter across the globe and infect the politics of countries far and wide. Most notably, these words would also guide the politics of Ronald Reagan and his tenure as president of the United States. "There is no alternative" would outlast Thatcher's (quite long) premiership in the UK and find its way into competing political parties whose calls for even modest government intervention would be replaced by an openly business-friendly approach. This short expression's far-reaching consequences would continue to reverberate after Thatcher died (in 2013), and it is possible that the human species as we know it will die without ever overcoming this belief.

It is possible that Thatcher was correct when she said that within a capitalist system government interventionism can have an iceberg effect that negatively impacts the economy. But we would be remiss to close our eyes to the fact that the state-promoted, profit-over-people form of capitalism that neoliberalism represents has its own *Titanic* effect, with an even larger iceberg.

If Thatcher saw the economic iceberg as a mass of unseen consequences stemming from government intervention, and if her premiere-ship helped to steer clear of that disaster, neoliberalism's path led it straight for the next iceberg. Below the surface of this iceberg lie the many bubbles attributed to the financialization of the economy and the profit-seeking imperative of capitalism.[6] It was this *Titanic* effect that produced the subprime mortgage crisis that started in 2007.

The *Titanic* was frequently invoked at that time: an unsinkable economy that came crashing down.[7] The irony is that such events seemed to be not only foreseeable, but inevitable. The neoliberal economists themselves had lost interest in preventing the busts that accompanied the stock market booms. Concern about economic crashes was for the Keynesians. During the Great Recession many fell into the cold sea of poverty and debt, while some managed to find a place on the few lifeboats available, but all this, according to Marxist economist David Harvey, was part of the neoliberal itinerary. Fundamentally neoliberalism was an ideological game played to bolster the position of capitalists at a time when the welfare state was facilitating modest measures of wealth distribution.[8] It was meant to reassert the dominance of wealth creation for the top 1 percent. To continue the analogy, it is as if the first-class passengers knew they would eventually crash into an iceberg and a few of them may find themselves at the bottom of the sea, but the majority of that elite who continued to survive would only strengthen their positions before and during the collision. They would stroll unperturbed to the lifeboats while the lower classes desperately scrambled to save their lives. (Incidentally, this is only an exaggeration of what actually happened in the case of the *Titanic*. The class of passengers was a strong predictor of survival.[9])

There is a still larger iceberg ahead. One much bigger than any stock market crash. A third reading of the *Titanic* effect. If the iceberg is the economy and above the surface is its readily visible form, then what we see is a wealth of material possessions and the advancement of all sorts of technologies. However, beneath the surface lies the waste that is produced, and the environmental degradation and destruction caused by the extraction, manufacturing, and disposal processes of capitalism. The waste serves no purpose. It is a world within capitalism that represents its contradiction, and one that may bury capitalism in its waste through the tide of climate change – a product of mass production reliant on mass disposal and rampant consumption. This iceberg threatens the Noah's Ark of *Titanics*. A ship containing human life as we know it. This is the unseen iceberg of the climate crisis, an iceberg that ironically is more representative of danger as it melts away.

This *Titanic* effect also holds within it a story of Margaret Thatcher. Thatcher was the first head of government of any country to sound the alarm of climate

14 Neoliberalism, TINA, and the *Titanic* Effects

change. Famously, she made a speech at the second World Climate Conference which was held in Geneva in 1990. She underscored the importance of taking (precautionary) action. Two years prior she had addressed the Royal Society about the issue of climate change, alongside other environmental concerns, but it is less well known that she had raised such concerns about the warming of the planet all the way back in 1979 when she first became prime minister.[10] Just one month after taking office, Thatcher joined the leaders of the other G7 nations in Tokyo where she raised the issue of climate change. The issue was noted in the declaration from the Summit, but it followed a much longer statement on the need to "increase as far as possible coal use, production and trade".[11] Though she was aware of the iceberg, Thatcher did little to stop it and only at the end of her tenure as prime minister did she use her position of power to do something about it. Any reduction in emissions during her time as prime minister was a result of political attacks on unionized coal miners, not a concern for the environment. Her track record as an environmentalist could be summed up by the epithet given to the United Kingdom while she was in charge: "the dirty man of Europe".[12]

If Margaret Thatcher pointed out the *Titanic* effect of government interventions in the marketplace and steered us clear of that iceberg, she found another, even larger iceberg – economic crises – and set a course for a head-on collision. On the way to market crashes, Thatcher warned us of a gigantic iceberg still further ahead, but nevertheless prepared new ships to take the surviving passengers of her own neoliberal disasters on a new crash course. It is as if there really is no alternative. However, it is ironic that Thatcher had originally used the metaphor of the *Titanic* to argue for an economic model in which the social safety net and regulations on businesses were to be removed. The more than 1,500 passenger deaths aboard the *Titanic* were largely a result of poor regulations in which the number of lifeboats required onboard a vessel was based on tonnage rather than the number of passengers. Even before the *Titanic* disaster the regulatory authority had considered changing the rules, but ship-owners had lobbied against this to avoid additional costs.[13] It was the sinking of the *Titanic* that forced the regulators to act.[14]

The Life Energy of Crisis

The phrase "There Is No Alternative" has become very influential. So influential that it has its own abbreviation – TINA. I would argue that while originally a false claim, the four words have become a self-fulfilling prophecy. By believing in their meaning, society develops a consciousness that prevents alternatives from coming into existence. Since Thatcher, commentators have often blamed the failures of the left on our inability to escape the hegemonic grip of the neoliberal ideology.[15] Like the 'extractors' from the Christopher

Nolan film *Inception* (2010), it is as if our common dreams have been infiltrated by neoliberalism and visions of alternatives have been replaced by an acceptance that radical change for the better is impossible. This idea has penetrated our subconscious and left us with only the hope of reforming the jagged edges of capitalism, which represents the worst economic system, except for all the others – ostensibly.

If state intervention in markets creates some problems, the neoliberal alternative creates even bigger problems once a boom turns into a bust. And when the economy crashes, as it has done fairly regularly since neoliberalism took hold in the 1980s, the government – in direct contravention to the neoliberal ideology – intervenes. This happened during the economic crash during the COVID pandemic and then again after the rise in inflation following Russia's full-scale invasion of Ukraine. Such crises create an alternative that neoliberals say does not exist. Certainly, commentators have claimed the death of neoliberalism and the reawakening of state intervention in the economic realm in these moments of crisis.[16] When the economy took a nosedive as a consequence of the subprime mortgage bubble bursting in 2007, commentators called it the collapse of neoliberal orthodoxy. Although some argued that the crisis itself was enough to generate a new consciousness, Slavoj Žižek's intervention held that some would not shift ideologically unless they began to see what the crisis truly meant. The changing of material conditions, he argued, was not enough to overcome our entrenched beliefs. In October 2011, addressing a large crowd at Occupy Wall Street, Žižek's words reverberated through the people's microphone:

> We are not dreamers. We are the awakening from a dream that is turning into a nightmare. We are not destroying anything. We are only witnessing how the system is destroying itself. We all know the classic scene from cartoons. The cat reaches a precipice, but it goes on walking, ignoring the fact that there is nothing beneath this ground. Only when it looks down and notices it, it falls down. This is what we are doing here. We are telling the guys there on Wall Street, "Hey, look down!"[17]

With the benefit of hindsight, we now see that people were perhaps dreamers if they thought the crisis – and our screams to notice the 'failure' of the system – could overcome the TINA mantra. Neoliberalism continued vivaciously afterward. The system did not destroy itself or create its own space for an alternative ideology. If Žižek believed the objective of Occupy was to provide the clarion call, it failed. We cannot expect crises themselves to bring an end to what is fundamentally an ideological issue. If we believe there is no alternative, then any response to a crisis will be more of the same. To get out of this trap requires not a shattering of upward stock market trends, but of our own deeply ingrained ideological positions.

16 Neoliberalism, TINA, and the *Titanic* Effects

Once the dust of a collapse subsides, business as usual returns and no ideological shift away from TINA can be found. Even as the government begins to intervene in the market, we continue to believe that there is no alternative despite seeing an alternative in action. This may be because, in practice, neoliberalism has never really been opposed to state interventions in the marketplace when it serves the interests of capital.[18] During the COVID crisis there were state interventions that helped ordinary people (such as stimulus checks in the United States or furlough schemes in the United Kingdom), but the majority of government intervention is just another bailout of failing businesses while refusing to substantially increase taxation on the skyrocketing wealth of oligopolies.[19] This is not even an alternative to the standard practices of the neoliberal state in better economic contexts, where regular corporate subsidization has led to the now cliché observation that we have capitalism for the poor and socialism for the rich.

Some argue that crises are more than just the unfortunate consequences of deregulated capitalism. "Capitalism", according to Žižek, "is all the time in crisis. This is precisely why it appears almost indestructible. Crisis is not its obstacle. It is what pushes it forwards towards permanent self-revolutionizing, permanent extended self-reproduction."[20] Here, Žižek seems to contradict his earlier point. Rather than crisis actually ending the neoliberal regime, the regular economic downturns we have seen in the era of TINA have only reinvigorated capitalism. When some businesses fail, other businesses expand and fill in the gap left behind. The Great Recession and the COVID pandemic have both shown us how profitable crises can be for some companies. Let us take J.P. Morgan as an example. During the financial crisis that began in 2007, J.P. Morgan swallowed up other banks that were experiencing financial difficulties as a result of the crisis for which these banks were responsible. J.P. Morgan absorbed Bear Stearns and Washington Mutual, eventually becoming the biggest bank in the world by market capitalization. During the COVID pandemic, J.P. Morgan's share prices reached an all-time high of $171.51.[21] For capitalism, crisis is just another opportunity.

The *Titanic* itself was a product of crisis. Following the abolition of the slave trade, ports that earned substantial wealth from the trade – wealth that effectively built the West – were in crisis and had to adjust their businesses to suit the new market. Liverpool, a central hub for its role in the slave trade, went on to host the company that built the *Titanic*[22] as an advanced transportation vehicle that sought to greatly expand travel across the Atlantic at a time when transatlantic commercial aviation was unimaginable. The company, the White Star Line, was owned by J.P. Morgan.[23] Even the wreckage at the bottom of the ocean that was once the great *RMS Titanic* represents an opportunity for capital, at least in a cultural sense. Its story served as the basis for one of the highest grossing films of all time,[24] a film whose own story does not shy away from crisis. The film *Titanic* (1997) follows the personal crisis of Rose (Kate Winslet), a 17-year-old from an upper-class background who is forced into marriage to preserve her family's economic and social status following her father's death. The situation leads her to contemplate suicide, but she is stopped by a young, handsome, working-class man named Jack (Leonardo DiCaprio). They begin a brief love affair that transgresses social norms until the *Titanic* sinks and Jack, having saved Rose, dies of exposure.

Žižek interprets the movie in the myth of Kipling's novel *Captain Courageous* where a wealthy character in crisis is rescued literally and metaphorically by the working classes. For Rose, Jack's function is to "reconstitute her ego".

> It's really a new version of one of the old favorite imperialist myths. The idea being that when the upper-class people lose their vitality, they need a contact with lower classes, basically ruthlessly exploiting them in a vampire-like way, as it were sucking from them the life energy. Revitalized, they can join their secluded upper-class life.[25]

Alternatively, the relationship exposes Rose to the realization that only the working class can engage in "sex-love", the term the socialist philosopher Fredrick Engels used to describe a monogamous marriage based on love rather than a relationship used for climbing the social ladder.[26] In such relationships men and women's desires are put on an equal footing and their bonds are built on their passions rather than their pocketbooks. In this interpretation, the sinking of the *Titanic* did not represent a way of saving Rose the embarrassment of leaving Jack soon after arriving in New York, newly revitalized and ready to return to her noble status. Instead, it suggests that the relationship could have continued, and she would have sacrificed wealth in order to be with him, albeit their romance would not have returned to the peak of its early, dopamine-infused stage. Through Jack's untimely death, the pinnacle of her love was forever immortalized because it was not allowed to survive beyond that chemical moment. In either reading, the iceberg that brings down the *Titanic* preserves Rose, either by allowing her to quickly dispose of Jack now that she has drained him of his lifeblood, or by keeping the memory of a perfect love intact by forbidding its continuation and inevitable (relative) decline. These readings allow crisis to serve a function as it does in capitalism: to revitalize and preserve.

Fear Unhooks the Bra of Capitalism

The relationship of Jack and Rose in this interpretation corresponds to the idea that the iceberg effect of neoliberalism is a planned crash course. This crash course may be avoiding a small iceberg earlier on represented by state intervention in the market, but it plans to crash nonetheless. Why

18 Neoliberalism, TINA, and the *Titanic* Effects

has this become the only possibility for our future, as far as our ideology is concerned? One answer may actually contradict the very question and it relates intimately to the third iceberg: climate crisis. That is to say, there *is* an alternative to capitalism that we do believe is possible but this alternative is crisis itself. Ecological devastation, societal collapse, apocalyptic destruction – these are ideologically almost as ingrained in our conceptions of the future as neoliberalism is in our present. First, it was the nuclear threat, one that is ongoing[27] and brought back in cultural form through the biopic of the creator of the atom bomb in *Oppenheimer* (2023). And now, our future visions are shaped by the severe threats of the climate crisis. But even before the climate crisis we had fantasies of global annihilation in the form of fiction: wars between human and machine, asteroid impacts, judgment day, plagues, pests, and pandemics.

Perhaps the crises of the 'Long Depression',[28] coronavirus, inflation, and war have not shaken our ideas of neoliberalism and its alternatives because we have been primed by fictional representations to imagine the future as crisis. Let us return momentarily to Žižek's speech at Occupy Wall Street.

> In April 2011, the Chinese government prohibited on TV, films, and in novels all stories that contain alternate reality or time travel. This is a good sign for China; it means people still dream about alternatives, so we have to prohibit this dreaming. Here we don't think of prohibition because the ruling history has even oppressed our capacity to dream. Look at the movies that we see all the time. It's easy to imagine the end of the world — an asteroid destroying all of life, and so on — but we cannot imagine the end of capitalism.[29]

Imagine the end of the world. It's easy if you try. We have seen it presented on film and television countless times. From *A Quiet Place* to *Zombieland*[30] and everything in between. The classics of *The Terminator* and *The Matrix* films represent[31] the action genre's apocalypse where science fiction provides a landscape where a hero ultimately defeats an enemy and prevents disaster or saves the few lives that remain. There is also of course the horror genre wherein the likes of *Bird Box* (2018), *Night of the Living Dead* (1968), and *Cloverfield* (2008) provide a series of frights that accompany the end of the world and terrorize its survivors. There is also the earth-destroying comedy sub-genre with the amazing *Dr Strangelove* (1964), *This is the End* (2013) and *The World's End* (2013) serving as excellent examples. We have seen the end of life as we know it enough times to have a vivid idea of what it might entail.

These fictional accounts of our possible future are artistic conclusions of our present state of being. With the state's development of and threat to

Neoliberalism, TINA, and the *Titanic* Effects **19**

use nuclear weapons, it is understandable why the cultural industry would develop representations of a nuclear holocaust. And with capitalism's constant demand for expansion (what Žižek described as "a strange religious structure" of the need to multiply itself at the expense of lives and nature),[32] it is no surprise we see regular representations of natural disasters leading to extinction-level events. The dark sides of real-life capitalism and of the state also serve as the very basis for the visible representations of these fictional apocalyptic futures. We can see it in the post-industrial capital flight that devastated cities across the United States, in failed enterprises such as Disney's dilapidated River Country, and the abandoned resorts of the 'Borscht Belt'. We see it in towns demolished by war and in nature's takeover of the human artifacts of Chernobyl. These serve as inspirations for the on-screen visions of apocalypse. *The Road* (2009), for example, used Pennsylvania as "a pleasing array of post-apocalyptic scenery: deserted coalfields, run-down parts of Pittsburgh, windswept dunes"[33] to set the scene for the end of civilization where only the family unit is worth preserving. An abandoned power station was used for the film *12 Monkeys* (1995) and the abandoned (and deadly) areas near Tallinn, Estonia set the scene for Tarkovsky's *Stalker* (1979). A graveyard of airplanes in the Mojave Desert actively advertises itself as the premiere "Apocalyptic Landscape for Film, TV, Commercial, Music Video or Photo Production".[34]

This is the alternative to capitalism and the state that we believe in, and it serves the function of reproducing the desire for capitalism and the state and provides a reason why we want to believe that there is no alternative, worried that the only other options will be worse. Even when capitalism is depicted as the culprit in producing this catastrophic landscape, as in the animated film *Wall-E* (2008), the only alternatives we see are destruction or reclamation, either the future of ever-abounding trash or our neoliberal present. Rather than providing a critical realization of what horrors capitalism is capable of, such representations reassert capitalism's importance. Although films such as *Don't Look Up* (2021) raise questions about the state and capitalism's assessment of risk and reward while a massive comet is hurling towards Earth, *The Day After Tomorrow* (2004) warns us of the dangers of continued greenhouse gas emissions, and *Snowpiercer* (2013) explores class inequalities when the geoengineering of the environment goes haywire, these films, and many other screen media texts like them,[35] only work to further ingratiate the current systems with the public. As the satirical comedy series *Corporate* (2018–2020) explains during its own brief representation of the end of the world, "fear is the steady hand that unhooks the bra of capitalism". The alternative futures of near extinction are ones we are happy to avoid and in doing so return to our own grim (but not as grim) realities with gratitude. It is not that we lack the ability to imagine the end of capitalism; it is that capitalism appears to be the best possible option.

20 Neoliberalism, TINA, and the *Titanic* Effects

In fact, such a marketing approach is nothing new for the state and capitalism. They have always positioned themselves not as ideal systems, but better than the alternatives. The French philosopher Alain Badiou stated:

> To justify their conservatism, the partisans of the established order cannot really call it ideal or wonderful. So instead, they have decided to say that all the rest is horrible. Sure, they say, we may not live in a condition of perfect Goodness. But we're lucky that we don't live in a condition of Evil. Our democracy is not perfect. But it's better than the bloody dictatorships. Capitalism is unjust. But it's not criminal like Stalinism …. Who indeed today would defend the Stalinist terror, the African genocides, the Latin American torturers? Nobody. It's there that the consensus concerning evil is decisive. Under the pretext of not accepting evil, we end up making believe that we have, if not the good, at least the best possible state of affairs—even if this best is not so great.[36]

Such a position was explicitly taken by politicians appealing to their constituencies in precarious times. Winston Churchill's famous remark, "democracy is the worst form of government except for all those other forms that have been tried from time to time" or, in the words of Ed Miliband, the former leader of the UK's Labour Party, "capitalism is the least worst system we've got". This was also paraphrased by the conservative public intellectual Jordan Peterson in his 'debate' with Slavoj Žižek: "capitalism is … the worst form of economic arrangement you could possibly manage except for every other one that we've ever tried".[37] These statements exemplify this defense of the status quo.

It is this perception that led Bono of the band U2, to sing the praises of capitalism in his speech at Georgetown University:

> Imagine, for a second, this last global recession, but without the economic growth of China and India, without the hundreds of millions of newly minted middle class folks who now buy American and European goods. Imagine that. … Rock star preaches capitalism. Wow. Sometimes I hear myself and I just can't believe it. But commerce is real. … Aid is just a stopgap. Commerce, entrepreneur capitalism takes more people out of poverty than aid.[38]

This speech led to praise from the capitalist press, with *Forbes* saying apparently without irony, that Bono "has the courage to go into the ideological lion's den of an American university to challenge the academic orthodoxy by declaring that capitalism is the answer. God bless Bono! There's hope for us yet."[39]

Although on different sides of the political spectrum, the *Forbes* quote gels with Žižek's argument about the importance of ideology in maintaining or changing the system. Žižek argued that the capitalist system was destroying itself, as evidenced by the economic crisis, but that the realization of the system's destruction went unnoticed by the powers that be. The economic system collapses but it continues under the delusion that all is well. When it comes to the realization that it lacks the foundation on which to stand, it crumbles. Žižek concluded his Occupy Wall Street speech saying, "Remember that our basic message is 'We are allowed to think about alternatives. If the taboo is broken, we do not live in the best possible world. But there is a long road ahead.'" For *Forbes*, it is also the ideological war that will determine the fate of the system. "There's hope" for capitalism, they say, because people are still preaching its benefits. Whereas Žižek argues that we are only just beginning to think about alternatives, *Forbes* believes that alternatives are dominant, and that capitalism is hanging by a thread. Why the disjuncture? Polls show that more and more young people report a decreased satisfaction with capitalism and an increased interest in socialism.[40] However, these understandings of socialism are often not built on a foundation of shared ownership of the means of production, not to mention the foundation of replacing the corporate division of labor.[41] Instead, it is a notion of socialism that entails increased regulation and protection by the state – alleviating the worst harms of capitalism (at least in the Global North) while maintaining a system of capitalism and state. Thus, we still find ourselves without either a revolutionary consciousness or a positive vision of a world beyond capitalism.

Perfect Moving Pictures

If ideology is a key battleground in a revolution beyond the state and capitalism, what role do cultural products play in this struggle? This cultural struggle is what the Italian Marxist Antonio Gramsci called the "war of position". While China banned alternate reality and time travel, these features appear frequently in Hollywood representations, and are even incorporated in romantic dramas.[42] However, such representations have not produced visions of alternatives.[43] This is why, according to Žižek, they need *not* be banned in the Global North. The system in place has "oppressed our capacity to dream".[44] But by what means is such a capacity oppressed? Žižek continues the quote above by making a somewhat tautological point – that it is in fact our movies that have made it easy to imagine the end of the world; that the mechanism is cultural consumption. Perhaps the Chinese government got it wrong. Maybe it's not the *sci-fi elements* that cultivate our imaginations to think beyond capitalism and beyond the state, but representations of better alternatives to the state and capital.

22 Neoliberalism, TINA, and the *Titanic* Effects

Of all the institutions of daily life, the media specialize in orchestrating everyday consciousness—by virtue of their pervasiveness, their accessibility, their centralized symbolic capacity. They name the world's parts, they certify reality as reality—and when their certifications are doubted and opposed, as they surely are, it is those same certifications that limit the terms of effective opposition. To put it simply: the mass media have become core systems for the distribution of ideology.[45]

While the quote above by Columbia University Professor Todd Gitlin focuses on the news media,[46] films and television series – no matter how fictional – also help to construct our understanding of the world in very real ways. Given that our cultural products have the capacity to shape our vision of the possible and desired, why is it that it is easier to imagine the end of the world than the end of capitalism? I argue that imagining the end of the world is exactly how we are now imagining the end of capitalism because, within popular culture, we lack representations of radical alternatives – and even radical critiques of our political and economic system. Our fantasies of global destruction and the post-apocalypse are the results of our engagement with the content of popular culture that fails to present us with radical critiques of society or alternative models, despite the possibility to do so. It is not only possible, but perhaps critical for art to play such a role.[47]

One of the most important Renaissance literary critics, Philip Sidney, elucidated the artistic creation of perfection as the very beauty art possesses. He wrote in *The Defence of Poesy* (1595),

Nature never set forth the earth in so rich tapestry as diverse poets have done: neither with so pleasant rivers, fruitful trees, sweet smelling flowers, nor whatsoever else may make the too much loved earth more lovely. Her world is brazen, the poets only deliver a golden.[48]

Sidney asserts the power of the poet to create a new world through art. This power of creation, God-like according to Sidney,[49] is greater than that of the philosopher or historian. The philosopher produces abstract and airy claims that are hard to imagine and might be divorced from the real world. The historian, on the other hand, is too concerned with the specific to consider the general and so focused on what has existed that they don't consider what *could* and *ought* to exist.

Now doth the peerless poet perform both: for whatsoever the philosopher saith should be done, he giveth a perfect picture of it in some one by whom he presupposeth it was done, so as he couplet the general notion with the particular example. A perfect picture I say, for he yieldeth to the powers of the mind an image of that whereof the philosopher bestoweth but a wordish description, which doth neither strike, pierce, nor possess the sight of the soul so much as that other doth.[50]

The artist has the capacity to imagine what ought to be in a way that perhaps no other could.[51] And although here Sidney speaks specifically for poets and their ability to produce "to the powers of the mind an image", screen media (i.e., film and television) provide the power to create that image, along with sound and motion, in a far more direct way. Indeed, as Francesco Sticchi writes of film but which we could extent to television, a screen media text "touches and surrounds the viewer, thus transforming her/him and allowing for the experiential configurations of new worlds".[52]

Sidney defined a poem as a "speaking picture – with this end to teach and delight".[53] We need only to add motion to produce the subject of the texts I cover in this book: films and television shows. But this definition also reminds us that the function of art is to educate and entertain. Art, according to Sidney, has the inherent ability to *teach* us. He was not alone in making this point. Hundreds of years later, the Russian revolutionary Leon Trotsky, in his contribution to literary theory, wrote: "art is always a social servant and historically utilitarian ... it educates the individual, the social group, the class and the nation".[54]

This notion continues to influence the field of cultural studies which has since incorporated psychoanalytic theory to strengthen the case that such 'learning' is an inherent characteristic of media consumption. If psychological health is rooted in the ability to create mental representations and to take existing representations from culture and internalize them, then the representations in cultural texts can shape the political imaginary.

When internalized, they mold the self in such a way that it becomes accommodated to the values inherent in those cultural representations. Consequently, the sort of representations which prevail in a culture is a crucial political issue. Cultural representations ... play an important role in determining how social reality will be constructed, that is, what figures and boundaries will prevail in the shaping of social life and social institutions. They determine whether capitalism will be conceived (felt, experienced, lived) as a predatory jungle or as a utopia of freedom.[55]

The *Titanic* not only serves as a metaphor but also as the grounds on which popular culture and reality converge to construct one another and shape our understanding of the world around us. This is exemplified by the story of one of the ship's passengers. Dorothy Gibson, a silent film actress, was excited to board the *Titanic* and get back to the studio where she had just been hired for a role in a new film, but after surviving the sinking of the unsinkable ship she had a change of heart about her next role. When she returned to New York she quickly wrote and starred in a film about her journey. *Saved from the Titanic* (1912) may have been the first time a real event was so swiftly turned into a motion picture. It was created in under a month – less than half the time of a typical film of its length. To increase its authenticity, Gibson wore the same clothes in the film as she wore when she was rescued. In the same month the film premiered, another film about the *Titanic*, the German film *In Nacht und Eis (In Night and Ice)* (1912) was being shot. The French film *La Hantise* (1912) was also released that same year featuring the fate of the *Titanic*. Few moving images of the real *Titanic* existed, so these films have become central to the social imaginary of the event itself, helping to generate endless interest in the story and shape our perceptions of what occurred on that fateful night.

On Culture's Consequences and Close(d) Readings

To understand why it is easier to imagine the end of the world than the end of capitalism it is worth further interrogating the role of popular culture. How have popular works of art produced 'a perfect picture' or an image of what ought to be? Is our imagination of an alternative socio-political and economic reality shaped and ultimately hindered by these artistic creations? Or is there promise and possibility in these texts that allow us to yield "to the powers of the mind and image" of a future without the crushing force of capitalism or the tyranny of the state? To answer these questions, we must look at a range of popular texts and evaluate the alternatives we find. In doing so we might develop a better understanding of why our ability to fathom a more collectivist end to capitalism has faded to near extinction. But we should also be open to the possibility that some sparks of hope in mainstream film and television might, if we are lucky, ignite our own radical imaginations.

How can we read (i.e. interpret) a film or television show (a screen media text) to gauge its relevance for the project of sparking a radical imaginary? The classical approach is attributed to the late Hungarian Marxist György Lukács who admired works of social realism. "The work of art must", he said, "reflect correctly and in proper proportion all important factors objectively determining the area of life it represents." This will make the text "re-experienceable" and "comprehensible from within and from without", producing an "intensive totality" that reflects on the world outside the text.[56] For critical theorist Theodor Adorno, the totality was conceived differently. It represented the way in which capitalism and the logic of the market was an all-consuming force.

> Behind the reduction of men to agents and bearers of exchange value lies the domination of men over men .... The form of total system requires

everyone to respect the law of exchange if he does not wish to be destroyed, irrespective of whether profit is his subjective motivation or not.[57]

Thus, according to Adorno, everyone, including artists, is subsumed into the capitalist system as both consumers and producers. Artistic creations are predigested by the culture industry. Just as a great work of fiction is condensed by *Reader's Digest* into a more 'readable' format, screen media texts – even those with lofty ambitions and radically different structures – are remade to be easily consumed, relieved of some of their more difficult or novel features. Films and shows are produced in a standardized process that resembles an assembly line. Their bare bones are replicas of stories that have been told before. Always seeing the same form on repeat produces an ideologically driven conception of the end of history, where alternatives in form are as impossible as alternative systems. For Adorno, the escape was a break in form which allows the audience to develop autonomous reflection and encourages new experiences. With such a break, the possibility of radical ideology becomes real. But just as crises fail to produce visions of alternatives, breaks from the standard form or constructions of the socially real cannot jolt us into an alternative political consciousness by themselves. The Marxist playwright Bertolt Brecht opposed this formalism as an "unwarranted confidence in the possibility of deducing political and ideological positions from a protocol of *purely* formal properties of a work of art".[58] In fact, if shaken to the point of opposing a culture of commodification, one can regress into appreciation of alternative economic relations which are no more ethical than that of late capitalism or of state powers that curtail commodification alongside civil liberties. Therefore, representations of alternatives still play an important role in developing a consciousness that is not only critical, but can conceptualize a *more just and equal* economic and political system.

As popular culture typically comes from the culture industry and is standardized, pseudo-individualized, and predigested, as Adorno argues, it is worth considering what role these texts play in shaping the political imaginary in the first instance. One of the goals of this book is to see if, *within* the content produced by the culture industry, there are alternative representations or even critiques of the present system – seeds of hope that can be planted – and if these do not exist, to try and decipher why not. These questions should be answered conclusively before a political project looking to improve society turns its attention to shaping ideology through culture by exiting the mainstream and consuming only 'authentic culture', as Adorno proscribes.

Of course, this examination is premised on the importance of culture in shaping ideology. It must be noted that others have disagreed with this formulation. For one, the social theorist Herbert Marcuse held the view that culture's separation from politics gives it the space to critique and imagine,

26 Neoliberalism, TINA, and the *Titanic* Effects

but it also means culture is an ineffective instrument.[59] Because culture can be seen as distinct from the political and economic realms it can always be trivialized and its contents can be ignored. If this is the case, then there is little point in focusing on film and television as a way of waking us from the coma brought on by the lullaby of TINA. Likewise, we need to consider Barthes' famous 'death of the author' argument. This tells us that regardless of the intended meaning of the author, a text can be read in a variety of ways and thus its meaning is not fixed. The cultural studies theorist Stuart Hall also subscribes to this notion, arguing against many of the early theories about the power of culture.

Early mass communication theorists argued for linear, straightforward conceptions of communication. Harold Lasswell's 'model of communication' argues that a communicator provides a message through a medium to a receiver with some kind of effect. This theory is now seen as simplistic and outdated.[60] Early media effects theories of the 1920s and 1930s such as the hypodermic needle and the 'magic bullet' theories were essentially proven false through empirical study. These theories argued that media has an immense, direct, and almost immediate impact on the viewer. The desired message of the media producer was viewed, in effect, as being injected into and received by the media consumer.[61] However, as Hall notes, "the television program is not a behavioral input, like a tap on the knee cap".[62] It is not just about the meaning placed in a media text (encoding). The meaning the viewer gives to the text (decoding) is also important. We must interpret what we see and hear. Likewise, the Italian semiotician Umberto Eco argues that the author writes something with an intended meaning but the reader, the 'addressee', always interprets it somewhat differently.

> The addressee is bound to enter into an interplay of stimulus and response which depends on his unique capacity for sensitive reception of the piece. In this sense the author presents a finished product with the intention that this particular composition should be appreciated and received in the same form as he devised it. As he reacts to the play of stimuli and his own response to their patterning, the individual addressee is bound to supply his own existential credentials, the sense conditioning which is peculiarly his own, a defined culture, a set of tastes, personal inclinations, and prejudices. Thus, his comprehension of the original artifact is always modified by his particular and individual perspective.

Viewers can provide endless decodings of texts, all giving rise to different social and political ideas. If this is the case, then we can hardly argue that culture is the cause of our collective belief that there is no alternative.

While it is true that reality is not as simple as those early theories of media effects suggested, in practice it is also not as complex as a million people producing a million different interpretations of what they see on television or in the cinema. Subsequent research into media effects has produced compelling evidence that mainstream US screen media texts give rise to some consistent attitudes and beliefs in their consumers. Those who watch large amounts of crime dramas were found to have heightened concerns about crime. People exposed to progressive dramas and sitcoms had higher levels of support for women's rights compared to those who viewed conservative traditional drama,[63] Content that has stereotypical images or representations can prime for stereotypical attitudes and watching television programs with thin female characters correlates with an increased drive for thinness.[64] Reports have found that some people who watch the medical television series *House M.D.* (2004–2012) self-diagnose their medical condition as a rare, life-threatening disease seen on the show and expect their doctors to run very expensive examinations to test for the disease.[65] Audience research examining the political television drama *The West Wing* (1999–2006) found that, after viewing one episode of the show, people were more likely to feel that "being compassionate, warm, funny, and loving" were important components of a president's success. In addition, both George W. Bush and Bill Clinton were viewed as being more principled presidents compared to those who did not watch the show.[66]

Other studies looked at people who view high rates of television, without paying attention to which specific programs, and compared them to those who watched less television. Watching a lot of television correlated with body dissatisfaction, a sense of ineffectiveness, increased fearfulness of specific environmental problems or issues, self-identification of holding "moderate" political views, a pro-war stance during the Persian Gulf War, positive attitudes to smoking, negative perceptions of mental illness, and greater approval of surgical body alterations. Despite their increased fear of environmental disasters and support for the Gulf War, high rates of television watching correlated with less knowledge about environmental and political issues. Those with high rates of television viewing were also found to have exaggerated perceptions of the frequency of violence in society, decreased trustfulness of others, increased views that others were selfish, and a greater likelihood to believe that criminal sentencing was race neutral. With regard to adolescents, studies found that high rates of watching television correlated significantly with an increased desire for high-paying and easy jobs with lots of vacation time and with a desire to get married, stay married to the same person for life, and have children.[67] Media studies have also found that the *behavior* of those with a high level of television viewing was affected. This included lower political participation, especially among those with progressive values, and a lower likelihood of being active on environmental issues.[68] Furthermore, the media helps to set the agenda for political and cultural discussion.[69]

28 Neoliberalism, TINA, and the *Titanic* Effects

One particular example from a movie can shed additional light on the effect of popular culture summed up in one line: "Fucking HMO bastard pieces of shit!" It is widely believed that viewers' reaction to this one line reverberated through their own experience and created a resonance of outrage. The co-founder of eHealthCare.com, Jeff Smedsrud, noted that "few movie scenes are as memorable as Helen Hunt's obscenity-laced rant against Health Maintenance Organizations (HMOs) in the 1997 Oscar winning movie, *As Good as It Gets* …".[70] The movie is a romantic dramedy that follows the unlikely relationship between an obsessive-compulsive (and bigoted) novelist, Melvin, and a waitress who has a son that suffers from acute asthma, Carol. Unbeknownst to Carol, Melvin arranges for an expensive doctor to help her son. When Carol meets the doctor, they begin to go over her son's medical history. The doctor is shocked to find that his previous healthcare providers did not follow standard protocols for this illness because those procedures were not in his health insurance plan. Carol reacts with obscenities. "But more striking than her performance", Smedsrud writes,

> was the audience reaction to the now infamous tirade. In movie theaters across the country, audiences applauded and cheered. The scene has been cited as a tipping point in consumer backlash against the restrictive provider networks of HMOs. It helped fuel the movement to give consumers more choice ….[71]

This connection between the film's representation and the audience's reaction was dubbed the 'Jack Nicholson effect'.[72] Of course, this critique is progressive at best and sits within a movie that is generally conservative. (The idea of being 'as good as it gets' is inherently stagnant as reflected in Carol's eventual acceptance that this racist and sexist man is as good as it gets as a partner; that she should not ask or hope or fight for more.) Regardless, this short tirade of expletives exposing HMOs is an example of the ideological, and subsequently material, impact film and television are capable of.

We can see that people *are* learning from these representations[73] and that culture *does* have a big impact on our ideas and beliefs. Mass media has a way of affecting our interpretations of the world, but not through a simple process. This is why the field turned to more complex theories in which common and repeated elements of the media environment cultivate certain worldviews in the audience, particularly in 'heavy' consumers of the media, and arguably in the world at large. The studies discussed above apply cultivation theory and in some ways this book makes the assumption which the theory implies: consumers of popular culture are likely to internalize the shared worldviews across a steady stream of media that they consume.[74]

Even while they argued for the interpretative capacities of the audience, neither Hall nor Eco were blind to the processes that limited the scope of those readings in practice. Hall understood that the reader is "only 'relatively autonomous' " in decoding a text.[75] Decoders are situated within a decoding culture[76] in which their interpretation is shaped by positionality and prior knowledge based partly on their previous consumption and decoding of texts. Hall writes that despite the more changeable nature of associated meanings that can be read from a text, "connotative codes are not equal among themselves. Any society/culture tends, with varying degrees of closure, to impose its classifications of the social and cultural and political world. These constitute a dominant cultural order".[77]

Audio-visual transmissions of film and television, Hall states, take the real world and transform it into a two-dimensional form through iconic signs. Iconic signs are signs that "mimic the character of objects in our daily perceptions" which "lead[s] to almost universal intelligibility".[78] The image presented before us on television of a beautiful house *represents* a beautiful house.[79] Thus, the audio-visual nature of film and television can allow for an 'easier' decoding process – in the sense that the decoding can relate more quickly to one's embodied, three-dimensional reality. While decoding is still an activity that is largely controlled by the reader, the form of data received *helps* the reader to decode a message one way rather than another. Of course, extracting values or deeper meanings from these texts still requires significant energy, but most popular texts within film and television are not 'open' in the Echian sense. For Umberto Eco, the semantic content of a text is open when the author provides space for the reader to interpret. Eco understands that art inherently has such a capacity and that "the form of the work of art gains its aesthetic validity precisely in proportion to the number of different perspectives from which it can be viewed and understood".[80] But this type of 'open text' isn't simply *any* artistic work. An author of open texts "subsumes [the different possible readings] into a positive aspect of his [or her] production, recasting the work so as to expose it to the maximum possible 'opening'.[81] Such a description rarely characterizes a Hollywood film or US television program which is far more structured and 'closed'.[82] They are not typically meant to be viewed and understood from different perspectives, but rather they are made to be easily digestible, as Adorno noted. This provides us with the opportunity to inspect them to understand the likely messages we receive.

Stuart Hall once wrote that ideology "concerns the ways in which ideas of different kinds grip the minds of masses, and thereby become a 'material force' ". On the one hand, ideology can help to "stabilize a particular form of power and domination; or ... reconcile and accommodate the mass of the people to their subordinate place in the social formation". On the other hand, ideology "has also to do with the processes by which new forms of consciousness, new conceptions of the world, arise, which move the masses of the people into historical action against the prevailing system".[83]

30 Neoliberalism, TINA, and the *Titanic* Effects

The prevailing system is already responsible for much destruction and devastation. The iceberg that hit us is now also melting alongside the glaciers that are leading to rising sea levels, thus hastening our submersion in the ice-cold waters of the end of history. Our sinking into the ocean can only be prevented with the help of a nearby vessel of ideology that can lift us out of what we accept is our inevitable doom. If we are saved, then this ideological ship can take us to the shore of the alternative. But we don't know if the ship will ever arrive. In the story of the *Titanic*, only the *Carpathia* arrived. But what if it didn't? Even the closest ship to the *Titanic* did not come to its rescue. Will this be the role of Hollywood – the biggest producer of globally consumed media? Will they be close to us but unwilling to help? Maybe it is apt that the ship that ignored the distress signals of the *Titanic* was called the *Californian*. Or maybe, like the sci-fi films that facilitate an imagination of the alternative in China, we can travel back in time and change the course of history.

Notes

1 I use 'businessmen' rather than businesspeople intentionally given the gendered nature of the workplace, particularly at the time.
2 Dunbar 2011.
3 Thatcher 1976.
4 Marx and Engels 2010[1848].
5 Thatcher 1976.
6 Wayne 2020, pp. 10–11.
7 E.g., Keen 2009; Ritholtz 2012; Stelzer 2010.
8 Harvey 2007.
9 Frey et al. 2011. In an extreme coincidence, the writer and self-styled anarchist Elbert Hubbard wrote on the subject, particularly as it pertained to women, just a few years before surviving the sinking of the *Titanic* and then sinking on the *Lusitania*. "Out in the great world women occasionally walk off the dock in the darkness, and then struggle for life in the deep waters. Society jigs and ambles by, with a coil of rope, but before throwing it demands of the drowning one a certificate of character from her Pastor, or a letter of recommendation from her Sunday School Superintendent, or a testimonial from a School Principal. Not being able to produce the document the struggler is left to go down to her death in the darkness" (Hubbard 1901).
10 Nulman 2015, pp. 8–10.
11 Declaration: Tokyo Summit Conference, 1979, p. 5.
12 Nulman 2015, pp. 8–10.
13 Battles 2001.
14 Following the new regulations, only 26 people died when the *Titanic*'s sister vessel – operating as a hospital ship during the First World War – sank after being torpedoed.
15 E.g., Monbiot 2016; Streeck 2016.
16 E.g., Sitaraman 2019; also see Palma 2009.

Neoliberalism, TINA, and the *Titanic* Effects **31**

17 This reminds me of the film *Atlantic* (1929) which probably inadvertently tells a similar story but replaces the animated cat with the *Titanic* (although technically the White Star Line did not permit the filmmakers to use the name Titanic, so they named the ship the *Atlantic* for legal reasons). The film recounts the sinking of the ship from the perspective of the proud elite passengers. After striking an iceberg the ship begins to take on water, but the main characters pay no attention to the warnings and are convinced the ship is unsinkable. Those who know better refrain from telling the others in order to avoid panic. Eventually word gets out and only when they become conscious of their own fate does the ship begin to capsize, and chaos ensues; men fight for places on board lifeboats meant for women and children; the lower classes join the first-class passengers, drinking away thoughts of their demise and fighting over money they can't take with them. In the end, after a brief moment of equality, the remaining passengers drown together whilst saying their prayers.
18 Harvey 2007.
19 Nulman 2021.
20 Žižek in Fiennes 2021.
21 Sen and Marshall 2012.
22 By the time the *Titanic* was being built, the White Star Line had moved from Liverpool to Southampton, a port town whose ships also participated in the slave trade.
23 J.P. Morgan had cancelled his trip on the *Titanic* before it set sail on its maiden voyage. This had led to unsubstantiated conspiracy theories regarding the Federal Reserve (Reuters Fact Check 2021).
24 At the time of writing, *Titanic* is the third highest grossing film behind *Avatar* (2009) and *Avengers: Endgame* (2019), and remains in third place when adjusting for inflation (behind *Gone with the Wind* (1939) and *Avatar*).
25 Žižek in Fiennes 2012.
26 Engels 2010[1884].
27 See the *Bulletin of the Atomic Scientists*. See Chapter 7.
28 Roberts 2019.
29 Žižek 2011.
30 *A Quiet Place* (2018), *A Quiet Place Part II* (2020), *Zombieland* (2009), and *Zombieland: Double Tap* (2019).
31 I.e, *The Terminator* (1984), *Terminator 2: Judgement Day* (1991), *Terminator 3: Rise of the Machines* (2003), *Terminator Salvation* (2009), *Terminator Genisys* (2015), and Terminator: *Dark Fate* (2019), *The Matrix* (1999), *The Matrix Reloaded* (2003), and *The Matrix Revolutions* (2003).
32 Žižek in Fiennes 2012.
33 McGrath 2008.
34 ACME: Directory for Film + TV n.d.
35 Post-apocalyptic films and television shows are too numerous to name, but here are a few popular ones of the last 15 years or so: *Mad Max: Fury Road* (2015), *The Book of Eli* (2010), *World War Z* (2013), *28 Days Later* (2002), *Zombieland* (2009), *I am Legend* (2007), *The 100* (season 1; 2014), *The Last Man on Earth* (2015–2018). These can fit the least-worst system critique.
36 Badiou 2001–2002. Badiou went on to say that "No intellectual will actually defend the brutal power of money and the accompanying political disdain for the

32 Neoliberalism, TINA, and the *Titanic* Effects

disenfranchised, or for manual laborers, but many agree to say that real evil is elsewhere" (Badiou 2001–2002).

37 Churchill 1947; Peterson 2019; Miliband 2012.

38 Bono 2012.

39 Of course, the speech was given at an event hosted by the Global Social Enterprise Initiative (GSEI) at Georgetown University's McDonough School of Business (Hendrickson 2013).

40 E.g., Newport 2018; Switzer and Jacobs 2018; YouGov 2017; Dahlgreen 2016. Albeit there is also a cross-national survey suggesting a relatively widespread increase of people who believe it is a "very good" or "fairly good" way to "run a country" by ""having a strong leader who does not have to bother with parliament and elections" (Foa and Mounk 2017). Some data has shown something of a decline in positive views toward socialism since 2019 (Pew Research Center 2022).

41 See Albert 2003.

42 E.g., *The Lake House* (2006), *The Time Travelers Wife* (2009), *Kate & Leopold* (2001), *About Time* (2013).

43 It's worth noting that the Chinese government may be taking such a position not because it facilitates the "capacity to dream" but because science fiction can more easily be used to indirectly critique the state than other forms of fiction (Landreth 2011).

44 Žižek 2011.

45 Gitlin in Kendall 2005, p. 6.

46 Also see Bourdieu 1996, e.g. "Television enjoys a de facto monopoly on what goes into the heads of a significant part of the population and what they think", p. 18.

47 Since Thomas More's *Utopia* in 1516 there have been over 6,000 literary utopias in the English language alone, with "virtually every European country enter[ing] enthusiastically into the enterprise" (Kumar 2010, p. 549). As I will argue, however, few can be found in popular film and television.

48 Sidney 2002[1595], p. 90.

49 "Neither let it be deemed too saucy a comparison, to balance the highest point of man's wit, with the efficacy of nature: but rather give right honor to the heavenly Maker of that maker, who having made man in his own likeness, set him beyond and over all the works of that second nature, which is nothing he sheweth so much as in Poetry; when with the force of a divine breath, he bringeth things forth surpassing her doings", Sidney 2002[1595], p. 90.

50 Unfortunately, Sidney's utopian vision was sprouted from reports of early colonization of the New World. He later devoted time and money to funding expeditions that would fund his nationalist Protestant ambitions. As Kuin writes, "there was, by this time, planted in his mind the enduring structure of an *other world*, a parallel, an alternative" (Kuin 1998).

51 Jameson (1992, pp. 53–54) reminds us that Aristotle made this point well before Sidney.

52 Sticchi 2021, p. 7.

53 Sidney 2002[1595], p. 86.

54 More problematically, Trotsky also discussed the application of state control over artistic creation within the case of the Soviet Union, stating in the same work that "the party will repel the clearly poisonous, disintegrating tendencies of art and will guide itself by its political standards" (Trotsky 2000[1924]).

55 Ryan and Kellner 1990, p. 13.
56 Lukács 1971, p. 38.
57 Cited in O'Connor 2013, p. 36. Also see Horkheimer and Adorno 2002.
58 Jameson 1995, p. 200, emphasis added.
59 Jameson 1995a, p. xv.
60 That said, some have argued this was due to misinterpretations of the theories (Sapienza et al. 2015)
61 Lim and Kim 2007; Borah 2015.
62 Hall 1993, p. 94. Even the empirical research on media effects have accepted that the relationship between media consumption and beliefs and behavior are not a simple behavioral mechanism, see Bryant and Oliver 2009.
63 Morgan et al. 2009.
64 For priming see Shrum 2009. For the drive for thinness see Harrison and Cantor 1997.
65 Kendall 2005, p. 10.
66 Holbert et al. 2003.
67 For correlates with body dissatisfaction and a sense of ineffectiveness see Harrison and Cantor 1997. For the rest see Morgan et al. 2009.
68 Morgan et al. 2009.
69 Petty et al. 2009.
70 Smedsrud 2015.
71 Smedsrud 2015.
72 Greene 2016, p. 232
73 van Zoonen, L. 2007.
74 Though I do not go into the details as to how media effect theorists argue this process occurs, you could consult Rodolfo Leyva's *Brains, Media and Politics* (2019) or Preiss et al.'s *Mass Media Effects Research* (2006).
75 Hall 1983.
76 See e.g., Ma 2003.
77 Hall 1993, pp. 95, 98.
78 Cohn 2010, p. 188. Also see Hall 1983, p. 95.
79 Hall 1993, p. 95. For iconic signs see Peirce 1998, p. 273. For such signs in animated form see Cohn 2010, p. 188.
80 Eco 1989, p. 3.
81 Eco 1989, p. 5.
82 Lykidis 2020, p. 13.
83 Hall 1993, p. 59.

References

ACME: Directory for Film + TV (n.d.) 'Ultimate Graveyard I 700 Acre Mojave Desert Film Location', https://www.theacme.com/directory/ultimate-graveyard-700-acre-mojave-desert-film-location.

Albert, Michael (2003) *Parecon: Life After Capitalism*, London: Verso.

Badiou, Alain (2001–2002) 'On Evil: An Interview with Alain Badiou', *Cabinet*, Issue 5. www.cabinetmagazine.org/issues/5/alainbadiou.php.

Battles, James B. (2001) 'Disaster Prevention: Lessons Learned from the *Titanic*', *Baylor University Medical Center Proceedings*, 14(2): 150–153.

34 Neoliberalism, TINA, and the *Titanic* Effects

Bono (2012) 'U2News – Bono at Georgetown University – Part 2', YouTube, https://www.youtube.com/watch?v=zh9NZqciQCs.

Borah, Porismita (2015) 'Media Effects Theory', in Gianpietro Mazzoleni (ed.), *The International Encyclopedia of Political Communication*, 1st Edition, Hoboken: John Wiley & Sons, Inc.

Bourdieu, Pierre (1996) *On Television*, New York: The New Press.

Bryant, Jennings and Oliver, Mary Beth (eds.) (2009) *Media Effects: Advances in Theory and Research*, 3rd Edition, New York: Routledge.

Churchill, Winston (1947) 'The Worst Form of Government', International Churchill Society https://winstonchurchill.org/resources/quotes/the-worst-form-of-government.

Cohn, Neil (2010) 'Japanese Visual Language: The Structure of Manga', in Toni Johnson-Woods (ed.), *Manga: An Anthology of Global and Cultural Perspectives* (pp. 187–203), New York: Continuum Books.

Dahlgreen, Will (2016) 'British People are More Likely to View Socialism Favourably than Capitalism', YouGov, Feb. 23, https://yougov.co.uk/topics/politics/articles-reports/2016/02/23/british-people-view-socialism-more-favourably-capi.

Declaration: Tokyo Summit Conference (1979) 'G7: Tokyo Summit Communiqué', June 28–29.

Dunbar, Polly (2011) 'How Laurence Olivier Gave Margaret Thatcher the Voice that Went Down in History', *Daily Mail*, Oct. 30, https://www.dailymail.co.uk/news/article-2055214/How-Laurence-Olivier-gave-Margaret-Thatcher-voice-went-history.html.

Eco, Umberto (1989) *The Open Work*. Cambridge, MA: Harvard University Press.

Engels, Friedrich (2010[1884]) *The Origin of the Family, Private Property, and the State*, London: Penguin Books.

Fiennes, Sophie dir. (2012) *The Pervert's Guide to Ideology*, Zeitgeist Films, DVD.

Foa, Roberto Stefan and Mounk, Yascha (2017) 'The Signs of Deconsolidation', *Journal of Democracy*, 28(1): 5–15.

Frey, Bruno S., Savage, David A., and Torgler, Benno (2011), 'Behavior under Extreme Conditions: The *Titanic* Disaster', *Journal of Economic Perspectives*, 25(1): 209–222.

Greene, Jeremy A. (2016) *Generic: The Unbranding of Modern Medicine*, Baltimore, MD: Johns Hopkins University Press.

Hall, Stuart (1983) 'The Problem of Ideology: Marxism without Guarantees', in Betty Matthews (ed.), *Marx: 100 Years On*, London: Lawrence & Wishart.

Hall, Stuart (1993) 'Encoding/Decoding', in Simon During (ed.), *The Cultural Studies Reader* (pp. 90–103), New York: Routledge.

Harrison, Kirsten and Cantor, Joanne (1997) 'The Relationship between Media Consumption and Eating Disorders', *Journal of Communication*, 47(1): 40–67.

Harvey, David (2007) *A Brief History of Neoliberalism*, Oxford: Oxford University Press.

Hendrickson, Mark (2013) 'U2's Bono Courageously Embraces Capitalism', *Forbes*, Nov. 8, https://www.forbes.com/sites/markhendrickson/2013/11/08/u2s-bono-courageously-embraces-capitalism/#1fe8e5a3575a.

Holbert, R. Lance, Pillion, Owen, Tschida, David A., Armfield, Greg G., Kinder, Kristin L. Cherry, and Daulton, Amy R. (2003) 'The West Wing as Endorsement of the US Presidency: Expanding the Bounds of Priming in Political Communication', *Journal of Communication*, 53(3): 427–443.

Horkheimer, Max and Adorno, Theodor (2002) *Dialectic of Enlightenment: Philosophical Fragments*, Stanford, CA: Stanford University Press.

Hubbard, Elbert (1901) 'The Better Part', in *A Message to Garcia and Thirteen Other Things* (pp. 147–155), New York: Roycrofters, https://archive.org/details/message togarciat00hubb/page/146.

Jameson, Fredric (1992) *Signatures of the Visible* (pp. 53–54), New York: Routledge.

Jameson, Fredric (1995) 'Reflections in Conclusion', in *Aesthetics and Politics* (pp. 196–213), London: Verso.

Keen, Steve (2009). 'Bailing Out the Titanic with a Thimble', *Economic Analysis & Policy*, 39(1): 3–24.

Kendall, Diana (2005). *Framing Class: Media Representations of Wealth and Poverty in America*, Lanham, MD: Rowman & Littlefield Publishers, Inc.

Kuin, Roger (1998) 'Querre-Muhau: Sir Philip Sidney and the New World', *Renaissance Quarterly*, 51(2): 549–585.

Kumar, Krishan (2010) 'The Ends of Utopia', *New Literary History*, 41(3): 549–569.

Landreth, Jonathan (2011) 'China Bans Time Travel Films and Shows, Citing Disrespect of History', *The Hollywood Reporter*, April 13, https://www.hollyw oodreporter.com/news/china-bans-time-travel-films-177801.

Leyva, Rodolfo (2019) *Brains, Media and Politics: Generating Neoliberal Subjects*, London: Routledge.

Lim, Tae-Seop and Kim, Sang Yeon (2007) 'Many Faces of Media Effects', in Raymond W. Preiss, Barbara Mae Gayle, Nancy Burrell, Mike Allen, and Jennings Bryant (eds.), *Mass Media Effects Research: Advances through Meta-analysis* (pp. 315–326). New York: Routledge.

Lukács, Georg (1971) *Writer and Critic and Other Essays*, New York: Grosset & Dunlap.

Lykidis, Alex (2020) *Art Cinema and Neoliberalism*, Cham, Switzerland: Palgrave Macmillan.

Ma, L. (2003) 'Is There an Essential Difference between Intercultural and Intracultural Communication?', *Journal of Intercultural Communication*, 3(2): 1–9, https://doi.org/10.36923/jicc.v3i2.388.

Marx, Karl and Engels, Fredrick (2010[1848]) *Manifesto of the Communist Party*, Marxist Internet Archive, https://www.marxists.org/archive/marx/works/downl oad/pdf/Manifesto.pdf.

McGrath, Charles (2008) 'At World's End, Honing a Father-Son Dynamic', *The New York Times*, May 27, https://www.nytimes.com/2008/05/27/movies/27r oad.html.

Miliband, Ed (2012) 'Ed Miliband: I Don't Mind the Rich, as Long as They Got There the Hard Way', *The Guardian*, Sept. 15, https://www.theguardian.com/politics/2012/sep/15/ed-miliband-nothing-against-the-rich.

Monbiot, George (2016) 'Neoliberalism – the Ideology at the Root of All Our Problems', *The Guardian*, April 15, https://www.theguardian.com/books/2016/apr/15/neoliberalism-ideology-problem-george-monbiot.

Morgan, Michael, Shanahan, James, and Signorelli, Nancy (2009) 'Growing Up with Television', in Jennings Bryant and Mary Beth Oliver (eds.), *Media Effects: Advances in Theory and Research* (pp. 34–49), New York: Routledge.

Newport, Frank (2018) 'Democrats More Positive about Socialism than Capitalism', *Gallop*, Aug. 13, https://news.gallup.com/poll/240725/democrats-positive-social ism-capitalism.aspx.

Nulman, Eugene (2015) *Climate Change and Social Movements: Civil Society and the Development of National Climate Change Policy*, Basingstoke: Palgrave.

Nulman, Eugene (2021) *Coronavirus Capitalism Goes to the Cinema*, Abingdon: Routledge.

O'Connor, Brian (2013) *Adorno*. Abingdon: Routledge.

Palma, José Gabriel (2009) 'The Revenge of the Market on the Rentiers. Why Neo-Liberal Reports of the End of History Turned Out to Be Premature', *Cambridge Journal of Economics*. 33(4): 829–869.

Peirce, Charles S. (1998) 'Sundry Logical Conceptions', in Nathan Houser, Jonathan R. Eller and Albert C. Lewis (eds.), *The Essential Peirce: Selected Philosophical Writings, Volume 2 (1893–1913)* (pp. 267–288), Bloomington: Indiana University Press.

Peterson, Jordan (2019) 'Marxism: Zizek/Peterson: Official Video', April 19, https://www.youtube.com/watch?v=lsWndfzuOc4.

Petty, Richard E., Briñol, Pablo, and Priester, Joseph R. (2009) 'Mass Media Attitude Change: Implications of the Elaboration Likelihood Model of Persuasion', in Jennings Bryant and Mary Beth Oliver (eds.), *Media Effects Advances in Theory and Research*, 3rd Edition (pp. 125–164), New York: Routledge.

Pew Research Center (2022) 'Modest Declines in Positive Views of "Socialism" and "Capitalism" in U.S.', https://www.pewresearch.org/politics/2022/09/19/modest-declines-in-positive-views-of-socialism-and-capitalism-in-u-s.

Preiss, Raymond W., Mae Gayle, Barbara, Burrell, Nancy, Allen, Mike, and Bryant, Jennings (eds.) (2007) *Mass Media Effects Research: Advances Through Meta-Analysis*, London: Routledge.

Reuters Fact Check (2021) 'CORRECTED-Fact Check – J.P. Morgan Did Not Sink the *Titanic* to Push Forward Plans for the U.S. Federal Reserve', *Reuters*, March 17, https://www.reuters.com/article/factcheck-titanic-conspiracy-idUSL1N2LF18G.

Ritholtz, Barry (2012) 'Repeal of Glass-Steagall: Not a Cause, but a Multiplier', *The Washington Post*, Aug. 4, https://www.washingtonpost.com/repeal-of-glass-steag all-not-a-cause-but-a-multiplier/2012/08/02/gJQAuvvRXX_story.html.

Roberts, Michael (2019) ' A Delicate Moment', The Next Recession blog, April 14, https://thenextrecession.wordpress.com/2019/04/14/a-delicate-moment.

Ryan, Michael and Kellner, Douglas (1990) *Camera Politica: The Politics and Ideology of Contemporary Hollywood Film*, Bloomington: Indiana University Press.

Sapienza, Zachary S., Iyer, Narayanan, and Veenstra, Aaron S. (2015) 'Reading Lasswell's Model of Communication Backward: Three Scholarly Misconceptions', *Mass Communication and Society*, 18(5): 599–622.

Sen, Anirban and Marshall, Elizabeth Dilts (2021) 'JPMorgan Edges Closer to Leaving Pandemic Behind, Its Earnings Show', *Reuters*, Oct. 13, https://www.reuters.com/business/finance/jpmorgan-profit-beats-estimates-ma-boom-loan-gro wth-2021-10-13.

Shrum, L. J. (2009). 'Media Consumption and Perceptions of Social Reality', in Jennings Bryant and Mary Beth Oliver (eds.), *Media Effects: Advances in Theory and Research* (pp. 50–73), New York, NY: Routledge.

Sidney, Philip (2002[1595]) *An Apology for Poetry (or, The Defence of Poesy)*, Manchester: Manchester University Press.

Sitaraman, Ganesh (2019) 'The Collapse of Neoliberalism', *The New Republic*, https://newrepublic.com/article/155970/collapse-neoliberalism.

Smedsrud, Jeff (2015). 'Do Healthcare Consumers Really Have a Choice? Is This as Good as It Gets?', HealthCare.com, https://www.healthcare.com/blog/do-healthc are-consumers-really-have-a-choice-is-this-as-good-as-it-gets.

Stelzer, Irwin (2010) 'Titanic-Style Problems for Euro Zone', *The Wall Street Journal*, Aug. 2, https://www.wsj.com/articles/SB1000142405274870470230457540293 0729180508.

Sticchi, Francesco (2021) *Mapping Precarity in Contemporary Cinema and Television: Chronotopes of Anxiety, Depression, Explusion/Extinction*, Cham, Switzerland: Palgrave Macmillan.

Streeck, Wolfgang (2016) 'A Problem with Democracy', Verso, Nov. 17, https://www.versobooks.com/blogs/2943-wolfgang-streeck-a-problem-with-democracy.

Switzer, Tom and Jacobs, Charles (2018) 'Millennials and Socialism: Australian Youth Are Lurching to the Left', *Policy Paper 7*, https://www.cis.org.au/app/uplo ads/2018/06/pp7.pdf.

Thatcher, Margaret (1976) Speech to Australian Institute of Directors Lunch, Sept. 15, Sydney, Australia, https://www.margaretthatcher.org/document/103099.

Trotsky, Leon. (2000[1924]) *Literature and Revolution*, Marxism.org, https://www.marxists.org/archive/trotsky/1924/lit_revo/index.htm.

van Zoonen, Liesbet (2007) 'Audience Reactions to Hollywood Politics', *Media, Culture & Society*, 29(4): 531–547.

Wayne, Mike (2020) *Marx Goes to the Movies*, Abingdon: Routledge.

YouGov (2017) 'Annual Report on US Attitudes towards Socialism', https://ct24.ceskatelevize.cz/sites/default/files/2020135-pruzkum.pdf.

Žižek, Slavoj (2011) 'Remarks at Zuccotti Park, October 9', in Astra Taylor, Keith Gessen, and editors from *n+1*, *Dissent*, *Triple Canopy* and *The New Inquiry* (eds.), *Occupy! Scenes from Occupied America*, London: Verso.

2
RESEARCH METHODS

As discussed in the Introduction, this book seeks to tackle two primary research questions. The first is whether or not radical, structural critiques of capitalism and the state are present in popular screen media texts. If there are a substantial number of radical representations, we could claim that as long as the screen media text makes money, producers do not care what content they produce, or may even be sympathetic to politics that undermines their own class. If few radical representations are present, this provides evidence that producers and studios are controlling the messaging of the content in their class interests. If radical representations are evident in the sample, we may be able to better understand what kind of radical content passes through the ideological filters that exist and what kind of content does not. The second question is about what, if any, positive alternatives to capitalism and the state are represented. This question is strongly linked to the first because screen media texts which are critical of current society in radical or structural ways may present these critiques by showing alternative social arrangements and institutions that don't suffer from the same problems that capitalism and the state do. They may have characters that fight against the present systems and build alternative institutions within the narrative of the text. However, some texts may simply show other ways of producing and distributing goods or making collective decisions without ever really discussing our present-day arrangements for doing this. Screen media texts that take place in different time periods, cultures, planets, or universes can demonstrate alternatives and serve as an *indirect* critique of our own society. If positive alternative representations are found it suggests that society's ideologies are either not substantially formed by popular culture or the belief in a positive alternative is not the key ingredient to overcoming the neoliberal ideology (and its

DOI: 10.4324/9781003514916-3

institutions). If there are few or no such representations, then we cannot reject the 'null hypothesis'. That is, the ideology produced by popular culture may be an important way of informing our collective political ideology and the representations of positive alternatives may be critical in overcoming TINA.

Chapters 3–6 look specifically at the question of what critical depictions of capitalism and the state are really representing. The results presented in those chapters are drawn from an analysis of over 400 screen media texts – although many more were viewed for the purpose of the project and over 100 other screen media texts are cited and discussed in the book. How were these screen media texts selected? How were they analyzed? This chapter looks at the methodological approach taken. First, to answer the two overarching questions discussed in the previous paragraph, I set out to analyze a large sample of popular screen media texts that included critical representations of capitalism and/or the state and investigate those representations. I also sought to use critical texts as a method of finding representations of alternative systems as they are more likely to be present in critical texts than in texts without such critiques. However, this was not the exclusive way of looking for alternative representations. Of course, it would be impossible to analyze all screen media texts. Data shows that between 2010 and 2022, the average number of released films in the United States and Canada[1] and English-language scripted series across all platforms (broadcast and streaming)[2] was roughly 1,060 per year (also see Figure 2.1). Consequently, to make sure the most likely screen media texts to have critical representations were being targeted, I used purposive sampling within a relatively wide but constrained pool. The screen media texts targeted were predominantly English-language and widely released in the

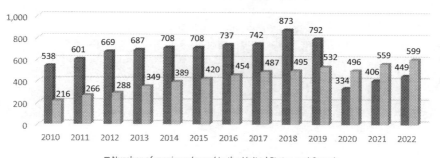

FIGURE 2.1 Film and Television Releases (2010–2022). Data from Box Office Mojo and Porter 2023.

40 Research Methods

United States between 1980 and the end of 2023. First, the criteria sought to focus on screen media texts that had large exposure and thus the potential to affect a large number of people's political ideology. This speaks mostly to English-language markets where American-produced texts are more easily distributed, but the international market also includes many cultural products created in the United States thanks to cultural neocolonialism.[3] A wide release is of course relative. The idea here was to focus on content that was on major television channels, streaming platforms, and cinemas. While a few short-lived (and thus relatively unpopular) television series were included, these were released on large networks. The sampling method did not actively exclude, for example, British or Canadian films if they otherwise fitted the criteria, however the vast majority of the screen media texts selected were American produced. Second, the date range was large – spanning nearly 45 years – in order to capture the period since roughly the rise of neoliberalism. Thus, any film or television text from 1980 up to the end of 2023 was considered. This was to demonstrate that the argument being made is not simply a short-term phenomenon and, at the same time, it limits the scope of the population to a manageable size.

Only fictional works were considered, and consequently news coverage or documentary films or series were not included. The sample of texts was limited to what I term screen media with political or economic content (SMPEC). To better understand SMPEC it is helpful to consider an existing framework for looking at political screen media.[4] Haas et al. developed a typography of political films which is also applicable to television series and can be expanded to questions about the economy. Haas et al. constructed a 2x2 table consisting of political content and political intent each with high and low levels (see Table 2.1). Political content refers to "depicting, more or less accurately, if not realistically, some aspect of political reality".[5] Here, the authors are referring to screen media texts that depict political institutions, such as the White House, Parliament, or courts; political processes, such as election campaigns and legislation; and political actors, such as policymakers. A broader reading of 'politics', which Haas et al. also subscribe to, includes institutions, processes, and actors such as the military, war, and the police, respectively. Whereas political content depicts political intent, "seeks to judge, prescribe, and/or persuade".[6]

TABLE 2.1 Types of Political Films Suggested by Dimensions of Content and Intent[a]

		Political Intent	
		Low	High
Political Content	High	Politically reflective	Pure political
	Low	Socially reflective	Auteur political

[a] Haas et al. 2015.

Given that both political content and political intent are a spectrum, they indicate the four ideal types in which screen media texts are either 'high' or 'low' in political content and intent. Screen media texts that are high in content and intent are labelled by Haas et al. as pure political which means that the "political nature of such films will be fairly evident to most audiences".[7] These are texts that are political in what they show and are politically 'active' in how they show it. Griffith's racist *The Birth of a Nation* (1915) (which was originally titled *The Clansman*) is given as an example. Films with high levels of political content but low levels of political intent are described as politically reflective in that they reflect "popular ideas about political phenomena"[8] and often use political institutions, actors, etc. ... as the context in which they focus on other, non-political themes and ideas. An example the authors present here is the romantic comedy *The American President* (1995) which uses the office of president to explore the human element, such as the romantic relationship the president forms with a lawyer. A television series such as *Veep* (2012–2019), a show about a fictional vice president, which is all about the laughs serves as another example. Texts with low political content but high political intent are referred to as 'auteur political' in that there is not a strong level of politics represented through institutions, processes, or characters but there is a *symbolic* discussion of political matters in the text. These texts feature little to no political characters; no one is voting; no one is talking about birth control regulations or Republicans and Democrats. Instead, they mask political referents in apolitical references. As an example, Haas et al. discuss the adaptations of Arthur Miller's play *The Crucible* which was a parable about communist witch hunts of the 1950s.[9] More contemporary examples may be the horror films by Jordan Peele (e.g., *Get Out* (2017), *Us* (2019)). Finally, where there is both low political content and low political intent there are 'socially reflective' texts. They do not speak about politics overtly in what they represent, nor do they have an intentional political message that focuses on other referents. As Haas et al. note, most Hollywood films (and we can extend this to popular television programming) fall into this category.

The research this book contains expands this typology to include economics. For example, a film with a character who owns a business – say, the film *The Company Men* (2010) – may not be high on *political* content if we think about politics in a narrow sense. It does, however, feature a lot of content (setting, characters, processes) that relate to a business and the economy. We see CEOs, unemployed workers, discussions about stock prices and hostile takeovers, etc.

Given that SMPEC is focused on content rather than intent, the types of screen media with no direct political or economic content were excluded. Part of the reason for this is a problem with the typology above. Consider the 'auteur political' category where political content is low, but political

42 Research Methods

intent is high. Here, movies are 'imparted' with political meaning without overt reference to politics.[10] But how are they imparted, by whom, and how do we know their 'intent'? The use of 'auteur' seems to suggest that it was perhaps the director who imparted the film with a deeper level of (political) meaning, as auteur theory usually places the director in this role.[11] However, the director of one of the examples used by Haas et al. for this category, the original *Invasion of the Body Snatchers* (1956) – a film widely discussed as an allegory about the McCarthy era -- denies the connection. Instead, he claims he wanted to show that "so many people have no feeling about cultural things, no feeling of pain, of sorrow".[12] It was an allegory, but not a political one. Perhaps it was someone else, such as the writer of the original novel, the screenwriter, or the producer who imparted the underlying political meaning. The head of Allied Artists Studio which produced the film, Walter Mirisch,[13] begged to differ. He stated in his autobiography, "From personal knowledge, neither [the producer] Walter Wagner nor Don Siegel, who directed it, nor Dan Mainwaring, who wrote the script, nor the original author, Jack Finney, nor myself saw it as anything other than a thriller, pure and simple".[14] Perhaps someone is lying here, but how else can we figure out an intention unless someone states it in some way? Thus, I argue that it is less about political *intent* than about interpretation. But when it comes to screen media texts that do not have a sufficient level of political *content*, how can we clearly see what the political meaning may be? Each viewer can draw political ideas from various films or television series. Although in later chapters I delve into my own readings and interpretations of texts to make wider points regarding popular culture and politics, most of the analysis presented in the book tries to steer clear of interpretations that cannot be defended with direct, explicit reference to politics and economics within the screen media texts themselves.

Given the discussion above, the sampling required screen media texts to include political and economic content. I did not restrict myself to high levels of such content and thus even brief but explicit references to politics and economics would qualify the text for inclusion. For example, in the romantic dramedy *As Good as It Gets* (1997) the issue of the healthcare system is raised very briefly, which serves to develop characters and their relationships. Despite its brief mention and the apolitical work for which it is used for – to advance the romantic storyline – this would fulfill the criteria for inclusion in the sample. However, most texts were biased toward having high levels of political or economic content because of the sampling method.

In order to produce a long list of potential films to include in my analysis, I utilized a number of different means. First, I found web-based lists of films and television programs using keyword searches such as 'political', 'radical', 'politics', 'economics', 'capitalism', 'money', and 'utopia' to generate a large number of films to consider. Many of the lists were user-produced via IMDb (Internet Movie Database). I selected only the screen media texts that met the selection criteria regarding origins and dates. These lists were not the only source of the sample, however. I asked others – colleagues, friends, and family – to provide examples of relevant texts. In addition, I scoured my memory for screen media texts I had already seen that met the criteria and went back to view them again. Of course, I was not able to find a copy or access all the films or shows in the long list that was generated. Typically, those I could not find were less popular texts and thus they were likely of less cultural importance when considering their ideological impact.

As mentioned above, the analysis was composed of 455 screen media texts. However, it may not be apparent as to what this number includes. Is every scene another 'text'? Is every episode of a television show another 'text'? Regarding the unit of analysis for texts, that depended on the screen media format. For standard films, each film was the unit of analysis. Sequels, spin-offs, or reboots would count as separate items. Films made for television (although there are only very few included here) are counted as films. No anthology films were included in the analysis (although Vittoria de Sica's *Yesterday, Today and Tomorrow* (1963) is discussed in the final chapter). For a standard television series, the unit of analysis was a season. Aside from pilots that do not get 'picked up', most television shows are structured and commissioned season by season and thus story lines are often developed on a seasonal basis. Even where characters, relationships, and settings are consistent throughout seasons, representations can change rather dramatically from one season to the next. *The Wire* (2002–2008) is in many ways a case in point. Each season expands the world of the show and many of the characters change substantially across seasons. Though a television show may be included in the analysis, not all seasons may have been included – partly because the book is likely to be published before additional seasons are released. Where a particular episode is of specific interest, I will indicate the matter but still count the season as the unit of study. Television shows where the season did not serve as the unit of analysis were episodic programs, in which each episode presents new characters, contexts, etc. A good example of this is *Black Mirror* (2011–). Even though the show is meant to take place within the same 'universe',[15] much like Quintan Tarantino films,[16] they present us with very different representations, each deserving of its own consideration. Because of this, each episode is the unit of analysis for an episodic show. For a mini-series, the whole of the mini-series forms the unit of analysis. These can be thought of as long films broken up in parts, but they are counted as a television series.

Not every text that meets the criteria above presented a critical perspective. Screen media texts with political content can be just setting up a context to explore something other than politics. Of course, even an exploration of

44 Research Methods

politics can be supportive of capitalism and the state. Thus, the long list was shortened as those texts that had no critical representations of these systems or their components were discarded. The full list of screen media texts used for the analysis presented here can be found in the Appendix. I use examples throughout the book, but some endnotes also include additional examples which may be helpful for the reader. The screen media texts that aligned to the criteria, and which were used for the analysis and cited in the book, are represented in Figure 2.2 broken down by year and media form – split between films and television series. This data is not meant to be representative. Years with higher numbers of texts, for example, do not necessarily indicate a year with more critical popular cultural content. Likewise, in my sample films outnumbered series (by seasons) by quite a large margin, but this too does not mean that films had more critiques than television shows.[17] We can also see that there are a larger number of examples from the 1990s onward, and thus the 1980s were probably underrepresented here (although it is possible that the 1980s had fewer relevant screen media texts). Data was collected between June 2015 and January 2024, representing almost 10 years of research.

Having described the sampling and the data collected, I now want to discuss the analysis. However, the selection of the unit of analysis is important in this regard. This is because the 'meaning' of a show – in relation to capitalism and the state – is read not on a scene-by-scene or even an episode-by-episode basis (unless the texts is episodic). The critique had to be interpreted from the whole of the text. Imagine a film in which a character says: 'capitalism is terrible'. This would not classify the text as being radically critical of capitalism in and of itself. Other information is important. What was the context of the snippet of dialogue? Perhaps the whole sentence was "Amusement parks are the embodiment of capitalism and capitalism is terrible". But what was the context of this sentence? Who was saying it? How was it said? Furthermore, there are many elements of film- and television-making that inform the audience about meaning without ever using dialogue to do so. Imagine that the line was said as the characters step into an enchanting amusement park and look around in wonder; uplifting music and laughing children are heard in the background. The characters have smiles on their faces and a glow in their eyes. Perhaps this scene is telling us that these jaded characters were wrong about their original anti-capitalist ideas or that they were speaking sarcastically. The *dialogue* tells us that capitalism is bad, but the *scene* tells us that capitalism is good. But imagine that, as the film goes on, we find out the characters in this hypothetical scene are actually the villain owners of the park. They truly love the park but later in the text we see tortured minimum wage employees who are the protagonists. Perhaps the film goes on to expose the environmental harms the amusement park causes, the

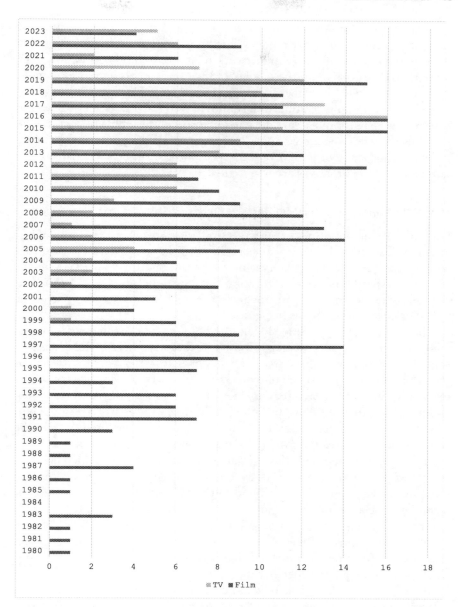

FIGURE 2.2 Number of Screen Media Texts Analyzed Organized by Year and Type

dangers it poses to people, the third world sweatshop labor used for all the gift shop items, etc. This tells us yet a different story and to 'read' this story we need to consider the dialogue, the characters, the images, the soundtrack, and much more.

46 Research Methods

This analysis draws on what Robert Spadoni argues is a combination of content and form, but what he refers to simply as form. "Think of form as the way the different parts of an artwork relate to each other and how they come together to make up the whole."[18] Spadoni is interested in looking at narrative and style altogether, where style includes, for example, mise-en-scène, cinematography, editing, and sound. He talks about "seeing the whole in terms of the parts and seeing the parts in terms of the whole".[19] In total, he calls this the 'viewer-centered approach' to screen media text analysis. I take a similar approach but with a very focused purpose on how capitalism, the state, and their alternatives are represented.[20]

The *RMS Titanic* and the HMO Bastard Pieces of Shit

Looking for representations of capitalism and the state raises a methodological question. Unlike the hypothetical example above, characters in screen media texts rarely talk about the *systems* of capitalism and the state. They might talk about specific policies or corporations, but how do we read this as a radical, systemic critique and not just a critique limited to the particular policy or corporation that is being discussed?

The word 'radical' is derived from the Latin *radix*, meaning root. People who are radical critics of capitalism, for example, believe that there is something wrong with the system of capitalism at its very roots rather than something that can be pruned into an acceptable form. But in terms of screen media representations, we are more likely to find something like the one-line attack of a particular part of the system – healthcare – as we find in the film *As Good as It Gets*. Cinematically pinpointing certain pressure points in the system – be it welfare, work/life imbalance, wage suppression, tax fraud, etc. … still leads us to focus on the particular and avoids the general. These are the wilted leaves on a tree that needs to be cut down at its root and a myopic focus on the leaves will leave us blind to the real rot. But the tree metaphor, from the perspective of the human eye, only takes us so far. We must consider the tree from the perspective of the ant. An ant may be able to 'see' the leaf, to interact with small branches and bits of bark, but it cannot visualize the tree as a whole. It may understand that it is there, that it exists, but it can't *see* it. It can only piece it together through its parts.

Likewise, for us *depictions* of capitalism or the state as whole systems are impossible to make. They cannot be represented themselves by themselves because they occupy a level of abstraction that make them inaccessible to average human imagining. Like a tree to the ant, they are in effect too big to see. This is because this level of abstraction goes beyond what cognitive scientists refer to as basic-level categories where words representing subjects "tend to be recognizable via gestalt perception, [to] be learned earlier, to be shorter (e.g., car vs. vehicle), to be more frequent, to be remembered more easily, and so on".[21] We can construct a mental picture of a generalized car, but we cannot construct an image of a generalized vehicle. The concept vehicle, like capitalism, is too abstract to 'picture'.

Film and television rarely discuss capitalism and the state in the abstract. So, how can we find critiques of these concepts in such texts?

> Abstract concepts, such as 'democracy' are considered to have an indirect basis in the sensory-motor system as representations of situations that are created from different individual experiences, such as 'voting in a voting booth'.... Thus, abstract concepts can be understood in terms of concrete concepts through metaphorical associations with concrete domains of experiences.[22]

That is, while we cannot conjure up an image of such concepts and they cannot be represented within an image, there are things that can be represented that stand in for these concepts. We can imagine a building (e.g., the White House or the Houses of Parliament) or a person (e.g., president, prime minister, a politician), or an event (e.g., voting in a voting booth, Senate hearing) that can stand in for the state. Equally we can imagine a brand logo, a corporate building, a workplace meeting, a boss, a banker, or a capitalist. These can act as representations of capitalism. This representational capacity is by no means limited to fictional circumstances. For example, Karl Marx uses individuals to stand in for classes in *The Class Struggles in France, 1848 to 1850* when writing about the French Second Republic. Writing about Napoleon III's Minister of Finance Achille Fould, Marx stated, "With the nomination of Fould, the finance aristocracy announced its restoration in the Moniteur".[23]

This view suggests that even a criticism of HMOs *could* be narrated in a way that produces a wider critique, where HMOs stand in for some broader process. However, not every bank, brand, or boss is used to represent a broader institution or system. Sometimes an HMO is just an HMO. Texts that include those broader representations need to be investigated using theoretically driven analysis to understand if the instance acts as a stand-in for the general within the textual analysis, and what exactly it stands in for.[24]

As in Chapter 1, let us take another screen media representation of the disaster of the *RMS Titanic* as an example, and also as a cautionary tale:

> Next week, the Titanic makes her maiden voyage over the big pond and you, gentlemen, will be aboard as my guests. On this trip you will experience a sensational surprise that will cause our shares to skyrocket. ... I ask all of you to trust me just as we all trust our Titanic, the proudest ship ever to sail soon to set to sea for the honor of the White Star Line and the glory of England.[25]

48 Research Methods

Sir Bruce Ismay, the president of the White Star Line, spent a large fortune building the *Titanic*, causing his investors to panic. But he didn't worry. He planned to buy low and then sell high after the *Titanic* had become "the fastest ship that has ever sailed the Atlantic". We know the ending to this story: the ship crashes and many people lose their lives. This story and quotation are from the 1943 film *Titanic* and while the representations are not the truth about what occurred, they present a kind of general critique using a specific case. Although the film's explanation was false, capitalism was at fault for the tragedy of the *Titanic*. There were not enough lifeboats to fit everyone and, due to the lack of training, many of the lifeboats were not full when they were released into the water. The profit incentive paved the way to poor regulations which may not have necessarily prevented the sinking of the ship but did mean that most of the passengers died as a result. The film shows that following the tragedy a trial was held and the captain of the ship, who was only following Ismay's orders, was at fault while Ismay was acquitted. The film represents the trial as a systemic political problem, as it ends by saying that "the deaths of 1,500 people remain unatoned for, an eternal condemnation of England's quest for profit".[26]

Here we can see how the particular can speak for the general. Reading the description above we may think that the White Star Line and President Ismay stand in for capitalism, and the Maritime Board of Inquiry which acquitted Ismay stand in for the state. However, if we develop a better contextualization of the film, its story, and its protagonists, we instead find that these representations stand in only for *British* capitalism and the *British* state. We should be wary of what this supposedly 'radical' critique is lining us up for as an alternative. Rather than being a systemic critique of capitalism and the state, it is a particular critique of Britain from an ethno-nationalist perspective. We know this both from the representations within the film and from the fact that the film was made in Germany at the time of Nazi rule. It was commissioned under the Minister of Propaganda Joseph Goebbels, passed the censors, and was declared a politically valuable piece of Nazi propaganda. While we can clearly read a critique of capitalism within the text, the implication is that German fascism was the superior economic system. This is hardly the alternative we are looking for, but it demonstrates a critique of critique. Even where capitalism or the state are positioned as wrong, corrupt, or immoral, the conclusion drawn might call for a different kind of capitalism or state – 'ethno-nationalist' dictatorship in the case of this film.

The case of *Titanic* (1943) also suggests the importance of deeper explanations of how and why I categorize and understand the level of critique for each text I examine. However, given the sheer number of screen media texts covered in the book, I cannot do this for each one. I try to present examples and highlight texts that are particularly relevant. That said, a viewer-centered approach is one that can be challenged by others' interpretations. Readers can view the screen media texts discussed in the book and cross-check my interpretation with their own perspective and with evidence drawn from the text. Although not freely available, the data used for this research is 'public' and thus this study is replicable, including by the use of other texts. People can challenge my categorization and placement of screen media texts within the categories. That is to say, I am trying to develop an argument that is verifiable but requires some level of subjective interpretation. For much of the argument, the interpretation is not only to be made from the screen media text's own formal elements but also through an interpretation that is in keeping with the way the viewer is 'directed' to interpret the text.

Finally, it should also be noted that in some places in the book, films, or television shows that fall outside the criteria discussed above were used to explore and make connections between ideas. Examples of films that presented conservative politics are discussed. Some older or foreign films, for example, are discussed to introduce new ideas such as *Saved from the Titanic* (1912), a film discussed in Chapter 1. Thus, not every screen media text cited in the book is used in the process described here.

Notes

1 Box Office Mojo 2023.
2 Porter 2023.
3 Butsch 2019, pp. 211–214.
4 Haas et al. 2015.
5 Haas et al. 2015, p. 9.
6 Haas et al. 2015, p. 10.
7 Haas et al. 2015, p. 11.
8 Haas et al. 2015, p. 13.
9 Haas et al. 2015, pp. 12–13.
10 Haas et al. 2015, p. 12.
11 E.g., Sarris 1963.
12 As quoted in Shultz 2015.
13 Mirisch 2008, p. 40.
14 Also see Bennett 2004, p. 243.
15 Bojalad 2019.
16 Hunt 2019.
17 It should be noted that in general, the number of television series was substantially lower than the number of released films until COVID restrictions meant a reduction of theatrical releases and moved more content onto streaming services (as can be seen from Figure 2.1).
18 Spadoni 2014, pp. 7–8.
19 Spadoni 2014, p. 7.
20 Chapter 6 is different from other chapters because, rather than seeking texts that contain explicit political or economic content, it looks for texts that represent not political or economic alternatives, but social or lifestyle alternatives. A similar

50 Research Methods

analysis is undertaken but a sampling of texts was not applied. Instead, some relevant texts served as examples.

21 Gallese and Lakoff 2005. For more on basic-level categories, see Laeng et al. 2003; Markman and Wisniewski 1997.
22 Dijkstra et al. 2014, citing Barsalou and Wiemer-Hastings 2005.
23 Marx 2010, p. 114.
24 See e.g., Stemler 2015.
25 From the film *Titanic* (1943).
26 In reality, the speed of the *Titanic* made avoiding the iceberg difficult (Howells 1999). However, the British inquiry into the *Titanic* did not find that the captain "had been under any pressure from White Star Line chairman J. Bruce Ismay" (Stemler 2015, p. 31).

References

Barsalou, Lawrence W. and Wiemer-Hastings, Katja (2005) 'Situating Abstract Concepts, in Grounding Cognition', in Diane Pecher and Rolf A. Zwaan (eds.), *The Role of Perception and Action in Memory, Language, and Thinking* (pp. 129–163), Cambridge: Cambridge University Press.

Bennett, Gillian (2004) 'The Bosom Serpent: Folklore and Popular Art', Book Review, *Folklore*, 115(2): 241–243.

Bojalad, Alec (2019) 'Black Mirror Shared Universe Confirmed – Here Is What It Looks Like', Den of Geek, June 5, https://www.denofgeek.com/tv/black-mirror-shared-universe-timeline.

Box Office Mojo (2023) 'Domestic Yearly Box Office', December 21, https://www.boxofficemojo.com/year/?grossesOption=totalGrosses.

Butsch, Richard (2019) *Screen Culture: A Global History*, Cambridge: Polity Press.

Dijkstra, Katrina, Eerland, Anita, Zijlmans, Josjan, and Post, Lysanne S. (2014) 'Embodied Cognition, Abstract Concepts, and the Benefits of New Technology for Implicit Body Manipulation', *Frontiers in Psychology*, 5: 757, doi:10.3389/fpsyg.2014.00757.

Gallese, Vittorio & and Lakoff, George (2005). 'The Brain's Concepts: The Role of the Sensory-Motor System in Conceptual Knowledge', *Cognitive Neuropsychology*, 22(3–4): 455–479.

Haas, Elizabeth, Christensen, Terry, and Haas, Peter J. (2015) *Projecting Politics: Political Messages in American Films*, 2nd Edition, Abingdon: Routledge.

Howells, Richard (1999) *The Myth of the Titanic*, Basingstoke: Macmillan Press.

Hunt, James (2019) 'Quentin Tarantino Movie Shared Universe Explained', Screen Rant, July 24, https://screenrant.com/quentin-tarantino-movie-shared-universe-explained.

Laeng, Bruno, Zarrinpar, Amir, and Kosslyn, Stephen M. (2003). 'Do Separate Processes Identify Objects as Exemplars Versus Members of Basic-Level Categories? Evidence from Hemispheric Specialization', *Brain and Cognition*, 53(1): 15–27.

Markman, Arthur B. and Wisniewski, Edward J. (1997). 'Similar and Different: The Differentiation of Basic-Level Categories', *Journal of Experiential Psychology: Learning, Memory, and Cognition*, 23(1): 54–70.

Marx, Karl (2003) 'The Class Struggles in France, 1848 to 1850', in Karl Marx and Frederick Engels, *Marx and Engels Collected Works, Volume 10* (pp. 45–145), London: Lawrence and Wishart.

Mirisch, Walter (2008) *I Thought We Were Making Movies, Not History*, Madison: University of Wisconsin Press.

Porter, Rick (2023) 'Peak TV Climbs Again in 2022, Nearly Reaches 600 Scripted Series', *The Hollywood Reporter*, Jan. 12, https://www.hollywoodreporter.com/tv/tv-news/peak-tv-2022-count-599-scripted-shows-1235298139.

Sarris, Andrew (1963) 'Notes on the Auteur Theory in 1962', *Film Culture*, 27: 1–8.

Shultz, Christopher (2015) 'Book vs. Film(s): "Invasion of the Body Snatchers"', *Lit Reactor*, May 29, https://litreactor.com/columns/book-vs-films-invasion-of-the-body-snatchers.

Spadoni, Robert (2014) *A Pocket Guide to Analyzing Films*, Berkeley: University of California Press.

Stemler, Steven E. (2015) 'Content Analysis', in Robert Scott and Stephan Kosslyn (eds.), *Emerging Trends in the Social and Behavioral Sciences*, Hoboken, NJ: Wiley, https://doi.org/10.1002/9781118900772.etrds0053.

3

EIGHT LIMITED CRITIQUES OF CAPITALISM AND THE STATE

Mapping the Terrain

Critiques serve as a starting point for developing alternatives. They help to locate our current position on the political map of possibilities, and they suggest alternative routes and potential destinations. Critiques provide a *reason* for alternatives, a collective rationale through which we can question the benefits of the social structures around us. Critiques are used to construct a discursive plane from which we can envision horizons, to our right and to our left. In this sense, a critique provides us with a utopia of sorts. As Marxist literary critic Fredric Jameson wrote, "works of mass culture cannot be ideological without at one and the same time being implicitly or explicitly Utopian as well".[1] That is, critique features in it a promise of something better that can lead to a radical horizon or, conversely, can be "a fantasy bribe to the public about to be ... manipulated".[2] Critique helps to shape the limits of our own imaginary in response to the faults within our current system. What are these faults? Can these problems be reformed, or do they require a revolution? Who is the revolutionary subject and how should the revolution be brought about? In a sense, critiques are like a compass where south is our past and north is the continuation of our present. Westward lie the possibilities on the political left and eastward the possibilities on the right. We look at each critique, each screen media text, from our present position and see what direction they point us to. If a critique is just a little west of the magnetic north, then the critique is calling for minor reforms. The further west, the more radical the critique. Once we have our trajectory, we can follow the text's critique to uncover new territories in our map of possibilities. Specifically, how far west do our film and television texts go?

The metaphor of compasses and maps relates to Jameson's notion of 'cognitive mapping'. For Jameson, the postmodern world in which we live

DOI: 10.4324/9781003514916-4

is a discombobulated and directionless place. Due to the ideology of TINA, we now see the world through an ahistorical lens. We are experiencing "the suppression of critical distance resulting from the completion of the global circuit of capitalism".[3] According to Jameson, a prerequisite for escaping capitalism is to have a cognitive map, a mental image of the social totality, and in order to do that we need aesthetics to allow people to connect the abstract understanding of the laws of capital that command our social existence with their own personal life experiences. Thus, art helps to produce a cognitive map that we can use to escape the ideology of TINA.

Let us think about each screen media text as a surveyor sent to draw the contours on a map of our social consciousness, our moral and ideological understanding. Often the surveyors find themselves mapping the same terrain – presenting us with the same critique. (Take, for example, how both *Detroit* (2017) and *LA Confidential* (1997) present a critique of police corruption.) These surveyors hike the same hills and cross the same channels, but in doing so strengthen the collective cultural viability of this route of passage into the future, a route for the collective migration of refugees from the present. But most surveyors rarely leave home, circling around what I will call Junkspace City that represents today.

When Žižek said it was easier to imagine the end of the world than the end of capitalism he was borrowing a phrase from Fredric Jameson who wrote it in his review of the Dutch architect Rem Koolhaas's notion of Junkspace. Junkspace is the built product of modernization. It is constant building without building anything worthwhile. The death of architecture. Our modern capitalist world is full of Junkspace, vacuous and ever in need of renovation. As soon as shopping malls, office buildings, and apartment blocks are built they need repairs. If they don't get repaired then "an entire Junkspace—a department store, a nightclub, a bachelor pad—turns into a slum overnight without warning".[4] The postmodern world around us looks like the end of the world itself. Jameson wrote, "Someone once said that it is easier to imagine the end of the world than to imagine the end of capitalism. We can now revise that and witness the attempt to imagine capitalism by way of imagining the end of the world".[5]

It is the Junkspace City of neoliberalism that we inhabit, and with it the idea that there is no alternative, with only the possibility of a few modifications in any direction. Junkspace City slopes and bends, covering our collectively clumped ideologies into the boroughs of Liberalism, Conservatism, Centrism, etc. .... The most populous of these is of course Apoliticism. It is here that we can invoke the director Wim Wenders who said:

> Every film is political. Most political of all are those that pretend not to be: 'entertainment' movies. They are the most political films there are because they dismiss the possibility of change. In every frame they tell you everything's fine the way it is.[6]

54 Eight Limited Critiques of Capitalism and the State

Thus, the surveyors – cultural texts – continually strengthen and expand the internal links within the city, connected by fat fettuccine freeways with signs reading "FORTUNE – 2 Miles", "ROMANCE – Next Exit". The roads are densely packed with drivers desperately seeking to reach their destination. The heavy traffic means most will never arrive, stuck in endless stop-and-go rotation.

Beyond the cities lie undiscovered beauty that the citizens of Junkspace City can hardly imagine. The presentation of critique helps to shape the direction in which we are looking out to those other horizons. The surveyors who dive into the depth of the ocean and slog through the snow-topped mountain peaks rediscover endangered species of hope and present us with radical vistas of the future. They are equipped with the compass of critique that gives them, and subsequently us, the angle we should take to move away from our starting point within the city and take us westward.

This postmodern world of today is today into the future because of the circular logic of capital itself. There is no alternative to today; Junkspace City will simply rebuild its own constantly dilapidating self forever into the future. But as reports come in from the surveyors who venture further afield, notions of other realms of existence outside the city become normalized, become destinations of possibility. However, these alternatives need not be places of rupture that abandon Junkspace City, but an expansion of the city itself. A municipal subsumption. The city reformed.[7]

This chapter presents the first set of findings from the research. It highlights a large number of screen media texts that feature a critique of capitalism and/or the state but which, in the various ways described below, are not systemic or radical critiques.

The Compass of Limited Critique

> The folly of men has enhanced the value of gold and silver because of their scarcity; whereas, on the contrary, it is their opinion that Nature, as an indulgent parent, has freely given us all the best things in great abundance, such as water and earth, but has laid up and hid from us the things that are vain and useless.[8]

Gold, the useless glistening mineral, is the valued possession of the flawed rich in Thomas More's *Utopia*, and likewise the dream of the city dwellers in the Liberal borough of Junkspace City. These citizens await the moment of westward expansion where they can make a home for themselves. Like the American myopia, they see the Pacific Ocean as one end of a globe. Gold mining towns represent limited critiques that lead us to the pseudo-utopias that lie not far from Junkspace City. Gold for a radical utopian is just fool's

Eight Limited Critiques of Capitalism and the State **55**

gold; a gold mining town discovered by one of our surveyors is just a critique that is easily enveloped into the bounds of the city itself. When discovered, the gold dust is spread on its citizens who in turn shower the mine owner and mayor with praise. *Black Panther*'s (2018) pseudo-radical representation is an example. It received applause for depicting a black, African superhero but really tells the story of collaboration with American imperialism and isolationism.

Below is a catalogue of the discoveries of gold mines surrounding the city. They represent the various critiques that are nothing more than a fool's paradise, limited critiques that do not demand a fundamental shift away from the Junkspace City that represents our system. Instead, they call for the expansion of the City through its incorporation of the mining communities (minor reforms, at best); they only further entrench the exploited citizens into further rebuilding their ever-breaking buildings.

Unlike gold, water is not a fool's treasure. This was the prized treasure of one fictitious entrepreneur, Dominic Greene, who made a deal to help overthrow the democratically elected Bolivian government in exchange for land that would allow Greene to dam up and privatize the country's fresh water supply – all with the help of the US government. If this sounds familiar to you then you probably remember it from the 2008 James Bond film *Quantum of Solace*. The film presents a seemingly radical narrative about the interaction between state and capital for the sake of power and profit[9] but we must follow the plot of the film to its conclusion. Yes, James Bond kills the bad capitalist, but the politics of the film are resolved when 'good' people are placed in senior positions within institutions of power. Justice is fully restored when the right people are promoted, and the bad ones are fired.

Many such critiques of the state and capital are presented in screen media texts. These critiques find problems with *particular* bosses or politicians, companies or administrations, economic or political sectors, or corporate or government policies. The critique within these texts is that which cannot easily be transposed onto capitalism or the state more broadly. Instead, they effectively signal that some aspects of capitalism or the state are good, and some are bad – we can refer to this as **the good, the bad, and the ugly critique**. Many other screen media texts utilize this limited critique (see Table 3.1).

Often this narrative is constructed within a plot in which all the major characters (both 'heroes' and 'villains') are part of the same institution and collectively they can represent the institution as a whole. In doing so, the critiques are often leveled at particular parts of the institutions or individuals within them and thus are limited. Regarding the representation of security services *Traitor* (2008), *The Americans* (seasons 1–6; 2013– 2018), *Sicario* (2015), *The Kingdom* (2007), and The *Bourne* series all fit this general

56 Eight Limited Critiques of Capitalism and the State

TABLE 3.1 Examples of The Good, The Bad, and The Ugly Critique

1917 (2019)	*9 to 5 (1980)*	*Accidental Love (2015)*
Air (2023)	*All the Money in the World* (2017)	*American Beauty* (1999)
American Dreamz (2006)	*American Gangster* (2007)	*Ant-Man* (2015)
Arrested Development (seasons 1–5) (2003–2019)	*Bombshell* (2019)	*Buffalo Soldiers* (2001)
City of Hope (1991)	*Escape from LA (1996)*	*Eye in the Sky (2015)*
Ford v Ferrari (2019)	*Free Guy* (2021)	*Frost/Nixon (2008)*
Fun with Dick and Jane (2005)	*Glass Onion* (2022)	*Horrible Bosses (2011)*
In the Electric Mist (2009)	*Kimi (2022)*	*Kingsman: The Golden Circle* (2017)
Mad City (1997)	*Medical Police* (season 1) (2020)	*Miss Sloane* (2016)
Mission: Impossible (1996)	*Mission: Impossible II* (2000)	*Mission Impossible III* (2006)
Mission: Impossible – Fallout (2018)	*Mission: Impossible – Rogue Nation* (2015)	*Money Monster* (2016)
Nick of Time (1995)	*Outbreak* (1995)	*Pain Hustlers (2023)*
Painkiller (2023)	*Philadelphia* (1993)	*Pokémon Detective Pikachu* (2019)
Ready Player One (2018)	*Richie Rich* (1994)	*Robocop* (2014)
Runaway Jury (2003)	*Runner Runner* (2013)	*Scrooged* (1988)
Severance (season 1) (2022)	*Speed Racer* (2008)	*Stranger Things* (seasons 1–4) (2016–2022)
Syriana (2005)	*Tetris* (2023)	*The Accountant* (2016)
The Americans (seasons 1–6) (2013–2018)	*The Assassination of Richard Nixon* (2004)	*The Boss Baby (2017)*
The Butler (2013)	*The Chamber* (1996)	*The Company Men* (2010)
The Contract (2006)	*The Distinguished Gentleman* (1992)	*The Founder* (2016)
The Ghost Writer (2010)	*The Menu* (2022)	*The Morning Show* (season 3) (2023)
The Office (US seasons 1–9) (2005–2013)	*Total Recall* (2012)	*Truth* (2015)
Vice (2018)	*Wall Street: Money Never Sleeps* (2010)	*War Dogs* (2016)
Working Girl (1988)	*xXx: State of the Union* (2005)	

profile.[10] Similar representations can be found in film and television texts that focus on the police and politicians.[11]

Other films may demonstrate how one component of the state or capitalism is significantly flawed, but the critique presented is challenged by other aspects of the system which work to reestablish justice, righting the wrongs displayed. This **counterbalanced critique** can be represented in the clash between the "good guy" FBI and the "bad guy" CIA such as in the miniseries *The Looming Tower* (2018); corrupt corporations vs the hardworking FBI, justice system, or Congress (e.g., *Gold* (2016)); or corrupt military and DEA officials vs. incorruptible police detectives (e.g., *American Gangster* (2007)). Steven Soderbergh's *The Informant!* (2009) is based on a true story about an oddball who is involved in price-fixing at his company but then turns informant for the FBI while still taking a cut from the company on the side. The company he works for could be construed as representing capitalism more broadly, but the critique is that the unethical actions of the business are mitigated through the hard work of the FBI, an organization that represents the state. This is very similar to the show *Billions* and the films *Miss Sloane* (2016), *The International* (2009), *Newsies* (1992), and *War Dogs* (2016), but similar counterbalanced critiques representing other stand-ins on either side of the scales of justice can be found in a wide range of screen media texts (see Table 3.2).

Another limited critique presents the problems in society as reformable. The most 'radical' variant of the **reformable critique** essentially calls for moving from a US-style of limited government spending on public services to a Nordic system of social democracy. Francis Ford Coppola's *The Rainmaker* (1997) features some scenes that are damning to corporations as they reveal how the profit motive overrides basic human interest, however in the end the film settles for easy reforms as its desired position. The courtroom drama shows how a medical insurance company went out of its way to deny a necessary bone marrow transplant so that it could save money. The protagonist of the film offers the following as his closing statement in the trial:

> I hope that you are astonished, as I am, at the lengths to which a wealthy insurance company like the defendant will go to take money from a low-income family, and then keep it, while denying a legitimate claim. It's no wonder they spend so much on their lawyers and their lobbyists, and their public relations machine to convince us we need tort reform, that we need to put an end to punitive damages.[12]

Public healthcare and the availability of tort litigation would effectively solve the problems presented in the film. The profit motive itself does not appear to be questioned more broadly (or only in industries such as health insurance

58 Eight Limited Critiques of Capitalism and the State

TABLE 3.2 Examples of The Counterbalanced Critique

A Civil Action (1998)	*Amsterdam (2022)*	*Black Mirror (season 4, episode 1) (2017)*[a]
Blood Diamond (2006)	*Broken City (2013)*	*Cloud Atlas (2012)*[b]
Crisis (2021)	*Enemy of the State (1998)*	*Erin Brockovich (2000)*
Evan Almighty (2007)	*Goliath* (season 1) *(2016)*	*Good Night, and Good Luck (2005)*
Gringo (2018)	*Homicide (1991)*	*Hot Shots! (1991)*
Independence Day (1996)	*Just Mercy (2019)*	*Man of the Year (2006)*
Michael Clayton (2007)	*Money Monster (2016)*	*Murder at 1600 (1997)*
Official Secrets (2019)	*Pain Hustlers (2023)*	*Quantum of Solace (2008)*
Ready Player One (2018)	*Richard Jewell (2019)*	*Richie Rich (1994)*
Robocop (1987)	*RoboCop 2 (1990)*	*The Accountant (2016)*
The Bourne Legacy (2012)	*The Bourne Ultimatum (2007)*	*The Constant Gardener (2005)*
The Expanse (seasons 1–5) *(2015–2020)*	*The Gunman (2015)*	*The Imitation Game (2014)*
The Infiltrator (2016)	*The Insider (1999)*	*The Manchurian Candidate (2004)*
The Net (1995)	*The Nice Guys (2016)*	*The Shawshank Redemption (1994)*
The Siege (1998)	*Tomorrow Never Dies (1997)*	*Traitor (2008)*
xXx: State of the Union (2005)		

[a] *Black Mirror* (2011–2023) is an episodic series.
[b] *Cloud Atlas* features several storylines. The Luisa Rey storyline fits this critique.

which can be nationalized through reforms). Perhaps due to the nature of the justice system, many films about court cases fit this limited critique, such as *Philadelphia* (1993) and *Runaway Jury* (2003) which focus on two specific issues of concern: anti-gay discrimination and gun control, respectively. Other examples of screen media texts that fit the reformable critique can be found in Table 3.3.

Eight Limited Critiques of Capitalism and the State **59**

TABLE 3.3 Examples of The Reformable Critique

Accidental Love (2015)	*Black Sheep (1996)*	*Blood Diamond (2006)*
Brooklyn Nine-Nine (season 8) (2021)	*Eagle Eye* (2008)	*Enemy of the State* (1998)
Good Night, and Good Luck (2005)	*Harold & Kumar Escape from Guantanamo Bay* (2008)	*Inception* (2010)
John Q (2002)	*Miss Sloane* (2016)	*Rendition* (2007)
Snowden (2016)	*Superstore* (seasons 1–6) (2015–2021)	*Terminator 3: Rise of the Machines* (2003)
The Bourne Legacy (2012)	*The Bourne Ultimatum* (2007)	*The Campaign* (2012)
The Distinguished Gentleman (1992)	*The Mauritanian* (2021)	

There are cases of more full-blown critiques of the system. Take this fascinating monologue from the comedy film *The Dictator* (2012):

> Why are you guys so anti-dictators? Imagine if America was a dictatorship. You could let one percent of the people have all the nation's wealth. You could help your rich friends get richer by cutting their taxes and bailing them out when they gamble and lose. You could ignore the needs of the poor for health care and education. Your media would appear free but would secretly be controlled by one person and his family. You could wiretap phones. You could torture foreign prisoners. You could have rigged elections. You could lie about why you go to war. You could fill your prisons with one particular racial group, and no one would complain. You could use the media to scare the people into supporting policies that are against their interests. I know this is hard for you Americans to imagine, but please try.

The film begins in a fictional North African country ruled by the dictator Aladeen. Aladeen is depicted as a stereotypical Arab leader which sets the scene for the film's various (sometimes racist) jokes as we follow the dictator on his trip to America. The quotation above is the words of Aladeen as he addressed a room full of American political and economic elites and showing us our hypocrisy. The monologue asks us to imagine America as a dictatorship, but shows us that it already has all the features of one. However, aside from this short critique, the film largely pokes fun at dictators in the Arab world, often by singling out their antisemitism, sexism, and brutality. In presenting us with this narrative, the film allows the viewer to say that

60 Eight Limited Critiques of Capitalism and the State

capitalist democracy of the Global North is still the best available option, even while knocking it (and at most calling for it to be reformed).

This representation mirrors the discussion presented in Chapter 1 – that of the **least-worst system critique**. Capitalism and the state may be flawed but there is nothing better out there. More typically, texts that fit this category are often (post-)apocalyptic film and television which partially blame the state (and less frequently capitalism) for initiating, facilitating, or failing to stop the impending doom but they return to the state (often of a heavily militarized variety) as either the annihilator of the existential threat or the utopian savior in the apocalyptic world. These apocalyptic images are often counterposed with our own time and space, and thus we are relieved to find ourselves not living in such a situation. Our own system and lifestyle are therefore glorified in comparison[13] (for other examples, see Table 3.4).

Sci-fi and fantasy screen media texts can depict the problems of the state or capital, but they often abandon their critique when they raise metaphysical questions or present a reality other than our own. This **obscured critique** can be found in *Total Recall* (2012). This otherwise typical action movie has a compelling political side plot that serves as the setting in which the characters operate. Briefly, chemical warfare has decimated the planet. All that is left is the United Federation of Britain (which includes Ireland, Spain, and part of France) and the Colony (Australia). This post-war world is heavily overpopulated and, the prologue in the film states, "[L]iving space is now Earth's most valuable resource". The Colony is poor and as the movie progresses, we find out that the government of the United Federation of Britain has hired a private military company to build robot soldiers in order to invade the Colony and take over the land. The ostensibly democratic government must provide a justifiable rationale for the invasion. So, the government commits terrorist attacks against its own civilians and blames the Resistance – a group of radicals seeking to improve conditions in the Colony. We begin to side with the resistance against the

TABLE 3.4 Examples of The Least-Worst System Critique

28 Days Later (2002)	*Chernobyl* (2019)	*Dark Phoenix* (2019)
I Am Legend (2007)	*In Dubious Battle* (2016)	*Independence Day* (1996)
Mad Max: Fury Road (2015)	*RoboCop 2* (1990)	*Snowpiercer* (2013)
Terminator 2: Judgement Day (1991)	*The Book of Eli* (2010)	*The Boss Baby* (2017)
The Day After Tomorrow (2004)	*World War Z* (2013)	

state, the military, and the private company that develops the robots. This setting provides an interesting look at the interaction between state and corporate interests in imperialism and invasion. Nevertheless, this setting is just that. The central plot is motivated by the main character's search for his identity. Douglas Quaid (Colin Farrell) keeps having strange dreams about being a double agent that he cannot understand, leading him to experiment with the company Rekall which implants memories. Quaid asks for memories that correspond with his dreams but as he is getting the implant, he is told the implantation fails if the memories they attempt to generate are true. As soon as he has received the implant, Quaid has to fight off security forces with combat skills that he did not know he had. Thus, we cannot tell if the company is implanting memories or if what is happening is real. It could be the case that Quaid has been a kind of sleeper double agent. He seeks answers and, in his search, the political subtext is exposed. The film never reveals the 'truth', leaving open the possibility that the majority of the movie is an implanted memory. Despite the film's indictment of the government and business, such a view may actually be explained in an imaginary reality. This option would present the critical worldview as a hallucination, undermining any of the political content presented. You will find additional examples of the obscured critique in Table 3.5.

Screen media texts can make substantial critiques and, rather than obscuring them, can ignore or contradict them. An argument presented but not sustained within the text is termed an **overlooked critique**. *In*

TABLE 3.5 Examples of The Obscured Critique

Game of Thrones (seasons 1–8) (2011–2019)	*Killing Them Softly (2012)*	*Men (2022)*
Severance (season 1)	*Starship Troopers* (1997)	*Star Wars: Episode I – The Phantom Menace* (1999)
Star Wars: Episode II – Attack of the Clones (2002)	*Star Wars: Episode III – Revenge of the Sith* (2005)	*Terminator 2: Judgement Day* (1991)
The Golden Compass (2007)	*The Last of Us* (season 1) (2023)	*The Lord of the Rings: The Fellowship of the Ring* (2001)
The Lord of the Rings: The Return of the King (2003)	*The Lord of the Rings: The Two Towers* (2002)	*The Matrix* (1999)
The Matrix Reloaded (2003)	*The Matrix Revolutions* (2003)	*The Peripheral* (season 1) (2022)

62 Eight Limited Critiques of Capitalism and the State

Dubious Battle (2016), based on the novel by John Steinbeck, presents this critique in two different ways so it is worth discussing at greater length. The film is set on a farm during the Great Depression to which people have traveled a long way to get a job picking fruit. Once they arrive, however, the pay they were promised is sharply reduced. "I can't live on a dollar a day" is a repeated line in the film, helping to solidify the angst amongst workers that the main characters, union organizers, use to foment a strike.

The film shows the battles between the farm owner and the fruit pickers, and in doing so depicts capitalism as a brutal force. The film presents this as a systemic problem through the dialogue between an old, scatter-brained union veteran, Joy (Ed Harris), and a young man who has just signed up to fight for the cause, Jim (Nat Wolff):

Joy: Who produces the goods?
Jim: Uh, the workers do.
Joy: And who takes the profit?
Jim: The bosses and the owner?
Joy: By what right? They don't produce nothing. What right do they have?

Despite the radical critique of capitalism, Joy is presented as a character who has fought the union fight for so long, and somewhat poorly, that he has more than a few loose screws. This short exchange is interrupted by the young but seasoned activist, Mac (James Franco): "Joy! You sound like a two-bit preacher in a one-horse town. Will you just stop trying to convince our own people and leave the poor boy alone?" The simplified – and yet important – economic understanding presented by Joy, perhaps because of its directness, is scoffed at. It is relegated to the ramblings of a moonbat.

There are other moments in the film when political discussions are held, but they often lack the same systemic approach. The characters discuss the "shit deal" bosses give to their workers who are "taken advantage of", but the discussion still hovers around the idea of better pay and working conditions – not inherent injustice and exploitation. Any articulated systemic analysis in the film comes from the deranged character Joy:

Why should we work for a man who think they own us? ... They think they can just chew you up, spit you out, take the profits from the work that you do with your sweat and your blood. And these cops, these pigs, you know what they do when you try to exercise your rights as a free American? They bash you in the skull, they knock out your teeth, they kick you in the ribs, call you a piece of shit. And now we're supposed to work for them?

Eight Limited Critiques of Capitalism and the State **63**

He says this immediately before he is shot by private security guards, Pinkertons. Joy is a hot-headed character and we as an audience hope he keeps his mouth shut so he does not get hurt. Consequently, the critique is overlooked in *In Dubious Battle* because the one espousing the critique is marginalized.

We later find out that Joy was likely set up by the union to shoot his mouth off in a hostile setting and get killed in order to rally the workers. Increasingly we see the union scheming and planning, throwing their own under the bus and hurting those they are there to help. Thus, the union is also placed under a shadow, and we side with the farmworkers themselves, although we rarely see them. Jim's love interest, Lisa (Selena Gomez), gives us the closest we get to a farmworker's perspective as she begins to fantasize about running away with Jim to live off the land. However, Jim becomes more enamored with the cause than with this idyllic escape.

Lisa (to Mac):	I was gonna ask Jim to build a house with me when this is all over with. I thought he'd make a good father.
Mac:	Well ... That ain't gonna happen. Kid's got the fever now.
Lisa:	He's gonna stay at this thing until he's arrested or shot, isn't he?

We feel sorry for the destruction of the couple, but not in a heroic way à la *Casablanca* (1942) (or *V for Vendetta* (2005), perhaps). Instead, we would rather see Jim run off with Lisa and save himself –be kind, but not a martyr. Thus, even if we accept that the critique Joy articulated is part of the union ideology, we begin to oppose the union and support a more individualistic lifestyle. The cause itself, and its analysis of capitalism, get overlooked in favor of the quiet life (see Table 3.6 for other examples).

In Dubious Battle's critique of the state is further limited by placing its story in a historical context that brackets its relevance. Not all films that are

TABLE 3.6 Examples of The Overlooked Critique

A Bug's Life (1998)
Admission (2013)
Gaslit (2022)
Jupiter Ascending (2015)
Shooter (2007)
The Hate U Give (2018)
The Other Guys (2010)

64 Eight Limited Critiques of Capitalism and the State

set in the past do this,[14] but *In Dubious Battle* closes with a message that takes a political position and turns it into a limited, **historicized critique**:

> Across the nation, countless workers engaged in battles like these in the ongoing fight for fair treatment. In 1934 alone, over 1.5 million workers took part in 2,000 labor strikes. Most ended in failure, with many of the strikers arrested, wounded, or even killed. But out of these struggles arose change. In 1935, Congress passed the Wagner Act guaranteeing workers the right to unionize, collectively bargain, and strike. In 1938, President Roosevelt signed the Fair Labor Standards Act establishing the federal minimum wage, overtime pay, and the forty-hour work week.

Thus, not only does the film overlook the criticism of capitalism made by one of its characters and through the stigmatization the union, but we are also left with an analysis showing that radical politics at that time improved the life of workers today and consequently, although "most [strikes] ended in failure" the unions won something, and we are now in a better place because of it. We now have a better, nicer capitalism thanks to the pressures on state powers to regulate unscrupulous business practices (see also Table 3.7).

The last limited critique presented here, the **overreaching critique**, is one that makes a *pseudo*-radical point. It is radical because it condemns the entirety of the system, but it is false in its interpretation of why and how the system is flawed. Typically, this refers to representations of conspiracy theories that overreach with their argument – creating further mystification about the way these systems operate, what their interests are, and thus how we can envisage an alternative.[15]

Since conspiracy theories are apt examples of this limited critique, it seems only natural to utilize the film *Conspiracy Theory* (1997) as its example. The

TABLE 3.7 Examples of The Historicized Critique

Free State of Jones (2016)	*Gangs of New York* (2002)	*Green Book* (2018)
Jojo Rabbit (2019)	*Malcolm X* (1992)	*Peterloo* (2018)
Schindler's List (1993)	*Selma* (2014)	*The Birth of a Nation* (2016)
The Boat That Rocked (2009)	*The Promise* (2016)	*Thirteen Days* (2000)
Trumbo (2000)		

Eight Limited Critiques of Capitalism and the State **65**

film's main character is a conspiracy theorist, Jerry, who believes that "They monitor everything. Absolutely everything." Who are "they"?

> There's lots of groups actually. Lots of initials. CIA. FBI. IMF. You name it. But really, they are part of the same two opposing factions ... which are 1) some of them are really, really wealthy families – their one thing is to maintain stability, or at least that's what they call it; the other group is Eisenhower's industrial military complex and they want to maintain instability, so they say. ... At some level they're at war but at other levels they're the same group. It's really scary. I mean it's hand in glove. Cold wars, hot wars. Then they sit back and watch the whole damn dumb show.

Jerry is presented in the movie as mad, but he is vindicated when we find out that not only are all his ideas "true" (e.g., Jerry Garcia is a "00" agent; Oliver Stone is George H.W. Bush's spokesman, earthquakes have become weaponized), but that his knowledge is derived from a conspiracy itself. He was a test subject in mind control research by the CIA and when the technology the researchers developed was stolen by some private organization, Jerry was placed under the control of that organization. When asked if he can prove his theories he says: "No. Absolutely not. A good conspiracy is an unprovable one. If you can prove it, I mean they must have screwed up somewhere along the line, and if that's the case, well ...." This notion of an unprovable conspiracy means that the state/capitalism is basically godlike: omnipotent, omnipresent, and omniscient. But this is an unrealistic and dangerous idea, based on a poor understanding of power.

While the movie mystifies the state and capitalism, it also utilizes the popular idea of conspiracy theorists being crazy as a means of branding the left with the same brush. (Jerry opposes right-wing extremists; he is a member of and advocates for membership in unions; he publishes a newsletter to a small group of interested parties in a kind of Leninist fashion.) While the film discusses major government institutions and intergovernmental organizations, the problems the film identifies are not actually real, so as an audience we would be worse off in understanding the role of capitalism and the state if we were to believe them.[16] Other examples of the overreaching critique include more grounded but nevertheless inaccurate representations, such as Oliver Stone's *JFK* (1991) (see Table 3.8 for additional examples).

Frontiers of the Bitter River

This chapter has revealed the major gold mining communities on the map of our possible futures. The attempt to solve the problems of our Junkspace City through gold actually only incorporates the mines and its contents into the jurisdiction of the city. The surveyors charted future possibilities in ways that

66 Eight Limited Critiques of Capitalism and the State

TABLE 3.8 Examples of The Overreaching Critique[a]

Antitrust (2001)
House of Cards (seasons 1–2) (2013–14)
JFK (1991)
The Pelican Brief (1993)
Total Recall (2012)
Wag the Dog (1997)

[a] Another older example is *The Parallax View* (1974), a film analyzed by Jameson (1995) and Fisher (2009), who suggest that it illuminates the limits of the individual rebel who becomes effectively coopted by the collective power of the institution and represents a social totality. However, the film in its barest sense represents a corporate/political conspiracy that is all consuming and omnipotent in a way that undermines a radical critique – one that provides a cognitive mapping of the capitalist (and state) system in its present form.

While Toscano and Kinkle (2015) compare the scenes within these conspiracy films of detectives and journalists sifting through piles of documents in order to find an order in the madness to Noam Chomsky going through news clippings and journal articles, Chomsky himself has poo-pooed the conspiratorial thinking that is represented in such films (see e.g., Robinson 2017).

are essentially no different from the present, but with a newfound sense of superiority. As such, the discursive plane revealed thus far mirrors our own inability to imagine the end of capitalism and the state. Take the anecdote told by Russell Jacoby as another example:

> I sometimes teach a course on utopianism. The students arrive on the verdant California campus in various colors and sizes but generally with the easy smile and open gaze of those to whom life has been good. I allot time for students to sketch out their own utopias. They come up with laudable ideas—universal health care with choice of doctors; free higher education; clean parks; ecological vehicles—but very little that is out of the ordinary. Their boldest dreams could be realized by a comprehensive welfare state.[17]

As we can see, the limited critiques presented above are visible in the real-life ideologies of even those privileged university students who are taking, with some degree of choice, a class on utopianism.

Needless to say, many also view the issues with the present state of things from a conservative position, even if they are also critical of the same institutions. Conservative critiques of the system found in screen media texts are surveyors venturing eastward into a hierarchical values system to chart maps promoting a different kind of future. Here, *The Dark Knight* trilogy is an excellent example. Wayne enterprises was once a family run business that benefited the city – Gotham. However, the city was sent into economic despair at the hands of the 'utopian' League of Shadows. Poverty became pronounced and people broke the law. Soon gangsters take over, eventually leading to the robbery that kills Bruce Wayne's parents and here begins his journey to becoming Batman. Batman, perhaps representing a conservative view of George W Bush, engages in an extraordinary rendition and mass surveillance and spying in order to catch a man terrorizing Gotham[18] – the name Irving Washington and others gave to New York City. Throughout the story the police are prevented (often by 'soft-on-crime' politicians) from delivering justice so someone not bound by the law must do it himself, a common theme in the superhero genre (e.g., *Luke Cage* (2016–2018), *Spider-Man* (2002)), among other screen media texts.[19]

Between the limited, progressive critiques and the conservative critiques we have scarcely surveyed much of the land. Instead, our surveyors have often found themselves at the same mining towns just on the outskirts of the city, redrawing the same lines into our cognitive maps. In the analysis presented thus far we see the formation of patterns, topographic demarcations that shed light on the fields and valleys in a not-to-distant land. But this is not without its own benefits. It could be argued that without such surveyors we may not have had the likes of Bernie Sanders and Jeremy Corbyn who represented a potential turn towards welfare capitalism amidst ongoing austerity and neoliberalism. The repetition of some of these limited critiques has perhaps made such small steps toward progress possible. But, in the Pangea of possible futures, we have scarcely explored beyond what could be the inner suburbs of our present Junkspace City.

Despite the many descriptions of the state and capitalism within the above texts they all share an understanding of these systems similar to what the cultural critic Edward Said called "latent Orientalism". The critiques are presented only in ways that reaffirm these systems in the long run through the discourse of the texts. Capitalism and the state are only problematic to the extent that small components or particular individuals in positions of power are undesirable; their flaws are counterbalanced, or nothing better can exist; they can be improved where flawed; their flaws can be overlooked; or they were only serious flaws in a particular historic context; they may not be real flaws at all; or they are presented as flawed in ways that are not true.

In each case, Thatcher's mantra, "There Is No Alternative", is echoed through the eyes, ears, and minds of the viewers – reverberating and resonating with already accepted truths that flow from a long lineage of discursive formations established by power to function as the mapmakers of our political imaginations. Of course, none of this process itself has to be understood or implemented consciously. This process simply 'makes sense' within the logic of the system imposed. But are we trapped in such a discourse? Is it impossible to work through existent discourses to structure a counter-hegemonic discourse and expand our map of possibilities? Can mainstream popular culture serve as a platform for such a discourse? Or can this be explained by a simplistic

68 Eight Limited Critiques of Capitalism and the State

understanding of a base-determined ideological superstructure? After all, the foremost critics of capitalism, Marx and Engels, stated:

> The ruling ideas are nothing more than the ideal expression of the dominant material relationships, the dominant material relationships grasped as ideas; hence of the relationships which make the one class the ruling one, therefore, the ideas of its dominance. The individuals composing the ruling class possess among other things consciousness, and therefore think. Insofar, therefore, as they rule as a class and determine the extent and compass of an epoch, it is self-evident that they do this in its whole range, hence among other things rule also as thinkers, as producers of ideas, and regulate the production and distribution of the ideas of their age: thus their ideas are the ruling ideas of the epoch.[20]

Is our restrictive map simply a product of the ruling class compass of consciousness? Certainly, there is an argument to be made here, but by what mechanism? The discourse constructed over time can be acting upon our popular consciousness, and we know its construction was no accident. For decades ideologies antagonistic to the state and capital have been systematically removed from the public sphere across many countries, not least in the areas of media and popular culture. Let us not forget the declarations chanted by the German Student Association in Berlin where they called for the burning of books not only by Marx and Kautsky, but also Heinrich Mann, Ernst Glaeser, and Erich Maria Remarque. Let us not forget the effect the McCarthy era had on Hollywood through the House of Un-American Activities Committee. Let us not forget that staff at the United Kingdom's BBC were vetted for their 'subversive' politics for decades until (at least) the 1990s.

These are quite stark examples, but such ideological construction occurs at a seemingly more innocuous level. If we return to Margaret Thatcher for a moment, we can see that her party campaigned for stripping government funding and claiming that no alternative existed because of the *Titanic* effect. Take her party's view on art in the 1979 manifesto – the election in which she became prime minister: "Socialist policies have placed the arts under threat. Lightening the burden of tax should in time enable the private sponsor to flourish again." Thus far we have the same mantra, but moments later in the same manifesto we are told a different story when it comes to the production of ideology. This story is one of government funding: "We favor the establishment of a National Heritage Fund to help preserve historic buildings and artistic treasures for the nation".[21] Over the next eight years Thatcher's government spent £100 million to purchase British art and architecture. In October 1988, Thatcher gave the opening speech for the grand opening of the project's culminating event – the Treasures for the Nation Exhibition at the British Museum. Praising the Lord and Trustees running the fund for their selection of artifacts representing great British craftsmanship, Thatcher continued: "But you haven't stopped at that,

Eight Limited Critiques of Capitalism and the State **69**

you've gone on to protect and to bring before us the examples of ... trying to go to the frontiers of what was possible." After all the money spent on looking at the 'frontiers of what was possible' she cited a speed car and a First World War tank. Is this the physical evidence of the possible in the world of no alternatives? Was this public funding for an ideological ruse?

Looking past the exhibition and further into the British Museum we can turn to one of their precious objects, The Map of the World. This 3 x 5 inch clay tablet from sixth century BC Babylonia depicts the world as Assyria, Bit-Yakin, Habban, Urartu, Babylon, and the Euphrates all surrounded by the cosmic 'Bitter River'. Two interpretations are feasible. Either the creators of this, the oldest surviving 'world' map, believed they had inscribed the truth of the whole inhabited world, or they were presenting a lie so as to produce an ideological 'truth'. Either they literally believed that only the cited lands held any human life, or the nations shown were the only ones suited to be labeled civilizations, and the others just mythical beasts.

We are left with many questions still to explore: Is the whole world Junkspace City? Are the frontiers of what was possible the speed car and the tank? Is all of popular screen culture simply a presentation of the inescapability of capital and state? Has not a grain of counter-hegemonic ideology survived the various attacks and reproduced itself through popular culture? Has nothing subversive slipped through the cracks? Is it not possible for one of our surveyors to make it to the mountain top and extend our map of the possible?

Notes

1 Jameson 2007[1992], p. 39.
2 Jameson 2007[1992], p. 39.
3 Wegner 1998.
4 Koolhaas 2001.
5 Jameson 2003.
6 Wenders 1992, p. 19.
7 If representations in film can be interpreted so that the specific is abstracted, then mapmaking is the reverse of this process. Cartographers necessarily use a level of abstraction to indicate the specific. "[T]he dominant paradigm of western cartography in the late twentieth century ... characterize[ed] the map as a communication model using abstraction, representation and design to convey a message to a community of users" (Fairbairn et al. 2001, p. 7). (The closest maps to being representational rather than abstract are perhaps Imhof's plaster terrain models, but a more ordinary map is far less representational and more abstract) (Fairbairn et al. 2001, p. 7). A pinkish blot is a hospital on the corner of Bath and Pine Street. Even highly realistic versions of political, physical, or topographic maps make real things abstract. In Jorge Luis Borges' one-paragraph-long absurd short story, "On Exactitude in Science", where he describes a map that is full scale and overlays the area it is representing "point by point". Even here the map can only tell you a partial, representational story of the geography of the space it covered. What exactly can be seen on a map made of "static polygons of

70 Eight Limited Critiques of Capitalism and the State

homogeneous value", as one geographer describes it (Roth 2009, p. 209), other than an illustration of the stable components (e.g., roads, buildings)? The utility of the spaces, their meanings and (sometimes multitudinous) functions cannot be directly represented. This can be better seen in Lewis Carroll's *Sylvie and Bruno Concluded*, the inspiration for Burges' short story:

> "What a useful thing a pocket-map is!" I remarked.

> "That's another thing we've learned from your Nation," said Mein Herr, "map-making. But we've carried it much further than you. What do you consider the largest map that would be really useful?"

> "About six inches to the mile."

> "Only six inches!" exclaimed Mein Herr. "We very soon got to six yards to the mile. Then we tried a hundred yards to the mile. And then came the grandest idea of all! We actually made a map of the country, on the scale of a mile to the mile!"

> "Have you used it much?" I enquired.

> "It has never been spread out, yet," said Mein Herr: "The farmers objected: they said it would cover the whole country, and shut out the sunlight! So we now use the country itself, as its own map, and I assure you it does nearly as well."
> (Carroll 2015[1894])

While abstraction is necessary in trying to represent the specifics of the referent in a map, we can abstract further from the totality of a map. The abstract spot on a map refers to a real place but also, in the process, generates an ideological positioning of the subject to the referent. In fact, many have argued that historically maps as we know them are "thoroughly bound up in the creation of nation-states and the expansion of capital" (Roth 2009, p. 209) because they were able to depict the relationship between state and territory. The same map could not easily translate African kingdoms whose control was not over territory, which was abundant, but people, who were in relative short supply. According to scholars of pre-colonial Africa, "strangers who settled in an unoccupied part of a guardian's territory could continue to be governed by their own headmen provided they recognized the ritual control of the original guardian over the land" (Harms 1987, p. 220, in Herbst 2000, p. 40). For this reason, mapmaking was relatively underdeveloped in most of the kingdoms of the African continent (Herbst 2000, p. 40) and arguably why the imposition of the ideology embodied in the European map as part of the colonial Scramble for Africa continues to be a source of conflict in the continent (Michalopoulos and Papaioannou 2016).

If traditional maps produce an ideology that facilitates state formation, imperialism, and capitalism, perhaps an alternative map of future possibilities can serve to construct an ideology that manifests in a reshaping of our political consciousness away from catastrophism and toward a new spirit of revolutionary potentialities.

8 More 1901[1516].

9 To some extent the filmmakers extend the radicalness of the critique in select scenes. For example, the villain, trying to convince the United States to support the coup against the Bolivian government, states: "You don't need another Marxist giving national resources to the people do you." The US government is shown aiding and abetting his corporate ambitions in exchange for one less Marxist government in Latin America. "You know, I was just wondering what South America would look like if nobody gave a damn about coke or communism. It always impressed me the way you [American] boys carved this place up", Bond says.

Eight Limited Critiques of Capitalism and the State **71**

10 For the Bourne series: *The Bourne Identity* (2002), *The Bourne Supremacy* (2004), *The Bourne Ultimatum* (2007), *The Bourne Legacy* (2012), *Jason Bourne* (2016). In addition, see *Fair Game* (2002), *The Sentinel* (2006), *Mission Impossible* (1996), *Mission Impossible II* (2000), *Mission Impossible III* (2006), *Mission: Impossible – Rogue Nation* (2015), *The Good Shepherd* (2006), *The Gray Man* (2022), *Breach* (2007), *Eraser* (1996), and *Tinker Tailor Soldier Spy* (2011).

11 For police see *Bad Boys* (1995), *Training Day* (2001), *Bright* (2017), *The Negotiator* (1998), *End of Watch* (2012), *Brooklyn Nine-Nine* (seasons 1–8; 2013–2021), *21 Jump Street* (2012), *22 Jump Street* (2014), *Freedomland* (2006), the *CSI* series (2000–2015), *Rampart* (2011), *The Departed* (2006), *Gangster Squad* (2013), *Homicide* (1991), *BlacKkKlansman* (2018), *L.A. Confidential* (1997), *Internal Affairs* (1990), *Cop Land* (1997), *Pride and Glory* (2008), *Detroit* (2017), and *Judge Dredd* (1995). For politicians see *The West Wing* (1999–2006), *Milk* (2008), *Dave* (1993), *The Manchurian Candidate* (2004), *BrainDead* (season 1; 2016), *W.* (2008), *Nixon* (1995), *Primary Colors* (1998), *The Contender* (2000), and *The Campaign* (2012).

12 At the same time, the defense attorney also exposes the bigger issues in his closing statement. "What will giving a judgement of $10 million accomplish? All insurance company premiums will spin out of reach, and it will pave the way for government-controlled health coverage." As if that would be a bad thing. For additional examples, see *Larry the Cable Guy: Health Inspector* (2006) and *No Sudden Move* (2021).

13 Krawczyk 2018. Also see *Leave the World Behind* (2023).

14 For an example of a film which overcomes the historical problem, but is nevertheless limited in its critique, see *BlacKkKlansman* (2018) and *The Last Duel* (2021).

15 Also see van Zoonen 2005, pp. 115–118.

16 At the same time, we know that the movie's star Mel Gibson is both a right-winger and a conspiracy theorist, stating the following in a 1995 interview for *Playboy* magazine: Somebody knew then that he [Bill Clinton] would be president now. ... I really believe that. He was a Rhodes Scholar, right? Just like Bob Hawke .... Cecil Rhodes established the Rhodes scholarship for those young men and women who want to strive for a new world order. Have you heard that before? George Bush? CIA? Really, it's Marxism, but it just doesn't want to call itself that. Karl had the right idea, but he was too forward about saying what it was. Get power but don't admit to it. Do it by stealth. There's a whole trend of Rhodes Scholars who will be politicians around the world.
 Talking about political assassinations, Gibson stated: "There's something to do with the Federal Reserve that Lincoln did, Kennedy did and Reagan tried. I can't remember what it was, my dad told me about it. Everyone who did this particular thing that would have fixed the economy got undone. Anyway, I'll end up dead if I keep talking shit" (Van Luling 2017). Unsurprisingly such conspiratorial thinking is often aligned with a deep-seated anti-Semitism even predating *The Protocols of the Elders of Zion*. Of course, we know that Mel Gibson himself has made anti-Semitic statements (Roth 2016; JTA 2016).

17 Jacoby 2005, pp. xii–xiv.

18 This point is also raised by Kellner (2010, pp. 10–11). However, while Kellner's argument that *The Dark Knight* (2008) depicts the seediness of the Bush-Cheney era where Batman's swerve to the 'dark' side – a kind of symbolism of a Republican

72 Eight Limited Critiques of Capitalism and the State

presidency (W. Bush's in particular) – this was represented as a problem in the films since the Joker was able to use this to his advantage. The point Kellner is making is weak as the film heroically concludes with both Batman using the mass surveillance system to capture the Joker (and then destroying the system, demonstrating that sometimes it can be worthwhile to trash civil liberties) and with Batman taking on the public persona of villain in order to give hope to Gotham (placing the blame on himself for deaths that the 'light' knight DA Harvey Dent committed). This representation seems to side with the Bush presidency rather than display its seediness.

19 E.g., *The Departed* (2006); *Dirty Harry* (1971); *Three Billboards Outside Ebbing, Missouri* (2017); *Mission: Impossible III* (2006); and *Mission: Impossible – Fallout* (2018). Other texts still present a critique in which the state is too ideologically *divided* and argues for a moderation and negotiation that inherently preserves the current system of state and capitalism (e.g., *My Fellow Americans* (1996), *BrainDead* season 1; 2016).

20 Marx and Engels 2004[1845], pp. 64–65.

21 Conservative Party (2000).

References

Carroll, Lewis (2015[1894]) *Sylvie and Bruno Concluded*, Project Gutenberg, http://www.gutenberg.org/ebooks/48795.

Conservative Party (2000) 'Conservative Party General Election Manifesto 1979', in Iain Dale (ed.), *Conservative Party General Election Manifestos 1900–1997, Volume 1* (p. 279), Abingdon: Routledge.

Fairbairn, David, Andrienko, Gennady, Andrienko, Natalia, Buziek, Gerd, and Dykes, Jason (2001) 'Representation and Its Relationship with Cartographic Visualization', *Cartography and Geographic Information Science*, 28(1): 13–28.

Fisher, Mark (2009) *Capitalist Realism*, London: Zero Books.

Herbst, Jeffrey (2000) *States and Power in Africa: Comparative Lessons in Authority and Control*, Princeton, NJ: Princeton University Press.

Jacoby, Russell (2005) *Picture Imperfect: Utopian Thought for an Anti-Utopian Age*, New York: Columbia University Press.

Jameson, Fredric (1995) *The Geopolitical Aesthetic: Cinema and Space in the World System*, London: BFI Publishing.

Jameson, Fredric (2003) 'Future City', *New Left Review* 21(May/June): 65–79.

Jameson, Fredric (2007[1992]) *Signatures of the Visible*, New York: Routledge.

JTA (2016) 'Mel Gibson: "It's Annoying" People Won't Let Anti-Semitic Rants Go', *Haaretz*, Nov. 1, https://www.haaretz.com/world-news/americas/mel-gibson-it-s-annoying-people-won-t-let-anti-semitic-rants-go-1.5455849. Accessed Oct. 16, 2018.

Kellner, Douglas (2010) *The Cinema Wars: Hollywood Film and Politics in the Bush-Cheney Era*, Malden, MA: Wiley-Blackwell.

Koolhaas, Rem (2001) Junkspace, https://www.readingdesign.org/junkspace.

Krawczyk, Staszek (2018) 'Do końca świata i o jeden dzień dłużej. O książce „Świat po apokalipsie" Lecha M. Nijakowskiego', *Kultura Liberalna*, https://kulturali beralna.pl/2018/10/16/staszek-krawczyk-recenzja-lech-nijakowski-swiat-po-apok alipsie. Accessed Oct. 16, 2018.

Marx, Karl and Engels, Fredrick (2004[1845]). *The German Ideology: Part One with Selections from Parts Two and Three and Supplementary Texts*, New York: International Publishers.

Michalopoulos, Stelios and Papaioannou, Elias (2016) 'The Long-Run Effects of the Scramble for Africa', *American Economic Review*, 106(7): 1802–1848.

More, Thomas (1901[1516]) *Utopia*, New York: Ideal Commonwealths. P.F. Collier & Son. The Colonial Press.

Robinson, Nathan J. (2017) 'Lessons from Chomsky', *Current Affairs*, July 30. https://www.currentaffairs.org/2017/07/lessons-from-chomsky. Accessed Oct. 16, 2018.

Rosenthal, Abraham M. (1999) *Thirty-Eight Witnesses: The Kitty Genovese Case*, Berkeley: University of California Press.

Roth, Daniel J. (2016) 'Jewish People Stole My Christ Movie, Mel Gibson Reportedly Tells Glenn Beck', *The Jerusalem Post*, September 6. https://www.jpost.com/Diaspora/Jewish-people-stole-my-movie-Mel-Gibson-reportedly-tells-Glenn-Beck-467243. Accessed Oct. 16, 2023.

Roth, Robin (2009) 'The Challenges of Mapping Complex Indigenous Spatiality: From Abstract Space to Dwelling Space', *Cultural Geographies*, 16(2): 207–227.

Toscano, Alberto and Kinkle, Jeff (2015) *Cartographies of the Absolute*, Winchester: Zero Books.

Van Luling, Todd (2017) Mel Gibson's Sexist Interview Answers from 1995 Are Relevant Again, *Huffington Post*, Jan. 24, https://www.huffingtonpost.co.uk/entry/mel-gibson-playboy-interview_us_581a2ea7e4b0c43e6c1d92c0?guccounter=1. Accessed Oct. 16, 2018.

van Zoonen, Liesbet (2005) *Entertaining the Citizen: When Politics and Popular Culture Converge*, Lanham, MD: Rowman & Littlefield Publishers.

Wegner, Phillip E. (1998) 'Horizons, Figures, and Machines: The Dialectic of Utopia in the Work of Fredric Jameson', *Utopian Studies*, 9(2): 58–77.

Wenders, Wim (1992) *The Logic of Images: Essays and Conversations*, London: Faber & Faber.

4

REPRESENTATIONS OF EVIL

A Cinematic Anthropology of Villains

On October 21, 2003, just over seven months after the US invasion of Iraq and eight years before it officially ended, retired Major General Robert H. Scales Jr. spoke before the House Armed Services Committee:

> Intelligence … is about understanding the enemy as he is and then tailoring strategic and operational approaches that turn his political framework to one's own advantage. Without this kind of political knowledge, which requires immersion in the language, culture, and history of a region, the [large amount of] data gathered by technological means can serve only to reinforce preconceived, erroneous, sometimes disastrous notions.[1]

With these words the decorated general called on the military to engage in anthropological research to ascertain actionable intelligence.[2] But we can reverse this inquiry and ask for an anthropology of the Major General and others in positions of power within the state and capital in order to better know the 'enemies' of freedom and equality: capitalism and the state. We can ask the same question UC Berkeley Professor Laura Nader asked in her search for a new anthropology: "What if … anthropologists were to study the colonizers rather than the colonized, the culture of power rather than the culture of the powerless, the culture of affluence rather than the culture of poverty?"[3] She termed this notion "studying *up*", and in this chapter we will study up to develop an understanding of our own popular cultural knowledge of our 'enemy'. We will look at the representation of political and economic enemies and villains within screen media texts to develop an idea of how popular culture shapes our critique of capitalism and the state.

DOI: 10.4324/9781003514916-5

Representations of Evil: A Cinematic Anthropology of Villains **75**

If our ventures into mapping futures come from a cartographic interpretation of the topography of cinema and television plotlines, then to understand the starting position from which we move into a possible future what is also necessary is an anthropological examination of the 'peoples' found in the newly discovered or retraced locations on the map of possible futures – the characters in the screen media texts. In this case, as we are interested in the critiques presented in these representations, the villains and representations of evil will be the focus of this anthropological investigation. This enemy can represent institutions of power within the context of a popularly used formal technique that helps distinguish the good from the evil and what should be cheered or booed. Seeing what is evil tells us its opposite: utopia. Or, as the introduction to the book *Anthropology of Evil* states, "the bad cannot be studied without also knowing the boundaries of the good".[4]

Perhaps the classic representation of a villain that most closely resembles evil is one that is furthest from our cultural definition of human – irrational, aggressive, and incapable of compassion. They do bad things without hesitation or remorse; in fact, they like it. Think of the 'barbaric' 'animalism' of a man who decapitates another and keeps the heads of the dead as trophies. This representation can be found in King Joffrey in *The Game of Thrones* series (2011–2019) and in the villain from the film *Se7en* (1995), for example. Of course, heads on spikes are not an unheard-of human phenomenon. Anthropologists know of the Munduruku headhunters in Brazil who engaged in the ritual as part of war feasts.[5] This 'evil', however, would not be seen as such by the Munduruku themselves. They, according to anthropologists, saw *others* as non-human, dangerous animals and their own violence as a necessity for survival.[6] The anthropologist seeks to understand a society from its own perspective and just as the anthropologist approaches a civilization to investigate its own view of evil[7] so our filmic anthropologies expose us to the evil as described within the text. After all, sometimes the one who beheads, often in the climactic fight sequence, is the 'good guy' such as in *Conan the Barbarian* (1982), *Kill Bill: Volume 1* (2003), *X-Men Origins: Wolverine* (2009), and *Game of Thrones* (2011–2019).

Of course, film and television villains do not often say much about capitalism or the state. The classic action film villain trope is usually a band of unscrupulous felons led by a sinister boss –think Hans Gruber in *Die Hard* (1988), Shredder in *Teenage Mutant Ninja Turtles* (1990), or Lex Luthor in *Superman* (1978). There are also the baddies who break social or legal rules to get their way, like Sensei John Kreese encouraging his students to injure their opponents in order to win a karate competition in *The Karate Kid* (1984) and *Cobra Kai* (2018–).[8] Think also of the school bullies from *Mean Girls* (2004) and *The Simpsons* (1989–).[9] The heroes'

76 Representations of Evil: A Cinematic Anthropology of Villains

job in these types of screen media texts is to prevent these bad *individuals* from doing bad things in otherwise acceptable institutional contexts. And there is a range of reasons that explain the evil-doers' behavior and desires. One set of reasons cluster together in *Psycho*'s (1960) Norman Bates, the baddy from *Se7en*, and the villains in the Hannibal Lecter series.[10] These villains are sometimes the reason why those films are classified as *psychological* thrillers. They are suffering some kind of psychological trauma and/or mental health issues that help to explore the mental stability of other characters or explain their own actions. While these villains do evil things, they are sometimes represented as being empathic light on these enemies of the peace.[11] With the *Star Wars* series, we also see this type of character within one of the most memorable and well-recognized villains in cinema history: Darth Vader. *Episode III* reveals the role the 'true' villain, Lord Palpatine, had in manipulating the youthful Jedi trainee at vulnerable moments in his life and *Episode VI* (1983) (re)establishes him as a victim of the powers of the dark side when Vader returns as a spiritual ghost alongside our dead protagonists Obi-Wan and Yoda following his death at the hands of Palpatine. Another set of villains are people (usually men) seeking vengeance on society or on particular individuals for real or perceived wrongdoing in their personal lives. Here you have your Two-Face, Magneto, and Captain Hook.[12]

Another classic villain trope is the master planner who has secretly amassed wealth, established their headquarters, and surrounded themselves with their minions. It is such an established trope that their parodies are big budget successes – e.g., the *Austin Powers* series,[13] *The LEGO Ninjago Movie* (2017). Often the heroes opposing these villains are part of the wider establishment, rooting out the evil interloper. These villains only represent the estranged from normal society, threatening us with their sinister schemes to gain power beyond the 'legitimate' hierarchy that is already present. They are a challenge to stasis, to the status quo – and thus the status quo is preserved as the desirable end. As villains represent what is wrong with the world around us, these different tropes leave us little to work with in pinpointing broader social problems.

Even when the villain does represent an institution or system, the analysis can be from a conservative perspective on evil. Again, we can look at Batman as an example, specifically Christopher Nolan's *The Dark Knight Rises* (2012). In the film, the villain Bane wants to destroy Gotham which he views as a cesspool. On the road to achieving this objective he promotes himself to the public of Gotham as a revolutionary who is returning the city to the people: the film, released soon after the Occupy Wall Street protests, shows Bane raiding Wall Street; he supports a vision of prison abolition and publicly releasing all prisoners, arguing that the city's prison is "a symbol of oppression …. Where a thousand men have languished …"; he calls on the collectivization of property and institutes death panels for those who disobey.

> We take Gotham from the corrupt, the rich, the oppressors of generations who kept you down with myths of opportunity, and we give it back to you, the people. Gotham is yours. None shall interfere; do as you please. Start by storming Blackgate [Prison] and free the oppressed. Step forward, those who would serve, for an army will be raised. The powerful will be ripped from their decadent nests and cast out into the cold world that we know and endure. Courts will be convened; spoils will be enjoyed.

Bane sounds a lot like what someone from the 'alt-right' may have thought of socialists – particularly at a time when a so-called socialist was in the White House, President Obama. Interestingly, at one point in the movie Bane states to a compatriot, "So, as I terrorize Gotham, I will feed its people hope to poison their souls." Hope, of course, being Obama's motto – a point that did not escape some anti-Obama memers who placed the mask of Bane over an image of Obama with the above quote.[14] This representation is perhaps not surprising considering that the co-creator of the character Bane was lifelong conservative Chuck Dixon who stated that Bane was "akin to an Occupy Wall Street type".[15] Bane's villainy in the text tells us that appeals to the masses and a rhetoric of radical justice and redistribution are actually calls for our own demise by opportunistic authoritarians.

Thus far, the villain tropes discussed tell us little about the negatives of capitalism or the state, but it is by no means uncommon to see the representations of villains as businessmen, bankers, lobbyists, politicians, heads of state, and government agents. In fact, in 2016 the *San Francisco Chronicle*'s television critic David Wiegand wrote:

> Film and TV have gone through a number of go-to enemies over the years, from the Nazis during in [sic] the '40s, communists in the '50s, the Soviets in the '60s and '70s, and, post-glasnost, Middle Eastern terrorists. This century, Hollywood's preferred villains increasingly wear tailored suits, natty ties and sleek wingtips. They don't kill people, for the most part, but they are merciless with people's money.[16]

This argument is corroborated by earlier research. In their 17-week analysis of 863 television shows and made-for-television movies, the conservatively biased media 'watchdog' Media Research Centre reported the following: businessmen are represented as criminals and murderers more than any other occupation; they are more likely to be represented as cheaters than positive contributors to society; and they are often depicted as unfriendly to workers.[17] The same could be said of politicians who are increasingly

78 Representations of Evil: A Cinematic Anthropology of Villains

portrayed as villains.[18] Consider the long list of television series and films with such representations, including *House of Cards* (2013–2014), *Murder at 1600* (1997), *Years and Years* (2019), and others.[19] But how exactly are these villainous elites represented?

The Ritualized Embodiment of Evil Institutions

Like the trophy heads of the Munduruku, evil – or our typical conception of it – can be ritualized. Rituals can be defined as a "formulaic spatiality carried out by groups of people who are conscious of its imperative or compulsory nature".[20] Rituals, according to anthropologists, can help us understand the "core of the social identity of all communities",[21] including the screen media communities of repeated actions across representations and texts. For our purposes here, reading the rituals of the evil actions of villains can pinpoint the social identity of the institutional problems that these characters represent, if any.

In the first three *Mission: Impossible* films, all starring Tom Cruise as protagonist Ethan Hunt, evil is depicted as a corrupt insider working for the otherwise positive Impossible Missions Force (IMF). The IMF is a group of well-trained spies working for the US government who are to meet the most challenging and often existential security concerns. Many of the problems arise, however, because one of the members of the IMF team turn on their agency during a mission, seeking power or financial reward as they know their identities are private and they are in close proximity to valuable information or technology. In these representations, the villains do not represent evil institutions. They are themselves the embodiment of the evil individual, of evil within these representations. In this case evil is the decayed moral character of individuals placed in a position of relative power and lucrative options.[22] Although these representations are not stand-ins for evil institutions, texts that do feature such characters can still suffer from the same ideological problem of *embodiment*.

Let's arrive at the problem of textual embodiment through a story that involves Tom Cruise himself. The same year Cruise was filming *Mission: Impossible III* (2006) he sat in front of the camera for a *Mission Impossible*-themed discussion of his belief in the religion of Scientology. The video was meant to be used for recruiting purposes for the Church of Scientology and three years after it was filmed, the video was leaked online. Those interested in Cruise's relationship with Scientology or in debunking the religion found it interesting, but it only made the news when the Church of Scientology began "firing off lawsuits alleging breach of copyright wherever the video pops up, notably on YouTube and Google Video".[23] Those concerned with protecting internet freedoms from such lawsuits came out in protest following a call to action by the decentralized hacktivist network

Anonymous. Over 7,000 participated in actions across 127 cities campaigning against what Anonymous called the Church's "misinformation, suppression of dissent, [and their] litigious nature".[24] To protect their identities during the demonstration, the activists donned plastic 'Guy Fawkes' masks. From then on, the masks became a prominent branding tool of Anonymous.

The masks worn by members of Anonymous were taken from the film *V for Vendetta* (2005), a film (based on a graphic novel) that features a revolutionary bandit who fights against an authoritarianism regime of a future Britain while himself wearing a Guy Fawkes mask. Guy Fawkes was a real person who in 1605 led a plot to blow up the Houses of Parliament in protest against the government's treatment of Catholics. Anonymous, a network that has also attacked the Catholic Church, does not need to address this irony because the film produced its own narrative of what the Guy Fawkes mask represents. Perhaps members of Anonymous were simply the first to adopt the Guy Fawkes mask as a symbol of their network but I would argue that the representation within *V for Vendetta* constructed and resonated with a view of the world shared by members of Anonymous. In part this is due to the representation of evil we read from the film's villain. Unlike other films that represent dystopian villains through a largely apolitical lens (think *Equilibrium* (2002), *The Hunger Games* series,[25] or the *Divergent* series[26]), *V for Vendetta* presents us with a particularly conservative authoritarianism. The central villain, High Chancellor Adam Sutler, is head of a fascistic police state of a future Britain where immigrants are unwelcome, and minorities are imprisoned and killed. The similarity between *V for Vendetta*, other dystopian texts, and the *Mission: Impossible* films is that the demise of the individual villains dismantles the evilness depicted. That is to say, there is no *systemic* problem presented, only a problem of specific tyrants and evildoers.

The story is archetypical precisely because of how revolutionary its representation appears to be. Our powerful protagonist V, who has been hiding underground, takes over a news studio to broadcast a message to the public, calling on those who oppose the establishment to come out in a year's time and break the curfew laws imposed by the regime to watch V blow up the Houses of Parliament. He uses that year to kill off most of the baddies associated with a prison in which he was confined and where he was turned into a mutant. Finally, the day comes when people are supposed to walk into the streets of London and oppose the authoritarian government. The regime is prepared. They set up a barricade with armed military personnel surrounding Parliament as the masses gather. The troops are just waiting to pull the trigger and fire on anyone getting close. In the meantime, V's final task is to kill off the High Chancellor and head of the secret police. He kills both but dies in the process. Nevertheless, the death of both the High Chancellor and the head of the secret police means that back at the barricades the military don't know what to do when they see droves of protesters come

80 Representations of Evil: A Cinematic Anthropology of Villains

up to them. They don't fire. They are effectively disarmed without their powerful leaders. They let the people pass without a fight and we know that the regime is over and, as Parliament gets blown up in a fantastic firework display, we know that justice and freedom are restored. In *V for Vendetta* there is no oppressive *system*, only oppressive leaders. If these leaders have all the power, then society is oppressive. If *those* leaders are gone, society is free.

These villains are puppet-masters who do not represent the evil institutions, they *embody* them. They are themselves the means through which the institutions function evilly. Such texts do not address the institutional and systemic problems of capitalism and state, only particular individuals that cause problems. Such an idea can be confused with 'propaganda of the deed', a term often used for violent action – such as the killing of individuals – that is meant to catalyze the public to revolt against the system.[27] 'Propaganda of the deed' is a concept used to describe the use violence against specific exemplars of the state and capitalism at a time when such actions would garner public sympathy and win adherents to a cause. It cannot be confused with thinking those particular individuals are *the* problem. The anarchist Alexander Berkman famously tried to murder the industrialist Henry Clay Frick after nine striking workers were killed in a scuffle with an armed private security force that Frick had hired. The deaths of those workers provided a very negative public sentiment against Frick and thus his murder, it was believed, could have led to support for the anarchist ideology and helped to fill the ranks of anarchist organizations. This support and increased membership could then go and address 'the system'. This was not how *V for Vendetta* discussed such acts of violence. In the film, violence against a handful of elites was the solution,[28] not a form of propaganda that could then be turned against the system. This, and its depiction of totalitarianism as the enemy, is perhaps the reason why the film's iconography was most powerfully taken up by Anonymous which holds strong right-wing cyberlibertarian positions but has little to say about capitalism, or power more generally.[29]

The *embodiment* of social ills can thus produce a narrative that reifies the non-social nature of the ills being discussed. They turn from social ills to personal and individual ills. In these cases, rather than serving as a stand-in for some broader problem, a villain simply stands themself. Another variation of this form of embodying evil speaks to the motivations of villains. Are the desires of villains being represented as a product of capitalism or the state, or of individual agency? In Disney's live action *101 Dalmatians* (1996), the notorious Cruella de Vil (Glen Close), head of a fashion company, is out to get her hands on Dalmatians in order to make the perfect fur coat for herself. However, the representation makes it easy to read her villainy as elite entitlement. She is so rich and powerful that she even feels entitled to killing the dogs of an employee. While this may be a statement about power and its effects on the powerful, it says little about the role of capitalism and, in this case, animal cruelty and slaughter. The narrowness of the discourse leads us to think that this *particular* rich person, rather than as the process of power itself, is cruel and devilish. At the end of the film, Cruella is carted off by police because the state is not in favor of this type of villainy, so we also know that it is not institutionalized. This supports the theory that Cruella as an individual is to be blamed, not the system that produced her. These villains are the types who abuse their position of power do so not as an indictment of systemic pressures, but for personal motivations.[30]

Shooter (2007) is an interesting example because a colonel and a senator who are depicted as villains for their role in decimating a village in Ethiopia in order to run an oil pipeline through the country are explained in the film as *not* embodying the evil and yet the film follows a logic that would indicate they do. Swagger, a retired military sniper, gets caught up in a conspiracy where he is accused of killing the Archbishop of Ethiopia. Over the course of the film, we find out that the archbishop was going to indict the US government for assisting in the slaughter of the villagers. Swagger is on the run, seeking vengeance and to clear his name. He finds out that the problem cannot be stopped just by getting rid of some bad individuals. "There is no head to cut off. It's a conglomerate. If one of them betrays the principles of the accrual of money and power, the others betray him." But the movie ends with Swagger killing off the Colonel and Senator as they plan another overseas campaign, with Swagger and his girlfriend escaping to freedom on the open road. This suggests that once those embodying evil have been killed, we are free.

A Desire to Annihilate

101 Dalmatians uses Cruella's evil status in cinema history as a plot point. The protagonist is a video-game designer who tries to pitch a game about Dalmatians escaping from an ordinary dogcatcher. This villain does not impress a respected child game tester. What makes for a good villain, the game tester is asked? "It's not hatred that's important. It's a desire to annihilate."

From an anthropological perspective, desire was once something that could be satiated through obtaining that which was craved. When it came down to the basic needs of the human appetite, obtaining those needs resulted in a "dignified and natural" life.[31] In the market – and by extension in capitalism – this ceased to be the case because "when markets are introduced, stimulating but never satisfying desire, the consumer becomes restless, acquisitive, never at peace with himself [or herself]".[32] In capitalism, desire cannot be satiated because there is always more to consume. Within the context of screen media, the desire to annihilate is something similar as its construction is constantly repeated: the establishment of an evil figure, the representation of their evilness, and their eventual downfall. This desire

82 Representations of Evil: A Cinematic Anthropology of Villains

to annihilate the villain creates a situation within the narrative where once annihilated, justice and peace are restored. It is this moment where the viewer engages with the 'unnatural', the indulgent, as they are relieved from the stranglehold the villain put on the fictional world of the text. But after one gasp of breath, the audience seeks more. The ideological component of representing evil to (temporarily) satisfy such a desire is that the evil embodied is no longer representational, but literal. Once the villain is slain, evil in the lifeworld presented on screen itself is destroyed. Such a consumer-driven approach perhaps assumes that a simplification of evil – one that is embodied and annihilated through the destruction of that body – allows the reader to more easily feel relief through this digestible fictionalized narrative. Evil itself is individualized. This simplification mystifies the systemic nature of true villainy.

While the desire for annihilation has led to more television programs and films featuring the characters' own desire for annihilating each other (e.g., *Game of Thrones* (2011–2019), *House of Cards* (2013–2018), *The Prestige* (2006), *Heat* (1995), and *The Pirates of the Caribbean* franchise) (2003–2011)), annihilation can be more meaningful for viewers if the rivalling characters represent institutions or systems within the narrative of the text, rather than simply standing in for 'themselves'. This is where *Billions* (seasons 1–7; 2016–2023) is a perfect example. Two characters, both seeking to annihilate the other (at least in some seasons), represent their respective fields: the state and capital. They act as surrogates of systems partially through the representation of their decisions coming out of institutional imperatives. Chuck Rhoades is a US District Attorney who exploits his power to destroy Bobby Axelrod, a hedge fund manager who does whatever it takes to amass wealth, no matter who it hurts. The dialogue between them demonstrates their representative character:

Rhoades: … you're a criminal, Bob. And it's my job to shut 'em down and put 'em in jail.

Axelrod: Well, if that's true, you're not very good at it. You're also full of shit. What have I done wrong? Really? Except make money. Succeed. All these rules and regulations: arbitrary. Chalked up by politicians for their own ends. And these fines you're always going after. Where do they go? Who gets them? The poor? No. The Treasury. The government. It's taxation by other means.

Rhoades: Save the civics lesson and the Ayn Rand bullshit. The fines are the minimum of what you should have to pay.

Axelrod: Oh, you decide what cases to take, and you only take the cases you won't lose. But you got it wrong with me, because this country was built on industry and competition. So they will always have a place for me.

Rhoades: Oh. And maybe a few generations from now, they'll tell stories about you, like they do Jesse James or Billy the Kid. Oh, the myth is so fuckin' romantic. The rugged individual who won't back down to the unimaginative, do-gooder authorities. Only in reality, those guys stole and hurt and destroyed lives. Now you say you don't think you've harmed anyone. I say that the effect is the same, worse even, because you infect the entire world. You throw the whole system off balance, leaving chaos and poverty in your wake.

Axelrod: I make the system run. I have contributed hundreds of millions of dollars in taxes and philanthropy. I employ hundreds of people directly, thousands indirectly. What do you do? Nothing besides suck from the municipality. Feed off of it. And in exchange, you what? Keep order? You're a traffic cop hiding in federal robes.

Depending on your perspective, as a viewer of the early seasons either Rhoades or Axelrod can be the villain or the hero. There's a moral ambiguity in the show which allows us to read the text in various ways and disagree on who to root for. In *Billions* we are surrounded by corruption both on Wall Street and in seats of power in the government. Axelrod engages in insider trading. Rhoades compromises his integrity to help his family one day and then throws his family under the bus in order to get Axelrod the next. Both main characters of *Billions* can be read to function in two ways – institutional representatives or ideal types. Bobby Axelrod is living the American dream. He came from a poor background and was able to 'pull himself up by his bootstraps'. He is a faithful husband and family man. He's also a ruthless businessman. Chuck Rhoades is a no-nonsense district attorney. He presents himself as a man of strong moral fiber who will not step out of line but will endlessly pursue white-collar criminals as a means of public service. But he is not as scrupulous as he presents himself to be. He breaks the law to advance his own career. These characters, in the eyes of viewers, could possibly sit as placeholders for any number of politicians and capitalists. At the same time, they could be seen as the best the system has to offer. These individuals pursue their paths but effectively *must* break moral and legal codes to continue to be successful in their respective fields. The system, in effect, is the problem.

However, while *Billions* depicts both capitalism and the state in negative terms, they also compete with each other. They are not represented as mutually exclusive by any means (Axelrod gets involved in politics and Rhoades gets involved in the stock market), but either character can be read as a flawed antihero and the other as a villain with likeable characteristics. Or perhaps we can see them both as antiheroes. Some seasons of *Billions* lean toward this latter analysis as the two enemies join forces.[33] In seeing them as antiheroes, we are presented with a different reading of the critique which is worth further exploration.

84 Representations of Evil: A Cinematic Anthropology of Villains

Greed *is* Good?

> As far back as I can remember, I always wanted to be a gangster. To me... being a gangster was better than being President of the United States. Even before I went to the cabstand for an after-school job ... I knew I wanted to be a part of them. It was there that I knew I belonged. To me, it meant being somebody ... in a neighborhood full of nobodies. They weren't like anybody else. They did whatever they wanted. They parked in front of hydrants and never got a ticket. When they played cards all night ... nobody ever called the cops.

Goodfellas (1990), quoted above, is an exceptional example of an antihero film. The film, based on a true story, is narrated by Henry Hill (Ray Liotta) who is shown rising through ranks of organized crime. While the film reveals the seedy underbelly of the gangster lifestyle, it also continuously shows us how positive that lifestyle was for those on the inside. It depicts the mob as a brotherhood, as a successful business, as a place of unlimited freedom to fornicate and use force. We see the film through the eyes of the characters, and this helps shape our judgement of them.

The antihero perspective was the go-to cinematic trick of the director, Martin Scorsese, used in his best films – *Raging Bull* (1980), *Taxi Driver* (1976), *Casino* (1995), and *The Irishman* (2019).[34] Before Scorsese got his break at filmmaking, he taught an introductory film module to young talents at the NYU film school. He may have passed on this trick to one of his precocious pupils, Oliver Stone, who went on to create one of Hollywood's most famous antiheroes, Gordon Gekko. Gekko famously said:

> I am not a destroyer of companies. I am a liberator of them. The point is, ladies and gentleman, that greed – for lack of a better word – is good. Greed is right. Greed works. Greed clarifies, cuts through, and captures the essence of the evolutionary spirit. Greed in all of its forms. Greed for life, for money, for love, knowledge has marked the upward surge of mankind and greed, you mark my words, will not only save Teldar Paper but that other malfunctioning corporation called the USA.[35]

Gekko, a financier and junk bond chaser from Oliver Stone's *Wall Street* (1987) and *Wall Street: Money Never Sleeps* (2010), is a character immortalized in cinematic history for this speech. Gekko goes from antihero to villain and back in the course of two films. In *Wall Street*, Gordon Gekko is the idol of our protagonist Bud Fox. Bud wants to work for Gekko and gets his chance after giving Gekko some insider information obtained from Bud's father, an airline company employee. Bud is asked to do some more insider trading and, in the process, becomes very wealthy. Things only turn sour after Bud proposes that Gekko buy out and expand the airline company where his father works. Gekko agrees to the idea but secretly plans to sell off the airline's assets, leaving Bud's father and his fellow employees out of work. News of this drives Bud's father to have a heart attack and Bud turns against Gekko. Bud finds a way to save the airline and get his former idol into legal trouble, even though it means going to prison for his participation in insider trading.

Constructing these representations of antiheroes for casual consumption can help create others in their image. Gekko is a rule-breaker who makes it big and lives the American dream.[36] Despite the film's conclusion labeling Gekko an antagonist, he serves as inspiration for others. The Gordon Gekko character became a hero for real-life stockbroker Jordon Belfort[37] who himself was depicted in a blockbuster Hollywood film, Martin Scorsese's *The Wolf of Wall Street* (2013). *The Wolf of Wall Street* takes the *Goodfellas* storyline and replaces gangster with stockbroker. Belfort (Leonardo DiCaprio) is shown rising in his career from promising stockbroker for L.F. Rothschild to founder of the brokerage house Stratton Oakmont. Belfort amasses his wealth through illegal dealings and when the Securities and Exchange Commission and FBI investigate him, he launders money. Not only are his business ventures questionable, but he also leads a lifestyle of non-stop drugs and prostitutes. Our disreputable antihero narrates his own introduction in the opening of the film, stating, "I also gamble like a degenerate, I drink like a fish, I fuck hookers maybe five, six times a week, I have three different federal agencies looking to indict me .... Oh yeah, and I love drugs." With a sense of pride, he continues:

On a daily basis I consume enough drugs to sedate Manhattan, Long Island, and Queens for a month. I take Quaaludes 10–15 times a day for my "back pain", Adderall to stay focused, Xanax to take the edge off, pot to mellow me out ..., cocaine to wake me back up again, and morphine .... Well, because it's awesome. But of all the drugs under God's blue heaven, here is one that is my absolute favorite.

He cuts some white powder on his office table. "See, enough of this shit will make you invincible. Able to conquer the world. And eviscerate your enemies." He snorts the drug through a rolled-up bill in delight, unrolling the $100 note. "I'm talking about this", he says as he directs our attention to the money which he wads up and throws into the trash.

The similarities between *Goodfellas* and *The Wolf of Wall Street* don't just lie in the antiheroes' sinful lives and attempts to evade the authorities. The two films end in very similar ways. *Goodfellas* concludes with Henry getting caught by the police and in exchange for his cooperation he is put into the Witness Protection Program. His punishment is to be one of us: an ordinary suburbanite.

See, the hardest thing for me was leaving the life. I still love the life. And we were treated like movie stars with muscle. We had it all, just for the asking. Our wives, mothers, kids, everybody rode along. I had paper bags filled with jewelry stashed in the kitchen. I had a sugar bowl full of coke next to the bed. Anything I wanted was a phone call away: free cars, the keys to a dozen hideout flats all over the city. I'd bet twenty, thirty grand over a weekend and then I'd either blow the winnings in a week or go to the sharks to pay back the bookies. Didn't matter. It didn't mean anything. When I was broke, I would go out and rob some more. We ran everything. We paid off cops. We paid off lawyers. We paid off judges. Everybody had their hands out. Everything was for the taking. And now it's all over. And that's the hardest part. Today, everything is different. There's no action. I have to wait around like everyone else. Can't even get decent food. Right after I got here, I ordered some spaghetti with marinara sauce and I got egg noodles and ketchup. I'm an average nobody. I get to live the rest of my life like a schnook.

Belfort is also caught and punished, but his punishment – and the contrast between the two outcomes – presents us with a different, more critical reading. The Feds eventually catch Belfort and he is tried and sentenced to three years in prison and a fine. "I'm not ashamed to admit it," the character begins, narrating the closing scene, "when we arrived to prison, I was absolutely terrified. But I needn't have been." They show him picking up a ball as the camera pulls out to show Belfort on a tennis court in prison. "See for a brief, fleeting moment I'd forgotten I was rich, and I lived in a place where everything is for sale." Here, the justice system does not restore harmony in the world. The capitalist still wins, and the state is all on board. Injustice prevails. However, one has to maintain a perspective of opposing the main character throughout the film for this message to be fully received. If we put the emphasis on 'hero' in 'antihero', then we get a situation in which we may be happy that this is the system we live in: hard-working entrepreneurs who oppose the justice system can earn enough to buy their way out of punishment.

Religious anthropologists have pointed out that, just as Belfort admired Gordon Gekko, Satanists become inspired by Milton's *Paradise Lost*.[38] But of course, Milton did not make Satan the hero, but the antihero. Antiheroes can blind audiences to the otherwise obvious message of a text. They can end up siding with and valorizing the antihero who is otherwise presented in the narrative negatively or, ultimately, reformed. Neo-Nazi representations in the film *American History X* (1998) are often referred to positively amongst real neo-Nazis[39]; the title character of Brian De Palma's *Scarface* (1983) is a now beloved popular culture icon,[40] the anarchists in *The Anarchist Cookbook* (2002), the title character in *Joker* (2019), and even the baby from *The Boss Baby* (2017) can fit this analysis.

Rituals and Magical Capitalism

Leonardo DiCaprio's Jordan Belfort enters the world of financialized capitalism after being hired by Mark Hanna, played by Matthew McConaughey. On Belfort's first day on Wall Street they sit down for lunch in a lavish modern dining room on one of the top floors of a Manhattan skyscraper. They sit in the middle of the restaurant surrounded by almost unobstructed glass windows that divulge the New York cityscape. Before any words are spoken Hanna rhythmically beats his chest with his fist while humming. Belfort does not know it, but he is being initiated into the industry. Hanna stops his ritual chant and snorts cocaine, explaining to the then strait-laced Belfort that drugs and prostitutes are the only way to do their job. But this initiation does not only include this seedy side of stockbroking, it also introduces the economic processes of its construction.

> Name of the game: move the money from your client's pocket into your pocket .... Number one rule of Wall Street: nobody, I don't care if you're Warren Buffett or if you're Jimmy Buffett, nobody knows if a stock is gonna go up, down, sideways, or in fucking circles. Least of all stockbrokers, right? It's all a fugazi .... it's a whazy, it's a woozy. It's fairy dust. It doesn't exist. It's never landed. It is no matter. It's not on the elemental chart. It's not fucking real .... We don't create shit. We don't build anything .... So if you got a client who bought stock at 8 and it now sits at 16, he's all fucking happy. He wants to cash in, liquidate, take his fucking money and run home. You don't let him do that. 'Cause that would make it real. What do you do? You get another brilliant idea. A special idea. Another "situation." Another stock to reinvest his earnings and then some. And he will, every single time 'cause they're fucking addicted. And you just keep doing this, again and again and again. Meanwhile, he thinks he's getting shit rich, which he is – on paper. But you and me, the brokers, we're taking home cold hard cash via commission motherfucker .... Revolutions .... Keep the clients on the Ferris wheel .... The park is open 24/7, 365, every decade, every goddamn century.

Hanna's speech concludes with the return of rhythmic chest thumping and humming, this time bringing in Belfort who joins in unison. Through this ritual Belfort is initiated into Wall Street, but in the monologue we also come to see the ritualized process of capitalism. While capitalism includes a range of rituals such as employee away days, international conferences, holiday sales, and the opening and closing bell of the New York Stock Exchange,[41] Hanna explains how the financial heart of the modern system itself is rooted in a ritual, magical means of exchange. As the editors of the book *Magical Capitalism* note, both capitalism and magic "are practiced under tenuous

88 Representations of Evil: A Cinematic Anthropology of Villains

conditions and, through many of their forms, use particular kinds of practices and ideology to deal with ambiguity and unpredictability while initiating processes of change".[42] Quoting a founder of social anthropology, Bronisław Malinowski, the editors note how magic becomes the explanation for "the unaccountable", the processes difficult to attribute to another actor or action.

Another founding father of anthropology, Marcel Mauss, stated that magic requires officers (magicians), actions (magical rites), and magical representations.[43] In the case above, stockbrokers are the magicians. They are demarcated by their occupation as having powers within the economic domain.[44] The magical representations consist of the ideas and beliefs that bridge the actor to the action and their affect. These ideological processes cannot be individualized and must be constituted within a community. The public's belief that stockbrokers increase their clients' wealth is one such notion. The magical rites are rituals that supposedly do work beyond the symbolic (e.g., beyond a contractual ritual in a court procedure). However, magic was often attributed to fields the wider public knew little about, but which produced a material result where the technique was undistinguished from other powers. For example, a surgeon's incisions were only of use to conjure some external force to help the patient.[45] The surgeon is a magician because the results are not perceived to be "achieved directly through the co-ordination of action, tool and physical agent" but because of "a world of ideas which imbues ritual movements and gestures with a kind of effectiveness".[46] In our case, stockbrokers' illocutionary acts – the process by which saying something produces that which is said[47] – helps to construct the collective value by which the stock itself is determined.

The magical qualities granted to agents of capital and state range from transformations "in share prices, in a patient's health, in defining 'fashion,' in the interpretation of a political event or criminal act",[48] etc. The actors use magical representation that feeds the ideological structures of their source of power (e.g., a balance chart forecasting real GPD growth).[49] But the magicians also confer magical powers on us, as individuals through the circular ideologies of capitalism and democracy. Through the invisible hand, representatives of capitalist institutions are so embedded in the ideology that they give magical powers to individuals to co-construct economic growth. In *The Wealth of Nations*, Adam Smith discusses the invisible hand as the force through which an individual pursuing his own interest is "led ... to promote an end which was no part of his intention", the economic growth of society. This magical force removes both the economic elite's own unequal role over the economy – and the need to figure in exploitation. Likewise, democracies confer magical powers on us through our electoral expressions as a means of granting legitimacy (even in cases where the plurality of the voting population refuses to grant such legitimacy by abstaining).

But the invisible hand is an ideology 'practiced under tenuous conditions' and, in a financialized economy, become process that is mystified. This is what Hanna exposes as a Ferris wheel amusement of constant rotations of wealth generated by systems of unpredictability. This is demonstrated by the inability of hedge fund managers to raise nearly the same amount as an index fund like the S&P500 over a long period[50] or, as one study notes, that "even a portfolio generated by [a] blindfolded monkey throwing darts outperforms the market".[51] The wealth they are generating is 'on paper' and calling in this wealth collectively would itself implode the market. The stockbroker's role in this process is also shown to be an illusion. Hanna is teaching a new magician how the trick is done.[52]

There is an entirely different ritual at play here, however. It involves not the rhythmic chest pounding or the magician's secret – in fact it is not even magical at all. This ritual is wider than the scene presented and the text itself. If we pull away from Belfort, pull away from the restaurant and from the Manhattan views and reverse the scene back to the observer we see another ritual happening in how we watch such a text. While the content presented here allows us to see how the magician's trick works, the form of this work positions this scene not as an anti-capitalist concern, but as an entrepreneurial opportunity.

According to the scholar Tony Wilson, when we watch screen media, "we draw on the viewer's knowledge of … patterns of activity",[53] which includes the standard interpretive ritual of cheering on the protagonist.[54] Although we see Belfort as the personification of finance capital and finance capital as problematic, our ritual of perspective-taking of the hero problematizes our interpretation of the economic and political context that they are placed in within an antihero text. We take their perspective and we sympathize with them. We become blinded by their actions hurting others because taking the protagonist's perspective, even an antihero, is a cultural norm in our reading of texts.[55] Thus, antiheroes can often become just plain 'heroes', just like Gordon Gekko was for the real-life Belfort and just like some gangster movies are for real-life gang members.[56]

Let us consider the reception of *The Wolf of Wall Street*. Exhibit A is an open letter to *LA Weekly* written by Christina McDowell – daughter of one of Belfort's real-life business associates and co-fraudster.

> You people are dangerous. Your film is a reckless attempt at continuing to pretend that these sorts of schemes are entertaining, even as the country is reeling from yet another round of Wall Street scandals. We want to get lost in what? These phony financiers' fun sexcapades and coke binges? Come on, we know the truth. This kind of behavior brought America to its knees. And yet you're glorifying it -- you who call yourselves liberals. You were honored for career excellence and for your cultural influence

90 Representations of Evil: A Cinematic Anthropology of Villains

by the Kennedy Center, Marty [Scorsese]. You drive a Honda hybrid, Leo [DiCaprio]. Did you think about the cultural message you'd be sending when you decided to make this film? You have successfully aligned yourself with an accomplished criminal, a guy who still hasn't made full restitution to his victims, exacerbating our national obsession with wealth and status and glorifying greed and psychopathic behavior. And don't even get me started on the incomprehensible way in which your film degrades women, the misogynistic, ass-backwards message you endorse to younger generations of men.[57]

There is additional evidence to suggest that others share McDowell's view, that the antiheroes are actually seen as heroes. At a time when the job market was generally cooling, researchers at the leading employment search engine in United States found that job searches for "stockbroker" skyrocketed soon after the release of *The Wolf of Wall Street* both in the United States, at the end of December 2013, and the United Kingdom, in January 2014 (see Figure 4.1).[58] This suggests that rather than presenting a critical look at the occupation and the downsides of such pursuits, the film actually highlights the job's positive attributes: money and power. This is further supported by a report for *Business Insider* that observed "the finance-heavy audience's gleeful reaction to [Belfort's] behavior and legal wrongdoings".[59]

The last scenes of *The Wolf of Wall Street* indicate that Scorsese knew what he was doing: Belfort picks up the tennis ball and says, "I lived in a place where everything is for sale" before asking the audience: "Wouldn't you like to learn how to sell it?" We then transition to the film's final scene showing Belfort in his new job: motivational speaker and sales trainer. What is most striking is the very last shot before the credits. The camera focuses on members of the large audience that have paid to see this criminal give them tips on becoming rich. This audience is a mirror image of the movie audience, and the scene asks us to reflect on our own complicity within this system that allows money to rule over basic notions of fairness and solidarity.[60] Could we, like the audience in front of Belfort, not see past this 'greed is good' mantra of capitalism? Can we avoid seeing Belfort as a protagonist?

Encoders (directors, screenwriters, producers, editors, etc.) have a variety of ways in which they can attempt to pull or push a reader from one type of reading to another. Encoders can adjust the music, color tone, lighting, sound effects, etc. in ways that correspond to existing meaning-making processes and interpretations. They can change the words and expressions, the camera angles, and the pace. All of these can contribute to our interpretation of the text. Take for example the openly racist silent film *The Birth of a Nation* (1915), directed by D.W. Griffith. The film spans the time of the US Civil War and Reconstruction, following the story of the Camerons and the Stonemans, two white families on opposite sides of the conflict. The film reinvents history

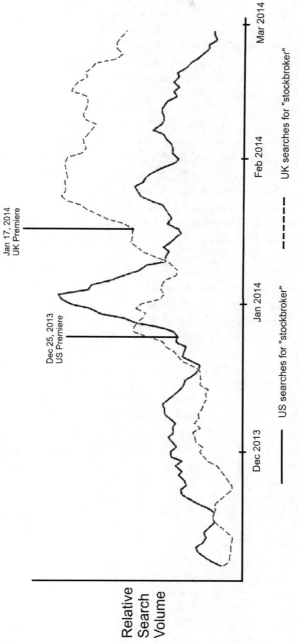

FIGURE 4.1 Indeed.com job Searches for "Stockbroker" Before and After the Release of *The Wolf of Wall Street* in the United States and United Kingdom. Reconstructed Graph Based on Indeed Blog (2014).

92 Representations of Evil: A Cinematic Anthropology of Villains

as it depicts the Northern victory releasing a plague of uncouth black people into the democratic system. Black people are shown as denying the vote to Southern whites and rigging the elections in their own favor. A black 'irregular force of guerrilla' is depicted raiding innocent and defenseless women who are chased inside their house. The Southern Camerons fear for their lives as animalistically-depicted black soldiers in Northern uniforms break into their home and chase after the young women of the estate. In response to what is represented as Northern punishment of the South during Reconstruction, Ben Cameron forms the Ku Klux Klan which becomes valorized in the film for their courage and moral certitude. Even today, over 100 years after its release and despite our more publicly anti-racist ideology, watching *The Birth of a Nation* can produce cheers for the Klan as they sweep through on horses to save the townsfolk from the menacingly barbaric hands of the black Northern troops. These are not the cheers of racists. I watched this film as an undergraduate student and heard young black women recount their own shock in supporting the Klan during the screening. The tone, mise-en-scène, and editing help make it easy for the audience to root for what we know is evil despite ourselves.

So, even if content is presented to show the fundamental flaws in the ideologies and actions of the protagonists, the interpretive ritual established by the formal elements encoded in the text allow most of us to reject these possibilities. Paul Verhoeven's *Starship Troopers* (1997), a film about human soldiers fighting intergalactic bugs, re-emphasizes this point. Verhoeven largely presents the humans in a positive light but drops ideas into the text that should reveal to the audience that the humans are actually meant to be the bad guys. For example, though the characters believe they are fighting in a war against aggressive aliens we find out that it is likely that the aliens "were provoked by the intrusion of humans into their natural habitat". The film's message, from the director's point of view, is really about the potential for fascism in America and how we as the audience can be complicit in this process. The director felt that "certain aspects of US society could become fascistic"[61] so he interlaced a teen sci-fi shooter with elements of a critique of war propaganda, chauvinism, and obedience. Although star actors like Mark Wahlberg and Matt Damon auditioned for the leading role, the director went with a relative unknown because the director "was looking for the prototype of blond, white and arrogant, and Casper Van Dien was so close to the images I remembered from [Nazi propaganda film director] Leni Riefenstahl's films." Verhoeven incorporated designs that resembled Nazi flags and SS uniforms. It more or less got past the studio execs.

> I borrowed from *Triumph of the Will* in the parody propaganda reel that opens the film, too. I was using Riefenstahl to point out, or so I thought, that these heroes and heroines were straight out of Nazi propaganda. No one saw it at the time.

Despite the fascistic elements, their position in the film – as heroes – blinded audiences to the film's politics. "I decided to make a movie about fascists who aren't aware of their fascism. *Robocop* was just urban politics – this was about American politics".[62] But not many saw it this way because of our interpretative rituals.

"F***ing Hypocrites"

One ritual that anthropologists engaged in was the pursuit of research funding and 'impact', but they often were blind to the harms they were contributing to in the process. The Major General who was discussed at the beginning of the chapter was not the first to call on the support of anthropologists for military purposes. In fact, since the beginning of the twentieth century the growth of anthropology as a discipline was a product of its role in working in the interests of the dominant institutions, or, in the words of anthropologist William S. Willis, Jr, "to provide data that might assist the imperialists".[63]

Anthropologists then began an inward turn, reflecting on their own role as researchers. The anthropologist Nancy Scheper-Hughes once declared that "if we cannot begin to think about social institutions and practices in moral or ethical terms, then anthropology strikes me as quite weak and useless".[64] Meanwhile, anthropologist Gerald Berreman called on his contemporaries to cease their hypocrisy[65] and, like Nader, to engage in anthropology from the bottom up. But the anthropologists that explore the mapped communities of antihero texts return with stories taken from the top. The antiheroes we focus on represent the systems of capitalism and the state and even if they tell tales that depict the problems of those systems, we as viewers become aligned to the interests of the storyteller and their perspective.

While we may also call on film and television creators to stop being hypocrites and create stories from the bottom up, it is possible to have a story led by an antihero and still make a radical point. In fact, it is the idea of hypocrisy that can produce the critical narrative we are looking for. Let's look at an example of a movie that successfully managed to create a narrative that subsumes their character into an indictment of something that is much bigger without having to rely on our antipathy for the leading role. *Casino Jack* (2010) explores the fall of 'superlobbyist' Jack Abramoff through his eyes. The film exposes aspects of the *systemic* nature of the political institution of lobbying with the most revealing scene being an imagined congressional testimony by Abramoff where, rather than pleading the 5th, he goes on a rant:

Jack Abramoff: No, I no longer wish to invoke the privileges. I have something to say and I'm gonna say it. No, no, no! In fact, if we want to talk all about the money, why don't we start with the four, five thousand dollar checks I personally handed to Senator Jarvis for his re-election campaign. And

94 Representations of Evil: A Cinematic Anthropology of Villains

we know what that money was all about, don't we, Senator. Or how about you, Senator Burman... I donated $30,000 to influence your vote to keep the Marianas opened for business, remember? What about you, Senator McCain... You should be sitting in the seat that I'm sitting in right now. For years, you've taken tens of thousands of dollars from lobbyists just like me representing competing Indian tribes who wanted to open up their own casinos that would have shut my clients down. This man ... this son of a bitch is guilty. And if he is allowed to go free, then there's something really wrong going on here.

John McCain: Sir, you're out of order.

Jack Abramoff: Out of order. You're out of order. You're out of order. You're all out of order. This whole Senate hearing is out of order. I've got a whole panel of Senators who loved to take money from anybody who's got a fucking bank account. And you call me a con Jew? Fucking hypocrites! You fucking hypocrites! You ought to stand for something. You should protect people.

In this scene, *Casino Jack* does what *Wolf of Wall Street* attempted to do but failed: place an antihero at the center of a film to expose a broader, institutional problem. It does this by suggesting that whatever we think of Abramoff – if we emphasis "anti" or "hero" – the bigger issue is that Congress and the justice system is complicit in corruption.[66] Had the film stopped there, *Casino Jack* would have had a much more radical message. Instead, the film shows who got punished and what happened to Jack Abramoff afterward, concluding with Abramoff writing a letter to Bill Clinton from prison, asking for the President's help in getting him released in exchange for "remind[ing] the world what a bunch of hypocrites [the Republicans] all are". Because Abramoff was a conservative and supported the Republicans the film ends up placing them in the crosshairs, backtracking from a broader system of legal corruption. It places the focus back on Jack and re-personalizes the story away from its wider political and economic critique. *Casino Jack* couldn't sustain a radical critique. Evil was assigned to Republican hypocrites, not the system.

Rocky's Horror and the Raison d'Être of Picture Shows

Simple notions of good and evil have been fan favorites of popular culture for some time. Semiologist Roland Barthes observed this during his research in the 1950s. Barthes conducted an ethnography of the daily life of France in search of myths, of the underlying ideology of the capitalist culture that was widespread but invisible. Barthes referred to this as "ideological abuse" that "transforms petit-bourgeois culture into a universal nature".[67] He observed a professional wrestling match in Paris and found it to be a "mythological fight between Good and Evil".[68] The story played out in combat is one of justice against evil presented through the most obvious of signs. Every moment, every action is exaggerated to clearly demonstrate its purpose and meaning, "constantly help[ing] the reading of the fight by means of gestures, attitudes and mimicry which make the intention utterly obvious".[69] Even the physical appearances of the wresters dictate to the audience who will play what role, like characters of the Commedia dell'Arte.

The drama in wrestling presents the audience with the visual exaggerations of suffering, defeat, and especially justice. The villain is shown as breaking the rules at whim, but complaining when rules are broken against him. Justice therefore is presented in the "blow which he received in return", and the more 'unfairly' he has behaved, the louder the crowd cheers when evil is punished. "Evil", Barthes writes, "is the natural climate of wrestling" and it is the "orgy of evil which alone make good wrestling".[70] The audience does not want to see a fair fight and enforced rules. They precisely want to see unfairness on display so that unfairness itself can be punished and justice restored. For Barthes, wrestlers in the ring are gods to their audience because "they are, for a few moments, the key which opens Nature, the pure gesture which separates Good from Evil, and unveils the form of a justice which is at last intelligible".[71]

In the American context this battle between Good and Evil is not one of justice but, according to Barthes, of politics. We have a range of examples of politics in American professional wrestling from Nikolai Volkoff and the Iron Sheik of the 1980s, to the Nation of Domination and Yokozuma in the 1990s, to Rusev the Putin-promoting Russian and #OccupyRaw in the 2010s, and the black bloc of Retribution. These examples point us to largely conservative representations and while there are few depictions of wrestling in cinema, boxing films often cover this same territory. Most famously we can see this in the Rocky films. The first film (1976) is about race politics, *Rocky II* (1979) is about masculinity, *Rocky III* (1982) is about class and habitus, and *Rocky IV* (1985) is about the Cold War – all from a conservative standpoint. Why, despite film and television often being political and dividing good and evil, is it so hard to find fictional screen media texts that present radical critiques of the state or capitalism?

In his documentary analysis of art, *Ways of Seeing*, John Berger argues that particular art forms have a historical and cultural raison d'être (reason to exist).

> We study other cultures far away as anthropology. That is to say, we study them from the outside. We don't judge them purely according to their own explanations of themselves. If we look at the culture of European oil

96 Representations of Evil: A Cinematic Anthropology of Villains

painting in the same spirit, leaving aside its claims for itself, I believe we will find that oil painting was, before everything else, a medium which celebrated private possessions.

Paintings display wealth but so does their content, Berger argued. Film and television are not about such private possession. Nor arguably are they about entertainment in its purest sense. Entertainment is the mythology behind film and television. I believe that an anthropological examination of screen media points us in the direction of the production of ideology as its raison d'être. Although Berger sees wealth and property on full display in European oil paintings, he finds exceptions that are more critical.[72] Surely then, we too can find exceptions of films and television shows that are critical of capitalism and the state.

Notes

1 Scales Jr. 2003.
2 Ribeiro 2007.
3 Nader 1972.
4 Parkin 1986, p. 3.
5 Schlothauer 2013–2014.
6 Staub 1993, p. 52.
7 Parkin 1986.
8 Also see Max from *Cape Fear* (1991), Biff from the *Back to the Future* films, or Trunchbull in *Matilda* (1996).
9 Also see *A Christmas Story* (1983), *Hocus Pocus* (1993), *Carrie* (1976), and *Easy A* (2010).
10 *The Silence of The Lambs* (1991), *Hannibal* (2001), *Red Dragon* (2002).
11 For a more nuanced depiction of 'bad guys' represented as – arguably – systemically abused – albeit not by state or capitalist institutions, see films such as *A Streetcar Named Desire* (1951) and *Primal Fear* (1996).
12 Also see *The Incredibles'* (2004) Syndrome, *GoldenEye*'s (1995) Alec Trevelyan, *Skyfall*'s (2012) Raoul Silva, and Khan in *Star Trek II: The Wrath of Khan* (1982).
13 *Austin Powers: International Man of Mystery* (1997); *Austin Powers: The Spy Who Shagged Me* (1999); *Austin Powers in Goldmember* (2002).
14 The Universal Spectator 2014.
15 Johnson 2012.
16 Wiegand 2016.
17 Lamer and O'Steen 1997. Rather than a watchdog, the Media Research Centre can be seen as a flak machine (Herman and Chomsky 2002).
18 Giglio 2005, 138; van Zoonen and Wring 2012.
19 Also, see *Absolute Power* (1997), *The Manchurian Candidate* (2004), *All the King's Men* (2006), and *Beyond a Reasonable Doubt* (2009). Similar representations were found when researchers explored British soap operas (Coleman 2008). Sometimes, rather than villains, these policymakers are represented as self-interested power-mongers (e.g., *Veep* (2012–2019), *In the Loop* (2009), *Jaws* (1975), *Wag the*

Dog (1997), *Bob Roberts* (1992), *Election* (1999)). This representation was also present in films of the 1940s, 1950s, and 1960s, following from a trend in literature (Fielding 2008).

20 Parkin 2003, p. 18.

21 De Coppet 2003, p. i.

22 Also see *GoldenEye* (1995) and *The Dark Knight* (1975).

23 Doyle 2008.

24 Anonymous 2008. For the widespread nature of the protest, see Coleman 2013.

25 *The Hunger Games* (2012); *The Hunger Games: Catching Fire* (2013); *The Hunger Games: Mockingjay – Part 1* (2014); *The Hunger Games: Mockingjay – Part 2* (2015).

26 *Divergent* (2014); *Insurgent* (2015); *Allegiant* (2016). These also work as examples of the obscured critique.

27 Fleming 1980.

28 Also see the movie *Shooter* (2007).

29 Fuchs 2013. The exception to the right-wing position is their opposition to intellectual property rights.

30 For other examples, see the "USS Callister" episode of *Black Mirror*, season 4, *Tinker Tailor Soldier Spy* (2011), *Jupiter Ascending* (2015), *The Wolf of Wall Street* (2013), *The Chamber* (1996), *Dick* (1999), *All the King's Men* (2006), *Chappaquiddick* (2017), *Blow Out* (1981), *Minority Report* (2002), *Gringo* (2018), *Luke Cage* season 1 (2016), *The House* (2017), and *No Way Out* (1987). Perhaps a more complex representation can be found in *Motherless Brooklyn*, season 1 of *Morning Show* and *Promising Young Woman* (2020).

31 Dio Chrysostom, quoted in Winkler 1990, p. 21.

32 Winkler 1990, p. 22.

33 This can be read through Jameson's development of binary opposition and reconciliation (see Wayne 2020, pp. 139–140).

34 For this point, also see Burnham 2016, p. 101.

35 From the film *Wall Street* (1987).

36 In the end, however, we see Gekko as *unscrupulous* capitalist, not a representative of the capitalist system per se. He is kept in check by federal authorities (similarly to the representation in *Billions*) and the main problem depicted in the film is *predatory* capitalism rather than capitalism itself. The airline was a good investment, but an unscrupulous financier decided to break it up instead.

37 Frith 2014.

38 "One prominent Satanist", notes *The Invention of Satanism*, found "Milton's Satan so clearly the hero of Paradise Lost that he was 'surprised it and its author were not summarily burned' " (Aquino 2013, p. 93, cited in Dyrendal et al., 2016, p. 28. "Church of Satan high priest Magus Peter Howard Gilmore announced in a statement that 'Having a conservative Christian likened to Lucifer – one who opposes equal rights for same sex couples and promotes the ability to deny services to any with different values – we Satanists see as besmirching the positive, heroic aspects of that character as portrayed by Milton in his epic *Paradise Lost*" (Danner 2016).

39 Lemons 2007.

40 Halima 2011.

41 Gudeman and Hann 2015, p. 3; Moeran and de Waal Malefyt 2018, p. 6.

98 Representations of Evil: A Cinematic Anthropology of Villains

42 Moeran and de Waal Malefyt 2018, p. 11.
43 Moeran and de Waal Malefyt 2018, p. 11.; Mauss 2001[1950], pp. 2–3.
44 Moeran and de Waal Malefyt 2018, p. 5.
45 The reference to the surgeon's incision was taken from Mauss 2001[1950], p. 24.
46 Mauss 2001[1950], p. 25.
47 Moeran and de Waal Malefyt 2018, p. 15.
48 Moeran and de Waal Malefyt 2018, p. 6.
49 Moeran and de Waal Malefyt 2018, p. 6.
50 Wattles 2018.
51 Arnott, et al 2013, p. 91.
52 Some would say that it is not a trick but, rather, an illusion.
53 Wilson 1995, p. 106.
54 Both Brecht and Jameson also talk our expectations and habits as central to our consumption patterns, see Lykidis 2020, p. 10.
55 Think also about films such as *Thank You for Smoking* (2005), *Bad Lieutenant* (1992), and *Cosmopolis* (2012).
56 Goodfellas has a track-record of attracting people to a life of crime – as do other antihero films such as *The Godfather* (Gambetta 2011). These films, unlike movies that also depicted criminal organizations but through the eyes of the police, are adored by criminal organizations (Gambetta 2011). According to Gambetta (2011), other mob movies were unpopular with real-life 'goodfellas'. For example, *Donnie Brasco* (1997), a film that follows an undercover cop getting dragged into the world of the mob, shows the gangsters getting out-conned by the police, and was unpopular amongst gangsters despite being a box office success. Gambetta writes, "advertising is not supposed to dwell on shortcomings." (Gambetta 2011, p. 273). This suggests that the narrative and representation matter and help to form judgements about the content of the text. Such texts not only bring in recruits but serve these organizations with self-confidence and legitimacy (Gambetta 2011, p. 273), demonstrating that antihero films can often be interpreted in ways perhaps unintended by 1heir creators. 'The absolute winner of the contest to supply the best free mafia advertising is undoubtedly *The Godfather*. That film had for the mafia the same effect that Marilyn Monroe's famous quip about her nocturnal dress had for boosting sales of Chanel no. 5. Mobsters loved it, and still do. "*The Godfather* is everything to these people," says David Chase, creator of *The Sopranos* (1999–2007). "It's their Bible, their Koran. Their Mona Lisa, their Eiffel Tower" ' (Gambetta 2011, p. 269). According to the book, "John Abbott, director general of the British National Criminal Intelligence Service, has openly blamed films, such as *Lock Stock and Two Smoking Barrels* (1999) and *Snatch* (2000), both by director Guy Ritchie, for glamorizing and thus encouraging organized crime" (Gambetta 2011, p. 270).
57 McDowell 2013. Others have disagreed with this analysis, e.g. Rosen 2013.
58 Indeed Blog 2014.
59 Perlberg 2013.
60 Although he references other techniques used in *The Wolf of Wall Street* (2013), Sweedler (2019) makes similar points.
61 This reality is even clearer in hindsight.
62 Verhoeven 2018.
63 Willis 1969.

64 Scheper-Hughes 1995, p. 410.
65 D'Andrade 1995, p. 407.
66 Also see *The Laundromat* (2019).
67 Barthes 1972, p. 10.
68 Barthes 1972, p. 21.
69 Barthes 1972, p. 16.
70 Barthes 1972, p. 21.
71 Barthes 1972, p. 23.
72 E.g., *A View of Het Steen in the Early Morning* by Peter Paul Rubens, *Woman Holding a Balance* by Johannes Vermeer, or the works of Adriaen Brouwer (Berger 1977, p. 103).

References

Anonymous (2008) 'Message to Scientology', YouTube, https://www.youtube.com/watch?v=JCbKv9yiLiQ.

Arnott, Robert D., Hsu, Jason, Kalesnik, Vitali, and Tindall, Phil (2013) 'The Surprising Alpha from Malkiel's Monkey and Upside-Down Strategies', *Journal of Portfolio Management*, 39(4): 91–105.

Barthes, Roland (1972) *Mythologies*, New York: The Noonday Press.

Berger, John (1977) *Ways of Seeing*, London: Penguin Books.

Burnham, Clint (2016) *Fredric Jameson and The Wolf of Wall Street*, New York: Bloomsbury.

Coleman, Gabriella (2013) 'Anonymous in Context: The Politics and Power Behind the Mask', *Internet Governance Papers*. The Centre for International Governance Innovation, Paper No. 3.

D'Andrade, Roy (1995) 'Moral Models in Anthropology', *Current Anthropology*, 36(3): 399–408.

Danner, Chas (2016) 'Satanists Reject John Boehner's Conflation of Ted Cruz and Lucifer', *Daily Intelligencer*, May 1, http://nymag.com/daily/intelligencer/2016/05/satanists-reject-ted-cruz-lucifer-comparison.html. Accessed Oct. 1, 2018.

de Coppet, Daniel (2003) 'Understanding Rituals', in Daniel de Coppet (ed.), *Understanding Rituals* (p. i), London: Routledge.

Doyle, Leonard (2008) 'Scientologists Try to Block Cruise YouTube Rant', *The Independent*, Jan. 17, https://www.independent.co.uk/news/world/americas/scientologists-try-to-block-cruise-youtube-rant-770649.html.

Dyrendal, Absjorn, Lewis, James R., Petersen, Jesper A. A. (2016) *The Invention of Satanism*, Oxford: Oxford University Press.

Fleming, Marie (1980) 'Propaganda by the Deed: Terrorism and Anarchist Theory in Late Nineteenth-Century Europe', *Terrorism: An International Journal*, 4(1–4): 1–23.

Frith, Maxine (2014) 'The Wall Street Wolf, His London Aunt and a £50m Scam', *Evening Standard*, Jan. 3, https://www.standard.co.uk/lifestyle/london-life/the-wall-street-wolf-his-london-aunt-and-a-50m-scam-9036566.html. Accessed Oct. 1, 2018.

Fuchs, Christian (2013) 'The Anonymous Movement in the Context of Liberalism and Socialism', *Interface: A Journal for and about Social Movements*, 5(2): 345–376.

Gambetta, Diego (2011) *Codes of the Underworld: How Criminals Communicate*, Princeton, NJ: Princeton University Press.

Giglio, Ernest (2005). *Here's Looking at You: Hollywood Film and Politics*. New York: Peter Lang.

Gudeman, Stephen and Hann, Chris (2015) 'Introduction. Ritual, Economy, and the Institutions of the Base', in Stephen Gudeman and Chris Hann (eds.), *Economy and Ritual: Studies of Postsocialist Transformations* (pp. 1–3), New York: Berghahn.

Halima, Maz (2011) 'How Scarface Dominated Pop Culture', *Flavourmag*, Aug. 31, http://www.flavourmag.co.uk/how-scarface-dominated-pop-culture. Accessed Jan. 10, 2018.

Herman, Edward S. and Chomsky, Noam (2002) *Manufacturing Consent: The Political Economy of the Mass Media*, New York: Pantheon.

Indeed Blog (2014) 'The Hollywood Effect & Other Recent Job Trends', March 28, http://blog.indeed.com/2014/03/28/the-hollywood-effect-other-recent-job-trends. Accessed Oct. 1, 2018.

Johnson, Ted (2012) 'Blockbusters Can't Escape Politics', *Variety*, July 21, https://vari ety.com/2012'fi'm/news/blo'kbusters-ca'-t-escape-politics-1118056853. Accessed Oct. 1, 2018.

Lamer, Timothy and O'Steen, Alice Lynn (1997) 'Businessmen Behaving Badly: Prime Time's World of Commerce', *Media Research Center*, http://archive.mrc.org/spe cialreports/1997/sum/sum19970616.asp. Accessed Oct. 1, 2018.

Lemons, Stephen (2007) 'Newsaxon.com, the Neo-Nazi MySpace, with Hot Racist Chicks Galore', *Phoenix New Times*, April 25, https://www.phoenixnewtimes. com/news/newsaxoncom-the-neo-nazi-myspace-with-hot-racist-chicks-galore-6503569. Accessed Oct. 1, 2018.

Lykidis, Alex (2020) *Art Cinema and Neoliberalism*, Cham, Switzerland: Palgrave Macmillan.

Mauss, Marcel (2001[1950]) *A General Theory of Magic*, London: Routledge.

McDowell, Christina (2013) 'An Open Letter to the Makers of *The Wolf of Wall Street*, and the Wolf Himself', *LA Weekly*, Dec. 26, https://www.laweekly.com/ news/an-open-letter-to-the-makers-of-the-wolf-of-wall-street-and-the-wolf-hims elf-4255219. Accessed Oct. 1, 2018.

Moeran, Brian and de Waal Malefyt, Timothy (2018) 'Magical Capitalism: An Introduction', in Brian Moeran and Timothy de Waal Malefyt (eds.), *Magical Capitalism: Enchantment, Spells and Occult Practices in Contemporary Economies* (pp. 1–44), Cham, Switzerland: Palgrave Macmillan.

Nader, Laura (1972) 'Up the Anthropologist – Perspectives Gained from Studying Up', in Dell Hymes (ed.), *Reinventing Anthropology* (pp. 284–311), New York: Pantheon Books.

Parkin, David (1986)' Introduction', in David Parkin (ed.), *The Anthropology of Evil* (pp. 1–25), Oxford: Basil Blackwell Ltd.

Parkin, David (2003) 'Ritual as Special Direction and Bodily Division', in Daniel de Coppet (ed.), *Understanding Rituals* (pp. 11–25), London: Routledge.

Perlberg, Steven (2013) 'We Saw "Wolf Of Wall Street" with a Bunch of Wall Street Dudes and It Was Disturbing', *Business Insider*, Dec. 19, https://www.business insider.com/banker-pros-cheer-wolf-of-wall-street-2013-12?IR=T. Accessed Oct. 1, 2018.

Ribeiro, Gustavo Lins (2007) 'Security for Whom? Anthropologists and Repressive State Elites', *Focaal—European Journal of Anthropology*, 50, 146–154.

Rosen, Christopher (2013) 'Here's One Reason Why You Didn't Like "The Wolf of Wall Street"', *HuffPost*, https://www.huffingtonpost.com/christopher-rosen/wolf-of-wall-street_b_4512756.html?guccounter=1. Accessed Oct. 1, 2018.

Scales Jr., Robert H. (2003) 'Statement by Mg (Ret) Robert H. Scales Jr. Before the House Armed Services Committee United States House of Representatives', Oct. 21, www.au.af.mil/au/awc/awcgate/congress/03-10-21scales.htm.

Scheper-Hughes, Nancy (1995) 'The Primacy of the Ethical: Propositions for a Militant Anthropology', *Current Anthropology*, 36(3): 409–440.

Schlothauer, Andreas (2013–2014) 'Munduruku and Apiaká Featherwork in the Johann Natterer Collection', *Archiv Weltmuseum Wien*, 63–64: 132–161.

Staub, Ervin (1993) *The Roots of Evil: The Origins of Genocide and Other Group Violence*, Cambridge: Cambridge University Press.

Sweedler, Milo (2019) *Rumble and Crash: Crises of Capitalism in Contemporary Film*, Albany, NY: State University of New York Press.

The Universal Spectator (2014) 'Obama and Holder Set to Release Thousands of Prisoners', https://theuniversalspectator.wordpress.com/2014/04/27/obama-and-holder-set-to-release-thousands-of-prisoners. Accessed Oct. 1, 2018.

van Zoonen, L. and Wring, D. (2012) 'Trends in Political Television Fiction in the UK: Themes, Characters and Narratives, 1965–2009', *Media Culture and Society*, 34(3): 263–279.

Verhoeven, Paul (2018) 'How We Made Starship Troopers', *The Guardian*, interview by Phil Hoad, Jan. 22, https://www.theguardian.com/culture/2018/jan/22/how-we-made-starship-troopers-paul-verhoeven-nazis-leni-riefenstahl. Accessed Oct. 1, 2018.

Wattles, Jackie (2018) 'Warren Buffett Beat the Hedge Funds. Here's How', CNN Business, https://money.cnn.com/2018/02/24/investing/warren-buffett-annual-letter-hedge-fund-bet/index.html?fbclid=IwAR099ijD95EmXJwLuVuirty_K0u1Ad4i 94AuRgi0cGFuZ5LWuJIou6ARv4o. Accessed May 31, 2019.

Wayne, Mike (2020) *Marx Goes to the Movies*, Abingdon: Routledge.

Wiegand, David (2016) "Billions' Takes Cynical Look at Corruption — on Both Sides of the Law', *SF Gate*, Jan. 13, https://www.sfgate.com/tv/article/Billions-takes-cyni cal-look-at-corruption-6756597.php. Accessed Oct. 1, 2018.

Willis, William S., Jr. (1972) 'Skeletons in the Anthropological Closet', in Dell H. Hymes (ed.) *Reinventing Anthropology* (pp. 121–152), New York: Random House.

Wilson, Tony (1995) *Watching Television: Hermeneutics, Reception and Popular Culture*, Cambridge: Polity Press.

Winkler, John J. (1990) *The Constraints of Desire: The Anthropology of Sex and Gender in Ancient Greece*, New York: Routledge.

5

STRUCTURAL CRITIQUES OF CAPITALISM IN FILM AND TELEVISION

Mr. Moneybags and the Hidden Abode

As part of his work *Mythologies*, the semiologist Roland Barthes examined Joseph L. Mankiewicz's 1953 classic film, *Julius Caesar*. Barthes' semiotic analysis found hair to be crucial, arguing that the 'insistent fringes' the characters wore indicated 'Roman-ness' to an American audience. But Barthes noted that this sign did not work for other audiences. "A Frenchman, to whose eyes American faces still have something exotic, finds comical the combination of the morphologies of these gangster-sheriffs [with the exception of Marlon Brando] with the little Roman fringe: it rather looks like an excellent music-hall gag".[1] This vignette says little about capitalism, but it expresses the importance of understanding that a sign only works if you are speaking the same language, so to speak. It is contextual and contingent on shared understanding. It is this understanding that leads to laughter when viewing comedies such as Charlie Chaplin's silent short film *The Count* (1916). In the film, Chaplin's tramp sneaks into an elite dinner party, pretending to be a count. He is accepted as one of the elites while he attempts to court a wealthy young woman named Ms. Moneybags. However, the tramp cannot embody ruling class distinction – failing to follow proper etiquette. For the rich guests around him, the tramp is viewed as a kind of comedian which allows us, the audience, to find both the continuation of this situation believable and funny. The other characters understand the situation one way while we in the audience realize that they understand it inaccurately. In this case we read the same signs differently because we are privy to different information – the inverse of an inside joke. But we can only fully appreciate this joke because we share information not only with Chaplin's character, knowing he is a tramp, but with the bourgeois guests, knowing what the proper etiquette is.

DOI: 10.4324/9781003514916-6

Structural Critiques of Capitalism in Film and Television **103**

Charlie Chaplin used the understanding of semiotics to develop a character who represents the poor and hungry but despite his destitute position, the tramp is never really politically aware. For this reason, Barthes argues that "no socialist work has yet succeeded in expressing the humiliated condition of the worker with so much violence and generosity" as Chaplin's *Modern Times* (1936).[2] In *Modern Times*, Chaplin "shows the public its blindness by presenting at the same time a man who is blind and what is in front of him".[3] If the language of revolution is not already understood, then the presentation of poverty and political blindness may have a stronger resonance. Similarly, we can look at the German film *Namenlose Helden* (*Nameless Heroes*), which premiered in mid-October 1925 in Berlin despite the efforts of the Reichswehrminister (Reich Ministry of Defense) to stop it. Released just six years after the communist-led Spartacist uprising in Germany, the film fought off an outright ban when Reichswehrminister appealed to the censors citing the film's anti-war and communist sympathies. What were the authorities so scared of? The film shows both the devastation of a family following the outbreak of the First World War and the senseless brutality of the war. Like the films of Chaplin, it also demonstrated class contradictions by contrasting the lives of the victims of war with the extravagant wealth of an ammunition manufacturer.[4] More importantly, it situated the context of the First World War within a series of other conflicts. Using archival footage, it showed scenes of the first Balkan War of 1912 and scenes of the German Revolution of 1918 and 1919, concluding with footage of the Kapp Putsch of 1920. For viewers at the time, these events were all too pertinent and they helped to effectively demonstrate the imperialist and capitalist causes of war and the consequences for ordinary families.[5] Viewed today without knowledge of this context, these archival scenes may have little meaning.

We can see the importance we must place on the contextual nature of the signs found in the media texts we explore when looking for radical critiques. Each enters the wrestling match of competing cultural discourses within a particular time and place that resonates with specific, although not uniform, readings of these texts. But this is further complicated by the fact that cultural texts themselves can play a role in shaping our understanding of the present, past, and future by helping both to create signs and to structure our interpretation of them.

The Shapeshifting of Spartacus

The radical German newspaper *Die Rote Fahne (The Red Flag)* celebrated the film *Namenlose Helden* (1925) at the time of its release.

This film honors the memory of the millions of victims of imperialism by turning sharply and clearly against the imperialist war and its causes,

104 Structural Critiques of Capitalism in Film and Television

capitalism. Just why the title "Nameless Heroes" for the unnamed murdered? They were not heroes in spite of their bravery, they could not be heroes because, beguiled and stunned, they had to die for the moneybag [Geldsack], they had to murder their brothers and classmates.[6]

The film was actually the only war movie to receive a positive review by the paper, showing the rarity of such radical representations.

The *Die Rote Fahne* newspaper was the organ of the Spartacus League, founded by Karl Liebknecht and Rosa Luxemburg. The famous revolutionaries led a general strike in a battle for power against the more moderate and ruling Social Democratic Party of Germany and armed combat between state forces and revolutionaries ensued. Although their uprising failed, they inspired future attempts at revolution.

The Spartacus League was named after the leader of a failed uprising of the past. Spartacus was a Thracian who fought in the Roman army and then was enslaved. He was brought to Capua where he was trained as a gladiator. After he assisted in an escape of 70 slaves, Spartacus was made a leader and led the fugitives to various victories against Roman forces. Others joined him and, according to the ancient historian Appian, at one point he was in command of approximately 120,000 warriors. Having realized the seriousness that this posed, with some accounts claiming the band of fugitives sought to overtake Rome, the Roman Senate put Marcus Licinius Crassus in charge of crushing the rebellion.[7] Crassus was a Roman politician who was noted for being one of the richest people on Earth, even by today's standards. (This led him to be nicknamed *Dives*, which roughly translates into Moneybags.[8]) Crassus expanded his wealth by buying up properties at a low price after they caught fire and securing skilled slaves to help rebuild on his newly acquired land. He reinvested his earnings into slaveholding which became his most lucrative enterprise. He used his wealth to amass power within the Republic and became one of the most respected public figures.[9]

In the historic documents that examine the slave revolt, Crassus is positioned not as the villain but as a military genius and someone to be feared. He disciplined his soldiers in a gruesome fashion, but he was effective as a military leader and "preserved our Roman honor". Likewise, Spartacus was not the hero we know him as today but was described as "a wholly disreputable person" and, like other slaves, a human of an "inferior type".[10] The Romans spoke the language of empire and not freedom or equality of humans. They read this rebellion in those terms. It was only later that Spartacus came to stand as a figure of freedom, listed (alongside Kepler) as Karl Marx's hero.[11] What brought about the image of Spartacus as a revolutionary figure to admire? Before Voltaire made his comments about Spartacus' Third Servile War being "indeed the only just war in history"; before the academic studies into the events and histories by Charles de Brosses

Structural Critiques of Capitalism in Film and Television **105**

and Jean Lévesque de Burigny; before the increased interest in slave revolts following the Haitian Revolution there was a play, *Spartacus: A Tragedy in Five Acts*. It was written by Bernard Saurin and performed at the Théâtre-Français in 1760. It was this cultural text that reinvented our view of this revolutionary.

The representation of him in the play fitted in with the movement of Enlightenment France with Spartacus driven by natural law and the rights of man. In the play, Spartacus falls in love with a woman who turns out to be Crassus' daughter. Crassus offers citizenship to the slaves and a senatorial post for Spartacus as well as his daughter's hand if he accepts the power of Rome. Spartacus refuses, choosing a liberty beyond the confines of the oppressive Republic that enslaved him in the first place.[12] The image of Spartacus that was partially shaped by this play came to resonate not just with the ideas of Enlightenment but with the revolutionary ideals of many within the radical left and has been a source of inspiration.

This was certainly not the first nor the last time that culture has helped to construct our imagination of the past, present, and future to the point of near universal acceptance. Few would now look at Spartacus as a rabble-rouser worthy of his brutal fate. He stands as a symbol of freedom and certainly this is due to our own socio-political hegemony of the 'rights of man' that paved the ideological way toward the quasi-democratic capitalist system we have today. These same 'rights of man' helped to justify colonialism and slavery, but some argue that liberal components of the ideology needn't necessarily lead to the negative outcomes of liberal policies that have come to accompany it. This is precisely why radicals have highlighted Spartacus. It is also why the radical academic and activist Noam Chomsky often draws on a classical liberal tradition, citing the works of Wilhelm von Humboldt and even the capitalist icon Adam Smith, in arguing for libertarian socialism.[13] Though Adam Smith is often a stand-in for rugged individualism and the benefits of an unregulated capitalism, Chomsky seeks to rewrite our understanding of him.

Rugged individualism is often envisaged in the gunslinging Wild West but, as Chomsky also points out, this too is a product of culture, not history. Citing Pamela Haag's *The Gunning of America*, Chomsky notes that the myths of the Wild West were produced by cultural texts that were then used by the gun industry to promote weapon sales after the First World War.[14] The heroism that was depicted was just a myth to serve particular interests. Likewise, the figure of Spartacus was interpreted differently by the powerful of his day, and through fiction grew to become what he is today. Though extremely popular in its time, the play that shaped the idea of Spartacus has long since been eclipsed in fame by Stanley Kubrick's *Spartacus* (1960).[15]

The film holds Spartacus in the highest of standing, a man of noble cause who is worth dying for. Although the heroes lose, Spartacus is positively

106 Structural Critiques of Capitalism in Film and Television

depicted as attempting to free himself and his fellow slaves. When pushed into a corner he strives for even wider liberation: "We have no choice, but to march against Rome herself and end this war the only way it could have ended: by freeing every slave in Italy". Evil is also represented in the film. While all the Romans are shown toying with lives for their political machinations, Crassus is presented as utterly evil. He purchases the Senate and maneuvers to make himself dictator, not only upending the slave rebellion but the Republic itself. Spartacus, on the other hand, is presented in direct contrast to Crassus. Spartacus calls for "a New Rome, a new Italy, and a new empire ... and the restoration of order ... throughout all our territories." Through the representation of Crassus, this screen media text attempts to comment both on the problems of order during a period of increased authoritarianism and on the establishment itself. *Spartacus* was based on a book written by Howard Fast, a communist who was imprisoned for contempt of Congress when he refused to name names before the House Committee on Un-American Activities (HUAC) during the anti-communist Red Scare of the McCarthy era. Fast was subsequently blacklisted and had to self-publish the novel. The screenplay was written by Dalton Trumbo, another 'communist sympathizer' who was blacklisted following his testimony before HUAC.[16]

The creators of *Modern Times*, *Namenlose Helden*, and *Spartacus* openly sympathized with a left-wing communist ideology. They produced works that reflected, in part, their political beliefs through critiques of capitalism and the state that were more substantial than the limited critiques presented in the previous chapters. But these sympathies and subsequent films were themselves coproduced by a context of possibility, the existence of a believed alternative – even if that alternative, found in socialist revolutions that largely devolved into authoritarianism, was not the utopia it was hoped to be. Those days are now over, and the pressures of context have shifted political allegiances. The Soviet Union, the Communist Bloc, the Third World Project are all essentially finished, certainly from the point of view of shaping the belief in positive alternatives. In their place we now have neoliberal capitalism with an ethno-nationalist twist. The long reigns of Putin's Russia and Netanyahu's Israel and the right-wing impulse to fight Islamist fire with their own brand of right-wing nationalist fire set the scene for Modi's India, Duterte's Philippines, Salvini and Meloni's Italy, Trump's United States, Bolsonaro's Brazil, and the growing neo-nationalism across the globe. If this persists, we expect to find it shaping the language of signs we see in the media, even if the texts do not openly advocate such positions. While media texts such as *V for Vendetta* (2005) and *Children of Men* (2006) foresaw this, others such as *Years and Years* (2019), spoke directly to this context. Although these representations are often critical of the new position, if this neo-nationalism continues, we can imagine discourses within film and television will become more supportive of this position. The pervasive ideological context is one in which there is no alternative – neoliberalism. And for some time such a context has had its grip on the ideological content of media texts.

Look at the difference we find between the Spartacus of the communists and the Spartacus of the Starz television series by the same name. In the latter, Spartacus is not driven by an urge for freedom but by individual (read: neoliberal) motivations. Initially the series focuses on Spartacus's enslavement and gladiatorial battles. The Roman's deceptions were largely political in the film whereas in the Starz series they too are driven largely by personal motives. The character of Spartacus, rather than being othered within the Republic, is depicted as popular due to his gladiatorial feats. He is pitted against a whole band of opponents in the ring. This unjust battle (echoing Barthes' analysis of wrestling described in the previous chapter) angers the crowd, but the Roman in charge contends that it is fitting for such a traitor whose punishment must be made an example of. When Spartacus successfully defeats all four gladiators the crowd cheers for the rebalancing of justice and Spartacus is hailed a sensation, adopting the position of hero even for the Roman audience whose privilege has enslaved him. This transformation locates him as a national hero, not a revolutionary.

Wrestling in the Marketplace

The gladiatorial scenes in the television series *Spartacus* (2010–2013) resemble a French view of wrestling, with its emphasis on producing justice, and the *Rocky* films, with its emphasis on the political battles between good and evil. Both depict the 'pure gesture', as described by Barthes. They present their conflicts on their sleeves and display them in exaggerated form to the audience, idealized myths about the realities of the day. The spectacles of the boxing matches and gladiatorial fights attempt to speak to the 'real' through the language of signs. In *Rocky IV* (1985), Rocky and Ivan Drago are the signifiers, and the United States and the Soviet Union are, respectively, the signified. The fight is supposed to tell us something about the world we inhabit. But in director Darren Aronofsky's *The Wrestler* (2008), the spectacle of the wrestling match is re-established as the un-real, the ideal, within the neorealist spectacle of the film.

The Wrestler understands the sporting component within the text as a text to be read itself, just as it was for Barthes. The film attempts to expose the superficial perspective on professional wrestling just as sociologist Loïc Wacquant attempted to do for boxing.[17] *The Wrestler* focuses on the fictional Randy 'The Ram' Robinson, a once famous professional wrestler who has become a broke and lonely grocery store employee who continues wrestling in front of small audiences on his days off. The film challenges the machismo politics of *Rocky* by presenting the problems that are a logical

108 Structural Critiques of Capitalism in Film and Television

extension of machismo's real-world manifestation. Randy is impoverished financially and socially, he has abandoned his daughter, and has no real relationships. Following a severe wrestling match, and just before a big rematch with 'his' archnemesis the Ayatollah, Randy suffers a heart attack and is told by his doctors that he can no longer continue fighting. His near-death experience leads him to reunite with his daughter and attempt a serious romantic relationship with a stripper he frequents and confides in. But his hypermasculinity continually disrupts his efforts to live a 'normal' life. The real world is too complex, and justice is unintelligible. Despite his doctors' recommendations and the desires of anyone who still cares for him, he proceeds to wrestle in the big fight.

Before his big moment, before scaling the ropes for his big 'Ram Jam' move that will surely result in a fatal heart attack, Randy speaks to the audience: "As time goes by, they say, 'He's washed up' .... But you know what? The only ones who are gonna tell me when I'm through doing my thing is you people here ... because you're my family." Here we see how the myth of the spectacle is even desired by the performers themselves, placing them at the center of a world that is easily delineated, a world where relations are easy to understand and maintain.[18] The realm of wrestling in the film represents an ideal world like the worlds of many films and television programs. But they are far from the ideals of those critical of the way things are. Their ideals are superficial and rooted in a shallow politics of simplicity – deinstitutionalized and devoid of understanding the oppressions produced by abstract processes that require more complex solutions, more creative ideals. Within these shallow ideals the problems that exist in their world reflect those represented by the marketplace in Marx's *Capital*.

In *Capital Volume I*, Marx describes the marketplace in which goods and labor are purchased as, ostensibly, "a very Eden of the innate rights of man" where "It is the exclusive realm of Freedom, Equality, Property and Bentham".[19]

> Freedom, because both buyer and seller of a commodity, let us say of labor-power, are determined only by their own free will. They contract as free persons, who are equal before the law. Their contract is the final result in which their joint will finds a common legal expression. Equality, because each enters into relation with the other, as with a simple owner of commodities, and they exchange equivalent for equivalent. Property, because each disposes only of what is his own. And Bentham, because each looks only to his own advantage. The only force bringing them together, and putting them into relation with each other, is the selfishness, the gain and the private interest of each. Each pays heed to himself only, and no one worries about the others. And precisely for that reason, either in accordance with the pre-established harmony of things, or under the

auspices of an omniscient providence, they all work together to their mutual advantage, for the common weal, and in the common interest.[20]

The world depicted in film and television discourses is effectively situated here, in Eden, where conflict is typically seen in the unjust behaviors of individuals and solved through the efforts of heroes and often backed by the realms of Freedom, Equality, and Property. These representations are not just competing in a field of possible interpretations about the world and politics as we know it – and therefore the type of utopia that stands in contrast – they are hegemonic. Even those that seem to attempt to contest the logic end up reiterating its central theses, as we have discussed in previous chapters.

The marketplace is not the true nature of things, it is only the (negative) ideology that blinds us to the truth. For Marx, the real story occurs in "the hidden abode" where "the secret of profit making" can be found, the shadowy underbelly of the system.

> Accompanied by Mr. Moneybags and by the possessor of labour-power, we therefore take leave for a time of this noisy sphere [the marketplace], where everything takes place on the surface and in view of all men, and follow them both into the hidden abode of production, on whose threshold there stares us in the face "No admittance except on business.[21]

Whereas in the marketplace the buyer and seller of labor were equals, in the hidden abode "He, who before was the money-owner, now strides in front as capitalist; the possessor of labor-power follows as his laborer. The one with an air of importance, smirking, intent on business; the other, timid and holding back, like one who is bringing his own hide to market and has nothing to expect but — a tanning".[22] Here Marx stands Plato on his head, putting the 'truth' in a cave and a mystification of capital in the open marketplace "in view of all men". It is in fact this visibility, as cultural sociologist Stuart Hall argues,[23] that allows the bourgeois ideology to take hold. The importance placed on 'freedom' and 'equality', for example, "may derive from the categories we use in our practical, commonsense thinking about the market economy", from "daily, mundane experience".

However, film and television interact oddly in this ideological space in at least two important ways. First, unlike being in a marketplace, watching a movie or show often means you are not having real human contact, or even contact with some material thing. You may be watching your television screen, but you are not aware of it. Usually, you are immersed in the world being presented to you. The movie or show is not an object and the human face of a "Mr. Moneybags"[24] is nowhere to be seen. In fact, the consumption seems to occur without an exchange of money. When an exchange happens, it is often in advance and it buys you a wide range of products you can

110 Structural Critiques of Capitalism in Film and Television

then choose to consume (e.g., internet access, a television, or a streaming subscription); therefore, any individual media product you consume often appears to be *free*. Thus the "daily, mundane experience" that is directly "in view" of the media consumer is often different from the description of the marketplace and could even lead to radical interpretations of 'freedom' without a reversion to the selfish spirit of Bentham.

Second, the content within media texts can itself provide a regular "experience" about the market economy (as well as the state) that emphasizes precisely what is inside the hidden abode. The mediums discussed here are not limited to the 'practical' considerations of exchange within the context of their content and can present 'mundane' scenarios in richer and 'truer' ways. In fact, most popular film and television texts avoid the representation of the mundane, producing an expectation of 'richness' (though perhaps even less true than the open marketplace). The potential for reshaping the ideological content of otherwise practical and mundane experiences lies in the very interest in consuming media texts. That is, we seek screen texts to 'escape' the mundane – not necessarily in an 'escapist' fashion, but to attempt to understand and 'live' that which is outside the realm of our personal experience in 'real life' (e.g., the 'marketplace'). If the remainder of Marx's *Capital* is a literary representation of a view into the hidden abode, can film and television provide a similar glimpse through fictional sights and sounds?

In the previous chapters we have answered this question in the negative when looking at the broad representations of capitalism and the state. In this chapter we will look at particular aspects of these systems to see if we can piece together a jigsaw puzzle of radical critique found in popular screen media. Like a good heist movie, this chapter will attempt to maneuver around the various obstacles that prevent entry into the vault, where each text represents another tactic to elude surveillance, decrypt passwords, and construct realistic disguises – all in order to find our way into the hidden abode.

Surplus-Value for Veridian Dynamics

In taking us into the hidden abode, Marx discusses the way in which the capitalist, having bought the necessary equipment and labor in the marketplace, goes about his business of converting his money into capital. Marx argues that the value added to the finished product is a result of the work of labor. The laborer, using the materials and equipment purchased by the capitalist, first does enough work to offset the cost of his labor and then continues to do more work to produce surplus-value. But, if the worker stops for a break, if the worker reduces her efficiency or degree of intensity, the capitalist may not achieve his surplus-value, or at least the amount of surplus-value that would have been possible had the worker been more severely scrutinized, under duress of future unemployment. The worker's energy

> must be applied with the average amount of exertion and with the usual degree of intensity; and the capitalist is as careful to see that this is done, as that his workmen are not idle for a single moment. He has bought the use of the labor-power for a definite period, and he insists upon his rights. He has no intention of being robbed.[25]

This closely resembles a fake commercial for Veridian Dynamics, a company that is the focal point of the television sitcom *Better Off Ted* (seasons 1 and 2) (2009–2010). In the show, Veridian Dynamics is presented as a mega-corporation that sells just about everything. Through parody, an instructional video for the company's employees reveals the aspect of surplus-value discussed above, masking surplus-value with the liberal notion of 'opportunity'.

> Veridian Dynamics.
> Friendship.
> It's so important.
> But it's different at work.
> Time spent with friends at work robs your employer of opportunity.
> And robbing people is wrong.
> Veridian Dynamics.
> Friendship.
> It's the same as stealing.

Even as capitalists ensure that every moment paid for labor is utilized for labor-power (rather than chitchat), increasing the efficiency of their paid and working time becomes crucial for the expansion of profit. If it takes less labor-time to produce the same amount of product, you have more to sell (even if the price of each product is reduced somewhat in order to increase demand) and thus the capitalist makes more profit. Therefore, "there is a motive for each individual capitalist to cheapen his commodities by increasing the productiveness of labor".[26] How can they increase productivity? Veridian Dynamics has an answer: the invention of a chair that is so uncomfortable that anyone sitting in it becomes more productive because they can no longer daydream. In this case as in most, the added efficiency also works in direct opposition to the conditions of the worker using it.

For the modern corporation, a wide range of costs such as pension contributions and health insurance are additional expenses. One way to increase profits is to reduce these costs which do not impact (substantially) on the quality or quantity of labor-power – meaning surplus-value should

112 Structural Critiques of Capitalism in Film and Television

increase. Here again, Veridian Dynamics has a solution: to pair genetically compatible employees. Why would this reduce costs? Here's the plan as outlined by a senior manager in the company:

> The company has thousands of employees, and every year, hundreds get married and have babies. If Veridian can ensure the breeding couple is genetically compatible, the company will save a huge amount of money on health care for their offspring.

Veridian Dynamics is less interested in what it produces and sells than in making sure it spends less to produce it than it gets from its sale. In order for this to happen, workers need to be squeezed (also see *Glengarry Glen Ross* (1992) and *Tropic Thunder* (2008)). As Marx wrote, "The value of a commodity is, in itself, of no interest to the capitalist. What alone interests him, is the surplus-value that dwells in it ...."[27]

The surplus-value is not just money that is pocketed by capitalists and shareholders. A portion of surplus-value is "reconverted" into capital, which is known as the accumulation of capital. In other words, "it takes money to make money", or as Marx wrote, "creating capital out of capital":[28]

> the development of capitalist production makes it necessary constantly to increase the amount of capital laid out in a given industrial undertaking, and competition subordinates every individual capitalist to the immanent laws of capitalist production as external and coercive laws. It compels him to keep extending his capital, so as to preserve it, and he can only extend it by means of progressive accumulation.[29]

We can see this is true even without *employing* labor per se. The movie *Newsies* (1992) demonstrates this nicely by covering the New York City Newsboys' Strike of 1899 which, according to the film, occurs after Joseph Pulitzer increased the price it charged newsboys for a bundle of newspapers. Newsboys have to sell papers to the public at a fixed rate, so the film shows Pulitzer increasing the price for newsies as a way of profiting and thus competing with newspaper magnate William Randolph Hearst. The film shows the capitalist's need to squeeze those with less power in order to increase their profits by utilizing the capital at their disposal – hiring thugs to bust the union and paying off politicians and police officers to do the capitalist's bidding. As depicted in the film, to produce the wealth to continually compete, the capitalist class must further exploit workers. If there are substantially more people destitute and looking for work, then it is much easier to increase exploitation.

This does not just mean wages might go down or jobs might be more precarious. An extreme form of exploitation, or super-exploitation, is comedically presented in the film *Sorry to Bother You* (2018). The film's

Structural Critiques of Capitalism in Film and Television **113**

plot leads to the main characters uncovering an extreme form of capitalism in which a company provides minimal living space and food in exchange for lifelong servitude, a kind of voluntary slavery. But the company that is providing this permanently indentured labor supply to another business does not stop there. They also develop a way of transforming people into horse-people who will have a greater capacity for physical labor and thus *even more* exploitation can take place.[30] Boots Riley, the director of the film, is openly a communist. He went on to direct the Amazon Prime series *I'm a Virgo* which explicitly spelled out the violence of capitalism and its need to exploit. Other representations of such forms of super-exploitation can be found in *Ready Player One* (2018) and the Sonmi-451 storyline of *Cloud Atlas* (2012).

The Alienation and Payne

Workers are not simply exploited through the logic of wage labor. They are also estranged and alienated under capitalism. Marx writes that capitalism "produces for the rich wonderful things". It creates "palaces", "beauty", and "intelligence" but "for the worker it produces privation", "hovels", "stupidity, cretinism", and "deformity".[31] What constitutes the alienation of labor?

> First, the fact that labor is external to the worker, i.e., it does not belong to his intrinsic nature; that in his work, therefore, he does not affirm himself but denies himself, does not feel content but unhappy, does not develop freely his physical and mental energy but mortifies his body and ruins his mind. The worker therefore only feels himself outside his work, and in his work feels outside himself. He feels at home when he is not working, and when he is working he does not feel at home. His labor is therefore not voluntary, but coerced; it is forced labor. It is therefore not the satisfaction of a need; it is merely a means to satisfy needs external to it. Its alien character emerges clearly in the fact that as soon as no physical or other compulsion exists, labor is shunned like the plague.[32]

Happyish (2015) demonstrates this unhappiness in satirical form. The comedy series follows the life of a married couple, Thom and Lee Payne, in their attempt to cope with an unhappy middle-class life. The episode entitled "Starring Josey Wales, Jesus Christ and The New York Times" is the best example of this. Thom is stuck on a train that stopped before the station and he's running late to work. Everyone on the train is pissed off. Sitting next to Thom is a woman on the phone with her secretary:

> Liz, hey, it's me. We're stopped. Dead stopped. Listen, I need you to move my 9:00 to 10:00, my 10:00 to 11:00, my 11:00 to 12:00, cancel my lunch with Bob and see if he can do drinks on Tuesday. I'll call in for my 4:00

114 Structural Critiques of Capitalism in Film and Television

on my way to my 3:00, but don't schedule anything after 5:00 in case my 4:00 runs long.

Suddenly, the train conductor makes an announcement. Someone had fallen onto the tracks. The train couldn't stop in time. The commuter is dead. This news naturally leaves the passengers in a state of shock. People on the train say prayers; another passenger tells the woman next to him that he would go back to church to get some perspective. They are hit by the knowledge that it could have been any one of them that died that day, and they start to realize how their work and their daily habits are not fulfilling. Instead, they are struck by the realization that they are merely running on a hamster wheel in hopes of a bigger hamster wheel in the future. Thom is pained by the idea that he did not hug his son Julius goodbye that morning. The woman who was on the phone to her secretary is changed.

Woman: I mean, should it take death to make you think about life? ...
          I picture myself doing all this stupid work. Happy as a pig in shit.
Thom: It doesn't matter how happy you are. It's still shit.
Woman: And if you're happy in shit ...
Thom: ...You're probably a pig.[33]

The experience forces Thom to contemplate how he is spending his time. An image appears on the screen showing a bar graph of "Kissing 2015" broken down by percentage: Julius – 15 percent, Lee – 30 percent, Corporate Ass – 55 percent.

We are seeing how he "does not feel content but unhappy" and that "in his work ... he does not affirm himself but denies himself". At the end of the episode, Thom rebels by taking the day off work, leaving his phone on for a conference call but pretending to still be on the delayed train even after the train arrives at its destination. He goes home to spend time with his wife and kid. Thom narrates his recurring thought, thinking back to the western film *The Outlaw Josey Wales* (1976) in which a man tracks down Josey in a saloon. Josey asks the man if he's a bounty hunter. "A man's gotta do something for a living these days." Josey replies, punctuating the realization that Thom continues to make, "Dying ain't much of a living, boy".

As Thom remembers and spends quality time with his family, our ears return to the headphones tucked in Thom's pocket, still connected to the meeting in the office. "This was a very productive meeting. I'm happy. Thom, are you happy?" Not getting a response, the owners of his company ask if they lost him and question his devotion to the company. "I really think

Structural Critiques of Capitalism in Film and Television **115**

Thom needs to get his priorities straight." Here, family is the escape from this alienation, restoring happiness and rehumanizing the worker. But capitalism has the ability to adapt and commodify – and this is also true in its relations with its own employees. We can return to another Veridian Dynamics 'commercial' to demonstrate, satirically, how this may be done.

> Veridian Dynamics.
> We're a family, just like yours ....
> We love our family which is why we work nights, weekends, and major holidays.
> Because that's when families should be together.
> Veridian Dynamics.
> Family.
> Yay.

Marx discusses this undermining of the family through the idea of transforming life-time into working-time.

> [W]ithin the capitalist system ... all means for the development of production undergo a dialectical inversion so that they become means of domination and exploitation of the producers; they distort the worker into a fragment of a man, they degrade him to the level of an appendage of a machine, they destroy the actual content of his labor by turning it into a torment; they alienate [enifremden] from him the intellectual potentialities of the labor process in the same proportion as science is incorporated in it as an independent power; they deform the conditions under which he works, subject him during the labor process to a despotism the more hateful for its meanness; they transform his life-time into working-time, and drag his wife and child beneath the wheels of the juggernaut of capital.[34]

A similar critique of this transformation of time can be found in the film *In Time* (2011). This sci-fi flick is set in the future where the aging process stops at 25 but humans are 'on the clock'. People are given one year of time beyond their twenty-fifth birthday and when their clock strikes zero, they die. Time operates like money. It can be exchanged, gambled, or stolen. Those with lots of time live completely different lifestyles from those who live day-to-day. They even live in different districts called time zones. You are paid in time and you buy goods and services with time while the cost of living seems to go up, as does the interest rate for borrowed time. This, combined with stagnant salaries, means you find people who have run out of time dead on the streets of the poorer time zones.

116 Structural Critiques of Capitalism in Film and Television

What the people in the poor time zones haven't figured out yet is how their economic system works.

Everyone can't live forever. Where would we put them? Why do you think there are Time Zones? Why do you think taxes and prices go up the same day in the ghetto? The cost of living keeps rising to make sure people keep dying. How else could there be men with a million years while most live day to day? But the truth is there's more than enough. No one has to die before their time.[35]

We can see how this also corresponds to Marx's observation that "It is precisely among the workers in large-scale industry that we meet with the shortest life-expectancy" while, quoting the Medical Officer of Health for Manchester, "the well-to-do classes had a lease of life which was more than double the value of that which fell to the lot of the less favored citizens".[36] The trend continues to this day, with levels of inequality skyrocketing further when we compare the Global North and South.

Losing time with one's family because of work can also be found in the sitcom *Better Off Ted*, alongside a range of ways that workers are alienated. The main character, Ted, is the head of research and development and his boss Veronica is all business. Ted's colleague in the product testing department, Linda, is the exact opposite – she openly hates the company. Phil and Lem are scientists within the research department. Each character, with the exception of Veronica, is presented as being alienated in one way or another by their employer throughout the series. Ted's work separates him from his young daughter. Phil is placed into a cryogenic freezer in order to test a new product. Lem is not able to use elevators or open doors because the company's upgraded sensors do not detect black people and the company doesn't care. Linda finds out that her personal calls are being monitored by the company. This just adds to the long list of what she hates about the company, but she relies on the income from the job. As Marx said, her labor is "not voluntary, but coerced; it is forced labor".[37]

As the worker is coerced into working for payment, the capitalist system must include a way of maintaining an efficient supply of labor-power extracted from the worker during the hours they are being paid to work. That process requires bosses, which establishes a hierarchical relationship between people that arguably further alienates people from each other. This relationship is not a necessary relationship in society – only one in which coercion helps to structure productivity (see *The Office*, season 7, episode 24). Let us have a look again at *Better Off Ted* to find a critique of this dynamic. In one episode (season 2, episode 4; 2010), the boss, Veronica, is having lots of sex with her boyfriend and it is tiring her out. This effectively leads to her underlings needing to do her work for her. One of them is irate: "So my boss gets to have all the sex-fun of a relationship while all the stress of being exhausted trickles down to me? Man, capitalism blows."

We can also find a critique of this relationship in one of the mock commercials in the show.

> Veridian Dynamics.
> Bosses.
> Everybody has one.
> Without bosses, we'd be like these worms: disgusting.
> Bosses make everything better.
> So listen to your boss and don't question them.
> Otherwise, you're no better than a worm.
> Veridian Dynamics.
> Bosses.
> Necessary.

We get a different view of this relationship in *Office Space* (1999) where the bosses are not represented as working to increase productivity or use their subordinates to do their work – they are depicted as policy enforcers to the point that productivity diminishes. The film's protagonist, Peter, has eight people who manage him, and they all continually remind him of the latest policy changes and demotivate him with demoralizing reminders if he makes a minor error. His will to work is completely broken by this managerialism to the point that he convinces some of his colleagues to help him rob their company. But the film is quite clear that the problem of managerialism is not simply one that is occurring in one strange company that he happens to work for. The character who is Peter's romantic interest in the film works at a restaurant and also deals with the same inefficient, alienating hierarchy between managers and their subordinates.

Profit Motive at Stockheed Barton

With the need to continually increase profits, capitalism ends up prioritizing profit over people. Reminiscent of the truth found in the hidden abode, Veridian Dynamics satirically places the truth in their company motto: "Money before people". Thus, as the rich get richer the poor get poorer. The capitalist class grows its wealth as the working class

> performs the most wearisome, the vilest, the most disgusting functions, which, in a word, takes on its shoulders all that is disagreeable and servile in life, and procures thus for other classes leisure, serenity of mind and conventional [c'est bon!] dignity of character.[38]

118 Structural Critiques of Capitalism in Film and Television

In the show *Incorporated* (season 1; 2016), which is set in 2074 following an ecological catastrophe, poor people who do not work for the mega-corporations that serve as the new state live in the dilapidated Red Zone while the rich live in the luxurious Green Zone. A similar representation can be found in the film *Elysium* (2013), which is described further in the next chapter. Both screen media texts show the resistance of the working class in their attempts to access miracle cures.

The profit motive, however, is not just put ahead of the workers, but also of the outcomes of their industry and the effect of its processes. From the anti-social effects of cost/benefit calculations to the military industrial complex, the inherent need for profit as part of the process of capital accumulation produces dire consequences that are highlighted in some screen media texts. Although largely a film about a broken family, *Class Action* (1991) depicts a feud between two lawyers, father and daughter, who represent different sides in a lawsuit against a car manufacturer. The prosecutors claim that a model of car was known to be defective and had exploded on numerous occasions, causing injuries and deaths of passengers. When the daughter – the lawyer for the car manufacturer – finds evidence of her client's knowledge of the defect she raises it with a senior manager of the company: "Why didn't you just change the [defective] blinker circuit?"

> I told [the former CEO] Flannery about the problem about a month or so before he died. He called in his head bean counter .... So, Flannery shows him the data and asks him how much it would cost to retrofit ... 175,000 units. Multiply that times 300 bucks a car, give or take. You're looking at around $50 million. So, the risk guy, he crunches the numbers some more. He figures you'd have a fireball collision about every 3,000 cars. That's 158 explosions .... So you multiply that times $200,000 per lawsuit. That's assuming everybody sues and wins. 30 million max. See? It's cheaper to deal with the lawsuits than it is to fix the blinker. It's what the bean counters call a simple actuarial analysis.

Another example is the first scene of *Better Off Ted*, where we are introduced to Veridian Dynamics through one of their 'commercials'.

> Veridian Dynamics.
> Every day, something we make makes your life better.
> Power – we make that.
> Technology – we make that.
> Cows – Well, no.
> We don't make cows.
> Although we have made a sheep...
> and medicines and airplane engines and whatever this is and all sorts of things.

Veridian Dynamics.
Every day, something we make makes your life better –
[We see a video of a building being bombed]
usually.
Veridian Dynamics.
Life.
Better.

In another scene from *Better Off Ted*, Ted points out to a senior manager how something the company did is morally problematic. The manager's sarcastic response is: "Gosh, you're right. How will we ever make the Fortune 500 list of the most moral companies? Oh, wait. They don't have that." The message here is that the profit motive drives capitalism regardless of the consequences.[39] We can also find this critique in *Happyish*. How does Thom's advertising company make its profit? By consistently pitching problematic suggestions to its clients as if they were good ideas (with the audience supposed to be in on the joke). Take, for example, this ad pitch for bottled water:

We all know the statistics: 38 billion water bottles wasted each year. 17 million barrels of oil annually to make those wasted plastic water bottles … yada, yada, yada.

But what if we're not the enemy? What if we're the savior? Mississippi River. Polluted. Ohio River. Polluted. According to the EPA, more than half of the rivers and waterways in the United States can no longer support life. 13,000 miles of riverways contain fish with elevated levels of mercury. This is not just ecological apocalypse; this is a wonderful opportunity for Nestle Waters.

The anti-tap water strategy worked for a while, but we need to expand that. Nowadays, you can't trust any water. Except ours. We're not polluters, we're environmentalists. Let's make pollution work for us. We are not the problem. We are the solution ….

So instead of being the evil plastic bottle makars, Nestle becomes the voice of environmentalism. "We just want you to have clean water. But there isn't any. So, we go out, we find it, and we bring it to your supermarket.

The advertising execs and employees in *Happyish* are all supposed to be so profit-oriented that they appeal to universally despised notions and yet everyone, including the big corporate and government clients, loves it. They talk about Al Qaeda and ISIS as amazing brands. They refer to a Nazi manual as their ad bible. Ethics are dropped for the sake of profit.[40] They even market war on behalf of the US army, a rather consistent theme in these satirical comedies. We see it again in the show *Corporate* (season 1, episode 2) where there is a competition for a contract to supply weapons to the US government

120 Structural Critiques of Capitalism in Film and Television

which is planning a secret war. The head of the show's central corporation is visibly upset as he talks about war. "I'm still haunted by the Iraq War. Stockheed Barton[41] stole that contract right out from underneath us. And for 15 years, I've had to watch the Middle East be destabilized by another man's bombs".[42] Similarly, *Better Off Ted* asks: "Is it wrong to invent a deadly pumpkin? Or an irritating chair that makes people work harder? [The] thing is work's not about right and wrong. It's about success or failure."

In this chapter we saw that there are some examples of screen media texts that identified problems with capitalism. Specifically, we explored representations of surplus-value, alienation, and the profit motive and the harms they do. These representations largely escaped the limited critiques or personalization of the problems that were discussed in the previous chapters. In the next chapter, I explore further examples of radical critiques with a particular focus on economic crises, colonialism, and consumerism.

Notes

1 Barthes 1972, p. 24.
2 Barthes 1972, p. 39.
3 Barthes 1972, p. 39.
4 It is a lost film and so it is difficult to know its exact content, but we can glean information from what has been written about it. See Kester 2003, pp. 125–127.
5 Kester 2003, pp. 125–127.
6 Quoted in Kester 2003, p. 126. Translated with the help of Ina Freisen.
7 Shaw 2001.
8 Naam 2013, p. 31.
9 Westermann 1942; Gruen 1995[1974].
10 Quotes from Florus, Appian in Shaw 2001, pp. 155, 144, 153 respectively.
11 Marx 1865.
12 Shaw 2001; Futrell 2005.
13 E.g., see Chomsky 1996.
14 Chomsky 2019; see Haag 2016, p. xix. Chapter 9 of Haag's book explores this argument in more detail.
15 Kubrick was brought in to replace the original director, Anthony Mann. Kubrick, however, essentially disowned the film and did not consider it his picture as he did not have the extent of control he wanted.
16 See *Trumbo* (2015) for a cinematic perspective despised by the conservative press.
17 Wacquant 2004.
18 Similarly, in *Fighting with My Family* (2019), one upstart wrestler explains that wresting is "an escape ... from the real world. And when I'm in that ring ... it feels like the world just disappears. And I sort of feel like I belong somewhere.
19 Marx 1982[1867], p. 280.
20 Marx 1982[1867], p. 280.
21 Marx 2015[1867].
22 Marx 1982[1867], p. 280.
23 Hall 1983, p. 70.

24 The reference to "Mr. Moneybags" first appears in the 1887 translation by Samuel Moor and Edward Aveling (Kemple 1995, p. 221). According to Robert Paul Wolff (2011), "the term translated by Aveling, Moore, and Engels as 'Moneybags' is geldbesitzer, whose standard translation is 'possessor of money.' But the etymology of 'geldbesitzer' suggests someone sitting on money, and that calls to mind the wonderful nineteenth century caricatures of Thomas Nast and others, who routinely represented capitalists as fat men in tails and top hats with big dollar or pound signs on their breasts, sitting on bags of money. The translation 'Moneybags' perfectly captures Marx's mocking tone."

25 Marx, 1982[1867], p. 303.

26 Marx, 1982[1867], p. 435.

27 Marx, 1982[1867], p. 437.

28 Marx, 1982[1867], p. 729.

29 Marx, 1982[1867], p. 739.

30 Also see Sticchi's (2021) analysis of the film in Chapter 2 of his book.

31 Marx 1964, p. 110.

32 Marx 1964, pp. 110–111.

33 Excuse the unfortunate anthropocentrism here.

34 Marx 1982[1867], p. 799. Also see *Hook* (1991).

35 Like the political economists, in Marx's view, the rich inside their time zones have their own mythologies. "Of course, some think what we have is unfair, the time difference between Zones," says one of the time rich elites. "But isn't this just the next logical step in our evolution? And hasn't evolution always been unfair? It's always been survival of the fittest .... This is merely Darwinian capitalism. Natural selection."

36 Marx 1982[1867], p. 795. Of course, this means the film misses the other major point, that the "time" is actually a product of the work of the laboring class.

37 Marx 1964, pp. 110–111.

38 Storch, as quoted by Marx 1982[1867], p. 801.

39 Also see e.g., *Erin Brockovich* (2000), *Don't Look Up* (2021), *Michael Clayton* (2007), *Promised Land* (2012), *Jurassic Park* (1993); *The Lost World: Jurassic Park* (1997); *The Insider* (1999), *Silver City* (2004), *Dark Waters* (2019), *Deepwater Horizon* (2016), and *The Boys* (seasons 1–3; 2019–2022).

40 In one episode of *Corporate* (season 2, episode 3), the CEO of Hampton DeVille states: "Americans are obese, drunk, and addicted to pills. Everyone is hooked on something. Addiction in this country is an epidemic. And it is fantastic for business. 90 percent of shopping is done by shopaholics. 90 percent of chocolate is consumed by chocoholics. 90 percent of alcohol is consumed by people addicted to alcohol. That's why I'm announcing an open call for pitches on new addictions." Also see *Thank You for Smoking* (2005), *The Boondocks* (2005) esp. season 1, episode 14; *The Gunman* (2015); *Fun with Dick and Jane* (2005), and *Corporate* (2018) season 1, episode 4.

41 A reference to the American aerospace and defense manufacturer Lockheed Martin.

42 Season 1, episode 3. Also see *Star Wars: Episode VIII – The Last Jedi* (2017) and *Eraser* (1996).

References

Barthes, Roland (1972) *Mythologies*, New York: The Noonday Press.

Chomsky, Noam (1996) *Class Warfare*, London: The Electric Book Company.

Chomsky, Noam (2019) 'Noam Chomsky: Life Expectancy in the US Is Declining for a Reason', *Truthout*, July 28, https://truthout.org/articles/noam-chomsky-life-expectancy-in-the-us-is-declining-for-a-reason.

Futrell, Alison (2005) 'Seeing Red: Spartacus as Domestic Economist', in Sandra R. Joshel, Margaret Malamud, and Donald T. McGuire, Jr. (eds), *Imperial Projections: Ancient Rome in Modern Popular Culture*' (pp. 77–118), Baltimore, MD: The Johns Hopkins University Press.

Gruen, Erich S. (1995[1974]) *The Last Generation of the Roman Republic*, Berkeley: University of California Press.

Haag, Pamela (2016) *The Gunning of America: Business and the Making of American Gun Culture*, New York: Basic Books.

Hall, Stuart (1983) 'The Problem of Ideology: Marxism without Guarantees', in Betty Matthews (ed.), *Marx: 100 Years On*, London: Lawrence & Wishart

Kemple, Thomas M. (1995) *Reading Marx Writing: Melodrama, the Market, and the "Grundrisse"*, Stanford, CA: Stanford University Press.

Kester, Bernadette (2003) *Film Front Weimar: Representations of the First World War in German Films of the Weimar Period (1919–1933)*, Amsterdam: Amsterdam University Press.

Marx, Karl (1865) 'Karl Marx's "Confession', https://www.marxists.org/archive/marx/works/1865/04/01.htm.

Marx, Karl (1982[1867]) *Capital: A Critique of Political Economy, Volume I* , Harmondsworth: Penguin Books.

Marx, Karl (1964) *Economic and Philosophic Manuscripts of 1844*, New York: International Publishers.

Naam, Ramez (2013) *The Infinite Resource: The Power of Ideas of a Finite Planet*, Lebanon, NH: University Press of New England.

Shaw, Brent D. (ed.) (2001) *Spartacus and the Slave Wars: A Brief History with Documents*, Boston: Palgrave Macmillan.

Sticchi, Francesco (2021) *Mapping Precarity in Contemporary Cinema and Television: Chronotopes of Anxiety, Depression, Expulsion/Extinction*, Cham, Switzerland: Palgrave Macmillan.

Wacquant, Loïc (2004) *Body and Soul: Notebooks of an Apprentice Boxer*, Oxford: Oxford University Press.

Westermann, William L. (1942). 'Industrial Slavery in Roman Italy', *The Journal of Economic History*, 2(2): 149–163, doi:10.1017/S0022050700052542.

Wolff, Robert Paul (2011) 'The Thought of Karl Marx Part Twelve', Archive of Wolff Materials, https://robertpaulwolff.blogspot.com/2011/02/thought-of-karl-marx-part-twelve.html.

6

REPRESENTATIONS OF CRISES, COLONIALISM, AND CONSUMERISM

Fat Cats, Starving Dogs, and Tulip Bulbs

On February 6, 1637, Joost van Cuyck entered the Menniste Bruyloft Inn in the center of Amsterdam where an auction was taking place as usual. David van der Cruijs was selling a pound of Switsers to the highest bidder. As van Cuyck stepped into the bustling room the bid reached 1,060 florins. The auctioneer looked around the room. "No one bids?" The price was considerable, enough at the time to buy a house in Haarlem. "No one?" The many men who had previously bid for the lot pondered the proposition, but no one raised their hand. "Once, no one further, twice no one?" The auctioneer, a man trusted by those in the room, was obligated to ask four times before a purchase was confirmed. Van Cuyck looked on with interest. "Third time, no one? Fourth time?" Just before the sale was confirmed Jaques de Poer stood up on the bench and raised the bid to ƒ1,065. De Poer had won the lot and the relatively unknown seller congratulated him. Van Cuyck, perhaps upon seeing this display of intense desire, became convinced that this was a good investment that he too should make. It could make him very rich indeed. As long as such passion for a pound of Switsers continued to grow as it had done in recent months, he was sure to be able to come back to the inn, perhaps the following year, and get a hefty return on his speculation. But first he needed to buy his own Switsers. Van Cuyck looked at the board of names placed at the back of the room of the inn. These names denoted sellers, one of which was the well-known Andries de Busscher who was offering to sell a pound of Switsers. After some haggling with other interested buyers, Van Cuyck successfully reached a deal with de Busscher in a more private affair: one pound of Switsers for ƒ1,100. Both men must have been happy with the deal, agreeing to confirm the transaction the next day.

DOI: 10.4324/9781003514916-7

124 Representations of Crises, Colonialism, and Consumerism

But the next day, February 7, proved to be an important day in the Netherlands. Experts in the trade had gathered in Utrecht to discuss a crisis. Apparently, as one account suggests, a man who had attempted to sell similar items in Haarlem a few days prior for ƒ1,250 was forced to lower his price to ƒ1,000 but still failed to find a buyer. For the first time, this precious commodity was starting to lose appeal and as soon as this news spread across the urban centers of the Netherlands things swiftly began to turn sour. Everyone knew the game was up. Van Cuyck backed out of the sale. "I need to think about it", he said, waiting to see how the market would play out the following day. De Poer also reneged on his promise to pay for his auction purchase. Van de Cruijs, who had sold him the Switsers, was furious and lodged a formal complaint, the first of its kind following the crash in prices. Money was lost, investments destroyed. Records show that by May a pound of Switsers, along with a pound of Centen, were worth just ƒ550, an enormous drop in market value in just a few months.

Switsers, Centen, Semper Augustus, Gevleugelde Coornarts, Admirael van der Eyck. These are all strange names for something that was very valuable at one point in seventeenth century Europe, particularly in the Netherlands: tulips. Tulips were collectables for the rich, beautiful flowers of various colors. The most precious tulips had variegated petals like the Switsers with their "gorgeous Coats of red and yellow".[1] But more than beauty, these flowers denoted wealth and status. Consequently, at the time tulips were what Karl Marx termed a "social hieroglyphic" and had what the cultural theorist Jean Baudrillard later called "symbolic exchange value".[2] This all took place during the Dutch Golden Age, with the Netherlands' colonial possessions in the East Indies bringing wealth and luxury to the mercantile class who had money to spend. But the cost of these expensive tulip bulbs was only partially a product of the social meaning they gave its owner and growing discretionary income. The price of tulips was high because of speculation, because as long as people believed the price would continue to rise purchasers kept on looking to buy low and sell high. However, if people stopped having faith that they could reap rewards for their speculation there would be a crash in price. This is what happened in an event known as Tulip Mania, the first economic crash of its kind depicted in the big budget failure *Tulip Fever* (2017).

This story connects economic crisis, colonialism, and consumerism, and, despite the passage of over 300 years, questions of economic crisis, colonialism, and consumerism still plague society. Recent economic crashes have reminded us of the cyclical nature of capitalism, and economists are already predicting another crisis soon.[3] Colonialism is still rearing its ugly head, having set the foundations for modern racism, and continuing in the form of economic dependency and the plundering of resources. Consumerism has ballooned since the 1600s, with symbolic exchange value determining

Representations of Crises, Colonialism, and Consumerism **125**

much of our social behavior, compelled as we are by the commercials and advertisements that continuously pop up everywhere we go. The chapter seeks to answer the question, what do movies and television programs tell us about crisis, neocolonialism, and consumerism and how do they help inform a critique of capitalism and the state?

The Really Existing Free Market

> 1637. 1797. 1819, 37, 57, 84. 1901, 07, 29, 1937, 1974, 1987. Jesus, didn't that fucker fuck me up good? '92, '97, 2000 and whatever we outta call this. It's all just the same thing, over and over. We can't help ourselves.

The infamous economic crashes are laid out for us in chronological order by John Tuld (Jeremy Irons), CEO of an investment bank at the heart of the film *Margin Call* (2011). While economic crises were not a frequent subject of big budget films and television programs, the Great Recession put the subject in the spotlight. Films like *Margin Call, The Big Short* (2015), and *Too Big to Fail* (2011) looked to explain what had happened and who had been responsible for the economic crisis and, in doing so, provided an additional glimpse into the hidden abode, not of production per se, but of the profit-making process more generally.

Margin Call looks at the day an investment bank realizes their mortgage-backed securities are about to be exposed as worthless and the bankers decide on a fire sale. It enlightens viewers by pointing out both the consistency of crises within capitalism as shown in the quote above, as well as the system's inability to do anything about it other than profit from them. Equality, fairness, and social mobility are skewered and placed in the flames of capital accumulation. In trying to convince his floor head that the fire sale, which will mean dumping toxic assets throughout the financial sector and creating an economic recession, is a good idea, the CEO presents us with a thorough critique of capitalism in the face of crisis:

> So you think we might have put a few people out of business today. That's all for naught. But you've been doing that every day for almost 40 years, Sam. And if this is all for naught, then so is everything out there. It's just money. It's made up, pieces of paper with pictures on it so that we don't have to kill each other just to get something to eat. It's not wrong. And it's certainly no different today than it's ever been. … And you and I can't control it or stop it or even slow it. Or even ever so slightly alter it. We just react. And we make a lot of money if we get it right. And we get left by the side of the road if we get it wrong. And there have always been and there always will be the same percentage of winners and losers, happy fucks and sad sacks, fat cats and starving dogs in this world. Yeah, there

126 Representations of Crises, Colonialism, and Consumerism

may be more of us today than there's ever been. But the percentages, they stay exactly the same.

The Big Short does a very good job of exposing the relationship between the state and capital in perpetuating the "really existing free market" discussed by Noam Chomsky.[4] *The Big Short* is based on a true story about the first people to predict (and bet on) the bursting of the housing bubble which led to the Great Recession. In the end, following the government bailout of the banks, the film lays blame at the feet of this "really existing free market doctrine" where the logic of capitalism and institutional forces of the state interlink to form class power unadulterated by ideology.

In the film, hedge fund manager Mark Baum (Steve Carrell) discusses the bailout with his colleagues who always thought the banks were just too stupid to see what was going on. Baum had a different theory.

Mark Baum:	[The banks] knew …. They knew the taxpayers would bail them out. They weren't being stupid, they just didn't care.
Colleague:	Yeah, 'cuz they're fucking crooks. But at least we'll get to see some of them go to jail. Right? I mean they're gonna have to break up the banks. The party's over.
Mark Baum:	I don't know. I have a feeling that in a few years people are going to be doing what they always do when the economy tanks. They will be blaming immigrants and poor people.

In steps our narrator, Jared Vennett (Ryan Gosling), a Deutsche Bank salesman.

> But Mark was wrong. In the years that followed, hundreds of bankers and rating agencies' executives went to jail. The SEC [Securities and Exchange Commission] was completely overhauled, and Congress had no choice but to break up the big banks and regulate the mortgage and derivatives industries.
>
> … Just kidding.
>
> Banks took the money the American people gave them, and they used it to pay themselves huge bonuses and lobby the Congress to kill big reform. And then they blamed immigrants and poor people. And this time even teachers. And when all was said and done, only one single banker went to jail. This poor schmuck: Kareem Serageldin from Credit Suisse. He hit a few billion in mortgage bond loses. Something most of the big banks did on a good day during the crisis.

Here we have a mainstream American film with an Oscar nominated cast and a big budget basically telling us the whole system is rigged.[5]. It is rigged

Representations of Crises, Colonialism, and Consumerism **127**

by a politics of class, with the state at the helm of the ship, bringing loot back to its queen, capitalism. It reinforces Chomsky's point when he says, citing Ruigrock and van Tulder, that "virtually all of the world's largest core firms have experienced a decisive influence from government policies and/ or trade barriers on their strategy and competitive position" and "at least twenty companies in the 1993 Fortune 100 would not have survived at all as independent companies, if they had not been saved by their respective governments".[6]

The state's subordination to the will of capital is theorized by Marx and Engels who wrote "The executive of the modern state is but a committee for managing the common affairs of the whole bourgeoisie",[7] with Lenin referring to the state as "a special force for the suppression of a particular class".[8] We can see how this is exposed in *Too Big to Fail* which looks into the detail of the bank bailout. In the government's attempt to keep the recession from sliding into a depression they decided to give a loan to the various banks that had made the bad investments in the first place in order to keep them financially stable. However, as shown in *The Big Short*, the banks knew they would be bailed out so they would not accept any real conditions on the bailout. As one character summarizes: "They almost bring down the US economy as we know it, but we can't put restrictions on how they spend the $125 billion we're giving them because ... they might not take it."

Kropotkin, a father of anarchist thought, argued that "the state organization, having always been, both in ancient and modern history ... the instrument for establishing monopolies in favor of the ruling minorities, cannot be made to work for the destruction of these monopolies".[9] In the age of capitalism, that minority is the capitalist class. This relationship between the capitalist class and the state is presented effectively in screen media texts such as *Sorry to Bother You* (2018), *The Wire* (seasons 1-5, 2002–2008), and *Bulworth* (1998).[10] *Sorry to Bother You* provides a radical critique in its depiction of the relationship between the state and capitalism, showing how the repressive forces of the state are used to quell a strike after telemarketers unionize and call for better compensation.[11] *The Wire* depicts the multiple and interrelated problems of the American political and capitalist system. In each season the world of the show is widened, starting with a critique of policing and an intercity struggling with poverty, then expanding to the class politics of dockworkers beginning in season 2, municipal politics in season 3, the education system in season 4, and the news media in season 5. The HBO original series explores how the problems of the characters, the city of Baltimore where the series takes place, and the United States more generally, are caused not by one institution, reformable policy, or bad guys. It shows a system in which the problems of capitalism and the state are interconnected (also see *Treme*, seasons 1–4 (2010–2013), another show by the same creator). In *Bulworth*, the protagonist Senator Bulworth (Warren Beatty),

128 Representations of Crises, Colonialism, and Consumerism

who is dealing with depression during his run for re-election, ends up telling the truth about the political establishment. This 'truth' is that corporations and the wealthy have financial power over politicians in the United States and that this is largely due to the election financing policies. Throughout, the film suggests that more social democratic welfare policies would be implemented if the government was not in the pocket of big business interests. This suggests, initially, that campaign finance reforms would democratize America and things like health insurance would be socialized. This largely falls within the reformable critique.[12] However, the conclusion of the film demonstrates that not only are there bad laws on the books that benefit big business, but that the capitalist class relies on the state to do its bidding and, if it doesn't, capitalists will go to extreme lengths to ensure that it does.

Senator Bulworth's rambunctious rapping about prospects in American ghettos and his positive, off-the-cuff comments about socialism to California's rich and famous leads him to a landslide electoral victory. The public like the politics he has to sell, even if the elites and corporations don't. He is the left populist. However, in the end the corporations effectively veto the popular vote. Shortly after his victory is announced, Bulworth is assassinated by an insurance company lobbyist.[13] The message is that the capitalist class will not allow democracy to play out if it means hurting their interests, and although an assassination may be over the top, the message of the film suggests the corporate supremacy over the state will remain regardless of campaign finance reforms.

Such political assassinations within the Global North have been attributed by some to the deaths or attempted murders of journalists such as Gary Webb, activists and union organizers such as Judi Bari, and whistleblowers such as Julian Assange and former Boeing employees. Representations of such assassinations can be found in *Kill the Messenger* (2014), *Michael Clayton* (2007), *Shooter* (2007), and *Silkwood* (1983).[14] We should not forget that some of this representation is rooted in real life, where an assassination may actually not be the most extreme consequence. Take, for example, the case of retired General Smedley D. Butler and the Business Plot of 1933:

> Smedley D. Butler, a retired major general of the Marines, a holder of two Congressional Medals of Honor, a Republican and a Quaker, whose devil-may-care personality might well have attracted people in search of a man on horseback. In 1933, Butler told a House committee, a New York bond salesman named Gerald C. MacGuire offered him $18,000 in one-thousand-dollar bills to defend the gold standard at the American Legion convention. Butler refused. MacGuire then took a trip to Europe on behalf of a group called the Committee on Sound Currency and a Sound Dollar. One purpose of the trip, judging by the reports MacGuire sent back to New York, was to study fascist veterans' movements …. Returning to the

United States, MacGuire asked Butler to head a similar group in America. A reporter testified that MacGuire had told him, 'We need a Fascist government in this country .... The only men who have the patriotism to do it are the soldiers and Smedley Butler is the ideal leader.' What about [President] Roosevelt? 'We might go along with Roosevelt and then do with him what Mussolini did with the King of Italy.' But Butler rejected the proposal with his accustomed pungency. 'If you get the 500,000 soldiers advocating anything smelling of Fascism,' he said, 'I am going to get 500,000 more and lick the hell out of you, and we will have a real war right at home.'[15]

This coup attempt, also represented in the film *Amsterdam* (2022), failed of course. However, other such plans have been supported by business which helped to overthrow democratically elected governments that ran against the capitalist class's economic interests. Take, for example, the US involvement in overthrowing the democratically elected governments of Iran in 1953, Guatemala in 1954, Chile in 1973, etc. Such representations can be found in *The Bourne Identity*, *The Bourne Supremacy*, and *War, Inc.* (2008).[16]

It must be said that states have their own geopolitical interests, such as expanding or maintaining their power. Such 'national interests' also produce the inherent problems of the state. An extreme version of this is found in the film *Rosewater* (2014) which is about an Iranian-Canadian journalist who is jailed and tortured in Iran, accused of being an American spy. This journalist's father was also tortured, and he realizes that the same torture methods were used by governments around the world "From the Soviets. From the CIA. From the Mossad. From all the fucked up secret services of the world." In *The Report* (2019) we see that the government will cover up its own wrongdoing in the service of 'national interests'.[17] In the context of the Cold War there was a particularly symbiotic set of 'national interests' between capital and the state because it was greatly in the state's interest to ensure a capitalist economic order across the globe. This included the use of soft power and military/counterintelligence operations – for example, Italy and Greece in the late 1940s, the Huk Rebellion in the Philippines from 1945, Syria in 1949, Egypt in 1952, etc. A fictitious account of this is seen in Amazon original *Patriot* (season 1; 2015).[18] Another intervention involved the US government engaging in drug running as a way of financing the distribution of weapons to the Contras to help them fight the leftist Sandinistas in Nicaragua. The representation of these events and its hypocrisy at the time of the war on drugs is put on full display in the film *American Made* (2017), as well as *Kill the Messenger*. For other examples of the state's preservation of 'national interests' in contravention of basic ethics see *Good Kill* (2014), *The Hunting Party* (2007), and *Jason Bourne* (2016). In addition, of course, we must consider the 'national interests' of neocolonialism.

130 Representations of Crises, Colonialism, and Consumerism

From the Dutch Indies to the New India

'Ho, Piet Van Doon,' the sailor cried, 'I've new thy heart to please,
Brought from the fragrant spicy isles that bask in Southern seas.'[19]

Thus begins a children's poem about a sailor returning to his Dutch homeland and giving news to the merchant trader Van Doon that a ship he commissioned to sail to the so-called Dutch East Indies was making its way back to port full of loot. Van Doon was delighted and prepared a feast of fish and wine to thank the sailor for the good news.

The sailor went, but ere he gained the merchant's portal-stone
He saw an onion on a shelf forgotten and alone
'I'll add it to the feast', said he, and drops it in his hat,
'Van Doon, I'm sure, would grudge me not a little thing like that,'
He reached the inn, was shown his chair: with zest sat down to dine,
Devoured the onion and the fish, then drained the glass of wine,
But ere the final drop was gone wild tumult shock the air.
Loud voices filled the village street; fierce footsteps climbed the stair.
'Hold him! Confine him! Thief and rogue!' the words with fury came.
As through the door burst Piet Van Doon, his eyes and face aflame.

Van Doon couldn't believe his eyes. It wasn't an onion the sailor took, but a tulip bulb bought with the loot onboard the ship. Despite his protests, the sailor was thrown in jail.

This story was told frequently following Tulip Mania and was similarly depicted in *Tulip Fever*, ruining the main protagonist's chance of escaping to the Dutch East Indies with her lover. The Dutch East Indies always seems to play some role in the discussion of Tulip Mania because it is hard to imagine how tulip bulbs could become such hot commodities without the merchant trade in the Dutch colonies. According to Anne Goldgar's *Tulip Mania*, "Dutch merchants in the seventeenth century engaged not only in trade, but in more adventurous trade than previously, exploring new markets and new areas, including the East Indies and the Americas".[20] The Dutch had effectively created the model for early European colonialism with the creation of the United East Indies Company (VOC) in 1602. VOC was a monopoly company built through the unification of merchant capitalists and the state with the aim of "global commercial and imperial dominance".[21] It served as an example for the creation of the East India Company and its French counterpart, the Compagnies des Indes Orientales.[22] The company was highly profitable and sent money back to the Dutch state which supported the VOC's monopoly privileges.[23] By 1619, the Dutch had taken control of Jakarta, which they renamed

Batavia,[24] its capital in the East Indies. A few years later the Dutch West India Company was formed.

By 1637, the year of Tulip Mania, the two companies had domain over settlements in mainland North American, South America, the Caribbean, Africa, and Asia. The Netherlands was a colonial empire to be reckoned with at the time, and the wealth extracted from the colonies and generated for the empire allowed luxury goods to be consumed and tulip bulbs to amass great value. It also meant the growth of capitalism itself. Colonialism has been explored in representations of the past (e.g., *Dances with Wolves* (1990), *The Mission* (1986), *The New World* (2005)) and in a fictitious present or future (e.g., *Avatar* (2009), *Avatar: The Way of Water* (2022)). Often, however, the representations take the perspective of the colonizer (usually a man) who realizes the err of his ways, but who still retains a perspective of superiority (although see *Black Panther* (2018), *Black Panther: Wakanda Forever* (2022), and *Waiting for the Barbarians* (2019), films with their own problematic perspective on colonialism).[25] Likewise, the slave trade and slavery that were part and parcel of colonialism were also depicted typically from the perspective of whites or featured white saviors. Similar types of representations can also be found in texts about the fight against slavery (e.g., *12 Years a Slave* (2013), *Amazing Grace* (2006), *Amistad* (1997), *Belle* (2013), *Free State of Jones* (2016), *Glory* (1989), *The Good Lord Bird* (2010), *Lincoln* (2012), *Underground* (season 1 and 2, 2016–2017); although some alternative representations can be found in, for example, *Emancipation* (2022), *Roots* (season 1, 2016).[26]

Colonialism has been contested by the subjugated throughout its history, with major victories coming in the form of the Haitian Revolution (Danny Glover had long wanted to make a film about the subject but no funding was forthcoming), Indian Independence (see *Gandhi* (1982)), the end of apartheid in South Africa (see *Catch a Fire* (2006), *Cry Freedom* (1987), *Escape from Pretoria* (2020), and – arguably – for a futuristic account, *District 9* (2009)), and the Algerian War (see *The Battle of Algiers* (1966)). The end of formal colonialism in the mid-twentieth century did not end this form of transnational exploitation. The legacies of colonialism remained (and were discussed in various ways and with mixed political representations in screen media texts such as episodes in seasons 4 and 5 of *Black-ish*,[27] *Hotel Rwanda* (2004), *Invictus* (2009), *Shooter* (2007), and season 1 of *The White Lotus* (2021)). In addition, capitalism found new ways in which the wealthy 'core' was able to extract wealth from the poor 'periphery'. All this became known as neocolonialism and continued the entanglement of capitalist and state interests in a process of control over other countries.

The essence of neo-colonialism is that the State which is subject to it is, in theory, independent and has all the outward trappings of international

132 Representations of Crises, Colonialism, and Consumerism

sovereignty. In reality its economic system and thus its political policy is directed from outside.

This simple yet effective definition is provided by Kwame Nkrumah, Prime Minister of Ghana and socialist who was later overthrown with the approval of the CIA to realign the country to the capitalist bloc.[28] After the coup, the International Monetary Fund (IMF) and World Bank were invited into (read: to exploit) the country.[29]

The problems of such global capitalist institutions were presented in *Our Brand is Crisis* (2015), a film that looks at the role of campaign strategists in effectively duping the public in Bolivia into supporting a candidate who sells out the country to the IMF.[30] What benefits accrue to those countries in the Global South who decide to, or are forced to, engage with these capitalist institutions? *Battle in Seattle* (2007) demonstrates how, during the chaotic World Trade Organization (WTO) negotiations of 1999, poorer nations' delegates were subjugated to the interests of colonial capital were prioritized over those working to reduce poverty and disease. The film portrays the WTO as a place to promote free trade in the interests of the corporations of the Global North.[31]

As jobs are moved from the Global North to the Global South where the cost of labor is cheaper, they are often located in free-trade zones and offer little protection for workers.[32] Even those jobs can be further outsourced to another country that decides to be competitive in the international marketplace by allowing wages to freefall. We see this presented in the 2006 film *Outsourced* where an American telemarketing division is laid off and outsourced to India and, shortly afterwards, the Indian workers are laid off and their jobs are further outsourced. "China is the new India. Twenty heads for the price of one."[33] Sometimes cheap labor is less important than land ownership and use and this often leads to the displacement or destruction of indigenous communities as we see in *Ace Ventura 2: When Nature Calls* (1995).

This global division of labor was articulated by segments of the black power movement. Summarizing the words of Huey P. Newton, a founder of the Black Panther Party, the sociologist John Narayan writes:

> The Second and Third World would increasingly become a site of capitalist production, technology and forms of consumption, but with an increased rate of super-exploitation. This centered on Western based multinational corporations penetrating these regions in order to create a global commodity and consumption chain. This disarticulated form of Fordism would see 'advanced technologies transplanted into these areas' but still under the control of Western interests. The result would be a new global geography of industrial production and the spreading of capitalist

ideology that would eradicate socialist alternatives to capitalist market societies.[34]

This form of super-exploitation was represented in the film *Elysium* (2013) where the Global North is represented as the utopia everyone should enjoy, where everyone should be made a citizen of the Global North. The year is 2154 and, because of pollution and overpopulation, the rich have flown off to a giant spaceship called Elysium which hovers over the planet.[35] The geography of wealth has morphed and expanded. Labor is still being extracted from the poor people left on Earth. Law enforcement still controls the movements of labor and employment continues to function under the rules of capital. Meanwhile on Elysium, there are large high-tech houses and lush green gardens and one important innovation: machines called Med-Bays which can cure diseases, regenerate lost limbs, and make you younger. Super-exploitation is depicted through our protagonist Max Da Costa (Matt Damon) who works on Earth in a plant that gives him radiation poisoning because of unfair treatment by the police and his boss. He needs to get to a Med-Bay on Elysium to save his life and he needs to do it quickly. On his journey he becomes involved in both a philanthropic mission to help others in a similar predicament and a political plot of which he is not fully aware. He eventually makes it up to the lush and luxurious planet where he ends up sacrificing himself to make everyone on Earth a citizen of Elysium, granting them access to universal healthcare as robotic AI medical units fly from Elysium to their rescue.

Huey P. Newton's argument was that this process of capitalism would mean that "even the populations of the Anglo-American Empire itself are in the process of being 'nativized' and pauperized".[36] Even the rich countries would start becoming poor. This is presented in films such as *Fun with Dick and Jane* (2005, *Sorry to Bother You* (2018) and *Up in the Air* (2009). Newton and the Black Panther Party were organizing in their community at a time when many different groups were calling for liberation from the grips of racial capitalism and neocolonialism. One such organization was the Symbionese Liberation Army (SLA) which famously kidnapped Patty Heart, the granddaughter of newspaper magnate William Randolph Hearst.[37] When the family refused or failed to have some jailed SLA members released, the SLA asked for food to be given to poor communities in Los Angeles and San Francisco, California. Two million dollars of food was distributed and, whilst simultaneously the organization robbed a bank with the help of the Hearst heiress. The bank robbery and wealth redistribution are portrayed in somewhat similar fashion in the film *In Time*, clearly inspired by those events. *In Time*, as discussed in the last chapter, replaced aging and money with time. The film's protagonist, Will, is on the run from timekeepers (police) because he is falsely accused of stealing time after a wealthy suicidal man gave him

134 Representations of Crises, Colonialism, and Consumerism

all his time, unbeknownst to Will. Will ends up in a wealthy time zone where the timekeepers track him down. In order to escape, Will kidnaps Sylvia, the daughter of a very wealthy time-loaning businessman (i.e. banker). Will holds Sylvia for ransom but her father refuses to pay, so Will and Sylvia have a new plan: they go from timebank to timebank robbing them and sharing the wealth with poor residents. Those once-poor citizens begin leaving the poor time zone, they stop working in their difficult jobs, and they begin to live a free life.

Commodity Fetishism and Hitler's Coca Cola

A year before Tulip Mania, Wouter Bartholomeusz Winckel, a tavern keeper who had a passion for growing tulips, died. He left behind seven children who had already lost their mother. The children were sent off to an orphanage which was a very undesirable fate. However, their guardian decided that they would auction off Winckel's tulip bulbs on the children's behalf. The auction was widely advertised and a sale catalogue of tulips in watercolors was commissioned for potential bidders to peruse. The auction was held on February 5, 1637 – two days before the crash. Evidence suggests that some of the highest prices were being offered for the tulips on sale. Winckel's collection of bulbs was sold for ƒ90,000, more than enough for his children to live off. Sadly, it was too late. Once the crash occurred buyers reneged on their promises to pay for the bulbs. But if people were still spending small fortunes on tulip bulbs on February 5, why did the crash become official just two days later? Perhaps this phenomenon can be explained through the notion of commodity fetishism.[38]

While the growing desire for and increased price of tulips in the Netherlands were predicated on a growing merchant class at a time of Dutch colonialism, it was transnational trade from the East and West that made all of this possible. Tulips became wildly popular for elites in the Ottoman Empire and became a transcultural commodity, making their way to Europe.[39] But the nature of this transcultural transaction, which involves 'production' in a rough sense of cultivation as well as the labor needed to establish trade, is hidden from view due to the negative ideology produced by what Karl Marx referred to as "commodity fetishism".

"Value does not stalk about with a label describing what it is", Marx wrote. "It is value, rather, that converts every product into a social hieroglyphic."[40] An object, even a cultivated tulip bulb, is a product of human labor. Hands got dirty and effort was exerted in order to produce the object. In its final form it is assembled or carefully plucked from the ground by the laborer. It is their product. That product has some kind of utility. A table is useful to eat food at or to work on, for example. The amount of utility an object has is for Marx its "use value". But once a price becomes attached to it the value that is given severs the link between that object and the labor involved in producing it. A tulip bulb worth $f1,100$ gains this new value from outside the relationship with labor. The value is based on supply and demand and the amount corresponds to an equivalence of whatever else $f1,100$ can buy. A pound of Switsers is equivalent to a house, or x number of tables. Once on sale, the bulbs, the house, and the tables become simply quantities and no longer useful.

The capitalist who is seeking to profit from the object, to exchange the object for something more valuable to them than they spent producing it, sees the object in this way. This new meaning of the object is known as 'exchange value'. Exchange value equates all objects to quantities that are equivalent to other products on the market, and money becomes the means of making the exchange. Things sold on the market acquire price tags of varying amounts which ebb and flow. The market's power to shift the exchange value of an object now makes it seem that the object's 'true' value is no longer based on its use and the work that was put into it by the laborer. By putting a price tag on objects that are a product of labor we get "commodity fetishism".

The world 'fetish' is derived from the Portuguese *feitiço*, or 'sorcery'. It is used to refer to magical objects and witchcraft.[41] Marx's use of the term, according to historian William Pietz, derived from a "notion of the fetish worshipper's desire-driven delusion regarding natural objects".[42] Thus, commodity fetishism can be understood as the process by which human interactions "appear as they are", which is "as material relations between persons and social relations between things".[43] In other words, society under capitalism, for Marx, means making things rather than relating to one another. And, at the same time, capitalism makes us blind to this reality. Instead, we come to believe that man-made objects have some kind of value that does not correspond to work and utility. Rather than an object's value being a product of labor, it is seen as a product of exchange.

For Marx, exchange value is fetishized, but use value is a positive way of understanding production and consumption. But for Jean Baudrillard it is not just exchange value that is fetishized but use value too. "Far from designating a realm beyond political economy, use value is only the horizon of exchange value".[44] Baudrillard questions Marx's assumptions, arguing that use of an object in itself is subjective and thus there is no use value contained within an object as Marx believed.[45] Use value is associated with social needs, but Baudrillard argues that our present-day consumer society is not predicated on the consumption of necessary objects and questions the idea that humans have needs that they are pledged to satisfy. In order to understand the active process of consumption, Baudrillard believes we must actually understand another form of value not found in Marx: *symbolic* exchange value – "the

136 Representations of Crises, Colonialism, and Consumerism

value of social prestation [prestige], of rivalry and, at the limits, of class discriminants".[46] What Baudrillard argues is that consumption, at least in our society, is manifested out of a desire for status or meaning via symbolic markers, not of utility. Tulips with variegated petals are a perfect example. What does one get out of these social markers, these consumed commodities? Here, Baudrillard combines Marx's "commodity fetishism" with Freud's psychoanalytic "fetishism".

Freud developed his theory of the fetish by utilizing Alfred Binet's meaning of the term which referred to erotic sensations toward objects such as shoes and linen.[47] "The fetish", according to Freud, "is a substitute for the woman's (the mother's) phallus which the little boy once believed in and does not wish to forego".[48] The fetishist concludes that, in effect, the object of fetish is the missing phallus. Baudrillard incorporates this into his argument by noting the substitutive property the object has for something immaterial. For Baudrillard, a fetish works like a sign. The object of obsession, the signifier, stands in for something other than themselves: a sexual desire, or the signified. In other words, a commodity that is consumed actually satisfies something outside itself for the consumer. It is not its use value that is being consumed, which allows the consumption and commodity production process to continue, but the symbolic element 'contained' within the object. The symbolic exchange value, unlike use value, is socially determined, rooted in our code, our social system of signs. Consider the example Baudrillard takes from the famed economist and sociologist Thorstein Veblen: "one does not dress a woman luxuriously in order that she be beautiful, but in order that her luxury testify to the legitimacy or the social privilege of her master".[49]

We can say the same about the tulips so prized in seventeenth-century Netherlands. We can also hypothesize that the crash in tulip prices was a result of the recalculation of the tulip's symbolic exchange value. Perhaps once the number of rare bulbs had mushroomed to such an extent that they no longer conferred the elite social status there was no desire for them. Such a status is social in nature and once the bulb failed to signify such prestige for some, it rippled into the consciousness of others. For example, a peppercorn merchant who is a central character in *Tulip Fever* never displayed any interest in tulips and described the whole trade as "madness". He preferred to exhibit his wealth through art and his wife. These 'objects' were of rarer quality to him and if this became true for others, these objects' value would increase while the value of tulips would diminish.

At this point in the economic development of the Global North, the function of conspicuous consumption – as termed by Veblen – "is to provide the economic stimulus for mass consumption".[50] Institutions have arisen to try and effect exactly this process of fetishization in order for the economy to

Representations of Crises, Colonialism, and Consumerism **137**

continue to function. Borrowing from the economist John Kenneth Galbraith, Baudrillard writes:

> the basic problem of contemporary capitalism is no longer the contradiction between 'profit maximization' and the 'rationalization of production' (from the point of view of the entrepreneur), but that between a potentially unlimited productivity (at the level of the technostructure) and the need to dispose of the product. It becomes vital for the system in this phase to control not just the apparatus of production, but consumer demand; to control not just prices, but what will be demanded at those prices. The 'general effect' – either prior to the act of production (surveys, market research) or subsequent to it (advertising, marketing, packaging) – is to 'shift the locus of decision in the purchase of goods from the consumer where it is beyond control to the firm where it is subject to control'.[51]

Entire industries, such as the marketing industry, are established to manipulate the social code of symbolic exchange value in order to suit their clients, creating demand. The sale catalog and advertising posters for the Winckel auction were precursors to the advertising industry.
Baudrillard also notes another function advertisers fill:

> advertising achieves the marvelous feat of consuming a substantial budget with the sole aim not of adding to the use-value of objects, but of subtracting value from them, of detracting from their time-value by subordinating them to their fashion-value and to ever earlier replacement.
> Here he is not referring to planned obsolescence but to changes to the *symbolic* exchange value of a particular commodity to increase consumption. And, as Herman and Chomsky note, there is an additional effect on the state as "the steady advance, and cultural power, of marketing and advertising has caused 'the displacement of a political public sphere by a depoliticized consumer culture' ".[52]

We can see how exposing the process of fetishism, as defined by Baudrillard, can work to undermine the entirety of capitalism (and bolster alternatives for the state) because "consumption … is a mode of systematic activity and global response which founds our entire cultural system"[53]. So, let us return to our original objective – to find out how popular film and television may be shaping our understanding of the processes that define and sustain capitalism and the state. As an example of a critique of consumerism, let's think back to *Happyish* (season 1; 2015) where Thom Payne is stuck on a train, and everyone is contemplating the value of their jobs because someone has just been fatally hit by another train. Everyone's life is seemingly changed by this event in which they recognize their own mortality. We cut to an hour or

138 Representations of Crises, Colonialism, and Consumerism

two into the future. The train passengers are now on a platform, waiting for the next train to take them to Grand Central Station. Two young suits are standing looking at their iPads.

Young suit 1: I hear she was reading her iPad when she fell in.
Young suit 2: So sad.
Young suit 1: I hear the new one's gonna have a better screen.

Here we see the instance in which the ideological strength of capitalism prevails and overpowers the brief moment of introspection that comes from the confrontation of mortality. The moment when the rhythm of capital skips a beat and provides the space to collectively skip the record to a different tune … but we all forget and keep listening.

Young suit 2: The old one already had retina display.
Young suit 1: I don't mean the display; I mean the screen.
Young suit 2: What about the screen?
Young suit 1: Split.
Young suit 2: Split?
Young suit 1: Split. You can have two windows open.
Young suit 2: No way!
Young suit 1: Way.
Young suit 2: I gotta get to the Apple Store.
Young suit 1: Me too. Where the fuck is this train?

On another occasion, Thom is the fetishist, using consumption as a way of dealing with his unhappiness:

> Sometimes on the way to work I like to imagine Samuel Beckett waiting, say, for the 6:47 to Grand Central. And Sam's pissed off. He hates his job. Wants to write. Wants to do something that matters. But he does his shitty job every day because Sam loves his wife; they love their child. Somehow Sam found a sliver of happiness in this shit-pile of a world so basically Sam's fucked. Because if he wants to keep that happiness Sam's gotta suck some cock. Same cocks we all do. So, Beckett takes his seat on the train, fires up his iPad and he thinks, I can't go on. I'll go on to Target. It's 30% off all skinny jeans 'til next mother fucking Monday.

Since Thom is an adman much of the show focuses on the industry that manipulates symbolic exchange value, which is presented in a critical way because Thom hates what he does. Thom knows what he does is wrong and occasionally lets us into his imagination which allows him to ridicule his entire profession. In one episode we are introduced to Coca Cola's brilliant

Representations of Crises, Colonialism, and Consumerism **139**

'Happiness' campaign featuring a commercial filled with extras smiling and laughing with exuberance. We swiftly cut to an imagined scene of Hitler directing the campaign and forcing everyone into being happier, allowing us to be exposed to the con of the production of commodity fetishism.[54]

Branded (2012) also presents these ideas of commodity fetishism in a very direct manner. The movie follows a Russian marketing expert, Misha, who becomes disgruntled with his job as he sees society increasingly fetishize consumer goods and be driven by moral panics created by the marketing industry. He retreats into a rural village and goes through a surreal spiritual journey which provides him with a vision of how to stop brand obsession and compulsive desires to consume using his marketing know-how. He begins to work for a vegetarian food company and tells them to invest in and sell an instant meat-testing product as there's a strange disease in meat that is spreading. The meat-testing product creates another moral panic where people oppose meat-heavy fast-food restaurants and go to these new vegetarian restaurants instead. He continues promoting a marketing strategy where rivals attack their competition.[55] Attack ads, and the marketing industry that develops them, become their own moral panic. People protest in the street. Marketers get attacked. People even lobby the government to pass legislation to get rid of advertising. Finally, after rioting takes place, the president issues an emergency broadcast banning advertising. Misha has completed his mission in life, the movie implies. At the end of the film, we see streets, roads, and major centers of the city, all billboard-less.[56]

Resistance and Glimpses into the Future

Despite the various representations which allow us to enter the hidden abode of capitalism and the state, we are still left searching for the alternative to these now less mystified (but not fully demystified) systems of domination. Some of these movies and television shows conclude in Hollywood fashion – a happy ending. But the problems entailed in these more radical representations require these endings to produce an alternative.[57] What utopian happy endings do we find?

Happyish concludes, having only been able to survive a single season, with the continuation of angst. Any possible salvation can only be found within an individualized context. Just as Thom decides to quit his job and set out for a career as a writer, his wife becomes pregnant, and he is forced to stay in his miserable job. In *The Wire*, we have a Greek tragedy of never-ending cyclical problems where younger characters fall into the role of the older ones. This demonstrates the systemic and social (rather than individual) problem, but it does not provide an alternative. *Office Space* (1999), discussed in the previous chapter, concludes with the protagonist being freed from a miserable office job to happily work in construction, while for others monotonous managerialism

140 Representations of Crises, Colonialism, and Consumerism

presumably continues until they too find themselves another form of wage labor. *Outsourced* and *Up in the Air* conclude with the characters finding themselves amidst ongoing economic hardships. Where there is a happily-ever-after moment it rarely includes an actual transformation that rids our world of the problems depicted. Instead, the characters that are lucky are able to individually escape the confines of those problems.

We may point to other critiques found in popular texts not discussed above which poke holes in the logic and defense of these institutions, but do not seem to entertain any solutions for these problems. For example, shows like Veep (seasons 1–7; 2012–2019) and *Archer* (seasons 1–4; 2009-2013)[58] and films like *Don't Look Up* demonstrate the incompetence of government officials and intelligence services, but they don't question whether representative democracy actually produces better results than more participatory structures.[59] Of the dozens of texts discussed above, only two seem to present some sort of alternative future beyond a general sense of hope: *Branded* and *Elysium*.

Branded clearly opposes the notion of marketing, branding, and overconsumption in capitalist society, although it is interesting that all this brand competition and the subsequent billboard-less society is set in Russia, a country that for many years was effectively billboard-less under communism. It is only in the very last seconds of the film that we are presented with this billboard-less alternative vision of society. While this alternative is certainly a major change from the present, highlighted by the narrator's concluding remarks about "a new era", what the alternative is remains unclear. Other than the visible signs of consumerism disappearing we are unsure of what has changed. Did the economy cease to be capitalist? Does "a new era" hint at Marx's view of epochs and the inherent contradictions within capitalism that will lead to socialism? Sadly, the movie is opaque on the matter. For all its attacks on branding it says little about capitalism as a relationship between ownership and production, placing the focus on the consumer side of the equation.

Additionally, the few images of the radical change that we see in the closing shots of the film present something almost disturbing. Rather than revolutionary, the new era looks a lot like the old era but just without the ads. Police officers, still in their usual roles, are now handing out parking tickets to cars that have their maker's logo on them and forcibly removing the car's emblem from the hood. Those same cars still fill the streets with stop-and-go traffic. The music, calm and serene, indicates the beauty of what we see, but the beauty is questionable. It looks familiar. Even the billboards, now ad-less, are still there. We suspect, however, that people will change. If marketing worked to manipulate people's desires, then no marketing works as a form of marketing itself – selling a future where desires are more organic. Even here we would be unsure of what the future then holds. Do we still

Representations of Crises, Colonialism, and Consumerism **141**

long to endlessly consume but will we no longer be told what it is we should consume? Or will we consume less?

The answer to this is perhaps indicated by a scene towards the very end of the film in which Misha plays with his son, a scene we had never seen before because his son was always on the hunt for a hamburger. Now that we are no longer driven by brand obsession and manipulation, we can enjoy human interaction at a more fundamental level, not one mediated through products. How radical is this rupture? We know one thing which is that the state seems to survive this experience. It was forced, through riots, to make a difficult decision, but the next day cops were still enforcing the state's laws. And the malleability of people to marketing campaigns also seems to suggest that a state is needed anyway, to ensure people are not molded incorrectly or to enforce the new anti-advertising code. The small glimpse we get of this post-marketing vision only happens in the early morning when we see few ordinary people: people cleaning up the advertising signs and posters; faceless police officers; a traffic jam; a garbage truck following its usual routine. Misha is now playing with his son, but this is the only change in the characters that is represented. There almost appears to be a class-based differentiation between the effects of this new ad-less world. The working class is still in the same boat. They might not have much discretionary income to spend on these branded goods anyway, so they are still cleaning up, removing trash, and driving to work in the early morning. Misha is a middle-class professional, however, and therefore for him and his son life seems to have changed. We simply don't see enough about what this "new era" means to really develop a vision of radical change. However, it may resonate with some who are beholden to conspicuous consumption and the representation we see may provide a vision of relief. That vision just does not appear to particularly rupture the perception of the state or capitalism more generally.

Elysium's representation of global citizenship, positive human rights, and geographic equality – fostered by the expansion of technological innovation – does present us with important components of an alternative system. The film, a story of the Global North and the Global South, migration, and free healthcare, presents a notion of enacting positive human rights – a radical notion in these neoliberal times. The heroes are able to make all the people of Earth citizens of Elysium and in doing so they can no longer be arrested by the robot police force, and everyone is afforded the healthcare with which only those on Elysium were previously provided. The film allows us to imagine away nation-states as health provision is universalized via access to Med-Bays which automatically relocate themselves to serve the new citizens. Citizenship itself is re-represented as *human* rights, and those human rights are positive as well as negative. That is, respectively, you are given access to universal healthcare, and you have rights to not be arrested by robots.

142 Representations of Crises, Colonialism, and Consumerism

This utopian payoff works so seamlessly because both the police force and Med-Bays operate as computers, inputting the data provided. Once the system was rebooted by the main character and citizenship was extended, the robots acted accordingly with no sense of inconsistency or the consciousness to behave in ways that lean more toward prejudice or simply habit. Had the police force been human they may have acknowledged the change regarding the formal rules as stipulated in the computer system, but they could have simply stated that this was a coup attempt and lacked legitimacy. "Yes," they may have thought, "these people are technically citizens but because there was no institutionalized process by which they became citizens I can ignore this technicality." In many ways, a wide range of oppression still operates in this way today, where rights are not, for example, gendered or racialized in law. Even if it were the case that the universalization of citizenship grew out of institutionalized means we could still expect other forms of institutional means of de facto discrimination. In *Elysium* we only accept this transformation because the robots in the film lack this sense of consciousness. The utopian dream of the film, therefore, seems to insist on vast technological progress that places vital services in the hands of hackable computer systems. We may be heading in that direction, but the key rights that were granted through the revolutionary efforts of the heroes in the film were those that were largely outside the scope of our current capabilities. Regarding healthcare provision, although it is conceivable that it would be possible to hack your way into some temporary form of drug (re)distribution, for example, actual medical procedures would not work this way. Nevertheless, the utopian representations in the film still provide us with a vision of an alternative, allowing viewers the ability to imagine something other and escape the curse of TINA.

Re-Transcoding Radical Ideas

As I have shown, *Tulip Fever* looks at a part of history that blends economic crisis, colonialism, and commodification. I've used the example of Tulip Mania and its filmic representation to explore screen media texts that brought to light some of the fundamental problems of capital and state. *Tulip Fever* itself only directly discusses the topic of crisis, ignoring colonialism and commodification. To understand why this is the case we can borrow a concept from critical and cultural theorists Michael Ryan and Douglas Kellner.

Ryan and Kellner coined the concept of *transcoding* to refer to the process of "[encoding] representations, discourses, and myths of everyday life into specifically cinematic terms".[60] Film and television do not reflect realities but are representations of discourses that occur in reality that are transcoded into film. Thus, the argument is that the creators and owners of the film decided to situate it within the discursive context of 'the moment', the economic crisis. *Tulip Fever* is an excellent case study because of how long it took for the film to be realized. Starting off as a book published in 1999, the film was quickly picked up by Hollywood. However, after a series of stops and starts, it was only completed and released in 2017. This allows us to compare the book which was published before the economic crisis and originally adapted by the author with the film that was written and released after the crisis, but still caught up in its discursive web.

The novel, also titled *Tulip Fever*, was written by Deborah Moggach who set a story of love, loss, and redemption at the time of Tulip Mania. It has little to say about the crash in tulip bulb prices and the economic effect this had. While the characters in the book engage in the tulip trade, the actual market crash does not affect the characters. It is only briefly introduced toward the end of the novel as a metaphor for the characters' progression over time. As soon as the book was written director and producer Steven Spielberg bought the rights, but he then shelved the project, which was then picked up again in 2005 with plans for a new script, although this also lost steam. It was only in February 2014 that the film was reconsidered for production. Prior to the film's September 2017 release, the film's producer – the notorious Harvey Weinstein – wrote an editorial for *Deadspin*, essentially trying to explain why the film had been delayed for so long and defending its quality. In the editorial he referenced the crisis and described commodities markets as "pretty nutty".[61]

In the film itself, crisis plays a big role, impacting on the characters and staging the film's climax. The impact it has on the characters gets translated into a lesson the film wishes to tell. This lesson, although not entirely historically accurate, was that the Dutch state made futures trading illegal following the crisis – and the implication is that we should too in our present circumstance. Weinstein himself wrote, "a thousand years from now we'll all be asking why people today bet on the futures of cattle and sugar".[62] This presents crises as manageable, able to align with capitalism as long as it is properly regulated by the state. The economic crisis inflected itself into the film with the discourse becoming transposed from 'real life' to cinema. The connection felt even stronger in 2008 when Deborah Moggach was hopeful the film would finally go into production: "it feels uncomfortably topical, what with the economy crashing around us … they experienced it all before, in Holland in 1636, but then it was tulips that brought the country to collapse".[63]

While social and political discourses are transposed into cultural texts, Michael Ryan and Douglas Kellner argue that cultural representations themselves "become part of that broader cultural system of representations that construct social reality".[64] We can think of this as *re-transcoding* – taking the discourses from the screen media text back out into the world. My objective in this chapter has been to explore screen media texts that brought

144 Representations of Crises, Colonialism, and Consumerism

to light some of the fundamental problems of capital and state. While these texts transcode existing discourses into film and television, they also have the capacity to re-transcode their more radical meanings back into our shared understanding of the world. Thus, these texts help to further build a discourse of radical critique that could be transformed into an ideology in search of alternatives. In the next chapter, I will take this idea of re-transcoding one step further.

Notes

1 Goldgar 2007, p. 357, n 3.
2 Marx 1982[1867], p. 167; Baudrillard 1981, pp. 64–65.
3 This is true at the time of writing, in early 2024, but is also likely true whenever you read this given the cyclical nature of the market.
4 Chomsky 1999.
5 Also see *Casino Jack* (2010), *The Laundromat* (2019), *The Other Guys* (2010), and *Too Big to Fail* (2011).
6 Chomsky 1999, p. 38.
7 Marx and Engels 1988[1848], p. 211.
8 Lenin 2014[1917], p. 80.
9 Kropotkin 1910.
10 Also see *City of Hope* (1991), *Silver City* (2004), *War, Inc.* (2008), and *Widows* (2018).
11 Largely, however, *Sorry to Bother You* deals with extreme forms of exploitation and where we may want to draw the line for capitalism's encroachment on civil liberties and freedom rather than a critique of capitalism itself. For this critique, also see *Cesar Chavez* (2014).
12 There are also similarities with *Head of State* (2004).
13 Also see *Zoolander* (2001).
14 Though older films, also see *Serpico* (1973) and *The China Syndrome* (1979).
15 Schlesinger (2003[1960]), pp. 82–83.
16 The film *Rosewater* (2014) briefly mentions the coup in Iran.
17 Also see *Shock and Awe* (2017).
18 Also in *Patriot*, a former police officer states "In the last 20 years, 17 police officers have been charged for killings for incidents that happened on the job in the U.S. None convicted. The system's bent, I guess."
19 Lea 1922, p. 523.
20 Goldgar 2007, p. 222.
21 Adams 1996, p. 13.
22 Adams 1996, p. 13.
23 Adams 1996, p. 17.
24 Taylor 2009.
25 See, for example, Kehinde Andrew's views on *Black Panther* (2018).
26 For an analysis and documentary film about such representations, see Andrews 2016 and *The Psychosis of Whiteness* (2018). For an older mini-series, also see the original *Roots* (1977) and for an attempt that fails, see *Django Unchained* (2012).
27 In particular, see season 4, episode 1 and season 5 episode 10.

Representations of Crises, Colonialism, and Consumerism **145**

28 Rooney 2007.

29 Gebe 2008.

30 The film only really deals with actual politics in its concluding scenes as the film's protagonist contemplates her role as a campaign strategist in electing someone who ends up being bad. She eventually quits that job and becomes the outreach coordinator for the 'Latin American Solidarity Network'.

31 Also see *War, Inc* (2008).

32 Rosa 1994.

33 Also see the television series *Outsourced* (season 1; 2010).

34 Narayan 2020.

35 Also see *The Hunger Games* (2012) and *Incorporated* (season 1; 2016).

36 Newton 2002 as quoted in Narayan 2017, p. 2487.

37 Hearst was one of the people that inspired another film critical of capitalism, *Citizen Kane* (1941).

38 Goldgar 2007; Dash 1999; Goldgar 2006, p. 185.

39 Salzmann 2000, p. 84.

40 Marx (1982[1867]), p. 167.

41 Dant 1996, p. 497.

42 Pietz 1993, p. 136, as cited in Dant 1996, p. 498.

43 Marx 1982[1867], p. 166.

44 Baudrillard 2001, p. 102.

45 "[T]he separation of the end from the means is the wildest and most naive postulate about the human race. Man has needs. Does he have needs? Is he pledged to satisfy them? Is he labor power (by which he separates himself as means from himself as his own end)?" Baudrillard 2001, pp. 98–99.

46 Baudrillard 1981, pp. 30–31.

47 Baudrillard 1981, pp. 30–31.

48 Freud 1971, p. 199.

49 Baudrillard 1981, p. 31.

50 Baudrillard 1999, p. 46.

51 Baudrillard 1999, p. 71.

52 Herman and Chomsky 1988, p. xviii quoting Robins and Webster 1999, p. 127.

53 Baudrillard 2002, p. 199.

54 Also see *Corporate* season 2, episode 3 (2019).

55 The film co-stars Jeffrey Tambor who plays in the show *Arrested Development* which features a similar competitive advertising battle for comedic purposes (season 3, episode 8; 2005) – drawing on a similar joke from the sketch comedy show *Mr. Show with Bob and David* (season 4, episode 4), co-starring David Cross who also played in *Arrested Development*.

56 Counterintuitively, the film blames Lenin for marketing. Misha states, "[I]t was Lenin who invented marketing in 1918. He found an absolutely unique way to sell people the idea of Soviet communism. The factories to the workers, land to the peasants, peace to the soldiers. He made the product promise one thing: happiness. That's marketing. Lenin hired just simply the best designers and copywriters. Rodchenko, ... Mayakovsky. The brand's official color: Red. The logo: The five-pointed star. Once they'd established the super brand, they designed campaigns for all the product lines to carry. So, chocolates for Red October, perfumes, Red Moscow .... The KGB came later, like a sort of brand police. See, it's the dream of

146 Representations of Crises, Colonialism, and Consumerism

every brand to make the competition's products illegal. That's exactly what they did. Seventy years of total domination of the market. Tragically, they had really shitty production, so ... the product failed to live up to its promise, and consumers fell out of love with the Soviet Union."

57 Of course, many of the movies mentioned above do not present such solutions. The movies depicting real events certainly, and sadly, cannot easily venture into the world of alternative. Neither do the more pessimistic representations such as *Happyish*.

58 In season 5, however, it is revealed that the agency represented in *Archer* was not approved by the US government, thus undermining even this critique. However, in season 6 they are contracted by the CIA after saving the day at the end of the previous season.

59 See e.g., Shalom 2021.

60 Kellner 1991, p. 9.

61 Weinstein 2017.

62 Weinstein 2017.

63 Moggach 2008.

64 Ryan and Kellner 1990, pp. 12–13.

References

Adams, Julia (1996) 'Principals and Agents, Colonialists and Company Men: The Decay of Colonial Control in the Dutch East Indies', *American Sociological Review*, 61(1): 12–28.

Andrews, Kehinde (2016) 'The Psychosis of Whiteness: The Celluloid Hallucinations of Amazing Grace and Belle', *Journal of Black Studies*, 47(5): 435–453.

Baudrillard, Jean (1981) *For a Critique of the Political Economy of the Sign*, St. Louis, MO: Telos Press.

Baudrillard, Jean (1999) *The Consumer Society: Myth and Structures*, London: Sage.

Baudrillard, Jean (2001) *Selected Writings*, Second Edition, Stanford, CA: Stanford University Press.

Baudrillard, Jean (2002) *The System of Objects*, London: Verso.

Chomsky, Noam (1999) *Profit over People: Neoliberalism and Global Order*. New York: Seven Stories Press.

Dant, Tim (1996) 'Fetishism and the Social Value of Objects', *The Sociological Review*, 44(3): 495–516.

Dash, Mike (1999) *TulipMania: The Story of the World's Most Coveted Flower and the Extraordinary Passions It Aroused*, New York: Three Rivers Press.

Freud, Sigmund (1971) 'Fetishism', in *Collected Papers: Volume 5* (pp. 198–204), London: The Hogarth Press.

Gebe, Boni Yao (2008) 'Ghana's Foreign Policy at Independence and Implications for the 1966 Coup d'état', *The Journal of Pan African Studies*, 2(3): 160–186.

Goldgar, Anne (2006) 'Poelenburch's Garden: Art, Flowers, Networks and Knowledge in Seventeenth-Century Holland', in Golahny, Amy, Mochizuki, Mia M., Vergara, Lisa (eds.), *In His Milieu: Essays on Netherlandish Art in Memory of John Michael Montias* (pp. 183–191), Amsterdam: Amsterdam University Press.

Goldgar, Anne (2007) *Tulipmania: Money, Honor, and Knowledge in the Dutch Golden Age*, Chicago: The University of Chicago Press.

Herman, Edward S. and Chomsky, Noam (1988) *Manufacturing Consent: The Political Economy of the Mass Media* , New York: Pantheon Books.

Kellner, Douglas (1991) 'Film, Politics and Ideology: Reflections on Hollywood Film in the Age of Reagan', *Velvet Light Trap*, 27(Spring): 9–24.

Kropotkin, Peter (1910) 'Anarchism', *The Encyclopaedia Britannica*, https://www.marxists.org/reference/archive/kropotkin-peter/1910/britannica.htm.

Lea, John (1922) 'The Sailor and the Tulip' in 'Boy's Own Paper' Office (eds.) *The Boy's Own Annual*, Volume 45, London: *Boy's Own Paper*, 523.

Lenin, Vladimir I. (2014[1917]) *State and Revolution*, Chicago: Haymarket Books.

Marx, Karl 1982([1867]) *Capital: A Critique of Political Economy, Volume I*, Middlesex, UK: Penguin Books.

Marx, Karl and Engels, Fredrick ([1848]1988) *Economic and Philosophic Manuscripts of 1844 and The Communist Manifesto*, New York: Prometheus Books.

Moggach, Deborah (2008) 'Autumn 2008', https://www.deborahmoggach.com/deborah-moggach-news/2019/11/18/14254552.

Narayan, John (2017) 'The Wages of Whiteness in the Absence of Wages: Racial Capitalism, Reactionary Intercommunalism and the Rise of Trumpism', *Third World Quarterly*, 38(11): 2482–2500.

Narayan, John (2020) 'Survival Pending Revolution: Self-Determination in the Age of Proto-Neo-Liberal Globalization', *Current Sociology*, 68(2): 187–203, https://doi.org/10.1177/0011392119886870.

Robins, Kevin and Webster, Frank (1999) *Times of the Technoculture*, London: Routledge.

Rooney, David (2007) *Kwame Nkrumah: Vision and Tragedy*, Accra: Sub-Saharan Publishers.

Rosa, Kumudhini (1994) 'The Conditions and Organisational Activities of Women in Free Trade Zones Malaysia, Philippines and Sri Lanka, 1970–1990', in Sheila Rowbotham and Swasti Mitter (eds.), *Dignity and Daily Bread: New Forms of Economic Organising among Poor Women in the Third World and the First* (pp. 75–102), London: Routledge.

Ryan, Michael and Kellner, Douglas (1990) *Camera Politica: The Politics and Ideology of Contemporary Hollywood Film*, Bloomington: Indiana University Press.

Salzmann, Ariel (2000) 'The Age of Tulips: Confluence and Conflict in Early Modern Consumer Culture (1550–1730)', in Donald Quataert (ed.), *Consumption Studies and the History of the Ottoman Empire, 1550–1922: An Introduction* (pp. 83–106), Albany, NY: State University of New York Press.

Schlesinger, Arthur S. (2003[1960]) *The Age of Roosevelt, Volume III: The Politics of Upheaval: 1935–1936*, Boston: Mariner Book.

Shalom, Stephen R. (2021) 'Decision-Making in a Good Society: The Case for Nested Councils', *méta*, Working Paper 8, https://metacpc.org/wp-content/uploads/2021/12/8EN-mWP-Shalom-Decision-Making-in-a-Good-Society-1.pdf.

Taylor, Jean Gelman (2009) *The Social World of Batavia: Europeans and Eurasians in Colonial Indonesia*, Madison: University of Wisconsin Press.

Weinstein, Harvey (2017) 'Harvey Weinstein on the Challenge of Growing "Tulip Fever"', *Deadline*, 31 August, https://deadline.com/2017/08/harvey-weinstein-on-the-challenge-of-growing-tulip-fever-guest-column-1202158947.

7

TRANSFERABLE RADICALNESS

Alternative Lifestyles in Film and Television

In the previous chapter, we discussed how the background of the film *Tulip Fever* was crisis, colonialism, and consumption. However, the foreground of the film was a tale of romance and deception. In summary, a woman, who is kept as a trophy wife by a rich merchant, falls for another man and deceives her husband in order to be with her true love. The merchant, who had developed genuine feelings for his wife, eventually discovers that she had faked her death to run away with another man. The merchant comes to the realization that he was using his wife as an object and deserved his fate. He leaves his wealth to his maid and goes off to Batavia in search of redemption and a new life. Like us, he is seeking an alternative. What kind of new life would this merchant seek? What alternative would he find? Although the character is presented as a man who destroyed his chance at love, we know that Dutch colonizers in Batavia often married native women. This is a tactful way of phrasing it of course. The Governor General of the Dutch East Indies, Jan Pieterszoon Coen, advocated the 'Romulus approach' – abduct and marry whichever woman you desire. This was somehow deemed ethical. The lifestyle and culture of the native Javanese, however, are described by outsiders in the following way:

> As it respects the manners of the natives, with their uncouth forms, their singular appearances, dwelling in hollow trees, and residing in caverns, with their woolly hair and tattooed bodies, their naked persons and uncooked food, and all such monstrous and unheard of matters, it is scarcely worth while wasting one's breath upon them.[1]

DOI: 10.4324/9781003514916-8

Transferable Radicalness: Representing Alternative Lifestyles **149**

This description presents the Javanese as beastly, a similar trope to the one we see in descriptions of indigenous peoples as they are being colonized. But not all representations appear negative on the surface. Let's take the example of early writings on European encounters with indigenous communities in the West Indies:

> As for the young girls, they covered no part of their bodies, but wore their hair loose upon their shoulders and a narrow ribbon tied around the forehead. Their face, breast, and hands, and the entire body was quite naked, and of a somewhat brunette tint. All were beautiful, so that one might think he beheld those splendid naiads or nymphs of the fountains, so much celebrated by the ancients.[2]

This passage discusses nudeness in a rather positive, idyllic way. However, this alternative form of living was not meant to be viable, merely exotic, and was therefore 'uncivilized'. The merchant in *Tulip Fever* would probably not have adopted this lifestyle. The idyllic quotation above comes from an anthology of reports of explorations of the 'New World' written by the Italian historian Peter Martyr d'Anghera between 1493 and 1525. Martyr's representation is a transcoding of his own context in which nudity is part of the 'state of nature' and in which the state of nature marks a moment prior to 'civilization'. In part, Martyr is developing this position from the discourses developed through prior texts and knowledge. It is noteworthy how he makes an analogy to the ancients, citing naiads and nymphs as points of comparison – not just for their beauty but for their otherworldliness, their uncivilized state.

Martyr's text is used by Stuart Hall in his famous essay "The West and the Rest" to show the power of discourse in shaping colonial Western powers' interactions and ideas about the New World and its inhabitants. Hall identified a contradiction in that discourse. Whilst vilifying indigenous peoples as "disgusting", "uncivilized", "barbarous and depraved" the West also represented them in the opposite way. The indigenous peoples "became the subject of the languages of dream and Utopia, the object of a powerful fantasy".[3] Despite the typically positive connotations, this fantasy also helps to shape other aspects of the discourse on indigenous people which are in line with the notions of a 'disgusting' and 'uncivilized' species of the earlier discourse. It is the 'othering' that produces a discourse that distinguishes 'the Rest' from 'the West' and produces a lens that ultimately led to genocide. The stories about the Rest became the basis on which people came to interpret the indigenous. Interactions between the West and 'the Rest' became almost a biproduct of the existing discourse that shaped the West's ideology. The main point here is that ideas are generated not just from our interactions

150 Transferable Radicalness: Representing Alternative Lifestyles

with the 'object' of evaluation, but with the representation of an 'object' reflected back onto the 'object' in question. Here we can refer to the idea of re-transcoding discussed in the previous chapter. This can also be applied to how we think about abstract concepts such as the state and capitalism, and their alternatives.

In the last few chapters we looked at screen media texts that paint the systems of state and capital in a negative light, showing how these are somewhat rare but nonetheless serve as a basis for a discursive starting point. This chapter will begin to put the focus on texts in which alternatives are represented. In particular, this chapter further bends Ryan and Kellner's notion of transcoding to help us make deeper inroads into a consciousness of radical alternatives. Where transcoding refers to the process of taking discourses from real life and coding them into screen media texts, and re-transcoding refers to the inversion of this process – whereby we read the context of our real lives from the discourses represented in such texts – *transferrable re-transcoding* suggests that we can transfer the discourses we find in screen media texts from one realm into another.

Let us simplify this concept by referring back to *Tulip Fever*. Transcoding allows us to understand *Tulip Fever* as partially deriving its discussion of the tulip trade from the lens of the Great Recession. Re-transcoding allows us to also read the uncritical representation of colonialism and commodification found in the film as an acceptance of those processes. Transferrable re-transcoding suggests that, for example, the relationships between the characters in the film can also provide the basis on which we can understand the relationships between publics and the systems of the state and capital, despite these relationships not being directly present in the text. In this way, ideas and understanding about love and loss, for example, can also become useful in understanding capitalism and the state. A man's wife runs away, he comes to the realization that he was actually using her and to find some sort of redemption he departs in search of a new life, leaving his wealth to his maid. The conclusion of the personal story in *Tulip Fever* can be transferred into the realm of politics and decoded as a message about redemption through reparations and an internally derived and peaceable process of redistribution.[4] In other words, the capitalist class – represented by the merchant – should realize the harms they have done and donate money to charitable causes or redistribute it to the poor – represented by the maid who is given the merchant's estate.[5]

With that in mind, this chapter focuses on the representation of alternatives not regarding state and capital but personal stories of relationships and lifestyles. Since most screen media texts are more interested in questions of personal life than social or political organization, it stands to reason that more examples of alternative relationships and lifestyles should be found among films and TV shows. If we find positive representations of

Transferable Radicalness: Representing Alternative Lifestyles **151**

such alternatives, we as viewers may then transfer those discourses to our thoughts about alternatives to state and capital. Thus, the aim of this chapter is to explore how non-conformist lifestyles are represented. This works in a similar fashion to Freudian displacement,[6] but in a way that enables us to ideologically develop an alternative. For Sigmund Freud, displacement was relocating a problem that is difficult to do anything about or even fully acknowledge to something within our domain of control. Capitalism and the state are big problems to tackle, but lifestyle choices are within our control. This may also apply to filmmaking. Alternatives that are easier to represent can actually be a form of positive displacement in that it enables us to develop a consciousness that rejects closing our minds to the assumption of what is normal and of normality equating to positivity. Thus, if alternative lifestyles can be shown positively, perhaps this opens up the possibility of considering positive alternatives in the realm of politics and economics. We shall begin our exploration with three contemporary comedies with representations of alternative lifestyles and relationships: *Admission* (2013), *Friends with Kids* (2011), and *Wanderlust* (2012).

Representations of a Brave New World

Admission (2013) includes numerous types of alternative lifestyles, even though they seemingly play a relatively small role in a larger plot about growing up as narrated through the eyes of Princeton University Admissions Officer Portia Nathan (Tina Fey). While our lead Portia has nothing particularly subversive about her, she is surrounded by alternative lifestyles. Portia's mother Susannah (Lily Tomlin) is a no-nonsense, independent, gun-toting author of *The Masculine Myth*.[7] Although Portia is a strong woman in her own right, her mother is much more fierce and stubborn. Susannah's fiery personality is part of her political ideology as a strong, unwavering feminist who says things like, "Did you know that women are the only exploited group in history to be idealized into powerlessness?" Susannah's personality and her lifestyle are in sync with her beliefs. She had Portia out of wedlock and did not even know the name of the man who had impregnated her. "I knew I needed his sperm, but I did not need him. . . I wanted a child but not some moody relationship. Sex with a stranger on the New Jersey transit was the answer to my problems." Repeatedly, Susannah is shown living out her philosophy in ways that counter the hegemonic norm. Despite aspects of rugged individualism demonstrated in Susannah's character, her (albeit white, middle-class) feminism is impressively embodied in the character. She is not merely a voice against patriarchy but a lived antagonist to it.

In some ways this embodiment of Susannah's ideals is mirrored in John Pressman (Paul Rudd), the male protagonist of the film, and his own ideals. John works at a high school and calls the Princeton University Admissions

152 Transferable Radicalness: Representing Alternative Lifestyles

Office in order to reach Portia and arrange an appointment for her to meet his students. He would also like her to speak to one student in particular who he thinks could be Princeton-bound. When Portia comes to visit the school, she gets to know John and his alternative lifestyle. John is a single father. He fell into the situation when a friend of his died in a car accident in Uganda where John was working at the time. The friend had a two-year-old son and no immediate relatives who could care for him. So, John adopted the boy. "Seemed like the only thing to do. All my friends thought for sure that I'd bail. That I was not ready to be a father. But, screw that." John chose a different path to having a child in more conventional, heteronormative circumstances and he acted in line with his values. But this goes beyond his caring role. He continues to live a lifestyle that he desires and finds fulfilling but that is 'abnormal' and admirable: he does humanitarian work around the world. "We've lived in Indonesia. We built a water purification system in Myanmar," to which Portia responds, "I'm sorry. So, you're just this single dad, travelling the world with his kid, doing good?" John jokes: "God. Well, when you put it like that it sounds so appealing." John also works at an alternative school called Quest. The school is located on a farm where the students milk cows, garden, and learn how to build sustainable irrigation systems.

The alternative school also promotes what John describes euphemistically as 'spirited debate'. Portia learns all about this when she delivers her Princeton pitch to the Quest students. In the film we had seen Portia go from one private school to the next, giving the same speech to attentive students who enthusiastically transcribed her every word in the hope of getting one step closer to being admitted to Princeton. Now at the alternative Quest School, she begins with her usual opener but gets a different response. "You all want to know the secret formula for getting in, right?" The students, sitting on makeshift seats in an understated room, respond with silence. 'Well, take out your pens,' she instructs. More silence until a hand goes up. "I'll tell you what I'd like to know,' a student confidently states. 'Why should I apply to an elitist institution with a history of anti-black, anti-gay, and anti-female oppression?' Portia is not phased. "Well actually, I reject that stereotype ...." But she is interrupted by another student who retorts, "Speaking of rejection, don't you reject 99.9% of your applicants? And don't you just want to drum up applications to keep your number-one position on *US News & World Report*?" And then another student interjects, "Don't people just need a college degree if you want to pursue the societally approved definition of success?" And John's son chips in, "Yeah. Wouldn't you be better off sitting in your room reading books instead of spending all that money?" As Portia tries to respond another voice is heard, starting a chorus of responses to the interloper from her elite institution. "Princeton is a corporation, no different than an oil company." "We should be educating ourselves to be citizens of

Transferable Radicalness: Representing Alternative Lifestyles **153**

the world and not of some guarded, suburban enclave." "What we want is to leave the planet better than we found it!" They all burst into applause. The students, informed by an alternative school, see a brave new world in front of them, where alternatives to the status quo exist.

Friends with Kids (2011) is another comedy that explores alternatives, this time solely within the sphere of parenting. The film follows a group of six friends: two married couples and two single, platonic friends – Jason (Adam Scott) and Julie (Jennifer Westfeldt). Flashing forward, the married couples have kids which leaves them living diminished social and sexual lives, while Jason and Julie stay single into their mid-30s. Jason and Julie both want to have kids but neither wants to settle for the sake of starting a family. As they see their friends' lives deteriorate into constant arguments, cleaning, and tiredness, they contemplate the pros and cons of trying to find a relationship that will eventually lead them into the same scenario. On the pro side, they both want to have kids. On the con side, they worry that kids will actually ruin the romantic relationships with 'their person', the 'one'. Julie wonders "how you get to be the most important person to your person and not miss out on having a kid". Jason's solution?

> So, what are you saying? You want to be already divorced, with a kid, so you can meet the man of your dreams? ... Actually, divorced people have it kinda great. They get all the toxic unsexy stuff out of the way with the first person, and then when they meet the person they really want to be with, they only have to deal with the kid half the time.

They come across an alternative, a loophole in what they see as the child/ marriage pit of despair. They decide that if they have a kid together then they can enjoy being parents but are also able to spend real quality time with the love of their lives – once they find them. "We love each other, we trust each other, we're responsible, gainfully employed, and totally not attracted to each other physically …. We have the kid, share all the responsibility, and just skip over the whole marriage and divorce nightmare.

After discussing it the next day they decide to go for it. While we can concede that this plan is probably too quickly committed to, it nevertheless represents an alternative lifestyle regarding parenting, love, and relationships. Upon hearing this idea one friend argues with her husband about the situation saying, "it's an affront to us … to all normal people who struggle and make sacrifices and make commitments to make a relationship work". But her husband is open to the new idea and understands why it might be the best thing to do.

> It's a brave new world, honey. There are test-tube babies and surrogate babies, Jon & Kate Plus 8. I don't think that two friends having a kid

154 Transferable Radicalness: Representing Alternative Lifestyles

together because it might be her last chance is the worst thing that I've ever heard.

The film cuts to Jason on a date with a young attractive woman we've not seen before. He gets a call and the next thing we know he's in the hospital trying to do what he can to ease Julie's pain as she's delivering their baby. They are then seen working together and making the situation as smooth as possible, while their friends continue to have a rough time. They seem to have 'beat the system', as Julie puts it, by opting for an alternative lifestyle.

The film *Wanderlust* follows a married couple in New York who are close to living the dream. George (Paul Rudd) and Linda (Jennifer Aniston) are your typical white, middle-class married couple who expect things to go their way because it usually does. George is looking forward to his bonus, maybe even a promotion. Linda is hopeful that her new documentary will be picked up by HBO. But just as many people in their position realized following the financial crisis, things do not always go well even for the privileged middle classes. Not only does Linda not get money for her documentary, but the company George was working for closes shop – we suspect due to white-collar crime at the top of the corporate food chain. So, soon after taking out a mortgage on a brand new 'micro-loft', they head back to their realtor, ask for it to be put on the market, and sell it at a loss. Homeless and unemployed, it is time for them to move out of New York. On their journey they unintentionally end up in Elysium, a hippie commune and 'intentional community'.

Among the large number of people in the commune are a nudist, a boy who thinks he is a butterfly, a socially awkward woman, and a shaman. The leaderless collective enjoys candlelit parties with exotic music, hallucinogens, skinny dipping, and free love. They share everything, they view clapping as too aggressive, and they don't have doors to close off rooms (even the bathroom!). While many aspects of the commune are used to supply the film's humor, the main characters are positively transformed by living there and choose to move in permanently.

Normal Boring Adults

Despite the alternative representations discussed above, all three films end on a negative note in relation to these alternatives. They conclude by reshaping the narrative to demonstrate that the alternatives are untenable, impracticable, or ultimately undesirable. Any nonconformist representations in these films are subverted and reduced to either comical contexts or failed experiments.

In the case of *Admission* (2013), our male lead who likes to travel the world with his adopted child reverses his plans. He cancels his trip to Ecuador – the

Transferable Radicalness: Representing Alternative Lifestyles **155**

next stage of his quest – because his kid, previously cheering on anti-capitalist positions against Princeton, now wants his father to be "a normal boring adult" who would take him to Chucky Cheese. The film begins to construct a discourse of the goodness of normalcy. What happens in the case of Portia's radical feminist mother, Susannah? First, we find out that her plan of getting impregnated by a stranger was just an accident she was covering up, essentially unmasking her feminist alternative as a fraud. Despite Susannah stating that one shouldn't rely too much on other people, she ends up with a philosophy professor and is finally happy as she becomes more 'normal'. By the end of the film, Susannah's radical personal and political views are shattered and her character is newly reconstructed into that of the norm. As for the alternative high school with all its progressive students? Well, the film ignores all those who protested against Princeton's elitism and focuses on one student who wants to go to a top-ranked university. And what of those radical points the students made about elite universities and their role in society? Portia actually concluded the exchange with a retort of her own:

> I have a question for all of you. Just how will you leave the planet better? Will you eradicate disease? You're gonna need a medical degree. If you want to create new drug therapies, that's a PhD. Do you want to defend the innocent and secure justice for all? I regret to inform you that you will have to go to law school. There are plenty of college graduates out there ardently hoping to leave the world better than they found it. We are looking for those people. Students with blazing minds and hearts who will change the goddamn world!

The students silently concede while John applauds, telling the students, "I bet you guys feel like a bunch of assholes." Even the teacher that seeks to promote alternative lifestyles and education comes to accept the hegemonic model of education, parenting, and lifestyle more broadly. He settles down, gets together with Portia, and – we assume – lives happily ever after in the world as it is.

The alternative parenting arrangement in *Friends with Kids* also collapses and reconstructs itself to fit the standard hegemonic mold. Jason and Julie are having a great time together with the kid, but Julie begins to have feelings for Jason and when her feelings aren't reciprocated, they begin to lead the life of a divorced couple, and we see it negatively impacting on their son. Eventually Jason too changes his mind and falls in love with Julie, but she is reluctant to have her heart broken again. They get thrust together when the child, representing a sort of natural desire, wants 'daddy to sleep at our house'. At this moment Jason convinces Julie that he also wants to sleep there and that she is indeed the one. They too live happily ever after in the world as it is. The lessons of the film are that men and women cannot be

156 Transferable Radicalness: Representing Alternative Lifestyles

best friends without being their ideal romantic partner and that alternative parenting arrangements cannot work because families are based inherently on a nuclear family model.

In *Wanderlust*, the lust and wonder of the commune soon fades after George and Linda set up their own publishing company and publish a best seller written by a member of the commune. They are back in New York in a very nice home, living the dream – the standard American dream. The film closes with the following words: "I think we're where we want to be." "So do I." As they kiss, Linda says: "Oh honey, shut the door." "Yes, the door. I love the door." And with this we are brought completely out of the commune and back into 'the real world' with the rules and values everyone knows and loves – because we haven't been presented with anything different.[8]

The Ethical Extremists

The three films above show that alternatives don't work, at least not for 'normal people'. But perhaps the most overt and recurrent ridicule of alternative living can be found in the sketch comedy show *Portlandia* (seasons 1–8; 2011–2018). Fred Armisen and Carrie Brownstein, two co-creators of the show, play the key roles of the recurring characters living in Portland, Oregon – specifically a kind of liberal, hipster representation of Portland. Many of the personae portrayed in the show are alternative to the mainstream, but – within the realm of the show – they are all too normal in the city of Portland. While these alternatives are represented, they are instantaneously ridiculed, driven to supposedly logical conclusions.

One famous sketch depicts a man and a woman at a restaurant asking their waitress about the ethical sourcing of the chicken. The waitress informs them that "the chicken is a heritage breed, woodland raised chicken that's been fed a diet of sheep's milk, soy, and hazelnuts ...". She's interrupted by another question: "Is this local?" The waitress responds affirmatively. "Is that USDA organic, Oregon organic, or Portland organic?" The waitress is bombarded with so many questions that she ends up bringing the couple a manila folder with all the information, including the chicken's name and photos. But the diners are not convinced. They head over to the chicken farm where they meet a man with a radiant aura who they immediately connect with as soon as they make eye contact. The sketch changes focus. The couple forget about the chicken and soon become mesmerized by this magus, and within minutes join him and his many wives in their cult. The ridiculous representation stretches the concern for ethical consumption into its most extreme form. They care so passionately about the ethics of their lifestyle choices that they cannot have a meal without interrogating the waitress. Even when she provides a plethora of information, they remain unconvinced. Their ethics are tied to a kind of hyper-skepticism that prohibits them from leading their lives. At the same time these individuals are depicted as susceptible to a cult of personality and emotionally driven into an extreme change of lifestyle. While the original characters are already extremes of the kind of ethical consumers which are counternormative, they are soon taken to a place where they are unrecognizable within society. Their counternormative position, the sketch tells us, is not simply a slightly odd behavior, but a start of something deeply problematic.[9]

Another set of recurring characters are Toni and Candace, owners of a feminist bookstore. These characters take on a similar role – they are counternormative in their views on gender and sexuality and the humor comes from deriding this perspective. Toni and Candace are offended by anything remotely resembling a phallus. One of them points to a customer's finger which is pointing at a bookshelf. "Can you put that away, please? Every time you point, I see a penis." These characters are shown facing an outside world that doesn't understand them, and the audience is positioned on the side of that outside world peering into the lives of these 'others' who they can see reflected in feminist discourses. They are portrayed as manhating, vagina-obsessed, self-righteous, and, at the same time, inconsistent. While most of their sketches take place inside their bookstore, Women and Women First, one skit takes them to a Portland Trailblazers basketball game where they are introduced to the concept of cheerleaders for the first time. They are (pretty rightfully) appalled, but the laughs are directed at them.

Candace:	"What is this? Why are they barely wearing anything?
Toni:	This is a private dance. This is a dance you do in your backyard, under the full moon.
Candace:	No. Cover your eyes everybody. This isn't a show.
Toni [to spectators sitting around her]:	Does anyone want to see my master's degree or my collection of books?!
Candace [as loud as she can in protest]:	Let them speak! Allow them to talk.

Irate, Toni and Candace want to meet the person in charge and the scene cuts to them sitting in the General Manager's office. The General Manager doesn't understand why they would be offended and defers to the desires of the fans, focusing us back on the main point: basketball. While Toni and Candace do present their point in an intentionally ridiculous way, their point is not outside the realm of a standard feminism critique of the objectification of women. But this logic is represented as extreme, a demand of a prototypical 'feminazi'. By denying a sensible feminist position and placing Toni and Candace as the only feminist voice, those who they encounter are those we

158 Transferable Radicalness: Representing Alternative Lifestyles

side with regardless of their position – which is invariably the uncritical status quo. We can actually see the uses of these representations helping to reproduce a reactionary narrative about feminists within the public discourse in the real world (re-transcoding). Here are just a few examples of people commenting on sketches of Toni and Candace:

> "This is Hilarious. Everyday feminazis. "

> "This documentary provides excellent perspective on every Leftist 'useful idiot' in America."

> "The scary thing is that actual feminists are probably even more insane than them, because they'd get mad that the bookstore owners even associated 'vagina' with 'women' which is transphobic. "

> "It's like a live-action re-enactment of a typical Jezebel comments page. .

> "... at it's core, feminism is every bit as corrupt, warped fear mongering hate ideology as portrayed here.

> "The sad thing is, this is exactly what many SJW [social justice warriors] are like. Special snowflakes that deny reality. "

> "Such a perfect rendition o[f] libtards. Amazing acting job."

> "I was a feminist. After watching these two, I may reconsider ...."[10]

While the creators of the show did not set out to ridicule the left, it is often decoded by viewers as a humorous critique of so-called "social justice warriors". *The Guardian* noted that the show "has succeeded where others have failed: scoring a hit (and laughs) in skewering earnest lefties and twee hipsters", while *The Portland Mercury* wrote: "If you're a person who feels disenfranchised from Portland's creative class ... you'll laugh your ass off. (Side note: The Republican uncle of a Mercury staffer LOVED IT.)"[11]

Tossed Salads and Scrambled Eggs

A few hours' drive from Portland is the city of Seattle where the TV sitcom *Frasier* (1993–2004) is set. The title character, Dr Frasier Crane, is a psychiatrist who hosts a call-in radio show. These callers have mixed up personal lives and psychological issues, what the show's theme song refers to as "tossed salads and scrambled eggs". But, Frasier, as the show's theme tune suggests, has them pegged and dishes out advice while struggling with problems in his own personal life. Although living a lavish lifestyle out of a penthouse apartment with a skyline view, Frasier is often interrupted by the intrusions of his grumpy, salt-of-the-earth father and his repugnantly snobbish brother. Frasier is a pompous and elitist holier-than-thou character whose assumed superior intellect allows him to delve into the miniscule mind of the commoner to solve their petty problems. This representation serves as part of the humor but only furthers the normalization of the common person, whose lifestyle is only marginally different from that of the doctor. Like *Portlandia*, the worldview depicted in *Frasier* helps to normalize the status quo – in this case by pointing fingers at the follies of the upper-middle classes, rather than the 'creative class'.

Frasier's career as a radio-psychiatrist helps to highlight the personal troubles of the wider public on top of his own family's troubles. We see that everyone suffers from something but because of this professional outlook, every solution is essentially a private one even as the problems are shared across the airwaves of the greater Seattle area to others experiencing the same symptoms. The world of *Frasier* does what most worlds in popular culture do, they ground us in a shared reality while blinding us to the structures that shape that reality, and the problems of those structures. When the issues of employment, work/life balance, and job satisfaction are addressed by callers, the overarching problem of capitalism and the state is never presented.

Sociologist C. Wright Mills wrote that an "essential tool of the sociological imagination" is the distinction between personal troubles and public issues. Personal troubles "have to do with his self and with those limited areas of social life of which he is directly and personally aware". Public issues, on the other hand, "transcend local environments of the individual" and "often involve[ ] a crisis in institutional arrangements".

> When, in a city of 100,000, only one man is unemployed, that is his personal trouble, and for his relief we properly look to the character of the man, his skills, and his immediate opportunities. But when in a nation of 50 million employees, 15 million men are unemployed, that is an issue, and we may not hope to find its solution within the range of opportunities open to any one individual .... Both the correct statement of the problem and the range of possible solutions require us to consider the economic and political institutions of society.[12]

Likewise, when the issues concern romantic and sexual relationships, as is the case more often in sitcoms like *Frasier*, the structures of gender-binary heteronormativity need to come into play because many problems, although seemingly personal, correspond to wider ideological and social-structural conditions that are actually shared by many.

In trying to imagine an alternate reality in relation to such questions we can get back in our car and take a cross-country road trip to New York's queer comedy series *Broad City* (seasons 1–5; 2014–2018). Creators Ilana Glazer and Abbi Jacobson play exaggerated versions of themselves in a

160 Transferable Radicalness: Representing Alternative Lifestyles

queer-friendly New York City, where lifestyle choices openly and actively go beyond the inhibitions of the conservative Courts of Appropriate Conduct that often govern the codes of the therapists' interventions in *Frasier*. In doing so, *Broad City* turns the otherwise-odd into the run-of-the-mill with the counternormative queer questioning of sexuality itself. Take, for example, a scene where Ilana describes her hypothetical marriage to her friend Abbi. When she refers to herself as the husband Abbi feels dejected, "I'm the wife??" "No," Ilana says, "you're the other husband." Ilana's sexuality is explored in an episode where, having instantly fallen in love with a woman, Ilana realizes the situation is wrong. The other woman looks just like herself. "It's too weird... I have sex with people different from me .... Different colors, different shapes, different sizes. People who are hotter, uglier, more smart, not more smart, innies, outies ... I don't know ... a Catholic person." But not people that are just like her. Not only does this representation depict the normalcy of her queer identity, but it demonstrates where the laughs are directed.

Unlike *Portlandia*, which asks us to laugh at the other, *Broad City* finds humor in the limitations of the present normativity of our real-life world. In this case we laugh with Ilana because what she perceives to be the *most* different from her Jewish self are Catholics. At the same time, she is empowered as a character by not seeing the more typical definitions of difference (e.g., gender, attractiveness). It is no surprise that this short, single-episode sub-plot received a wealth of positive commentary amongst feminist and queer publications praising it for transcending these traditional categories of sexuality.[13] Ilana and Abbi's worldview is also normalized in the show, which further prevents us from easily laughing at them. This is perhaps best exemplified in an episode that explores Abbi's more hesitant queerness. Abbi's first date with a crush, Jeremy, ends with them sleeping together. During intercourse Abbi inadvertently asks to "mix it up a bit", exciting Jeremy to no end. He jumps out of bed and comes back with a strap-on dildo for her to wear. Upon hearing this story Ilana dances with glee and cries tears of joy. In the show the unusual becomes the desirable and all within a feminist framework of consent and respect. Later, Abbi meets up with Ilana and Ilana's parents and gay brother, Elliot. Ilana's dad, Arthur, asks, "Pegged? What's pegged?"

Ilana: Pegging is when a woman with a strap on, with a dildo, penetrates a man.
Arthur: Oh, but wouldn't that be more like a gay thing, Elliot?
Elliot: No, I mean, how would I put a dildo on top of my dick?
Arthur: That's true.
Elliot: Straight men and gay men alike both enjoy prostate stimulation.
Ilana: And it's very popular with married couples.
Arthur: Oh ....

Transferable Radicalness: Representing Alternative Lifestyles **161**

The casualness of the conversation demonstrates how the representation of the lifestyle politics in the show creates a utopian world where the present social norms of sexuality cease to exist and openness to new experiences are prized. The 'scrambled eggs' of *Frasier*, with their psychological problems that cause them to behave outside the norms, are no longer mixed up in *Broad City*. They are the new norm, and they aren't for Frasier to peg down psychologically.

Of course, the social norms we live with today are not erased from the show in their entirety. Instead, they are othered – in an inverse fashion from *Portlandia*. The status quo of our society becomes the oddity in the worldview of *Broad City*. Take the example of one episode in which Abbi loses her phone and, using an app to track it down, discovers that it is somewhere in the affluent Upper East Side. "I ... I don't wanna go there", Abbi says as they both cringe. "Must we?" Ilana asks. But they must, and when we see them walking down the posh streets of one of New York's most wealthy neighborhoods we hear background music befitting a menacing scene from *The Phantom of the Opera*. We see Ilana and Abbi walk slowly and carefully through the eerie streets of the elite, keeping a safe distance away from those anonymous monsters who speak of horror stories as they walk by:

"My son in law is such a disgrace. He went to Cornell!"

"I'm fine with a tsunami but not in St. Barts. Anywhere else is fine."

"It's the tenth horse that's died this year. That's ten horses I've had to replace."

Ilana turns to Abbi. "Why does anyone come here? It's a horrible, vapid wasteland." The show turns desirable into disgusting and normal into abnormal. They check the tracking app and Abbi's phone now appears to be somewhere in Central Park, so they make their way over to a green field dotted by people lounging on the grass enjoying the summer day. One of them must have Abbi's phone, but who? "I have an idea", Ilana says as she begins to unbutton her crop top shirt.

Abbi: Ilana, are you kidding me? Stop. What are you doing?
Ilana (while unhooking her bra):
No. This park is full of pervs. Get ready, because everybody is gonna whip their phone out and we're gonna find yours. Three. Two. One.

As Ilana begins to dance topless, Abbi tries to draw a crowd: "This is crazy right now. Only in NYC. If I were you, I'd pull my phone out and

162 Transferable Radicalness: Representing Alternative Lifestyles

take a pic." Neither Abbi's shouting nor Ilana's nude dance draws much attention. "Why is no one taking a picture of her?" Abbi wonders. A man relaxing at the park points in another direction: "That girl's been here for hours." The camera pans and we see a topless middle-aged woman twirling hula hoops. That which is 'outrageous' becomes commonplace. No one's head is turned, and people are free to be themselves without shame or ridicule.

The Authentic Status Quo

Our limited belief in alternatives to capitalism and the state is partially a product of the unavailable representations of positive alternatives more generally, such as the alternative lifestyles discussed in this chapter. If we are not presented with alternatives even to lifestyles, how can we blame our imagination for having limited views of alternative economic and political systems? And where alternative representations do exist, they typically work to further separate them from modern normativity, othering these alternatives as unviable, unnatural, or unhealthy. Thus, we are liable to make the jump from ostracizing alternative lifestyles to ostracizing alternative economic and political systems. But as we can see with *Broad City*, there are *some* depictions of alternative lifestyles that do create a positive space for our radical imaginations. These representations could have an important impact on the perception of the lifestyles and their normative counterparts. The representations in *Broad City* can be compared to Ellen DeGeneres outing herself and her character as a lesbian on her sitcom *Ellen* (1994–1998) over 20 years ago. Ellen's revelation came in the fourth season of the show, allowing viewers to fall in love with the character before she exposed them to a sexuality they may have previously seen as unacceptable. One could ask, "If I liked Ellen and then found out she was gay then why should I not accept other people who are gay?" Or "If I'm seeing it on TV, and it's not a bad thing, maybe it's also not a bad thing in real life?" Ellen was not the only positive representation of homosexuality, but she contended with many negative representations at the time.[14]

While these positive representations of 'otherness' can have important outcomes, and while accepting otherness in one field can expand elsewhere, we should ask ourselves how transferable is transferable re-transcoding for our purposes? Specifically, how transferable is re-transcoding in a context where the capitalist system can readily incorporate alternative lifestyles and sexualities into its own operations? The economic system we find ourselves in can quickly treat something once alien as a new norm and we have seen this demonstrated across iconic cultural products for decades. Slavoj Žižek discusses this phenomenon with reference to Italian director Michelangelo Antonioni's *Zabriskie Point* (1970), a film that closely follows in the footsteps

Transferable Radicalness: Representing Alternative Lifestyles **163**

of the hippie movement. Regarding a scene featuring an orgy in the dusty Death Valley desert, Žižek writes:

> It's crucial that Zabriskie Point was made in 1970 when the authentic revolutionary energy of the sixties was already losing its strength. This orgy is somewhere between subversion of the existing social order and already the full aestheticized reincorporation of these allegedly transgressive activities into the hegemonic ideology. Although Antonioni meant this as a kind of transcendence of the existing constraints, we can easily imagine this shot in some publicity campaign.[15]

Here Žižek is saying that these counternormative representations, and their real-life inspirations, can be incorporated into hegemonic ideology because they do not directly challenge the powerful institutions. The direct challenge to these institutions is what Žižek refers to as "authentic", but other kinds of alternatives do not necessarily challenge other oppressive aspects of society. In fact, previously *alternative* lifestyles can be appropriated by the establishment and used for their own ends. So, sex in the desert can go from being a subversive act to an advertising gimmick. More generally, the hippie counternormative lifestyle was refashioned, branded, and commodified. While its commodified versions typically did not absorb all of the more radical features of such a lifestyle, it was able to refashion such a cultural identity into a consumer identity. Burning Man has replaced Woodstock, and the hippie attire is repackaged by major clothing brands. The symbols of peace and love are now incorporated into advertising slogans, their meaning devoid of their political messages and now signifying nothing more than a state-of-mind that is content with the way things are.

Years after the hippie generation, Nirvana tested the limits of the grunge scene's power to stay true to itself while signing a deal with the corporate 'devil' to broadcast its subculture to a wider audience beyond basement venues and backstreets. According to Mark Andresen's *All the Power*, the Nirvana album *Nevermind* marked "an end of one era of mainstream rock and inaugurating another".[16] The album rose to the top of the charts as they tried to maneuver their rebellious band through the thicket of commodification, attempting to evade that corporate 'r' that was attempting to invade them – by turning their band into a brand. They agreed to play live music at MTV Video Music Award and were awarded Best New Artist and Best Alternative Video but trashed the stage during their gig. They agreed to appear on the cover of *Rolling Stone* but lead singer, guitarist, and songwriter Kurt Cobain wore a T-shirt reading "Corporate Magazines Still Suck".

The consistent message of punk and grunge music was one of independence and 'authenticity', appealing to young people who were seeking an identity and lifestyle outside the status quo. This alternative scene did not refer to a

164 Transferable Radicalness: Representing Alternative Lifestyles

particular political project, or even an object of defiance more specific than simply 'the mainstream'. According to Andersen, " 'authenticity' could just as easily lead one to allegiance to the capitalism-loving, individual-exalting theories of Ayn Rand as to Karl Marx".[17] In the end, even this broad vision of 'authenticity' largely translated into torn up designer jeans and the chain retail store Hot Topic. Now anyone, including those who are lost and confused, can consume their way to security, identity, and 'authenticity'.

We can see a similar situation occur in *Broad City*, our key example for positive representation of alternative lifestyles. Although representing an alternative lifestyle, Ilana and Abbi's New York still sells out. In an episode that aired around the time of the 2016 Democratic presidential primaries for the state of New York, Ilana ends up getting an unpaid internship at the Hillary Clinton campaign headquarters. Ilana expresses her ecstatic admiration for the most famous female politician in the country. Throughout the episode Ilana is portrayed as going gaga for Hillary and just as Ilana is about to end her internship for financial reasons, Hillary Clinton (the real Hillary Clinton) shows up. The show quickly turns into an infomercial for her primary. "Secretary Clinton. Madam ... Présidente. She-king. I can't afford to volunteer here full-time, but I still want to get the word out, so I vow to tweet once a week, 'Vote for Hillary. Yas, yas, yas.'" Hillary responds, clearly lacking the acting acumen of the cast, "That would be great. We need to drum up some excitement for the campaign. Do everything that we possibly can." The scene closes with Hillary putting her arms around Ilana and Abbi as they lay their heads on her shoulders.

This obscene political advert for a hawkish Democratic presidential nominee demonstrates the limits of *Broad City*'s alternative lifestyle and sexuality politics. Clinton's primary rival was the consistently progressive and self-styled socialist candidate Bernie Sanders who, although his LGBTQ+ credentials have not been unblemished, supported civil unions for gay couples for nearly 20 years prior and advocated for gay marriage a full four years ahead of Hillary Clinton. By supporting any political candidate, the queer politics of the show negated its potential for a more radical transferring of its alternative transcoding. But by supporting Hillary over Bernie – who had been independent of the Democratic Party for much of his career – the show became fully integrated into and absorbed by the hegemonic political and economic institutions.

Billions (2016–2023), the show about the battle between a district attorney and a hedge fund manager discussed earlier in the book, plays on this same notion very subtly. In season 2 a new character, Taylor, is introduced. Taylor starts out as an intern stock analyst and makes their way up the hedge fund ladder. Taylor is gender non-binary and uses the pronouns 'they', 'theirs', and 'them'. Taylor's character is developed through revealing a history of their support for progressive causes. The prosecutors who are trying to catch the

Transferable Radicalness: Representing Alternative Lifestyles **165**

hedge fund committing corporate crimes think Taylor's progressive streak may make them susceptible to exposing information for the sake of the greater good. But Taylor is no dove and reaffirms their devotion to the company, Ax Capitol, and to the hedge fund manager, Axelrod. Later Axelrod asks Taylor to take over as the manager. The character of Taylor, discussed in the press with much fanfare,[18] was situated as a counternormative person within the context of egregious capitalism by the creators of the show as part of a deepening of the storyline. Devid Levien, one of the creators and executive producers, stated that "Wall Street and hedge funds are some of the slower changing institutions".[19] "We thought it would be great to introduce somebody to Ax Capital who's quite different. Could Ax[elrod] see through this exterior to notice that which is exceptional?", said Brian Koppelman, co-executive producer and co-creator of *Billions*.[20] Taylor epitomizes how radically different lifestyle choices or identities can be usurped of their broader challenges to society's conservativism, reducing its potential to see through such radical lifestyles to see radical political and economic changes.

This is not to say, of course, that radical lifestyle changes and their representations are not important in themselves. In fact, it is crucial that such advances are made, and these characters provide diversity and detract from the negative representations usually attributed to anything counternormative. By adding to the fabric of our social world, perhaps these discourses can lead to interpersonal freedoms and life-changing possibilities. But in relation to imagining the end of capitalism and the state, such representations – even if expanded through more diverse and frequent representations – do not appear to provide substantial space for reimagining the political and economic. As Joseph Heath and Andrew Potter put it in their book *The Rebel Sell: Why the Culture Can't be Jammed*, "For generations now, countercultural rebels have been pumping out 'subversive' music, 'subversive' art, 'subversive' literature, 'subversive' clothing .... So much subversion, and yet the system seems to tolerate it quite well".[21]

Claims of being subversive, anti-racist, pro-LGBTQ+, environmentally friendly, etc. ... can simply turn into whitewashing, pinkwashing, greenwashing, etc. They cover over the bloodstained walls of their castles with a veneer of color that tricks the public into accepting the justified supremacy of the sultan. The remake of *Aladdin* (2019) is a good example of purplewashing because it makes appeals to liberal feminism by giving the female lead a much stronger voice than in the original. However, it happens to be a voice of a princess who in the end rules over the land and its people without even a wink to the unwarranted powers of divine rule that people have struggled and died to destroy and replace with (representative) democracy – betraying even its own liberal message.[22]

Just as Taylor provides a queer face to diversify an exploitative economic institution, and *Broad City* is used to endorse a hawkish political future,

166 Transferable Radicalness: Representing Alternative Lifestyles

their forward-thinking and groundbreaking predecessor provides an example of how radical steps forward regarding identity, just like lifestyles, can be quickly incorporated into the status quo. Ellen DeGeneres, an important cultural icon of gay rights, invited (war criminal) George W. Bush on to her variety talk show *The Ellen DeGeneres Show* (2003-2022) in 2017. The appearance was to promote his new book and there was no sign of displeasure at having him on the show – and no real mention of his political career. Instead, Ellen discussed how she loves his whole family, including his dad (another war criminal) and said how the media was tough on the W. Bush presidency. (Yes, the same presidency that lied about weapons of mass destruction in Iraq, a story that the media promoted and which subsequently led to a quagmire and over 600,000 deaths,[23] was being treated too harshly by the media, apparently.) This budding friendship resurfaced in 2019 when the two were spotted attending a Dallas Cowboys game. Ellen's response to the flak was to claim kindness toward others, even if they disagreed politically.[24] Although once suppressed by the political system, now that she has been fully incorporated and welcomed into the elite circle, the wider critique fades.

A Beamer, a Necklace, or Freedom?

The films and TV shows discussed above demonstrate how counternormative identities and alternative lifestyles can be incorporated into the capitalist ideological structures without losing their essence. These alternatives can become new 'products' for consumers to buy. They did it with Ellen, it did it with *Broad City*, it did it with punk, grunge, and hippies. As Fredric Jameson explained, they also did it with art.

> [T]he masterpieces of the most recent schools of American painting are now sought to embellish the splendid new structures of the great insurance companies and multinational banks (themselves the work of the most talented and 'advanced' modern architects), are but the external symptoms of a situation in which a once scandalous 'perceptual art' has found a social and economic function in supplying the styling changes necessary to the societe de consommation of the present.[25]

But while these temporary challenges to the system become incorporated, they also get visibility, acceptance, and at times even desirability. We can see that at the very basic level of product placements. When his own government suspects him of treason during a mission to stop terrorists from setting off nuclear bombs in *Mission: Impossible – Fallout* (2018), Ethan Hunt needs a capitalist-sponsored partner. In steps BMW and a series of vehicles, new and old, that Hunt uses to save the day. In return for paying to have eight minutes of screen time chasing down baddies, BMW brought in $11 million, according to one source.[26] People were 'converted' to buying BMW cars. However, product placement isn't always so successful, as Lexus can attest. When they paid for a concept car for the futuristic *Minority Report* (2022) to be Lexus branded, they did not get much return on investment despite its prominent role in the film. Arguably, this is because you couldn't actually buy the model being advertised. Though it may have not helped its brand, what Lexus did help produce is a vision of what the future should look like, just as reference to flying cars was an idea that was fueled by representations of such futuristic fantasies.

The goal of product placement is to answer a question for the viewer: Would you rather have a Lexus or a BMW? But if we had depictions of futures that got rid of state and capitalism and replace them with positive alternatives, the placement of these radical representations would pose a different question: "you would rather have a Lexus or justice? This is precisely the question posed by the radical, anti-capitalist duo Dead Prez in their hit "Hip Hop" in which they rap about the abolition of the police and taking over city hall. But even that song has been integrated into the consumer capitalist system, featured, rather ironically, on a TV commercial for Volkswagen. The song is used to sex-up a compact family SUV to the viewer. Of course, the car commercial fails to broadcast the radical anti-capitalist lyrics, but the song is there selling the slogan "Cool. Calm. Connected".

Capitalism can take what it wants and spit out the rest. It will incorporate diversity, queer identity, and alternative lifestyles as long as, ultimately, capitalism and the state are preserved. But even if popular culture under capitalism isn't (typically) willing to entertain subversive ideas, it still has the potential to build a radical imaginary. Sometimes subversive ideas provide a premium for selling products. Grunge started off as an underground scene but reached the point of mass consumption. Those bands whose content are overtly political, as Andersen states, have the potential to "bring radical ideas into the mainstream".[27] In this case radical bands can start fitting their radical content into fashionable forms. Punk, hip hop, and pop all have their examples. Capitalism can cut a profit selling Che Guevara T-shirts made in sweatshops, but it means Che's legacy and his politics will live on.[28]

What's the difference between a T-shirt of Che and a blank T-shirt? What's the difference between a Dead Prez song and an Eminem song? While both are exploitative and profitable for capitalism, and the same in form, the difference is content. Dead Prez's "Hell Yeah" finds loopholes to escape poverty, stealing from your employer who "got me flippin' burgers with no power, can't even buy one off what I make in an hour". Sometimes we have to accept the form, and the exploitation, as a means to an end: the spread of ideological content. This is the loophole and this very book is a case in point. If people are transformed by the content, they may come to see an alternative to the form in which the content arrived. If the content represents

168 Transferable Radicalness: Representing Alternative Lifestyles

the economic and political alternative, then it'll be easier to imagine the end of capitalism and the state.

While the Dead Prez song talks about the problems of capitalism, the music video shows them getting beaten up by police before, all of a sudden, they wake up and are on an African beach, leading a life of leisure and safety – a utopian dream that imagines away colonialism. Another radical dream is represented in the famous film *Titanic* (1997). Rose is an old woman and the only living survivor of the disaster. She's brought on board a ship to tell the crew about the story of a coveted necklace with a rare Heart of the Ocean diamond that they are in search of. Rose was engaged to a wealthy man who she did not love but had to marry to maintain her wealthy status. The necklace was an engagement present presumed to be left somewhere among the rubble at the bottom of the ocean but is never found. When the crew give up their search at the end of the film, Rose goes to the edge of the ship and reveals that she had kept the necklace all along, a symbol not of her love for her fiancé, but for that which wealth could not buy. On her voyage, Rose met a working-class man, Jack, with whom she fell in love. That experience changed her life and made her realize the problems class differences place in front of people searching for something more to life. Now in her old age she throws the necklace to the bottom of the ocean, and we cut to her lying in bed in her room sleeping, perhaps dreaming for the very last time. In her dream she is once again on board the *Titanic* surrounded by the other passengers as she makes her way up a beautiful staircase for the first-class passengers. Something is different in this dream however, because all the passengers are now mixed. No longer are the poor contained in their lackluster lower decks but share the same privileges as the other passengers. A ship that represented a class hierarchy, and the damage that the class system did – even to those elites – is reimagined in the final scene as a classless utopia. For Rose, as presaged by Engels' concept of sex-love, the class suicide represented by the throwing away of the necklace actually meant a freedom to marry and live for love, not for social status.

This big budget picture presents us with a brief glimpse of a classless society and poses a question about the importance of our own capitalistic values. Just like seeing a BMW star in a film makes us want to buy one, or seeing a futuristic Lexus makes us think that is what the future could look like, seeing alternatives, utopian images, can help us 'buy in' to a radical future and a revolutionary present. So Dead Prez ask us rhetorically, "You would rather have a Lexus or justice? A dream or some substance? A beamer, a necklace, or freedom?"[29]

Notes

1   Ong-Tae-Hae 2012, p. 232.
2   Quoted in Hall 1995, p. 300.

Transferable Radicalness: Representing Alternative Lifestyles **169**

3 Quoted in Hall 1995, pp. 300, 306, 308.

4 Also see the analysis of *Knives Out* (2019) in Nulman 2021.

5 This all seems a particularly ironic reading given that the film's producer, Harvey Weinstein, was embroiled in allegations of sexual harassment and rape just a month after the release of *Tulip Fever*.

6 For a look at the use of displacement within the context of reading films, see Wayne (2020, p. 140).

7 The role, which Tomlin was well cast for, was essentially reprised by Tomlin in *Grandma* (2015), a film that fits the reformable critique.

8 An economic alternative is presented in the show *Alex, Inc.* (season 1; 2018) with similar effect. Alex, a progressive guy, is trying to set up his new small business as anything but the typical boss. His two employees are given decision-making power and, although it is unstructured, Alex institutes a policy of workplace democracy. Within the very same episode the show depicts this policy as disastrous as the two workers disagree with each other and Alex is forced to reassert his decision-making powers as the boss. Also see *The Anarchist Cookbook* (2002).

9 In *Forrest Gump* (1994), the desire for an alternative lifestyle (and left-wing politics) is a by-product of something problematic. The film is largely about the title character, an intellectually disabled person whose kind-heartedness (and sometimes ignorance) leads him on a wild adventure that sees him meeting with celebrities and presidents and accidently influencing major world events. An important subplot to these adventures is his love for his childhood sweetheart Jenny. In the film Jenny is shown at different points in her life as sexually transgressive, a peace activist, a Black Panther supporter, and a hippie – always living an alternative lifestyle. We also learn that as a child Jenny was abused by her father and became psychologically damaged. This abuse, the movie shows, leads her to explore alternatives. Along with Jenny being a left-wing activist she is depicted as a heroin user and a stripper who eventually contracts AIDS, presumably from all the free love and drugs she has enjoyed. Her 'deviance', something depicted as wholly undesirable, was a product of abuse.

10 Malcolm Nicoll 2016; Jim Dandy 2018; Marty _ 2016; Mitch Morrison 2014; castro sherwood 2017; strontiumXnitrate 2015; ERIC GRANBERG 2018; Patrick EH 2018. Some of the worst comments including references to 'gender terrorists' and Auschwitz were not included.

11 Alston, 2012; Humphrey 2011. Others also make similar points. Grant McCracken, writing for the *Harvard Business Review*, asks: "[Will] Portland see the humor of *Portlandia*? The Women & Women First skit suggests not. The proprietors have no sense of humor. (And this is too often true of cultural innovators. They gorge themselves on moral certitude and righteous indignation.)" (McCracken 2011).

12 Mills 2000, pp. 8–9.

13 E.g., Hakala 2015; Kutner 2015.

14 The same could be said also of the representation of transgender people in films like *The Crying Game* (1992) or *Dallas Buyers Club* (2013), which had to challenge depictions of trans people as mentally ill or vomit-inducing (e.g., *The Silence of the Lambs* (1991), *Dressed to Kill* (1980), *Ace Ventura: Pet Detective* (1995), *Naked Gun 33⅓: The Final Insult* (1994)).

15 *The Pervert's Guide to Ideology* (2012).

16 Andersen 2004, p. 40.

170 Transferable Radicalness: Representing Alternative Lifestyles

17 Andersen 2004, p. 37.
18 E.g., Hibberd 2017.
19 Showtime n.d.
20 Showtime n.d.
21 Heath and Potter 2005, p. 35.
22 Ironically, the man she marries is a common thief who has to 'steal to eat' but the system that produces his and others' predicament is never questioned.
23 Burnham et al. 2006.
24 While many celebrities supported her position, Mark Ruffalo did not accept this excuse, tweeting:

> "Sorry, until George W. Bush is brought to justice for the crimes of the Iraq War, (including American-lead torture, Iraqi deaths & displacement, and the deep scars—emotional & otherwise—inflicted on our military that served his folly), we can't even begin to talk about kindness."

25 Jameson 1995, p. 209. Along with Schoenberg's pupils who went off to write scores for Hollywood films, the rest of the 'creative class' had been incorporated into the system. Crucially, they are incorporated without bringing with them the radical break from the status quo that, according to Theodor Adorno, creativity was meant to foster.
26 Concave 2019.
27 Andersen 2004, p. 45.
28 To spread his political message the anarchist anti-art artist and poet Ben Morea effectively adapted his work to fit today's popular form of the written word: the tweet. This capitalist-driven form of communication still provides a space for radical, anti-capitalist content. Even with a limit of 140 characters, Morea can still send a provocative political message.
29 Dead Prez 2000.

References

Alston, Joshua (2012) 'Look Out, Liberals: *Portlandia* Returns for a Second Season', *The Guardian*, Jan. 6, https://www.theguardian.com/tv-and-radio/tvandradioblog/2012/jan/06/portlandia-liberals-second-season-tv.
Andersen, Mark (2004) *All the Power: Revolution without Illusion*, Chicago: Punk Planet Books.
Burnham, Gilbert, Lafta, Riyadh, Doocy, Shannon, and Roberts, Les (2006) 'Mortality after the 2003 Invasion of Iraq: A Cross-Sectional Cluster Sample Survey', *The Lancet*, 368(9545): 1421–1428.
'castro sherwood' (2017) Re: *Portlandia LGBTQ Community* [Video file], https://www.youtube.com/watch?v=c8O7FICOm4c.
Concave (2019) 'Top 10 Brands in 2018 Movies – Product Placement', http://concavebt.com/top-10-brands-2018-movies-product-placement.
Dead Prez (2000) 'Hip Hop'. *On Let's Get Free*. [Audio file].
'ERIC GRANBERG' (2018) Re: *Portlandia – Feminist Bookstore's Intern* [Video file], https://www.youtube.com/watch?v=wmEXWRCDTGE.
Hakala, Kate (2015) 'Thank You, "Broad City," for Finally Proving How Unnecessary Sexual Labels Are', *Mic*, March 13, https://www.mic.com/articles/112734/thank-you-broad-city-for-finally-proving-how-unnecessary-sexual-labels-are#.qrMrvX5g7.

Hall, Stuart (1995) 'The West and the Rest: Discourse and Power', in Stuart Hall and Bram Gieben (eds.), *Formations of Modernity* (pp. 275–320), Cambridge: Polity Press.

Heath, Joseph, and Potter, Andrew (2005) *The Rebel Sell: Why the Culture Can't be Jammed*, Chichester: Capstone.

Hibberd, James (2017) 'TV's First Gender Non-Binary Character Introduced in Billions Premiere', *Entertainment Weekly*, Feb. 19, https://ew.com/tv/2017/02/19/billions-non-binary-asia-kate-dillon.

Humphrey, William Steven (2011) 'The Paradox of *Portlandia*', *Portland Mercury*, Jan. 20, https://www.portlandmercury.com/portland/the-paradox-of-portlandia/Content?oid=3273589.

Jameson, Fredric (1995) 'Reflections in Conclusion', in Ernst Bloch, Georg Lukacs, Bertolt Brecht, Walter Benjamin, and Theodor Adorno (eds.), *Aesthetics and Politics* (pp. 196–213), London: Verso.

'Jim Dandy' (2018) Re: *Portlandia – Season 3 – Candace's Son Visits the Feminist Bookstore* [Video file]. https://www.youtube.com/watch?v=e9r2o5ZnSHo.

Kutner, Jenny (2015) '"I Have Sex with People Different from Me": On "Broad City," Ilana's Sexuality Continues to Defy Neat Labels', *Salon*, Mar. 12, https://www.salon.com/2015/03/12/i_have_sex_with_people_different_from_me_on_broad_city_ilanas_sexuality_continues_to_defy_neat_labels.

'Malcolm Nicoll' (2016) Re: *Portlandia – Toni and Candace – ep.2* [Video file], https://www.youtube.com/watch?v=5ch1kXp3mQA.

'Marty _' (2018) Re: *Portlandia – Season 3 – Candace's Son Visits the Feminist Bookstore* [Video file]. https://www.youtube.com/watch?v=e9r2o5ZnSHo.

McCracken, Grant (2011) 'The Genius of *Portlandia*', *Harvard Business Review*, Jan. 27, https://hbr.org/2011/01/the-genius-of-portlandia.

Mills, C. Wright 2000. *The Sociological Imagination* (pp. 8–9). Oxford: Oxford University Press.

'Mitch Morrison' (2018) Re: *Portlandia – Season 3 – Candace's Son Visits the Feminist Bookstore* [Video file], https://www.youtube.com/watch?v=e9r2o5ZnSHo.

Nulman, Eugene (2021) *Coronavirus Capitalism Goes to the Cinema*, Abingdon: Routledge.

Ong-Tae-Hae (2018) 'Selections from *The Chinaman Abroad: An Account of the Malayan Archipelago, Particularly of Java*', in Leonard Blussé and Nie Dening (eds.), *The Chinese Annals of Batavia, the Kai Ba Lidai Shiji and Other Stories (1610–1795)* (pp. 229–237), Leiden: Brill.

'Patrick EH' (2018) Re: *Portlandia – Feminist Bookstore's Intern* [Video file], https://www.youtube.com/watch?v=wmEXWRCDTGE.

Showtime (n.d.) 'Billions: Meet Taylor' [Video file], https://www.sho.com/video/53199/billions-meet-taylor.

'strontiumXnitrate' (2015) Re: *Portlandia LGBTQ Community* [Video file], https://www.youtube.com/watch?v=c8O7FICOm4c.

Wayne, Mike (2020) *Marx Goes to the Movies*, Abingdon: Routledge.

8

RADICAL RESISTANCE IN
THE LEGO MOVIE

The Building Blocks of Utopia

> It is proven that amongst them the land belongs to everybody, just as does the sun or the water. They know no difference between meum and tuum, that source of all evils. It requires so little to satisfy them, that in that vast region there is always more land to cultivate than is needed. It is indeed a golden age, neither ditches, nor hedges, nor walls to enclose their domains; they live in gardens open to all, without laws and without judges; their conduct is naturally equitable, and whoever injures his neighbor is considered a criminal and an outlaw.[1]

This quotation comes from Peter Martyr d'Anghera who was discussed in the previous chapter. Reading it now, we are invited to an early representation of a utopia, a civilization without private property or state authority. But Martyr's interpretation was different, shrouded by his own ideological mask. He goes on to discuss how an 80-year-old native of that land first encountered Christopher Columbus, wanting to ascertain the explorer's intentions.

> What occasioned him great surprise was to learn that a man like Columbus recognized the authority of a sovereign; but his astonishment still further increased when the interpreter explained to him how powerful were the kings and how wealthy, and all about the Spanish nation, the manner of fighting, and how great were the cities and how strong the fortresses. In great dejection the man, together with his wife and sons, threw themselves at the feet of Columbus, with their eyes full of tears, repeatedly asking if the country which produced such men and in such numbers was not indeed heaven.[2]

DOI: 10.4324/9781003514916-9

We do not know how truthful these accounts are, but we can see how Martyr approached his understanding of the indigenous from a worldview that he unconsciously possessed. For Martyr there was a progression from the "state of nature" to being "civilized", something that required the presence of the European colonizers. It is for this reason that the great cities and strong fortresses ruled over by kings could be interpreted as heavenly, rather than hellish, and the alternative as something that could only exist among those not *yet* civilized. In a way, this ideology forces Martyr to represent these encounters as he does. When the colonizers kill, Martyr suggests, they only kill the most uncivilized; when they take land, they do so with the elders' consent because these elders are closer to a state of civilization.[3]

Utopia isn't 'present', it must be read and interpreted as such. The benefit of most popular cultural texts is that they often represent their worlds in such a way that the audience is aware of the author's proposed interpretation. We know that the future world of militarized robots and scattered human soldiers depicted in *The Terminator* (1984) is a dystopia, but sometimes even utopias are seen as dystopian. "Few would claim that freedom leads to slavery or that frigid water will boil" writes cultural historian Russell Jacoby, "but many do argue that utopia leads to dystopia—or that little distinguishes the two in the first place".[4] Thus, utopian representations have disappeared, used only as an ideological mask within dystopias such as *Demolition Man* (1993), *Pleasantville* (1998), and *The Giver* (2014).

With regard to literary fiction, for Fredric Jameson utopias serve a function in certain historical contexts.[5] Historically, he argues, utopias become prominent and popular in "transitional periods" or "pause[s] in the all-encompassing forward momentum of differentiation which will sweep [enclaves of utopian mental space] away altogether".[6] Arguably, we are in such a moment – where communism and revolution appear discredited and capitalist markets are spreading far and wide, particularly since the fall of the Soviet Union. In such a historical space, the only alternative to no alternative is utopia.[7] That is, we are in a moment where no forward progress seems actionable and therefore the only hope that can be maintained is purely imaginary – "a utopian imagination". However, in our analysis so far, utopia representations have been almost entirely absent. Instead, as sociologist Krishan Kumar says and Jameson acknowledges, fantasy has replaced science fiction as the genre of imagination and that fantasy leans toward nostalgia – a backward rather than forward looking genre.[8] Instead, Kumar argues, "imagining a better or more perfect future" has been replaced by the "imagination of disaster" which "fares infinitely better, and this at least means that utopia's cousin – or alter ego – the dystopia, continues to flourish".[9] While thus far we have few examples of screen media texts that have representations of utopia, we certainly have many examples of

174 Radical Resistance in *The Lego Movie*: Building Blocks of Utopia

dystopias – from *The Hunger Games* series (2012–2015) to *Children of Men* (2006) and from *Wall-E* (2008) to the original *Matrix* trilogy (1999–2003).[10]

Jacoby's book, *Picture Imperfect: Utopian Thought for an Anti-Utopian Age*, argues that utopias became disfavored in our culture for at least three reasons. The first is in direct opposition to Jameson's argument regarding the transitional periods in which utopias flourish. Jacoby writes that the collapse of communist states negatively impacted utopian writing because "[t]o many observers, Soviet Marxism and its knockoffs symbolized the utopian project. The failure of Soviet communism entailed the end of utopia".[11] The second reason for the demise of utopia, according to Jacoby, is that the notions of utopianism became intertwined with notions of totalitarianism. Thus, authors such as Isaiah Berlin, Karl Popper, and Hannah Arendt "have thrown communism, Nazism, and utopia into one tub", arguing they all lead to the same conclusions of totalitarian rule and widespread bloodshed.[12] The catastrophic outcomes of the communist countries mentioned previously were a result of the utopia vision embedded in those grand projects. A utopian grand project leading to a dystopian end of history is exactly the challenge Emmet and his friends face in *The Lego Movie* (2014), the centerpiece of this chapter.

Nubicuculia

The intertwining of utopian and dystopia in the film *The Lego Movie* begins with the representation of President Business, President of the LEGO world of Bricksburg *and* the head of the Octan Corporation which, as stated in the film, owns "music, dairy products, coffee, TV shows, surveillance systems, all history books, voting machines", and a construction company.[13] Although he seems nice, always greeting his employees and telling everyone that he loves them, President Business has a dark side that few know. Behind closed doors President Business is fitted with retractable long legs, a light-up suit, and a helmet that shoots flames – turning him into Lord Business bear in mind that essentially all the characters in the film are meant to be made of LEGO blocks). Lord Business, a character who wonderfully describes the interconnection between state and capital, rules over nearly the entire LEGO universe and has a secret plan to permanently freeze everything in its perfect place. How does he plan on doing this? Aside from his vast wealth, he derives power from his collection of 'relics', mythical objects in the LEGO universe which are actually everyday human objects such as an X-Acto blade, a cotton swab, and nail polish remover. The most powerful relic is called the Kragle – an opened tube of Krazy Glue with the "zy" and "u" covered over in paint. With this relic, Lord Business plans to glue every LEGO piece in the universe in place, making it by-the-(instruction)-book and therefore perfect in his eyes – a permanent hegemonic order.

Thus we can see how Lord Business's utopia is a dystopia for all other LEGO characters. He wants to create a precisely prescribed order, imposed on everyone else, as a means of obtaining 'perfection'. This corresponds to what Jacoby argued was popularly understood as the result of 'blueprint utopias' in the twentieth century. For Jacoby, blueprint utopias are detailed visions which often prescribe a future in the finest detail, leaving little space for human freedom within those spaces. The regimentation within those blueprint utopias has become interpreted as necessitating totalitarianism, and certainly we see this as being the case in *The Lego Movie*. The audience sees Lord Business's plans and hears him talk of blueprints. He uses instruction manuals to create the perfect societies he would like to freeze. The vision, from our perspective, is purely maniacal and totalitarian.

However, Jacoby insists that the utopias of fiction did not advocate totalitarianism. He gives Aristophanes' *The Birds* as an example. In the play, two men who are fed up with Athens have left looking for a better place to live. They eventually find the Hoopoe, formerly the mythological Tereus who was changed into a bird by the Olympian Gods. The two men convince the Hoopoe that the birds should create their own city in the sky which they call Nubicuculia, or literally "Cloud Cuckoo Land", a utopian place – which works as a perfect setting to critique Greek society at the time.

> Aristophanes paints Cloud-cuckoo-land in broad strokes. As the classicist Victor Ehrenberg writes, the wandering Athenians wish to establish a place where 'food and love' reign supreme. To this end, they reject numerous new arrivals who want to join but who would strangle the new utopia with the old terrestrial problems .... While the utopianism in The Birds remains vague, it would be difficult to construe it as implicitly or explicitly advocating violence—or even 'totalitarian' control. Indeed, one hopeful settler is a mathematician, who arrives with a plan 'to subdivide the air into square acres.' He is advised to depart and 'subdivide somewhere else."[14]

Although President Business's designs on the future are dystopian, *The Lego Movie* does present us with a truly utopian vision that is worth exploring in more detail. We are introduced to this utopia as a secret place where characters known as MasterBuilders are due to meet and come up with a way to defeat Lord Business before he executes his plan. MasterBuilders are characters of the LEGO universe who have the ability to quickly build different things from various LEGO pieces that make up everything in their world. Given their power and disposition to change things into essentially whatever they want, they represent a direct threat to Lord Business's plans. Consequently, Lord Business hires a police force (the Super Secret Police) led by Bad Cop who does his best to hunt down, capture, torture, and imprison the

176 Radical Resistance in *The Lego Movie*: Building Blocks of Utopia

MasterBuilders[15] who have all gone into hiding. Lord Business's apocalyptic plans are imminent so the MasterBuilders come together in their preferred location, a dog-shaped dome in a secret place that can only be reached by driving up a rainbow. This secret realm is called Cloud Cuckoo Land.

Cloud Cuckoo Land is the only place that is overtly outside the control of the state and capital. Our team of LEGO heroes enter the land, presented in a heavenly aura, and, when the cloud doors open, we see a rainbow-colored light blazing through the entrance, accompanied by dance music. There's an eclectic combination of LEGO characters, pulsating lights on the wall, and a white dance floor where LEGO Dracula is grooving with LEGO Cleopatra. Everyone is living a colorful, carefree life in a world without rules and where everyone is welcome. The film's central protagonist is Emmet, an ordinary construction worker from Bricksburg who, though not a MasterBuilder, is taken to Cloud Cuckoo Land because he discovered a relic, the Piece of Resistance (actually the cap to the Krazy Glue). Emmet is unfamiliar with this world of MasterBuilders and has always followed the rules, so he is visibly bewildered by the happy anarchy he sees in Cloud Cuckoo Land. It doesn't make sense to Emmet because it's not supposed to make sense in the logic of the fixed-LEGO worlds like Bricksburg, and the world Bricksburg reflects - our own.

Emmet is introduced to Cloud Cuckoo Land by Princess Unikitty, a MasterBuilder who is half kitten, half unicorn, and all princess:

Emmet:	I'm just gonna come right out. I have no idea what's going on ... or what this place is at all. ... there's no signs or anything. How does anyone know what not to do?
Princess Unikitty:	Here in Cloud Cuckoo Land there are no rules. There's no government. No babysitters. No bedtimes. No frowny faces. No bushy mustaches. And no negativity of any kind.

Here we can see what a utopia may look like, although one outside the human realm. However, even here the utopia is critiqued. Like classic utopian literature, Cloud Cuckoo Land in *The Lego Movie* serves as a representation of perfection, a critique of society, and a satire of its own impossibility. Here, Emmet's love interest and MasterBuilder WyldStyle steps in: "You just said the word 'no' like a thousand times." Princess Unikitty retorts but only to further this utopia's contradictions: "And there's also no consistency .... Any idea is a good idea ... except the not happy ones. Those you push down deep inside where you'll never, ever, ever, ever, find them." Despite the contradictions, the utopia presented within *The Lego Movie* still poses an existential threat to the wishes of Lord Business. It is the land which shouldn't be preserved because 'perfection' is not possible in a land meant to be anarchic. So, Lord Business's police force is sent to destroy Cloud Cuckoo Land. The cops secretly plant a tracking device on Emmet and when he reaches the secret destination the police come in with LEGO guns blazing. In the ensuing chaos most of the MasterBuilders are either destroyed or arrested and Cloud Cuckoo Land, like the end of utopian thought itself, burns and eventually crumbles into the ocean.

Machines without Imagination

Jacoby posits that the third and last reason for the end of utopia is the "Western imagination".[16] Jacoby argues that "imagination nourishes utopianism",[17] something that Yevgeny Zamyatin understood when he wrote the science fiction classic, *We*.[18] The book tells the story of a state striving to create perfect people who would have the "pendulum-precision" of machines. Although people are "nurtured from earliest infancy on the Taylor system", humans are one element short of the perfection of machines: "machines have no imagination". This leads the state to discover a way of removing the part of the brain responsible for imagination so they can cure people of this "sickness".[19]

Thus, Jacoby poses a question: "If imagination sustains utopian thinking, what sustains imagination?" Jacoby undertakes a brief sociological analysis in his search for an answer. "Imagination probably depends on childhood—and conversely, childhood depends on imagination", noting that this was accepted as true by the romantics such as Rousseau and Wordsworth "who idolized the child as a creature of imagination and spontaneity".[20] Looking at the historical changes in childhood, Jacoby finds that the institutions of forced schooling, the improvements in healthcare that led to lower child mortality rates and subsequently smaller family sizes, and the increase of mass production and consumer culture all had a role in shaping modern childhood.

> A "fall of childhood" literature has emerged that posits a thinning of the emotional and psychic space that enveloped the growing child. A protective zone—always delicate—succumbs to marketing forces. "The modern make-up of society," wrote Max Horkheimer in the 1940s, "sees to it that the utopian dreams of childhood are cut short in earliest youth."[21]

He goes on to add, quoting the scholar David Buckingham, "Not only have merchandisers targeted children, but due to increased affluence and anxiety about external dangers, 'the principal location of children's leisure has moved from public spaces (such as the street) to private spaces (the bedroom).'" Jacoby believes that the lack of unstructured playtime has had a large impact on our imaginations. Not only are the toys that children play with replacing their own imaginative play with objects made by adults,[22] but the objects themselves contain ideological content. "New playthings embodied dreams of growing up fast to a glamorous world of consumption or a heroic realm of power and control".[23]

> If unstructured childhood sustains imagination, and imagination sustains utopian thinking, then the eclipse of the first entails the weakening of the last—utopian thinking …. [I]t seems likely that the colonization of children's space and time undermines an unfettered imagination. Children have more to do, more done for them, and less inclination—and perhaps fewer resources—for utopian dreaming.[24]

Jacoby's argument appears to have been mirrored by the co-authors and directors of *The Lego Movie*, Phil Lord and Chris Miller, when, during a presentation, they asked the audience, "What happens between the age of 7 and 17?".

> You ask a bunch of year two students how many of you sing and dance and everybody raises their hand. And you ask anybody 17 and older and very few people, some drama geeks, will raise their hand …. Is it that … you learn how to be embarrassed …?
>
> You start to understand the social implications of telling a joke that doesn't land or having an idea that other people don't like. And the other thing that happens is you start to learn about 'the classics'. You start to learn about masterpieces, and you go from thinking that anyone can be creative to thinking that … creative people have to … be really good at what they do.[25]

This was the major question Phil Lord and Chris Miller asked themselves when making *The Lego Movie*. And this fascination with imagination and the space for creativity become clear focal points in the narrative of the film.

The narrative of LEGO characters such as Emmet and the MasterBuilders trying to stop Lord Business's plans to glue the universe into perfect permanence is actually an allegory within the film for the 'real world' relationship between a boy, Finn, who wants to play creatively and use his imagination, and his father who wants to maintain order. We are introduced to these 'real-world' characters toward the end of the film. Our LEGO protagonist Emmet is captured by Lord Business who is on his way to release the Kragle and glue every LEGO piece where it belongs with the help of robots, known as Micromanagers, designed to ensure perfection. Since this frozen dystopia is near completion Lord Business decides to electrocute the MasterBuilders and Emmet using another relic, a battery. The battery is set on a timer and just in the nick of time, Emmet decides to sacrifice himself in

Radical Resistance in *The Lego Movie*: Building Blocks of Utopia **179**

order to save the MasterBuilders by jumping out of the window of the Octan building, taking the battery with him.

Emmet believes this to be a leap to his death as outside the Octan building is the "Infinite Abyss of Nothingness". However, the abyss turns out to be a portal into the live-action world. At this point we get introduced to Finn (Jadon Sand) who is playing with LEGO and imagining this whole story of the MasterBuilders in the basement where his father has built a variety of perfectly structured LEGO worlds that he plans to glue together so that Finn will not be able to play freely and destroy what Finn's father sees as a "highly sophisticated interlocking brick system" made for adult hobbyists. In the end, Emmet convinces Lord Business – as a reflection of Finn convincing his father – that playing in an unstructured way is more desirable than building the kind of perfection that requires an instruction manual. Within what will be referred to as the 'internal allegory', the MasterBuilders represent the free and imaginative subject. Thus, the film clearly speaks to the importance of allowing our imaginations to wander in play – a criterion which Jacoby argues is essential for the development of a radical imaginary.

Citing other scholars, Jacoby argues that children are increasingly spending more time in front of televisions and computers and billions of dollars are being spent advertising aimed at them. Outside the hours of media consumption and playing with structured toys under constant supervision, children have little time for imagination. Jacoby's argument raises an important point for us to consider: if childhood is an important moment for the development of imagination, then time children spend watching films and television, regardless of its ideological content, is not ideal if it detracts from vital creative time.

Well-Ordered Houses and Ticking Atomic Clocks

For the very reason that artistic work, particularly film and television, can "giveth a perfect picture" – returning to the words of Sidney – they restrict space for imaginative thinking, at least within the time of their direct consumption. Perhaps this is one reason why Jacoby's book referenced above is entitled *Picture Imperfect*. Rather than producing an over-structured space, time, and text Jacoby argues for a period of unencumbered freedom to be imaginative, without controlling the process and thus not knowing what the results may be. He compares this to the philosopher Gershom Scholem's "anarchic breeze".

> The great scholar of Jewish mysticism, Gershom Scholem, once wrote that Jewish messianism can be described 'as a kind of anarchic breeze.' He alludes to the 'profound truth' that 'a well-ordered house is a dangerous thing.' In that house, 'a window is open through which the winds blow in, and it is not quite certain just what they bring in with them'.[26]

180 Radical Resistance in *The Lego Movie*: Building Blocks of Utopia

But this anarchic breeze, and the book's title, also refer to something else in Jacoby's opinion: the essay's defense of iconoclastic utopias. Unlike blueprint utopias, iconoclastic utopias are "imageless" but "laced with passion and spirit" that "did not entail a puritanical severity";[27] they do not fall prey to the same problems of the blueprint utopias, according to Jacoby. "Inevitably, history eclipses or ridicules the most daring plans; it makes them appear either too banal or too idiosyncratic".[28] To illustrate iconoclastic utopianism, Jacoby quotes Heinrich Heine:

> We are fighting not for the human rights of the people, but for the divine rights of mankind. In this and in many other things we differ from the men of the Revolution. We do not want to be sansculottes, nor simple citizens, nor venal presidents; we want to found a democracy of gods, equal in majesty, in sanctity, and in bliss.[29]

But such a spirit of utopia may have made more sense in a time before dystopia became central to our thinking. The word 'dystopia' was coined by John Stuart Mill but became popularized – and used to describe such works of fiction as Orwell's *1984* and Huxley's *Brave New World* – after its use by J. Max Patrick in *The Quest for Utopia: An Anthology of Imaginary Societies* in 1952.[30] If the sixteenth century gave us the term 'utopia' and the twentieth century gave us 'dystopia' then perhaps it is the widespread realization of manmade apocalypse that brought an end to utopian thinking? If so, how do we couple this with the lack of *embodied* recognition of the potential extinction of mankind as a species?[31] Because if we had such recognition, perhaps it would lead to rebellion or radical change?

In recent times Noam Chomsky has repeatedly emphasized that life as we know it is currently being threatened like never before. Two major issues haunt our very existence as a species: climate change and nuclear war. At the time of writing, the Science and Security Board of the *Bulletin of the Atomic Scientists* has placed the Doomsday Clock at 90 seconds to midnight (where midnight corresponds to the end of the world). The clock has never been closer to midnight than it is now. Even in 1953, when the Soviet Union achieved a thermonuclear explosion which meant that the two superpowers at that time had the means of mutual annihilation, the clock was 2 minutes to midnight.[32] According to the *Bulletin of the Atomic Scientists*, we are now closer to apocalypse than we were then. And yet, look outside. No one seems too bothered. We don't see anyone wearing dog tags so they can be identified after a disaster like American schoolchildren did in the 1950s,[33] nor widespread public concern about nuclear weapons despite the box office success of *Oppenheimer* (2023), a movie that explicitly raised concerns about nuclear weapons. Even climate change fails to elicit much concern relative to other issues.[34] Even though we are hurling the world into annihilation, we continue living our lives – with a smile. Why? Chomsky has an explanation:

> In the contemporary United States there has been an increasing growth in the power of the ideology of short-term gains, whatever the consequences. The US business classes have been admirably forthright in announcing publicly their intention of running huge propaganda campaigns to convince the public to ignore the ongoing destruction of the environment, by now quite hard to miss even for the most blind.[35]

Many other countries could be described the same way. Such is also the world in *The Lego Movie*. The film begins with Emmet following all the standard operating procedures of the instruction manual. Like everyone else that morning, he wakes up, breaths in and out, primps himself, and gets ready to go to work. He greets his neighbors and turns on the news. Like our real-life news, we are briskly made aware of our impending doom before moving on. For Emmet, the news has President Business reminding everyone to follow the rules "or they'll get put to sleep!" before quickly talking about Taco Tuesday "where every rule-following citizen gets a free taco". Emmet thinks about how great President Business is, but realizes he just said, "put to sleep" and its implications. The TV quickly moves on to everyone's favorite sitcom "Where's My Pants?" and rather than questioning the president, Emmet begins to laugh hysterically. "What was I just thinking?", he asks himself. "I don't care."

The citizens of Bricksburg are being fooled by the distractions of pop culture and consumerism while the world around them is about to be destroyed. They ignore the warning signs and go on with their day and everyone seems to be doing pretty much the same thing. Like everyone else, Emmet gets in his car and follows all the traffic laws. He turns on the radio and listens to everyone's favorite song "Everything is Awesome". He is nice to everyone and, like everyone else, he waits happily in line for his overpriced coffee. He goes to work where, as a construction worker, he takes instructions from the Octan Corporation. He happily follows their orders when they tell the workers to "take everything weird and blow it up", replacing them with standard structures that fit their modern city. We can see how Chomsky's analysis coincides with the narrative in *The Lego Movie*. We know the world will end, but we continue our lives in an orderly fashion. In this sense, the LEGO world in the movie mirrors our own and produces a radical critique of the state and capitalist systems as well as society at large. Even the way we engage in activism against the system can be found in the text.

182 Radical Resistance in *The Lego Movie*: Building Blocks of Utopia

From Normal to Ground-breaking

Emmet is the protagonist in the film, but he isn't some special superhero. In fact, he doesn't even stand out among the normal LEGO people he knows. He does not fit in with either the MasterBuilders, or the people of Bricksburg. Despite seemingly being just like everyone else, Emmet lacks companionship. He has no friends, and we learn the reason for this through his co-workers' and acquaintances' descriptions of Emmet:

> "[He's an] average, normal kinda guy but … he's not like normal like us. He's not that special."

> "Look at Randy here. He likes sausage. That's something. Gail is perky. That's something."

> "When you say 'Harry' I go 'hahahaha'. When you say the other guy [Emmet] I go … [he stares silently]".

> "He's a little bit of a blank slate I guess."

> "We all have something that makes us something and Emmet is … nothing."

Although Emmet isn't special, we can see these other workers are not particularly special either. Their love of sausage or perkiness gives these ordinary citizens enough to differentiate themselves and thus have self-esteem which allows them to easily go about their day. They are co-opted by this pseudo-specialness into the system which is slowly waiting to glue them into immobility. Emmet, in turn, is co-opted by seeking their approval, particularly by attempting to be normal, so much so that he does not display even superficial levels of 'specialness'.

MasterBuilders on the other hand *are* special and they look down upon the ordinary people of the LEGO lands like Bricksburg. These normal people are viewed as followers who lack the creativity to realize that they are being enslaved by a system that keeps them isolated in their own little LEGO worlds and drains them of the imagination that would make them fully actualized beings. This was also the view they had of Emmet, which further alienated him from others.

We are first introduced to a MasterBuilder when Emmet comes across a stranger who is looking for the Piece of Resistance in the construction yard where Emmet is working. Upon seeing this hooded trespasser, Emmet follows the rules and begins to make a call to the authorities but when she turns around, he falls in love with her instantly and ends the call. For the first time, Emmet breaks a rule. The beautiful stranger, WyldStyle, flees after being seen and Emmet chases after her and serendipitously finds the Piece of Resistance. Within the LEGO universe it had been prophesied that the person that finds the Piece of Resistance would be 'The Special', "the most important, most talented, most interesting, and most extraordinary person in the universe". Soon, however, WyldStyle realizes he's none of these things. First, Emmet will not contravene the 'instructions' (the laws of Bricksburg). Dumbfounded, Wyldstyle, wants to double-check to see if he is The Special:

Wyldstyle: Wait, what's your favorite restaurant?
Emmet: Any chain restaurant.
Wyldstyle: Favorite TV show?
Emmet: *Where Are My Pants?*
Wyldstyle: Favorite song?
Emmet: Everything Is Awesome.
Wyldstyle: Oh, no! ... You're not The Special!"

Emmet admits that he is not particularly special, spending his whole life just trying to fit in. We can see how he describes himself when he gives a less-than-inspirational speech to the MasterBuilders in Cloud Cuckoo Land:

I may not be a MasterBuilder. I may not have a lot of experience fighting or leading or coming up with plans. Or having ideas in general. In fact, I'm not all that smart. And I'm not what you'd call a 'creative type'. Plus ... generally unskilled. Also ... scared and cowardly. I know what you're thinking: 'He is the least qualified person in the world to lead us.' And you are right.

The MasterBuilders begin booing him at this point, having hoped that he could come up with the answer to defeating Lord Business after their previous failures. Emmet is a working-class character who represents the ordinary, whereas the MasterBuilders represent the unique. In the allegory outside the film, the MasterBuilders are the activists we often encounter in radical political struggles. They represent anti-establishment norms through their radical habitus. Habitus, according to the sociologist who coined the term, Pierre Bourdieu,

is a set of dispositions, reflexes and forms of behavior people acquire through acting in society. It reflects the different positions people have in society, for example, whether they are brought up in a middle class environment or in a working class suburb.[36]

But rather than focusing on class, we can consider the notion of activist or radical habitus[37] – dispositions, reflexes, and forms of behavior *activists* acquire. As part of such a habitus, sociologist Nick Crossley writes, "activists tend to perceive their lifestyles in political terms and arrange them

184 Radical Resistance in *The Lego Movie*: Building Blocks of Utopia

accordingly",[38] citing examples of pacifists sporting beards and feminist clothing trends. The activists have lifestyle differences that set them apart from others because they become political, not just personal, choices. In the context of *The Lego Movie*, it is clear that the MasterBuilders claim their 'specialness' as part of their identity developed through their MasterBuilder habitus. Emmet, in contrast, is looked down on by the MasterBuilders due to his 'normalness'. This attitude and the way in which the film concludes its central conflict reflect on our world as it pertains to activists and their struggle against capitalism and the state – the systems embodied by Lord Business.[39]

While the Super Secret Police are trying to round up the MasterBuilders and are destroying Cloud Cuckoo Land, our MasterBuilder heroes try to protect Emmet. They huddle together and, with their own unique ideas, they develop a high-tech submarine that they plan to take into the ocean to hide from Bad Cop.[40] Emmet also chips in to add the only original idea he's had in his life: a double-decker couch with cup holders and under-seat coolers. As you can imagine, his contribution to the submarine is not appreciated by the others. Despite the prophecy, he still appears anything other than special, but it doesn't take them long to recognize that his normalness is an asset. The police successfully sabotage our heroes' efforts to hide underwater. The submarine gets flooded and is about to explode. With nowhere else to go, the whole team hide in the coolers of Emmet's invention which floats to the surface. Robot drones scouring the surface of the ocean cannot detect any life. The only thing they find is a useless double-decker couch which they ignore, assuming that both Emmet and the Piece of Resistance have sunk. The heroes survived purely because the drones never suspected such a silly object would serve any practical purpose, and the MasterBuilders realize that in order to defeat Lord Business they need to use otherwise silly or rudimentary ideas because, as with the couch, they would go undetected – unlike the MasterBuilders' complex and creative ideas. So, Emmet has a plan: "What's the last thing Lord Business would expect MasterBuilders to do? ... It's follow the instructions." The MasterBuilders all sigh in disappointment.

> No, wait. Listen. You guys are all so talented and imaginative. ... I'm just a construction worker. But when I had a plan and we were all working together, I mean we could build a skyscraper. Now, you're MasterBuilders. Just imagine what can happen if you did that! You could save the universe.

He develops a plan for them to follow. They'll take an ordinary, Octan delivery spaceship to get inside the Octan building, and then they will disguise themselves as one of the many robots or ordinary inanimate objects in order to sneak past the guards. By doing normal things they won't attract

Radical Resistance in *The Lego Movie*: Building Blocks of Utopia **185**

attention. Although in the end they don't succeed in their plan, they get closer than ever before. This suggests a strategy of resistance that involves the 'clandestine' approach, one in which those with a radical habitus make gains by blending in and subverting the system from within, disguising their own lifestyle preferences. The "anti-normal" norms of the MasterBuilders is shown to limit their abilities to achieve the world they want. They can't get through the security systems of the Octan Corporation because they stick out like sore thumbs.[41]

Despite the progress made through working clandestinely *through* the system, ultimately, the film suggests that a popular revolution is the only solution. This too gets played out through an incorporation of the notion of specialness and, for our purposes, taking into account activist habitus. Toward the end of the film, Lord Business began to use the Kragle to glue people who are running away in fear of Lord Business while the micromanagers chase after them and try to catch them. Back in the Octan Corporation, the MasterBuilders are caught but Emmet saves them by sacrificing himself, falling into the Infinite Abyss of Nothingness. The Masterbuilders are free but, believing Emmet is dead, have run out of ideas as to how to save the LEGO universe. "Emmet had ideas", says one MasterBuilder, Benny. "Arr. If only there were more people in the world like he (sic)", replied another. And then WyldStyle realizes that there are more people like him. The MasterBuilders quickly hijack the filming of "Where are My Pants?" and WyldStyle sends out a live broadcast to the people of different worlds who are trying to escape the glue-spraying micromanagers:

I know things seem kind of bad right now. But there is a way out of this. This is Emmet [Emmet's image is projected]. And he was just like all of you. A face in the crowd following the same instructions as you. He was so good at fitting in, no one ever saw him. And I owe you an apology because I used to look down on people like that. I used to think they were followers with no ideas or vision. Because it turns out Emmet had great ideas. And even though they seemed weird and kind of pointless they actually came closer than anyone else to saving the universe. And now we have to finish what he started by making whatever weird thing pops into our heads. All of you have the ability inside of you to be a groundbreaker. And I mean literally! Break the ground! Peel up the pieces, tear apart your walls! Build things only you could build. Defend yourselves. We need to fight back against President Business' plans to freeze us!"

The citizens take up arms in the form of LEGO blocks and begin to construct absurd planes and weapons to use against the Kragle-blasting robots. The MasterBuilders join them in their fight, taking a spaceship from the Octan Building to Bricksburg.

The spaceship is also special in this context as it's the only one that the MasterBuilder astronaut Benny got to invent on his own. Benny is obsessed with building spaceships but throughout the movie he is not allowed to make his own by the other MasterBuilders. The only other time they build a spaceship together, it has to be an ordinary Octan delivery spaceship, so they can sneak into the Octan building. The Octan delivery spaceship and Benny's original spaceship represent the difference between the clandestine and revolutionary strategies. Benny is allowed to express his specialness within the revolutionary context, after they obtain mass support and mobilization.

MasterBuilders and the Multitude

We can see that the division that was established through the exceptionalization of the MasterBuilders led to the previous failures in stopping Lord Business. In our world it may be that the activist habitus is holding back resistance to state and capital as it creates a fissure between dispositions and cultures that reduces the potential for mass mobilization. It helps us to understand the limits the MasterBuilders' activist habitus may put on them in their views of other, ordinary people – placing the ordinary working-class individual back into a position of being a radical subject within the multitude.

While this reading of *The Lego Movie* may suggest that the MasterBuilders, with their activist habitus, are somehow homogenous in their beliefs, dispositions, and cultures, this is certainly not the case. Our LEGO hero team is composed of characters from a diverse range of worlds, creative in different ways, which resemble what the Marxist philosophers Michael Hardt and Antonio Negri call "the multitude", or "the living alternative that grows within Empire".[42]

> The multitude is composed of innumerable internal differences that can never be reduced to a unity or a single identity – different cultures, races, ethnicities, genders, and sexual orientations; different forms of labor; different ways of living; different views of the world; and different desires. The multitude is a multiplicity of all these singular differences .... The multitude is many-colored, like Joseph's magical coat. Thus the challenge posed by the concept of multitude is for a social multiplicity to manage to communicate and act in common while remaining internally different .... The multitude, in contrast [to 'working class'], is an open, inclusive concept .... The multitude is thus composed potentially of all the diverse figures of social production.[43]

There are further parallels between the film and Hardt and Negri's work. Both emphasize internationalization as a political goal. In the film, internationalism was both the prior state of things and the future ideal:

Radical Resistance in *The Lego Movie*: Building Blocks of Utopia **187**

All the people of the universe were once free to travel and mingle and build whatever they wanted. But President Business was confused by all the chaos. So, he erected walls between the worlds and became obsessed with order and perfection. And he stole the mysterious secret super weapon called The Kragle!"

And now from Hardt and Negri:

The struggles ... were expressions of the force of living labor, which sought to liberate itself from the rigid territorializing regimes imposed on it. As it contests the dead labor accumulated against it, living labor always seeks to break the fixed territorializing structures, the national organizations, and the political figures that keep it prisoner. With the force of living labor, its restless activity, and its deterritorializing desire, this process of rupture throws open all the windows of history.[44]

In their work, Hardt and Negri contrast the multitude (MasterBuilders) with Empire (Lord Business). For them, Empire is "a new Leviathan" that rules over its subjects. While the multitude can create everything within that world, Empire feeds off the multitude like a leech.[45] In the world of *The LEGO Movie* Lord Business's profits and grand plans are predicated on the instruction manuals he gives to workers who follow them. Even the manuals themselves are the ideas from captured MasterBuilders who are thrown into the "Think Tank" where their ideas are forcibly extracted.[46] In the original script of the film, this point is made even more directly. The villain reveals a huge robotic monster to Emmet who realizes it was built by his fellow construction workers. The villain stands up proud: "It's my best work". "But you didn't do anything", retorts Emmet. The villain replies, "Are you kidding? You think the MasterBuilders just up and forced themselves to think of this? Did those guys force themselves to build it? No. I did. Ergo, it's mine." In other words, as Hardt and Negri state, "the multitude is the real productive force of the social world".

Because of the chronic exploitation, MasterBuilders attempted to escape into the tunnels between worlds and created the hideout that was Cloud Cuckoo Land. They used their creative forces to effectively produce a world outside the control of Lord Business. For Hardt and Negri, "The creative forces of the multitude that sustain Empire are also capable of autonomously constructing a counter-Empire, an alternative political organization of global flows and exchanges".[47] As we can see, *The Lego Movie* is not only a useful representation of an allegoric utopia found in Cloud Cuckoo Land, but full of other interesting parallels through which we can strengthen our strategic and tactical knowledge of how to overcome the powers of the state and capital that are embodied in the President Business villain. Despite the critical

188 Radical Resistance in *The Lego Movie*: Building Blocks of Utopia

content found in the film, there is something that prevents this interpretation from being the closed reading of the text. The internal allegory in the film minimizes the critique because through the non-animated characters of Finn and his father we figure out that the LEGO world doesn't mirror our world. Instead, it is a metaphor for a fragile father-son relationship. The internal allegory seemingly ruins the critical analysis. However, it could be argued that the film can still be saved from itself and repurposed for radical use.

A Rope of Sand

The creators of *The Lego Movie*, Phil Lord and Chris Miller, presented a master class on screenwriting for the British Academy of Film and Television Arts in which they discussed the importance of relationships in filmmaking. By this they meant two things: first, the making of a film is a collaborative process requiring good relationships with everyone involved and, second, at their core the story of all films is about relationships. Phil and Chris learned these lessons the hard way. Their road to stardom started with the animated film *Cloudy with a Chance of Meatballs* (2009). In the early stages of production both screenwriters were fired from the project. The studio execs didn't like their approach to the story which was centered on a scientist who was isolated in his town. Other writers were hired and shortly afterward they too were fired. The screenplay just didn't work, but the studio had invested too much in the film to drop it altogether. Phil and Chris were rehired, and they set out to make the project work by listening to others' ideas about what the film should be.

Eventually Phil and Chris realized that the problem with the original script was that it did not have a compelling relationship. They redrafted the story to feature a relationship between a father and son, something they had previously wanted to avoid because it was too cliché. The execs liked the film and its success led to their next projects, including *The Lego Movie*. In some ways *The Lego Movie* is a combination of the two versions of *Cloudy with a Chance of Meatballs*. The LEGO world focuses on Emmet who is isolated and lonely in his city – which provides a context for critiquing society. The 'real' world in the film is all about the relationship between father and son, the framework that Phil and Chris previously did not want to incorporate but needed to in order for the film to work. In this way it could be said they hid the radical critique and utopian representation inside a story about family.

This radical subterfuge brings to mind Fredric Jameson's analysis of the film *Videodrome* (1983). David Cronenberg's cult-classic is about the CEO of a small-time softcore porn channel who seeks to acquire smut films that he comes across. His drive to obtain the films leads him to unravel a conspiracy and get trapped in hallucinations. The film presents its subtext as a battle

Radical Resistance in *The Lego Movie*: Building Blocks of Utopia **189**

between small business and big corporations while its "deepest allegorical impulse", according to Jameson, is

> an articulated nightmare vision of how we as individuals feel within the new multinational world system. It is as though the narrowly economic had to be thematized and thereby marginalized, in order for the deeper socio-economic allegory to pass the censorship.[48]

In *The Lego Movie* something closer to the reverse can be interpreted. Without considering the internal allegory, the narrative of the film is about a revolutionary uprising against a tyrannical but (ostensibly) democratically elected leader and captain of industry.[49] Popular culture is heavily critiqued throughout the film; internationalism is praised while borders are shown as oppressive structures. And, on this rare occasion, the central protagonist is a working-class manual laborer. Is it not possible that such a representation, particularly one geared toward children, required obscuring in order to "pass the censorship"? If we take Lord/President Business as a stand in for Finn's father, do we not remove the otherwise radical, overt message? Through this internal allegory, any 'rebellion' is simply seen as Finn's attempt to get along better with his father, and ruin his LEGO structures in the process; Cloud Cuckoo Land is morphed from utopia to a box of LEGO pieces Finn's father has discarded and therefore Finn is free to play with; internationalism and the deconstruction of borders is simply the desegregation of LEGO constructions in the basement of a man's garage; and the MasterBuilders are really a representations of Finn and his imaginative construction of LEGO blocks.

Beyond the difficulties this film may have had in being produced without this internal allegory, it is interesting that the film speaks to this very problem. That is, there may be *another* allegory we need to look at. The MasterBuilders were unable to get to Lord Business's office in all their previous attempts. They were only able to advance and finally penetrate the army of robots and a minefield of security measures using Emmet's ideas of fitting in and slipping undercover by using the ordinary structures, spaceships, and persona in order to bypass security. If they had come in with their special creations and guns blazing, they would have been easily spotted and defeated. Perhaps that was the same logic behind *The Lego Movie* itself, and its radical message. Perhaps Phil and Chris's script would have been shot down easily otherwise. Perhaps they were attempting to make some progress in providing a radical message while working within the system but needing to hide behind the allegory in order for the film to be produced. Or perhaps, and most likely, this is all a stretch. Of course, that is the downside of allegories.

The popular song from the movie *Everything is Awesome* is a critique of how we ignore the problems around us, thinking everything is awesome instead of realizing we face existential problems. The internal allegory removes this critique and turns the song into simply a catchy tune. But, if we remove the internal allegory, *The Lego Movie* is far more radical than most other films because it presents us with an alternative. As this book has demonstrated, in the last decades mainstream film and television have produced few instances in which alternatives are presented favorably, if at all. Even positive representations of alternative lifestyles are rarely presented, and if they are presented, they seem to be drained of any overt radical political content. In general, the political or economic critiques of these mainstream visual media texts lack a radical edge, often falling into one or more limited critiques. The more radical critiques are often presented in quite banal or brief ways. Similarly, most alternative, utopian visions are presented in brief flickers. Only a few frames are reserved for the sacred. Perhaps this speaks to Jacoby's iconoclastic utopia, expressed in *The Lego Movie* as a society where "All the people of the universe [are] free to travel and mingle and build whatever they [want]". Or perhaps Phil and Chris have pointed us in the right direction: only those texts which can successfully subvert the subversive can be created. (Let us not forget that *The Lego Movie* is just one giant commercial for LEGO.)

Lenin is paraphrased in the oft-stated line "the capitalists will sell us the rope with which we will hang them".[50] However, it does not look as if the capitalists will sell the cultural products that contain the ideological tools that may lead us to wanting to "hang them" in the first place. For that purpose, the capitalists will only sell us a rope of sand. To reiterate this lesson learned from *The Lego Movie* we should consider another film, William Dietrich's aptly titled film *Rope of Sand* (1949). The film, set in the diamond-rich deserts of South Africa, begins as a critique of money and power. Diamonds are, according to the film, "the hardest of all matters . So hard, in fact, that whatever it touches must suffer: glass, steel, the human soul." The diamonds, essentially a stand in for capitalism, make everyone around them greedy and corrupt. We are presented with scenes of thievery, police brutality, torture, super-exploitation, and lies. A 'rope of sand' refers to the social bonds that dissipate in the social conditions that promote such behavior: the promise of wealth in the face of poverty and the promise of power at the cost of morality. At the same time a rope of sand refers to the sand barrier that divides the South African town from a land so diamond-rich that you can dig them out with your bare hands.

These two interpretations of the metaphor provide two seemingly contradictory objectives for the film: to re-establish a moral social order and to obtain the diamonds. The diamonds are seemingly easy to reach – one must simply cross the desert. But the simple rope of sand is actually a highly guarded terrain patrolled by a private corporate army. The protagonist, Mike, is plotting a scheme to get the diamonds when he falls in love with a woman who is planning her own get-rich-quick scheme. This love marks the beginnings of a progressive social order where eventually trust and sacrifice replace a politics of selfishness and competition. The film could have easily concluded on the note that love breaks the bonds of the socially oppressive force of wealth, which eats at the soul from the inside. Instead, after our heroes make sacrifices for each other and escape what would have been an otherwise ugly fate, they are rewarded with the very object of corruption: diamonds. We are then retold that old line about diamonds with a new twist: a diamond is "so hard in fact that whatever it touches must suffer. Glass, steel, the human soul. *Except of course under unusual circumstances and in the right hands.*"[51] Unlike *Titanic* (1997), where wealth must be sacrificed to enable real love to form, *Rope of Sand* must bury its critical politics in the comfort of liberal warmth. If you are well-intentioned, both fortune and fidelity can be obtained. If you are worthy, the economic system will not corrupt you.

Rope of Sand can't present us with the radical notion that we are people shaped by the material forces that surround us and that capitalism corrupts our very soul. To avoid this, the film – like *The Lego Movie* – subsumes its critique through a story about relationships, absolving it of its radical message.[52] Also like *The Lego Movie* it is a self-reflective critique of society, because just as it is covering up its radical message it tells us as much through its own narrative. The auteurs want to create a movie with a radical critique (diamonds). According to the pluralist, liberal model of the media they should be able to with a bit of effort (travelling across the rope of sand). When they attempt to, they are prevented by the repressive institutions that control property (the corporate army). Therefore, the only way to reach the masses with such a message is by disguising the movie as something else – a story about relationships. In *Rope of Sand*, Mike is only able to reach the diamonds when he disguises himself as one of the trusted mining company men, just like Emmet's plan to destroy Lord Business required the team of MasterBuilders to pretend to be company employees and make normal things rather than making eccentric LEGO tools.

It is entirely possible that mainstream culture will simply not allow the utopian imaginary to easily grow. It may be the case that only the guerrilla gardening of utopian ideas will allow seeds to sprout. Seedlings may germinate in the moments when we read texts in radical ways. But if these plants cannot blossom into flowers for a large number of people, we will face the danger of escaping into a bubble of radical habitus that may preclude the collective mass mobilization needed for change.

We may find such seedlings in small pockets of the web, creeping into platforms such as YouTube and TikTok and we don't have to be professionals in order to make them and put them out there in the world. The creators of *The Lego Movie* entitled their BAFTA presentation the "Non-master Class Regarding Writing Things Down for Money: A Rope of Sand". Their point was that every human has the innate capacity to tell stories and that no

192 Radical Resistance in *The Lego Movie*: Building Blocks of Utopia

one can call themselves a 'master'. But if we want to create something for Hollywood, maybe we need to engage in Emmet's tactic of subversion: do something they wouldn't expect – make something 'normal'.

Notes

1 D'Anghera 1912, p. 103.
2 D'Anghera 1912, p. 103.
3 The native was described as being a religious man who understood heaven and hell and thus was more civilized than people of other nations.
4 Jacoby 2005, p. 7.
5 Kumar 2010, p. 550.
6 Jameson 2005, p. 16.
7 Jameson 2005, p. xii.
8 Kumar 2010, p. 553; Jameson 2005, p. 71. Here we have *Game of Thrones* (2011–2019), *The Lord of the Rings* 2001–2003), etc.
9 Kumar 2010, p. 555.
10 The list is long: *The Divergent* series (2014–2016), *Equilibrium* (2002), *Snowpiercer* (2013), *The Handmaid's Tale* (2017–2022), *The Man in the High Castle* (season 1, 2015), *V for Vendetta* (2005), *Incorporated* (season 1; 2016), etc.
11 Jacoby 2005, pp. 5–6.
12 Jacoby 2005, p. 13.
13 We can also assume that the company profits from the sale of gasoline as Octan is originally the name of the oil company that LEGO used in its building sets since the early 1990s. In the original screenplay, the company controlled by the villain was called Empura and was described as "a company which apparently owns everything" (Lord and Miller n.d.).
14 Jacoby 2005, p. 39.
15 Bad Cop shares his body with Good Cop which Lord Business feels is making him soft. Lord Business can't risk ruining his plans, so he uses the Fleece-Crested Scepter of Q-Teep and Po'leesh Remover of Nai'eel to erase the face of Good Cop, and then asks Bad Cop to show his loyalty by using the Kragle to glue his own parents in place. Bad Cop is no longer of two minds about it: "Sorry, Dad. I have a job to do." Through this employer/employee relationship we see how Bad Cop is reshaped by his job, one that requires taking orders regardless of the consequence while we, as an audience, see the horror of such behavior.
16 Jacoby 2005, p. 5.
17 Jacoby 2005, p. 22.
18 Zamyatin 1987[1924].
19 Zamyatin 1987[1924], p. 179.
20 Jacoby 2005, pp. 23–24.
21 Jacoby 2005, p. 25.
22 Jacoby 2005, p. 29.
23 Cross 1997, as quoted in Jacoby 2005, p. 29. Jacoby argues that even outdoor play is being cannibalized by sports that are structured, coached, and monitored by adults. Jacoby 2005, p. 30.
24 Jacoby 2005, p. 30.
25 Lord and Miller 2017.

Radical Resistance in *The Lego Movie*: Building Blocks of Utopia   **193**

26 Jacoby 2005, p. 31, quoting Scholem 1995 [1971].
27 Jacoby 2005, p. 33.
28 Jacoby 2005, p. xv.
29 Heine 1985[1834], pp. 180–181, quoted in Jacoby 2005, p. 34.
30 J. Max Patrick thought he was coining the term and it is likely he had not come across Mill's use of the term nearly 100 years earlier. Mill's use of the term was recorded by Hansard as it was used in a parliamentary debate in which he stated "I may be permitted, as one who, in common with many of my betters, have been subjected to the charge of being Utopian, to congratulate the Government on having joined that goodly company. It is, perhaps, too complimentary to call them Utopians, they ought rather to be called dys-topians, or cacotopians. What is commonly called Utopian is something too good to be practicable; but what they appear to favour is too bad to be practicable" (Mill 1868, as quoted in Jacoby 2005, p. 154).
31 See e.g., Karger et al. 2023.
32 Rabinowitch 1953.
33 Kelly 2017.
34 See Nulman 2015; Gallup's 'Most Important Problem' page notes that from September 2023 to March 2024 climate change has received a maximum of 3 percent identifying it as the most important problem as compared to 28 percent identifying immigration as the most important problem in March 2024 (up from 13 percent in September 2023) (Gallup 2024).
35 Chomsky and Polk 2013.
36 Bourdieu 2000.
37 See Crossley 2003.
38 Crossley 2003, p. 53.
39 This embodiment, as mentioned in Chapter 4, certainly limits the obvious reading of the critique, also making it fit into the overreaching limited critique mentioned in Chapter 3, if we overlook the internal analogy.
40 In the original script a similar scene occurs but the collaboration is explained as collective meditation.
41 This is presented on various occasions in the film. One such occasion is when Bad Cop – the head of the Super Secret Police – interrogates Emmet, who he now believes to be The Special since he discovered the Piece of Resistance. Emmet denies this by demonstrating his lack of specialness but the more he denies it the more Bad Cop believes it is the perfect cover. When Emmet later escapes, Lord Business tries to find him, but Emmet's face is so generic that it matches all the others in the computer system, a ploy President Business thinks is "diabolical".
42 Hardt and Negri 2004, p. xiii.
43 Hardt and Negri 2004, pp xiv–xv.
44 Hardt and Negri 2000, p. 52.
45 Hardt and Negri 2000, p. 62.
46 The Think Tank can be read as a critique of the intellectual class serving the capitalist/state system in a similar way that the anarchist anthropologist David Graeber described the role of academia in relation to the working class.
47 Hardt and Negri 2000, p. xv.
48 Jameson 1995, pp. 26–27.
49 We can assume the voting is rigged in favor of Lord Business because we are made aware that his Octan Corporation owns the voting machine systems.

50 The original quotation is actually supposed to be from Lenin's manuscripts which I. U. Annenkov had examined, copying some quotations, shortly after Lenin's death. The original is "They [capitalists] will furnish credits which will serve us for the support of the Communist Party in their countries and, by supplying us materials and technical equipment which we lack, will restore our military industry necessary for our future attacks against our suppliers. To put it in other words, they will work on the preparation of their own suicide."
51 Emphasis added.
52 Also see the reading of *Antz* (1998) in Barker 2000, p. 78.

References

Barker, Martin (2000) *From Antz to Titanic: Reinventing Film Analysis*, London: Pluto Press.

Bourdieu, P. (2000) 'The Politics of Protest: Bourdieu Interview', *Socialist Review*, 18–20 June. http://pubs.socialistreviewindex.org.uk/sr242/ovenden.htm.

Chomsky, Noam and Polk, Laray (2013) *How Close the World Is to Nuclear War*, New York: Seven Stories.

Crossley, Nick (2003) 'From Reproduction to Transformation: Social Movement Fields and the Radical Habitus', *Theory, Culture and Society*, 20(6): 43–68, https://doi.org/10.1177/0263276403206003.

Gallup (2024) 'Most Important Problem', https://news.gallup.com/poll/1675/most-important-problem.aspx. Accessed May 5, 2024.

Hall, Stuart (1995) 'The West and the Rest: Discourse and Power', in Stuart Hall and Bram Gieben (eds.), *Formations of Modernity* (pp. 275–320), Cambridge: Polity Press.

Hardt, Michael and Negri, Antonio (2000) *Empire*, Cambridge, MA: Harvard University Press.

Hardt, Michael and Negri, Antonio (2004) *Multitude: War and Democracy in the Age of Empire*, New York: Penguin Press.

Humphrey, Wm. Steven (2011) 'The Paradox of *Portlandia*', *Portland Mercury*, 20 Jan https://www.portlandmercury.com/portland/the-paradox-of-portlandia/Content?oid=3273589.

Jacoby, Russell (2005) *Picture Imperfect: Utopian Thought for an Anti-Utopian Age*, New York: Columbia University Press.

Jameson, Fredric (1995) *The Geopolitical Aesthetic: Cinema and Space in the World System*, London: BFI Publishing.

Jameson, Fredric (2005) *Archaeologies of the Future: The Desire Called Utopia and Other Science Fictions*, London: Verso.

Karger, Ezra, Rosenberg, Josh, Jacobs, Zachary, Hickman, Molly, Hadshar, Rose, Gamin, Kayla, Smith, Taylor, Williams, Bridget, McCaslin, Tegan, Thomas, Stephen, and Tetlock, Philip E. (2023) *Forecasting Existential Risks: Evidence from a Long-Run Forecasting Tournament*, Forecasting Research Institute, FRI Working Paper #1. https://forecastingresearch.org/s/XPT.pdf

Kelly, John (2017) 'Duck and Cover: Did D.C. School Students Get Dog Tags during the Cold War?', *The Washington Post*, Aug. 5, https://www.washingtonpost.com/local/duck-and-cover-did-dc-school-students-get-dog-tags-during-the-cold-war/2017/08/05/5c1b8958-7796-11e7-9eac-d56bd5568db8_story.html.

Kumar, Krishan (2010) 'The Ends of Utopia', *New Literary History*, 41(3): 549–569.
Lord, Phil and Miller, Chris (n.d.) *LEGO: The Piece of Resistance*, www.screenplaydb.com/film/scripts/lego.pdf.
Lord, Phil and Miller, Chris (2017) 'Phil Lord & Chris Miller | Screenwriters' Lecture', British Academy of Film and Television Arts, http://guru.bafta.org/phil-lord-chris-miller-screenwriters-lecture.
Nulman, Eugene (2015) *Climate Change and Social Movements: Civil Society and the Development of National Climate Change Policy*, Basingstoke: Palgrave.
Rabinowitch, Eugene (1953) 'The Narrowing Way', *Bulletin of the Atomic Scientists*, 9(8): 294–296.
Scholem, Gershom (1995[1971]) *The Messianic Idea in Judaism: And Other Essays on Jewish Spirituality*, New York: Schocken Books.
Zamyatin, Yevgeny (1987[1924]) *We*, New York: Avon Books.

9

UTOPIAN CONCLUSIONS

Yesterday, Today, and Tomorrowland

There are two wolves,
and they're always fighting.
One is darkness and despair.
The other is light and hope.
Which wolf wins?
… Whichever one you feed.[1]

The small amount of light and hope projected onto the silver screens and through pixels in your TV, laptop, or tablet screens means that everything else that is broadcast effectively continues to feed the wolf of darkness and despair. Under such circumstances it is no wonder that it is easier to imagine the end of the world than the end of capitalism. Or an end of capitalism that is not the end of the world. We are constantly being provided with images of our own destruction that effectively feed into a self-fulfilling prophecy because we are ideologically blinded from seeing that alternatives can exist.

"Mutually assured destruction. Today, any nuclear country or terrorist is capable of inflicting damage on a massive scale with weapons of …"

"Environmental entropy. The polar ice caps aren't waiting for us to decide if climate change is real. Rising coastal waters, intensifying weather patterns, they're all punching our one-way ticket to …"

"Dystopia. By definition, 'not perfect.' Huxley's Brave New World, Bradbury's Fahrenheit 451, Orwell's 1984. Once considered fiction, these futuristic novels are actually happening right now, and they seem to be getting worse."[2]

DOI: 10.4324/9781003514916-10

Utopian Conclusions: Yesterday, Today, and Tomorrowland 197

We are used to hearing such messages. In schools, in books, and certainly in popular film and television. What these messages seem to lack is a positive answer to the question, "Can we fix it?" This is the question that Casey Newton (Britt Robertson) asks in the film *Tomorrowland* (2015) after her teachers give the apocalyptic prognoses quoted above.

Casey maintains hope in the face of a futile future. Her dad is facing unemployment and every time she turns on the news twisters and floods are shown wreaking havoc on the environment. Worst of all, everyone accepts the doom they are heading into. No one seems to think they can do anything about it. For most people, there is no alternative. However, Casey's hopefulness leads her to mysteriously receive a special pin. When she touches the pin, she is transported into another world where technological innovation has blossomed. Gravity can be shifted, clean energy is found in endless supply, and everyone seems to be an astronaut flying light years through space. Her belief in an alternative future appears as a real future that she can tap into in the present – a beautiful parallel world. But the world she sees through the pin is just a science-fiction mirage, a hologram. Even so, hope is not lost. An alternate world does exist, just in another dimension to which she must travel. After meeting an audio-animatronic robot and an old inventor, Frank (George Clooney), who once lived in the alternate universe, Casey eventually finds herself in a spaceship launched from the Eiffel Tower, traveling to another dimension, and arriving in Tomorrowland.
How did this futuristic, utopian place come about?

> Have you ever wondered what would happen if all the geniuses, the artists, the scientists, the smartest, most creative people in the world, decided to actually change it? But where? Where could they even do such a thing? They'd need a place free from politics and bureaucracy, distractions, greed. A secret place where they could build whatever they were crazy enough to imagine.[3]

This is fully automated luxury communism, existing within the confines of another world and simultaneously representing an alternate future. But not everything is rainbows and spaceships. Tomorrowland has come under the control of Governor Nix (Hugh Laurie), a man with authoritarian tendencies in a world meant to be free of politics. He doesn't welcome the newcomers Casey, Frank, and the robot. His main concern is making sure that no one from Earth comes back to Tomorrowland because humans "are driven by savagery", which has led them to destroy their own planet.

Governor Nix's analysis of the problem mirrors a real-world discourse regarding climate change – the 'Anthropocene'. This is the idea that humans are so destructive to society that they, as a species, are the problem. However, this idea fails to understand that it is not the species that is at fault, but the

198 Utopian Conclusions: Yesterday, Today, and Tomorrowland

systems of state and capitalism. Decades of scientific research led scientists to approach policymakers to solve the problem. International conferences were held but the states were not interested in making serious, long-term changes in the face of short-term costs. The financial costs to mitigating climate change are large and require a synchronized effort that countries (particularly the United States) were not willing to make. And what about the economic benefits? There was little profit to make from decarbonization and much to lose. If governments did not force industry into mitigation efforts, they certainly are not going to do them on their own. And what about a sharp cut in production and consumption that would be needed until alternative sources of energy were found? It's unthinkable in a capitalist economic system. The whole thing would collapse if profit couldn't take precedence over populations, human and otherwise. So, if Governor Nix is wrong, what do our heroes think about this impending doom?

Consciousness of Catastrophe

Many years ago, Frank invented a machine that calculates the time and probability of the Earth's apocalypse based on the discovery of tachyon particles. Tachyon particles can travel faster than light and therefore allow us to see into the future. The system is hooked up to the Monitor – located in Tomorrowland – which projects the devastation. We see scenes of major cities being flooded and massive mushroom clouds engulfing metropolitan areas. Riots break out amidst the storms of horror. The doomsday clock is ticking and there are only 58 days left.

Frank knew the end was near and his equipment assured him that this future was 100 percent certain. That was until Casey, never having ever met Frank, ended up at his door in our world, in search of answers about her secret pin. When they started talking, Frank asked her: "If I could tell you the date, the exact date that you're gonna die, would you wanna know?" Her response was, "I would want you to tell me. But I wouldn't believe you .... Don't we, like, make our own destiny and stuff?" Her comments spark a change in Frank's equipment. The probability of doom went down to 99.9994 percent. Maybe there's hope after all?

But even Casey, after arriving in Tomorrowland and seeing the devastation projected through the Monitor, loses faith. There was no more ice left to melt that would feed the internal spring of hope. The Monitor made that crystal clear. Casey regrets receiving the pin which gave her a vision of an alternate future and affirmed her belief that anything was possible, a belief Frank too once had before he made his discovery. But then it hit her like a bucket of ice-cold spring water. If the pin projected a vision that anything was possible, what if the Monitor was actually projecting a vision of doom? "What if it's not just predicting the future?" "What if the Monitor is just a giant pin? But instead of

Utopian Conclusions: Yesterday, Today, and Tomorrowland **199**

making you think positive, it makes you think negative ... and it's convincing the whole world to feed the wrong wolf. We need to turn that thing off ...."

Casey and Frank realize that the Monitor is the problem, and they try desperately to convince Governor Nix what's happening.

Frank: It isn't just receiving tachyons. It is taking a possible future and ...
Casey: And amplifying it, transmitting it, like a feedback loop.
Frank: It's a self-fulfilling prophecy that's coming from right there.
Casey: But it's not just showing people the end of the world, it's giving them the idea over and over again until they just accept it!
Frank: It's a ticking time bomb, and we're the ones that lit the fuse.

It turns out that Nix knew this all along. In fact, he intended people to see this dismal future. Nix was no villain in his attempt. He didn't set out to convince everyone in the world of their inevitable demise. He was doing it for precisely the opposite reason – he was trying to save the world. Nix's monologue is worth quoting at length.

> Let's imagine: if you glimpsed the future and were frightened by what you saw, what would you do with that information? You would go to .... Who? Politicians? Captains of industry? And how would you convince them? With data? Facts? Good luck. The only facts they won't challenge are the ones that keep the wheels greased and the dollars rolling in.

> But what if ...? What if there was a way of skipping the middleman and putting the critical news directly into everyone's head? The probability of widespread annihilation kept going up. The only way to stop it was to show it. To scare people straight. Because what reasonable human being wouldn't be galvanized by the potential destruction of everything they have ever known or loved? To save civilization, I would show its collapse.

> But how do you think this vision was received? How do you think people responded to the prospect of imminent doom? They gobbled it up, like a chocolate eclair. They didn't fear their demise, they repackaged it. It can be enjoyed as video games, as TV shows, books, movies. The entire world wholeheartedly embraced the apocalypse and sprinted towards it with gleeful abandon. Meanwhile, your Earth was crumbling all around you ....

> In every moment, there is the possibility of a better future. But you people won't believe it. And because you won't believe it, you won't do what is necessary to make it a reality. So, you dwell on this terrible future and you resign yourselves to it. For one reason: because that future doesn't ask anything of you today. So, yes, we saw the iceberg, we warned the *Titanic*. But you all just steered for it anyway, full steam ahead. Why? Because you want to sink. You gave up.

200 Utopian Conclusions: Yesterday, Today, and Tomorrowland

Nix won't stop the Monitor because he doesn't believe it matters. Humans are doomed because they don't seem to care about their own survival. The Anthropocene. But we as the audience can't discount the role of the Monitor in constructing this ideology of inevitable doom rather than it being something hardwired into the human species. The good guys team up and destroy the Monitor.

It is obvious what the Monitor stands for – film and television. In the fantasy world of *Tomorrowland* just as in our world, the Monitor broadcasts dystopia and we internalize it and accept our fate. But the dystopia need not be the hellscape of *Mad Max* (1979) or the catastrophes of *The Day After Tomorrow* (2004). It can be the simple sameness that saturates the texts throughout our popular culture – the *Friends* and the *Family Matters* of television and the *Friday*s and *Fargo*s of film. In which ever form, we are always presented with the same message: There Is No Alternative. *Tomorrowland* points a finger at the film and TV studios, the writers, and the producers for not only failing to inspire, but creating a consciousness of catastrophe. Despite the brilliant ways in which films like *The Player* (1992) and *Adaptation* (2002) turn inward in producing a self-referential critique of Hollywood, *Tomorrowland*'s subtler critique is more effective because it critiques while constructing that which it claims others fail to construct. Whereas popular screen media texts usually give us catastrophe and complacence, *Tomorrowland* gives us hope. But this hope is not simply presented in the futurist possibilities of the alternate dimension of Tomorrowland, or in the climax of the Monitor's destruction, but also in the film's final scenes.

The film does not end with the prevention of apocalypse through the destruction of the Monitor. "It isn't hard to knock down a big evil building that's telling everyone the world is going to end", Frank tells us. "What is hard is figuring out what to build in its place." Casey and Frank are standing in front of a group of humanoid robots when he delivers this line. The robots are tasked to find "dreamers", "the ones who haven't given up. They're the future." We then see a montage of robots appearing in various landscapes secretly handing out the pins that will guide those with hope to a mission to save the future by building something new out of the wreckage of the old. In these "dreamers" we see the multitude. A young busking guitarist in Asia. A female engineer developing the latest car prototype. An old elephant conservationist in Africa. A black woman planting trees on urban sidewalks. A judge in Hong Kong. A female sidewalk chalk artist. An African American mathematician. An Asian wind turbine engineer. A ballerina. An astronomer. A hiker. They all get a pin which transports them to a new world, free of capitalism and the state that had restricted their creativity and ingenuity. But it's not quite utopia yet. That's what they are there to build.

Utopian Conclusions: Yesterday, Today, and Tomorrowland **201**

The Community, the Banker, and the FBI

The ending of *Tomorrowland*, like *The Lego Movie* (2014), points us to the collective as a basis for hope, the revolutionary subject. In doing so it moves us away from the narratively easy protagonist-driven conclusion in which the lead character's achievement, freedom, enlightenment, courtship, or death concludes the story or represents justice.[4] The true protagonists of films like *Tomorrowland* are not Frank and Casey, because the world constructed in these representations *requires* collective action for their conclusions. It is this collective, these quasi-intentional communities, that are the real heroes.

Such representations are not particularly new phenomena. In fact, they seem far more common in popular culture of old – before neoliberalism. Take Frank Capra's film *It's a Wonderful Life* (1946) as an example. In the film, George Bailey sacrifices his ambitions and pleasures to do what is right for his community of Bedford Falls. But in the end, it's the community that saves George from going to jail. The film borrows its Christmassy surrealism from Charles Dickens' *A Christmas Carol* where Ebenezer Scrooge, the grumpy and miserly businessman, is visited by ghosts who take him to the Christmases of yesterday, today, and tomorrow. The experience changes him into a man of goodwill. Unlike Scrooge, George Bailey is already a man of goodwill and precisely for this reason he is destroyed by a business rival, Henry Potter. Potter, like George, is a banker but his unscrupulous nature means he'd throw everyone in Bedford Falls out of their house if it meant cashing in. George doesn't even want to be a banker – not even for the small Bailey Brothers Building and Loans that runs like a credit union. He wants to explore the world and become an architect. He ends up running a small community bank when his father passes away and George is left with a choice: either he runs the company, or it becomes dissolved by Potter. In order to protect the community from Potter, George gives up his dreams and runs the bank.

Every step of the way, George gives up privileges and comfort to do what is right only to eventually be double-crossed by Potter. Potter effectively steals money from George's bank without anyone noticing. He then refuses to lend George money when a bank examiner audits George's books. If George doesn't pay the hefty amount soon, he'll go to jail. Realizing that his life insurance policy means he's worth more dead than alive he sets out to commit suicide, seeing no other alternative. He regrets making all the sacrifices in his life only to end up in this position. Just as George is about to jump off a bridge, he is 'rescued' by his guardian angel (a literal angel). George wishes he'd never been born, so the angel makes George a ghost in a world in which he was never born, showing how the entire community has fallen prey to Potter without him. Potter ruins George's beloved town and its community. After waking up from this nightmare George regains

202 Utopian Conclusions: Yesterday, Today, and Tomorrowland

his joy for life regardless of the consequences. His spirit is saved even if his body will be locked away. *It's a Wonderful Life* could have easily stopped at George's personal salvation and perhaps Potter's eventual enlightenment and admission of guilt. But George isn't a spiritual martyr and Potter's soul is never saved. Instead, the community comes to the rescue: in order to repay George's debt, everyone in the community chips in and donates to the cause, even the police who were there to arrest him.

This Christmas classic, made in 1946, wasn't a success story at the time. It lost its studio money and had middling reviews. It was hardly the beloved picture it is now. In fact, it only became a Christmas classic after its copyright lapsed and it entered the public domain in 1974, getting screened on TV networks during the holiday season because it was cheap to air. In between its release and its success, it was attacked for being dangerous.

> With regard to the picture It's a Wonderful Life, [REDACTED] stated in substance that the film represented a rather obvious attempt to discredit bankers by casting Lionel Barrymore [playing Potter] as a 'scrooge-type' so that he would be the most hated man in the picture. This, according to these sources, is a common trick used by Communists.
>
> In addition, [REDACTED] stated that, in his opinion, this picture deliberately maligned the upper class, attempting to show the people who had money were mean and despicable characters. [REDACTED] related that if he had made this picture portraying the banker, he would have shown this individual to have been following the rules as laid down by the State Bank Examiners in connection with making loans. Further, [REDACTED] stated that the scene wouldn't have 'suffered at all' in portraying the banker as a man who was protecting funds put in his care by private individuals and adhering to the rules governing the loan of that money rather than portraying the part as it was shown. In summary, [REDACTED] stated that it was not necessary to make the banker such a mean character and 'I would never have done it that way.'

The redacted names probably make it obvious that the quotation came from an FBI memorandum which was produced shortly after the film's release as part of a large investigation into the communist infiltration of Hollywood. Some have posited that the right-wing individualist author Ayn Rand was involved in this process and may have been the 'Redacted' in question.[5] If Rand did bring *It's a Wonderful Life* to the attention of the scrutiny of the House of Un-American Activities Committee, it would not be a surprise. Her book *The Fountainhead*, published three years before *It's a Wonderful Life* was released, follows the life of a young crusader against collectivism, precisely the idea which Capra's film upends. In *It's a Wonderful Life*, the

Utopian Conclusions: Yesterday, Today, and Tomorrowland **203**

same young, enthusiastic aspiring architect puts his individualism aside precisely *for* collectivism. The hero sacrifices his own desires for the benefit of the community, and they return the favor – something they are never asked to do and never do begrudgingly. The community, not the ego, is the savior. The film produces a representation of what ought to be, which is what the FBI and Rand were so worried about. In a letter to the Motion Picture Alliance for the Preservation of American Ideals in 1947, Rand wrote:

> If you wish to protect your pictures from being used for Communistic purposes, the first thing to do is to drop the delusion that political propaganda consists of political slogans.
>
> Politics is not a separate field in itself. Political ideas do not come out of thin air. They are the result of the moral premises which men have accepted. Whatever people believe to be the good, right and proper human actions – that will determine their political opinions ....
>
> The purpose of the Communists in Hollywood is not the production of political movies openly advocating Communism. Their purpose is to corrupt non-political movies – by introducing small, casual bits of propaganda into innocent stories – and to make people absorb the basic premises of Collectivism by indirection and implication.[6]

Perhaps this collectivism is worth exploring further as we see it continually emerge within the texts that also provide us with radical utopias. In fact, some representations of collectivism itself can be seen as microcosms of radical utopias.

Lars and the Rural, Kitty in the City

If *It's a Wonderful Life* represents collectivist justice, then *Lars and the Real Girl* (2007) represents collectivist wellbeing. In *Lars and the Real Girl*, the title character is unable to be romantically involved because he develops a fear of intimacy as a result of difficult childhood experiences of abandonment. Lars finds a loophole to overcome his loneliness by ordering himself a life-sized sex doll, who he names Bianca and treats like the woman of his dreams. He gives her a complete backstory and personality of her own. He even laughs at all of 'her' jokes.

Although at first alarmed and bemused, his brother and sister-in-law eventually persuade their small Wisconsin community to pretend that Bianca is real. They integrate her into the community where she gets a 'job' as a mannequin in a clothing store, goes to church, and 'volunteers' entertaining children. "Every person in this town bends all backwards to make Bianca feel at home.... Why do you think she has so many places to go and so

204 Utopian Conclusions: Yesterday, Today, and Tomorrowland

much to do, huh? … Because all these people love you," Lars is told. Because the community treats her as real, Lars is able to cautiously live through his anxieties and overcome his fears, eventually enabling himself to open up and become romantically involved with a co-worker, a real woman.

Both *Lars and the Real Girl* and *It's a Wonderful Life* are set in small towns and while communalism is praised in both, they don't have to be seen as antithetical to systems of state and capitalism which produce individualism and greed. They can be explained through the compassionate conservatism of a small town. There is some truth to this town versus city dichotomy. Study after study have found that rural residents are more helpful than people in the city.[7]

Social psychological research into empathic behavior among urban and rural people began in 1968 following John M. Darley and Bibb Latané's study of bystander interventions during emergencies.[8] The researchers ran an experiment in which a participant would think they were part of a group discussion with each discussant in their own private cubicle speaking over a communication system that only allowed one person to speak at a time for two minutes. In reality, all the voices except for the participant's were recordings. One of the recorded voices tells the 'group' that he is prone to seizures and later in the recording is heard having a seizure, then sounding as if he is choking, followed by silence. The study was set up to test how quickly the participant would leave the room to report the seizure to the research assistant. The research recorded the actions of participants under different circumstances, particularly based on the number of people the participants thought were in the discussion. The more people believed to be in the discussion, the less likely the participant was to go and get help. When the experiment only included the person with the seizure and the participant, 85 percent of participants reported the incident to the research assistant before the end of the recording (125 seconds). If the participant believed there was one other person who could hear someone having a seizure, the number fell to 62 percent. If the participant thought there were five others in the group, only 31 percent of them reported the incident.[9] The researchers found that even those that did not report the incident were still distressed by the situation and did not show signs of apathy. This wasn't a difference in personality, they argued, but in context. People were less likely to report incidents when they thought that someone *else* might do it instead, which might save them from an awkward situation or being blamed for negatively affecting the experiment. This social force became known as the 'bystander effect'.

The researchers undertook this study after being inspired by real-life events. They began their published paper on the experiment by outlining the case of Kitty Genovese. Four years prior to the study, Kitty had been stabbed multiple times as she tried to enter the front of her apartment building in Queens, New York. As she was attacked, she screamed. Neighbors turned on their lights. One neighbor even shouted, "Let that girl alone!" After stabbing

Utopian Conclusions: Yesterday, Today, and Tomorrowland **205**

her the attacker drove off and Kitty dragged herself to the back of the apartment for safety, but ten minutes later the attacker returned. He stabbed her again and raped her. Eventually the police were called, an ambulance arrived but she died soon after she arrived at the hospital.[10]

Though it became widely known and even led to several documentaries, the story of Kitty Genovese did not become big news right away. A reporter began to investigate the case and he found that 38 people had witnessed the murder and failed to do anything about it. This was the ultimate bystander effect, and the city of New York began to stand in for general urban detachment in the public consciousness. Darley and Latane's study further testifies to what some have referred to as "simple folk wisdom: 'Country people are more helpful than city people' ".[11] Based on this knowledge, one could argue that *Lars and the Real Girl* is not a proto-utopian representation of collectivism, but a reflection of rural communities. Individualism is not a byproduct of capitalism and the state, but an urban problem. It is the geographic psychology that leads to the withering of even basic solidarities.

Looking back at *It's a Wonderful Life*, it is precisely this urbanness that represents George's worst nightmare. When his guardian angel shows George the world as it would be without him, we see a garish and drunken urban image. In the real Bedford Falls that George has devoted his life to, the bars are quiet, and families are home at night. But in the ghostly vision presented to George, the townsfolk are always out and rowdily about, drinking the night away while ignoring the plight of beggars. As George stumbles towards his home, he sees just how much his town has changed. He passes one bar after another. He looks across the streets: "Bowling Alley", "Pool Tables", "Fights every Wednesday nite". George's nightmare is the urban, represented as immoral. We are thus faced with some questions: Is the metropolitan of today the revolutionary subject of a collectivist future? Can the citizens of the urban even be redeemed? More to the point, do such collectivist representations only serve a *conservative* communalism based on small town simplicity?

Adelina and Oskar

For years the fiction author Harlan Ellison was obsessed with the case of Kitty Genovese. He imagined how someone could see such violence and not do a thing. Unable to get it out of his head, he put it on paper. In his short story about the incident, Ellison blames the city through the interactions of bystanders who also exhibit violent tendencies. One rapes the other and goes on to explain why.

> I'm like this because I'm a New Yorker, baby. Because I live in this fucking city every day .... Because I've lived in this great big snapping dog of a city all my life and I'm mad as a mudfly, for chrissakes! ... [D]o you expect

206 Utopian Conclusions: Yesterday, Today, and Tomorrowland

> kindness and gentility and understanding and a hand on your hand when the smog burns your eyes? I can't do it, I haven't got it. No one has it in this cesspool of a city. Look around you; what do you think is happening here? They take rats and they put them in boxes and when there are too many of them, some of the little fuckers go out of their minds and start gnawing the rest to death. It ain't no different here, baby![12]

Ellison's reading paints the urban as a slum that breeds sinister slovenliness in its inhabitants. This argument seems to contradict the forms of working relations among the proletariat that capitalist urbanity should have fostered according to Marx and Engels. They argued that the increase of the urban population under capitalism "rescued" people from "the idiocy of rural life" and with increased "development of industry, the proletariat not only increases in number; it becomes concentrated in greater masses, its strength grows, and it feels that strength more".[13] Cities were supposed to create solidarities, not selfishness. Some urban representations of communal solidarities and cooperation do exist, but they are situated in particular contexts. Take, for example, the beautiful Italian film from 1963, *Yesterday, Today and Tomorrow*, which features radical collectivist justice within an oppressive system in the urban center of Naples, Italy.

Vittorio de Sica's film is composed of three short stories themed in the respective periods in three Italian cities. 'Yesterday' corresponds to 'Adelina of Naples', the story of a woman in the neighborhood of Forcella who gets fined for selling contraband cigarettes on the street. She and her husband, with their child and another on the way, can't afford to pay her fine from their small income, so the next step is the confiscation of their furniture. But when the repo men enter her flat, they find the family's furniture is gone and the house is empty. There's nothing the authorities can do so they leave the flat, and as soon as they have gone neighbors begin to return Adelina's furniture which they had been hiding. Dressers and chairs hoisted down from balconies. Cabinets carried through the streets, making their return. Everyone in the community helps, satisfied that they were able to pull one over the state that is punishing them for trying to get by. But the charges against Adelina have not dropped. If she can't pay the fine, she will go to jail. She finds a loophole: she cannot be imprisoned as long as she is pregnant. After having seven kids in a row, she still ends up in jail, but the community doesn't give up. In each little business – from contraband cigarettes to barbershops, from lemonade stands to prostitutes – everyone charges an extra tax that they collect to buy Adelina's freedom. As in *It's a Wonderful Life*, even police officers participate. "The people of Forcella are out of this world! They've risen up in a gesture of solidarity!", says Adelina's husband. Through the collection of donations and pressure on the president, the neighborhood is able to get Adelina released and the neighbors decorate the streets to celebrate her return. While it presents a bygone era, the film undermines our views of a conservative past and a self-interested urbanity.

Comparing the work of the directors of *It's a Wonderful Life*'s with *Yesterday, Today and Tomorrow*, film director Michel Gondry found significant political difference. Regarding the films of Frank Capra, Gondry said: "They feel good. And they're great. But if you look at what's being said, it's really very, very conservative." Arguably this is because Capra presents the urban as a backward space and time that destroys communities. Gondry contrasts the work of Capra with the socialist films of de Sica.[14] As we see in *Yesterday, Today and Tomorrow* the urban does not preclude solidarity, and breaking with common perceptions and social mores of the time was not represented as evil but a form of justice under the oppressive circumstances. Gondry himself was keen to undermine common perceptions in his films, creating "elaborate, homemade worlds of lonely boys" such as *The Science of Sleep* (2006) and *Eternal Sunshine of the Spotless Mind* (2004). But these failed to touch on socialistic representations, choosing love as their central narrative. A film that replicates Gondry's evocation of such dream worlds, however, is a film that in contrast to the rural setting of *Lars and the Real Girl* represents the collectivist provision of wellbeing in the urban streets of New York City: Stephen Darldy's *Extremely Loud and Incredibly Close* (2011).

Extremely Loud and Incredibly Close follows a nine-year-old boy with Asperger's named Oskar and his idyllic relationship with his father. His father sets up various scavenger hunts for Oskar to complete. These 'reconnaissance expeditions' are created to help Oskar overcome his own fears – partially, we surmise, as a product of his neurodivergence – and deal with them within the hustle and bustle of New York City. These fears are exponentially enlarged when his father goes to a meeting in the Twin Towers on September 11, 2001, and dies in the tragedy. In the aftermath, Oskar stumbles upon 'The Greatest Reconnaissance Expedition': he finds a key but does not know what it belongs to and he is left with a solitary clue – the last name "Black". To try and preserve his father's memory, Oskar undertakes an impossible mission to find the lock to which the key belongs and whatever contents it safeguards. He attempts to do this by creating a list of everyone with the last name "Black" in New York and going to visit them to find out if they know anything about the key. Behind the scenes, Oskar's mom finds out about his plans and, rather than stopping him, she goes to the addresses and informs the residents that a young kid is coming, that his father died in 9/11, and that he's trying to find a lock that fits his key. In the context of the tragedy the individuals of the city known for the bystander effect come together to form a community that fosters the mental and emotional health of a nine-year-old boy who has just lost his father. When Oskar knocks on the door, they invite him in, they empathize with his story, they provide hospitality, and they tell him their own story. Through this experience Oskar's phobias and frustrations are resolved.

208 Utopian Conclusions: Yesterday, Today, and Tomorrowland

In the examples above we see solidarity unfolding outside the norms. In the Forcella community of Naples, we see people living outside the law out of economic necessity. Forcella, famously a stronghold of the Camorra – the mafia of Naples – is never presented in such a light in the film. A strongman is never present. Instead, solidarities in the midst of deprivation and collective law-breaking (engaging in the black market) create a need and a new norm of true solidarity. In the case of Oskar, it is 9/11 that breaks the norm and creates a more communal space of solidarity within tragedy. Although critics argued that 9/11 was introduced unnecessarily, even cynically, into the film and that the same story could have been told through the loss of a father by other means,[15] there is something within the 9/11 narrative that may help to preserve a realism within the urban landscape of New York. Through media representations, especially following the Kitty Genovese story, New York has often been painted as a rat-invested cesspool. This view of the city sets the ideological limits to what is possible. 9/11 is invoked in *Extremely Loud and Incredibly Close* because the urban solidarities can only realistically be explained through collective trauma.

> When inward life dries up, when feeling decreases and apathy increases, when one cannot affect or even genuinely touch another person, violence flares up as a daimonic necessity for contact, a mad drive forcing touch in the most direct way possible.[16]

This passage closes Ellison's fictionalization of the Kitty Genovese story. It is a quotation from existential psychologist Rollo May who was also interested in the Genovese case. May discusses Genovese's murder in an attempt to understand the callousness of modern life. But May does not believe that it is simply a case of rats put into boxes. The urban itself is not to blame, according to May.

> It is not difficult to appreciate how people living in a schizoid age have to protect themselves from tremendous overstimulation – protect themselves from the barrage of words and noise over radio and TV, protect themselves from the assembly line demands of ... industry and gigantic factory-modeled multiversities. In a world where numbers inexorably take over our means of identification, like flowing lava threatening to suffocate and fossilize all breathing life in its path; in a world where "normality" is defined as keeping your cool ... it is not surprising that will and love have become increasingly problematic and even, as some people believe, impossible of achievement.[17]

Here, May explains that it is the continued progress of capital and state interests that blindsides us off the cliff of inward vitality. The numbers and the industries toughen our skin to the sensitivity of others. In the case of Lars in *Lars and the Real Girl*, the familial angst which was likely a byproduct of such systems stripped his skin bare, making him hypersensitive and incapable of human contact. It is not the city, but the city's stand-in as the apex of capital and state power that create such problems. It is not a problem of the urban, but of state and capitalist 'progress'.

Rollo May focuses on processes of production and consumption in advanced capitalism as the problem. People were turned into numbers and exploited until they could be replaced. When May was writing, computers became what machinery was to the Luddites – a form of capitalist expansion that represented the supremacy of profit and the ruling class over life and everyone else. Where the Luddites represented the resistance of their time, May argued that the student activists represented resistance of the 1960s – the time of Genovese's murder. The student activists had not yet internalized the system and so they raged against the dying of the inward light. May, quoting student activists, saw that institutions were pushing people "towards something worse than mediocrity – and that is absolute indifference. An indifference towards perhaps even life itself." Another student said "We were all divided up into punches on an IBM card …. We decided to punch back in the riots of 1964, but the *real* revolution around here will come when we decide to burn computer cards as well as draft cards."[18]

Computer cards were an old-fashioned way of coding software. Punching was the means of coding. Immediately before May discussed the burning of computer cards in his book *Love & Will*, he had mentioned the Genovese murder. However, he had not been able to piece together the harrowing connection. Kitty's assailant was a murderer by night and a computer punch-card operator by day. The Remington Rand machines that he used at work had the motto "Methods that keynote the future of business". Just as Governor Nix got it wrong about the Anthropocene, we got it wrong with urban crime. Kitty's murder wasn't a glimpse into a dystopian future of urbanity, but of a future shaped by the logic of capital.

The Monitor of Past and Present

Rollo May's discussion of the "barrage of words and noise" of the TV, accompanied by concerns that the media increases isolation,[19] points us to a further object of dehumanization beyond the factory machine and the computer punch cards. Unlike those tools, television (and, as we are increasingly watching them at home, film) constructs a loneliness in which we are not 'alone'.

> In the alienated state of mass communication, the average citizen knows dozens of TV personalities who come smiling into his living room of an evening – but he himself is never known. In this state of alienation

210 Utopian Conclusions: Yesterday, Today, and Tomorrowland

and anonymity, painful for anyone to bear, the average person may well have fantasies which hover on the edge of real pathology.... [The viewer] sees thousands of other people every day, and he knows all the famous personalities as they come, via TV, into his single room .... [T]hey bandy about in a 'we're-all-friends-together' mood on the screen which invites him to join them and subtly assumes that he does join them. He knows them all. But he himself is never known.[20]

The real pathology discussed by May relates to Winston Moseley, the murderer of Kitty Genovese. Though he earned himself a decent living, Moseley "routinely broke into people's houses and stole television sets".[21] Five days after the murder of Genovese, his compulsion to steal televisions led an urban bystander to call the cops, which resulted in a murder confession. For May, the television had become the enemy of a healthy society. The Monitor of *Tomorrowland* served the same purpose. And if the hope for May was the student activists burning the computer punch cards, then for the protagonists of *Tomorrowland* hope lies in the destruction of the Monitor, a television screen that pumps out hopelessness setting into motion that which it broadcasts – the apocalypse. But the destruction of the Monitor did not signal a happy ending. In its concluding scenes, the film sets out the utopia of the future we can be hopeful for – a world without the interference of government or greed. But this utopia is still iconoclastic. We do not know what will replace the Monitor.

In our own world the Monitor not only presents us with dystopia, but also with an ideology that replicates the ideas of the ruling class. After all, as Marx and Engels argued:

the ideas of the ruling class are in every epoch the ruling ideas, i.e. the class which is the ruling material force of society, is at the same time its ruling intellectual force. The class which has the means of material production at its disposal, has control at the same time over the means of mental production, so that thereby, generally speaking, the ideas of those who lack the means of mental production are subject to it.[22]

We have seen that although they exist, there are few popular screen media texts with truly radical critiques that oppose the interests of capitalism and the state. Even more rare, almost unseen, are representations of positive alternatives to those systems. We could argue that the book has demonstrated that such ruling ideas are found in the content of film and television, but the argument should also apply to its early days.

In relation to television, those early days started off in a large former pickle factory in Passaic, New Jersey where DuMont Laboratories developed what some believe were the first home television sets sold to the general public. The company was named after owner Allen DuMont who previously worked as chief engineer and then vice president of the De Forest Radio Company. From its experimental station W2XCD in Passaic, De Forest was the first company to transmit picture and audio into people's homes.[23] Although this gave Passaic the label "The Birthplace of Television",[24] De Forest went bankrupt and DuMont set up his own business which improved on the picture and sound of television transmissions. Due to DuMont's engineering innovations and their control over a major network – the first to provide regular daytime programming, DuMont Laboratories was set to be a major player in television in the postwar era.[25]

How did DuMont sell themselves to the well-to-do public? "[E]ven in 1943, the company's ads typified corporate America's bid to shape the TV environment in ways that made the buyer of a receiver [TV] feel modern, more than that, Utopian."[26] DuMont Laboratories pitched television as "the biggest window in the world" and "the greatest show on earth". "You'll sail with television through vanishing horizons into exciting new worlds."[27] But this utopianism was firmly rooted in both the futurist capitalist enterprise and patriotism.[28] This was wartime technology and to the victors go the spoils. According to these ads, television even bridged the gap between city and country as they quoted Winston Churchill's line that with television "life in the country and on the land ought to compete in attractiveness with life in the great cities".[29]

The utopianism of the commercials was undermined by the perpetuation of the state and capital that was actually being pumped out of the television. The 1950s followed an economic depression and war when people were taught the lesson of frugalness which created "psychic, moral, and political obstacles to consumption among the public at large".[30] At the same time, the country wanted people to consume more, enabling the economy to grow. This was the context in which televisions were arriving in homes. As American Studies Professor George Lipsitz notes, "television's most important economic function came from its role as an instrument of legitimation for transformations in values initiated by the new economic imperatives of postwar America".[31] The government's policies meant that while the technological innovations of war were used for civilian purposes in television sets, corporations were also able to deduct from their taxable income the cost of advertising. Advertising thus became the major revenue source for television, and advertising interests would go on to shape the contours of television content. Advertising on television put consumerism front and center in the everyday lives of American families and television "provided a locus redefining American ethnic, class, and family identities into consumer identities".[32]

212 Utopian Conclusions: Yesterday, Today, and Tomorrowland

Will Play Jazz for Housing

The message on television was to buy more to help the country, but at the same time watching television meant being passive. Sitting, doing nothing, and letting the airwaves wash over you. The famous filmmaker Orson Welles once said this of 'the Monitor':

> You can be a complete paralytic, you watch it .... You can be drunk, you watch it. You can be making love, you watch it. You can be eating, you watch it .... But, with every other form [of entertainment] you have to collaborate with it in some way .... When we had only 'blanc et noir' in the cinema we demanded something from them. When we had no sound, we demanded something. The closer we got to an approximation of life the less was asked of the public and therefore the less [positive] impact it had upon the public.[33]

For Orson Welles, this can be read as self-criticism. As a film director, Welles' works at least asked his audience to leave their house and go to the cinema. But when film studios stopped giving him money to make movies, he began to make television programs. *The Orson Welles' Sketch Book* (1955), for example, was a mini-series that prefigured the age of YouTube and TikTok. Welles sat in front of the camera and told the viewer a story. This was essentially the entire show, which arguably asks even less of its audience than television shows.

Despite his own professional work falling into the trap of the Monitor, Welles was a passionate fan of jazz music, an art form that forces us out of passivity. Jazz asks something of its audience. The physical movements and the inevitable dancing springing from jazz can be understood, as it is for Rollo May, "as a ritual to express one's exhilaration and freedom".[34] Beyond its ability to actively engage the listener, jazz becomes a way of exhibiting one's own freedom. It not only expects participation but encourages a new lived experience. According to May, "Human beings dance ... jazz ... as an expression of aesthetic possibilities" .[35] The movement produced by jazz allows us to become aware of those possibilities, these personal freedoms. The history of jazz itself speaks not only to those freedoms and possibilities, but also to the solidarities in struggle.

The antecedents of jazz stretch as far back as nineteenth-century slave dances with music rooted in African rituals and the work songs of enslaved Africans.[36] Under extremely dehumanizing conditions these 'movements' provided enslaved people with a limited expression of freedom. But jazz also required "seasoning", as jazz pioneer Jelly Roll Morton put it. This seasoning came in the form of Spanish influence that was readily found in New Orleans.[37] In a radio broadcast, Orson Welles laid out a concise history of jazz:

Utopian Conclusions: Yesterday, Today, and Tomorrowland **213**

The whole thing started in that good time, wide-open, all night carnival city which was New Orleans before the last war. Jazz then swam the river boats and carried this new kind of music up to Chicago. From there it spread, all over the world and influenced all popular music and the greater part of what's called serious music. I'm not going to try and explain what it is, but I would like to point out that jazz is art for art's sake if ever there was such a thing, it's music musicians play for themselves, for their own satisfaction, the way they like it.[38]

Welles described this music for musicians in his introduction of a new band that he had assembled called the All Star Jazz Group, headlined by one of New Orleans' greatest talents, Kid Ory. Jazz musicians from New Orleans developed their talents at lawn parties and fish fries. With large open spaces, big jazz bands could form. As the music made its way up to densely populated urban areas such as Chicago and New York City, these big bands grew smaller, and sometimes there would be just a single pianist, like the legendary Fats Waller, pushing the keys as 100 people danced around him.[39]

Fats Waller and other prodigious jazz talents grew popular through a phenomenon known as rent parties which could be found in different cities where jazz put down roots. As is still the case, wages at the time were low, employment was often difficult to find, and yet you still had to pay rent. Racism compounded these problems. So, people organized big events with live jazz, dancing, and drinking and they invited their friends and neighbors to chip in a nickel or quarter which were used to pay the rent. These became known as rent parties and some of these parties ended with over 100 people packed into an apartment, overflowing into the corridors, and all to pay off someone's rent amidst poverty and racism. "Saturday nights were terrific in Harlem, but rent parties every night were the special passion of the community".[40] Rent parties weren't extravagant affairs. Musicians often played unrefined arrangements on heavily used equipment[41] but they were still the talk of the town, particularly in Harlem where Fats and other greats played. However, within a short amount of time jazz went from ramshackle rent parties to mainstream radio, and from the music of freedom to the sound coming out of the old-school Monitor.

The legendary Duke Ellington grew out of the rent parties of Harlem but began searching for greater fame, unintentionally leading jazz into what some may argue was an artistic abyss. Leaving the rent parties behind, Ellington went to play in the famous Cotton Club where, starting in December 1927 and through to 1933, his music was broadcast via radio across the United States. Duke Ellington's ascendency to stardom appropriately represented the period in between the 'jazz age' and the 'radio age' of American history.[42]

In the early years of radio much of the programming was produced by organizations such as universities, religious groups, political parties, and

214 Utopian Conclusions: Yesterday, Today, and Tomorrowland

newspapers. In 1927, only 7 percent of stations were commercial broadcasters that sought to maximize profit like the New York's WHN radio station, the station that first broadcast Ellington's performances.[43] WHN was driven to have a mass audience, which it telegraphed through its slogan "Serving the Masses, not the Classes". Just as the radio was seeking wider audiences, so was Duke Ellington. In those years, according to Professor of Radio and Popular Music Studies Tim Wall, Ellington and his band had no problem appealing to the stereotypes of "jungle music"; they "played their horns like baying animals, and performed in a club that signaled—through its name, decor and performances—the past of African Americans as slaves".[44] The musicians presented themselves through the primitivism that their white audience wanted.

The mutual striving for large audiences meant that jazz and radio began to co-construct their images to fit a broad, popular form of entertainment.[45] Ellington began to adapt himself to fit radio, composing "Mood Indigo" explicitly for electrical transmission.[46] Ellington eventually moved into swing which became jazz's most popular form. By the swing era, however, white bands were dominating the jazz scene. As Professor Wall states,

> Radio and film company executives now took the view that the media experiments with black culture had been dead-ends, a perspective which led to the exclusion of African American artists from the networks and mainstream cinema for at least the next fifteen years.[47]

Long before then, however, Ellington stopped exemplifying the spirit of jazz that Welles attributed to it: "it's music musicians play for themselves, for their own satisfaction, the way they like it".[48] With radio, jazz moved from being what Theodor Adorno referred to as "authentic culture", to the culture industry.

As argued in the book *The History of Jazz*, the radio that popularized jazz music also represented its decline in dynamism and collective spirit. Radio was the Monitor of old. Partially due to radio, by the mid-1930s "the whole ethos and ambiance of jazz culture were demystified".[49] The broadcasting of jazz over the radio nationwide meant that just one band could entertain hundreds of thousands. This "catapulted a few jazz players to a level of celebrity that would have been unheard of only a few years before".[50] However, this also meant that fewer and fewer musicians were needed for entertainment. At the same time that jazz started to become a more lucrative enterprise for those few who could make the cut, rent parties died out.[51] When you could sit at home and listen to the best jazz musicians, you did not need to go to a rent party to hear a decent one. And now that jazz had moved from crowded apartments and dance halls to your living room, you could also have a more passive relationship with the music.

The Sweding of Passaic

The rent parties of jazz were like the lively urban collectivist solidarity seen in De Sica's *Yesterday, Today and Tomorrow*. Both embraced the stretching of mores and legalities in their form of communal uplift. The communal uplift of Capra's *It's a Wonderful Life*, on the other hand, painted such boundary shifts as urban excesses that would put an end to solidarity itself, leaving only individualism in its wake. This is why director Michel Gondry saw significant differences in the political messages of the directors of these two films. "I like Capra, but he's very conservative .... I prefer Vittorio De Sica; he's warmer, he's on the side of poor people".[52]

Gondry made this comparison in interviews following the release of his film *Be Kind Rewind* (2008). The comedy is set, quite fittingly, in the hometown of television – Passaic, New Jersey. Once a town of innovation, the home of the first television station and one of America's biggest television companies, by the time Gondry made his film Passaic had become a post-industrial shadow of itself. Boarded-up buildings and closed shops represented the realities of an economic system that thrives off change and innovation without any concern for those eating the dust of capital flight. The dust of underemployment, of dilapidated tenements, and of eventual rejuvenation in the form of gentrification. First capital left their town, and now the poor residents are forced to leave it too.

This sets the scene for Gondry's film: from the creation of television, which brought viewers the "wide-eyed utopian optimism" of yesterday,[53] to the struggles of post-industrialization of today, to the ominousness of 'urban renewal' staring at us from the land of tomorrow. On Passaic's Main Street there is the old pickle factory that became the research office of DuMont Laboratories and just down the road, on 261 Main Street, there is a fictional place where past, present, and future intersect in the shop that serves as the film's namesake: Be Kind Rewind Video & Thrift Store. This VHS-only rental store (at a time when DVDs were very popular) is placed at the center of the film. It is introduced in the opening scenes, which are shot in black and white to look old but it is still clear to the audience that they were recently filmed. Two men hold a tape recorder interviewing an older African American man in front of the store.

It was all happening in the little town of Passaic, New Jersey. Passaic was the capital of jazz in the '20s and '30s because of its own native son Thomas "Fats" Waller, one of the greatest entertainers of all time .... It all began right here, a hundred years ago in Passaic, New Jersey. Right here, on this block. It was a different neighborhood then, but look here: he was born at 261 Main Street.

216 Utopian Conclusions: Yesterday, Today, and Tomorrowland

We soon cut to a modern, color film where the two men who were holding the tape recorder before, Jerry (Jack Black) and Mike (Yasiin Bey, aka Mos Def) are now spray painting a large mural reading "Fats Waller says Be Kind Rewind". They go back to the video store and we are introduced to the owner, Mr. Fletcher (Danny Glover). Mr. Fletcher is distressed because the city is arguing that his building is in a bad state. It violates modern building and regulatory standards and it is eventually condemned. Mr. Fletcher has 60 days to bring the building up to code or it will be demolished – turned into gentrified apartments along with the rest of the block.

Jerry and Mr. Fletcher hope that the mural will help draw in more customers to save the store, but Mike is more interested in telling people about the history of the neighborhood. Mr. Fletcher gives them some more history:

> A rent party was the place to be in the '20s and '30s. They were jumping. If you didn't have enough money to cover your rent ... you'd invite a few musicians, charge for drinks, and you'd get it on. Everybody would throw just a little bit in the pot. A dollar, whatever they could spare.

Mr. Fletcher is a jazz aficionado with a love for Fats Waller. On the sixtieth anniversary of Waller's death he joins a small commemoration with his friends on an abandoned train, supposedly where Fats died. During the intimate gathering, with Fats' record playing in the background, Mr. Fletcher describes his troubles with the store. The others, some of whom had some minor successes in business, recommend he emulate successful video rental stores instead of sticking to his failing model. One friend tells him, "just give the people what they want".

So, Mr. Fletcher goes to New York City on his own reconnaissance expedition to find out how the big chain store, West Coast Video, is able to be profitable. He goes in and asks the employees some questions that give him some ideas for adapting his business: "Less choice, more copies of the same movie, simplified categorization of genre ..., no specific knowledge required [by the employee]". Additionally, he finally decides he should replace his VHS tapes with DVDs. While Mr. Fletcher is out doing market research, Mike has been put in charge of the store. Mike has never had this much responsibility before and he is keen to impress his father figure, Mr. Fletcher. Before leaving to attend the commemoration, Mr. Fletcher tells Mike to follow one crucial rule: Keep Jerry Out. While Mr. Fletcher tolerates Jerry, he knows that he's accident-prone and he doesn't want anything to happen to the store. Mike does his best to prohibit Jerry from entering the shop, but Jerry starts to vomit right outside the store. In order to clean up and help him, Mike takes Jerry inside. Unbeknownst to either of them, chaos is about to ensue.

The reason Jerry is sick is because he tried to sabotage a nearby powerplant the night before, thinking that the plant was a conspiracy causing a lot of problems in the local area. In attempting to shut down the plant, Jerry got magnetically charged. His illness comes as a result and – having entered the store – Jerry accidentally erases all the movies on the tapes with the magnet force emanating from him. Mike and Jerry panic when a loyal customer comes in and asks for the classic 1984 movie *Ghostbusters*. Mike promises to deliver the movie before the end of the day but fails to find another VHS copy. In desperation, Mike comes up with the idea of filming their own version of the movie.

> She doesn't know what the movie's supposed to look like. The only thing that she knows is what's on this [VHS] box. She's never seen it before. If we stay 10 feet away from the camera, she's not gonna recognize us.

So, Mike and Jerry set out to make their version of *Ghostbusters* with nothing but an old-school camcorder, bits and bobs from Jerry's junkyard chop-shop, and the city of Passaic. Their version is ridiculous, but Jerry is proud of his efforts and wants to make more movies. Luckily for him another customer walks into the store requesting *Rush Hour 2*. For this film they set out to recruit a few Passaic locals to play other characters in the film, including a young woman named Alma (Melonie Diaz). Eventually their movies become more popular in the city, and, with Alma's business acumen, the store starts charging $20 for each rental, justifying the expense by saying the films are custom-made and imported from Sweden. They are "Sweded".

Customers start pouring in from all over the city to see these Sweded movies. When Mr. Fletcher comes back, he insists that his DVD idea is more sensible than the idea of Sweding movies, but Mike, Jerry, and Alma are persistent. Alma argues that if they cut the length of the films, they can make more of them and therefore make more money. "People will feel swindled", Mike retorts. "Not if we include them in the films. We'll give them parts to play. This way, A) with their help, we can make more movies; B) the films can be shorter, and they won't feel swindled." So, they start to bring people in to create movies for themselves as a way of saving the store. This is the point at which Gondry ties together the store and Fats Waller. Fats Waller was a product of rent parties and Gondry replicates this idea in relation to movies. In the process of independently making their own movies the community discovers a new, true art form in which, as Gondry said – mirroring Welles' comments about jazz– "people [make] their own entertainment". Or, as the movie puts it, "[people] become the stockholders of their own happiness".

Mike, Jerry, and the rest of the gang "Swede" dozens of old films. Then, one day, a representative from the movie studios of Hollywood walks through their door. She's not there to launch their film careers; she's there

218 Utopian Conclusions: Yesterday, Today, and Tomorrowland

to "assess the damage" of copyright infringement. The fees come to $3.15 billion and/or 63,000 years in prison. "The entire film industry is crumbling because of pirates and bootleggers. And we intend to stop it", the rep says. They argue that it's not the "formulaic big movies" that people are there to see but the new Sweded versions. Despite the protestations, the studios confiscate the tapes and destroy them. All hope seems to be lost. Not enough money was raised through renting Sweded films, and it looks as if the store has come to an end. But the business is not the end goal. Before the building is demolished, the gang set out to make one more big movie; a new original picture with the whole community playing a role. The movie is filmed in a black and white, old-school documentary style like the one in the first scene of *Be Kind Rewind*. It fictionalizes the life of Fats Waller, creating meaning for a town through their collective efforts. In creating this film-within-a-film, Gondry also sets out to integrate the local community in the production. A large number of the actors in the film came from the community of Passaic.

Together, the characters of the film and the community make their own Fats Waller film that ends up being projected out of the window of the store for all the passersby to see before the iconic shop gets demolished. They crowd around the street watching, enchanted by the film. In the process, the collectivist spirit was reawakened and, although Hollywood remained, the big-budget studios were symbolically defeated in the battle.

The Monument, The Monitor, and Marx

Be Kind Rewind incorporates a story of past, present, and future along with an exploration of urban and suburban space through the concept of the new evil, the DVD. The VHS-only store is seen as a relic of the past, one that is crumbling from the inside, from its own natural entropy. Despite this, it still has a place in the suburban city of Passaic which is struggling with its own economic, post-industrial decay and the decay of its community through gentrification. The DVD represents the edge of the present. It is a modern form of viewing film which Mr. Fletcher observes when he is in the fast-paced urban space of New York City, just across the Hudson River.

Fletcher eventually embraces the present and wants to adapt to the current market. But Passaic would have to be pushed along. Its residents are also behind the times, which is why Mr. Fletcher plans to sell affordable DVD players as well as renting out movies. In entering the 'present', Passaic would also need to gentrify, which is why the city wants to convert the old video store into luxury apartments. The city is caught up in the storm of philosopher Walter Benjamin's *Angelus Novus*: "The storm is what we call progress".[54]

If the past is represented by both VHS tapes and suburbs and the present is represented as DVDs and urban centers, then what of the future? In The Monuments of Passaic", the artist Robert Smithson wrote, "If the future was 'out of date' and 'old fashioned,' then I had been in the future."[55] He wrote this in 1967 after taking a short journey to Passaic with his Instamatic camera. He snapped pictures of what he referred to as monuments but what were really the semi-completed constructions of industrial society. Pipes gushing water into a river. A parking lot. A sand box. Smithson chose to look at Passaic because of the splendor it exuded to the urbanites of the nineteenth century in search of natural scenery, like the Passaic Falls.[56] It had obviously since developed into an industrial suburb and then, 20 years after Smithson's essay, become a struggling post-industrial settlement. Many of the sites that Smithson described have been altered. His first monument was a swing bridge of "ramshackle" beams over the Passaic River which he described as being of "an outmoded world". The bridge has been replaced and it no longer swings. Another monument divided the city "turning it into a mirror and a reflection". This was a parking lot which was built over old train tracks. The height of innovation of its time was buried under the asphalt of "progress". For Smithson, progress is "a form of obsolescence".[57] From a bridge convenient for boats to one for cars. From a railroad to a parking lot. The latest technologies of transportation (like the radio, television, and internet or the VHS and DVD) spelled both dystopia and utopia, depending on your perspective. "The windows of City Motors auto sales proclaim the existence of Utopia through 1968 WIDE TRACK PONTIACS—Executive, Bonneville, Tempest, Grand Prix, Firebirds, GTO, Catalina, and Le Mans— that visual incantation marked the end of the highway construction."[58] The highways were passages to the future and their unfinished nature marked what Smithson referred to as "holes". "[T]hose holes in a sense are the monumental vacancies that define, without trying, the memory-traced of an abandoned set of futures."

We have a past, we have a present, but we always have futures in the plural. These futures are ambitions that, once achieved or even once started, collapse into the present. And there is always either progress or "progress" – either a movement toward something better, or just a movement forward into a future no better than the past, or even worse. Technological advances that we experience, or even the imagined Monitor of *Tomorrowland*, do not embody in them which progress we speak of. Their mere existence does not uproot the natural environment, displace populations, or lead to starvation. The Monitor only shapes our ambitions for the future – annihilation – because of *what* it is broadcasting.

The pasts before capitalism could not have developed the technologies which represent the many pasts we have *within* capitalism – the pasts of the radio and railroad are quickly replaced, as Marx and Engels remind us in *The Community Manifesto*.[59] The pasts are still linear, but each new present presents us with varied possibilities of what is to be. However, before

220 Utopian Conclusions: Yesterday, Today, and Tomorrowland

these productive forces can be turned into positive possibilities, their default application for the masses grinds them down.

> Owing to the extensive use of machinery, and to the division of labor, the work of the proletarians has lost all individual character, and, consequently, all charm for the workman. He becomes an appendage of the machine, and it is only the most simple, most monotonous, and most easily acquired knack, that is required of him.[60]

The demand for something to build the worker back up was there and capital filled the void with other forms of technology such as radio, film, television, etc. .... These worked for the purposes of social reproduction. They provided enough distraction to rebuild the strength to get up early the next morning and go back to one's rudimentary job. Although such technology can be seen as an "opiate of the masses", these technologies, from a Marxian position, do not determine in themselves how and for whom they will operate. But just as the technologies within a workplace default to further oppress labor, the advances of cultural technologies, by default but not necessity, further the interests of the ruling class. For Smithson, who was looking at the culturally built environment as nature, there is always an endless "negotiation between nature and culture in which each became a reflection of the other".[61] But culture is not one of our equal co-creations. Culture is often imposed on us, by force, through the forms of state and capitalism. The technologies are under their control, and they are largely shaping the function and use of those technologies.

The Revolutionary Actor

If our culture and imagination is co-produced by 'Hollywood capitalism', what modes of media production can replace it? *Be Kind Rewind* provides us with an alternative. It is the collective creative process itself that may free us from the debilitating message of the Monitor. Returning to Orson Welles, he argues that "man cannot escape his destiny to create whatever it is we make – jazz, a wooden spoon, or graffiti on the wall. All of these are expressions of man's creativity, proof that man has not yet been destroyed by technology."[62] The benefit of the acceleration in technological advances is that we are now well into the age where the co-construction of screen media texts is possible. It is inexpensive to access and easy to use. Perhaps in this age we cannot only produce texts that can expand artistic creativity but we can also develop radical potentials both within the text and through our interactions with it.

YouTubers and TikTokers can make films and shows with radical messages, but we are still passive consumers of these products. They may provide us with a radical worldview, but we may still hesitate to seize power. This is a byproduct of how we engage with our media – and other forms of consumption. We don't participate proactively but through the selection process. You want a radical message, pick a radical film. Although there are few made by Hollywood, there must be many available online and meant for free public consumption. You want a radical alternative, pick a 'radical' political candidate. Bernie Sanders. Alexandria Ocasio-Cortez. Jeremy Corbyn. But only social democracy would result from this and even that would likely be on the backs of the Third World. The idea of collective Sweding primes us to *act* in our own collective interests beyond making a simple choice and in doing so turn ourselves into the revolutionary subject we should desire to be, a revolutionary actor.

In the first episode of *Orson Welles' Sketch Book*, Welles talks about his first great passion: the theatre. Unlike film and television, the theatre asks the audience to engage, to do some work. Welles discussed his performance, at the age of 15, as Duke Karl Alexander in a production of *Jew Suss* at the Gate Theatre in Dublin. Welles describes himself as having no nerves at all during his performance until, soon after he delivered a line, someone from the audience shouted at the stage. Welles recollects his feelings at that very moment, returning to Žižek's cartoon metaphor from Chapter 1.

> "You've all seen Donald Duck and Pluto the Pup in the Disney cartoons when they run off the edge or a roof or off the ledge of a cliff, run quite a distance. Then they happen to glance down and when they realize where they are, there's nothing under them, they fall .... At that moment, the sound of that voice [from the audience] was my first experience of feeling like someone unfortunate at Disney.

The collective co-creation of culture gives us two positive potentials. One is to bypass the limitations of the culture industry's grip on our ideas. To construct new realities that represent our own visions and our own challenges. As demonstrated, occasionally film and television allow this, but it is hardly a drop in the dead sea of distraction, filled with the sodium chloride of complacency in capital and state. The second potential is to fall, like Orson, but not into fear – into possibility.

The psychologist Rollo May concludes his book *Freedom and Destiny* saying: "We all stand on the edge of life, each moment comprising that edge. Before us is only possibility". But the Monitor can block our vision of these possibilities. By actively engaging in culture construction, we can prefiguratively expose ourselves to alternatives to the models we know, to radical horizons and possibilities. For May, possibility equates to freedom and is in a dialectical relationship with destiny. Destiny puts limits on freedom and this in effect makes freedom viable. These limits, however, are the limits of responsibility and community. Destiny drives us to be free in ways that restrict unwanted worlds of hedonism at other people's expense.

"In the freedom of being, new possibilities continually surge up, possibilities of new discoveries about oneself, new flights of imagination, new visions of what the world and living in it might be."[63]

But are we ready for this challenge of freedom, of being the revolutionary actor, as we build up to the revolutionary rupture? May writes,

> Every human being experiences this anxiety when he or she exercises the freedom to move out into the no man's land of possibility. We can escape the anxiety only by not venturing – that is, by surrendering our freedom. I am convinced that many people never become aware of their most creative ideas since their inspirations are blocked off by this anxiety before the ideas even reach the level of consciousness.[64]

If we take a leap of faith in *taking action* – including in co-producing culture, we might then finally be able to more easily imagine a world beyond capitalism than the end of the world itself.

Notes

1 From the film *Tomorrowland* (2015).
2 From the film *Tomorrowland*.
3 From the film *Tomorrowland*.
4 Also see *C'è ancora domani* (*There's Still Tomorrow*) (2023).
5 A letter from a Special Agent in Charge of the Los Angeles Office of the FBI to then Director of the Federal Bureau of Investigation, J. Edgar Hoover, notes that "Rand published a booklet which was designed for furnishing information concerning the type of Communist propaganda used in motion pictures" (BACM Research n.d.). She also testified in front of the House of Unamerican Activities Committee as a friendly witness.
6 Rand 2014[1947].
7 Steblay 1987.
8 Darley and Latané 1968.
9 Even those who did respond to the emergency when they believed four other people had heard the seizure taking place, they were slower in leaving the room and telling the research assistant.
10 Rosenthal 1999.
11 Steblay 1987.
12 Ellison 2001, p. 207.
13 Marx 1982[1867], Ch. 13; Marx and Engels 1988[1848], p. 218. However, of the great revolutionary movements – even those adopting a Marxist analysis – most have been by peasants and those in rural areas. Thus, we need not see rural solidarities as inherently conservative even in the age of capitalism.
14 Phipps 2008.
15 Green 2012.
16 Ellison 2001, p. 213.
17 May 2007, p. 32.

18 May 2007, p. 30. Emphasis in original.
19 May 2007, p. 22.
20 May 2007, pp. 31, 161–162.
21 Lemann 2014.
22 Marx and Engels 1998[1846], p. 67.
23 Myers 2000, p. 58.
24 Sullivan 1975.
25 Spigel 1992, p. 76.
26 Tichi 1991, p. 12.
27 Tichi 1991, p. 15.
28 Tichi 1991, p. 13. In its ads "the company familiarized the televisual process in wartime patriotic figures of electrons moving in 'squads' under the direction of 'sergeants'" (Tichi 1991, p. 13), and appealed to the 'highest national values' (Tichi 1991, p. 13).
29 Tichi 1991, p. 16.
30 Lipsitz 1986, p. 361.
31 Lipsitz 1986, p. 359.
32 Lipsitz 1986, p. 361.
33 From *The Orson Welles' Sketch Book*.
34 May 1981, p. 65.
35 May 1981, p. 62.
36 Gioia 1998.
37 Gioia 1998, p. 6.
38 Welles quoted in French 2006.
39 Lester 2012.
40 Lester 2002, quoting David Levering Lewis, p. 174.
41 Lester 2002, quoting David Levering Lewis, p. 145.
42 Wall 2012.
43 Wall 2012, p. 204.
44 Wall 2012, p. 206.
45 Wall 2012, p. 206.
46 Wall 2012, p. 213.
47 Wall 2012, pp. 220–221.
48 From *The Orson Welles' Sketch Book*.
49 Gioia 1998, p. 135.
50 Gioia 1998, p. 135.
51 Boyd 1938.
52 Daly 2008.
53 Butsch 2000, p. 253.
54 Benjamin 1940.
55 Smithson 1967.
56 Menard 2014.
57 Menard 2014, p. 1031.
58 Smithson 1967, p. 50.
59 "The bourgeoisie, during its rule of scarce one hundred years, has created more massive and more colossal productive forces than have all preceding generations together. Subjection of Nature's forces to man, machinery, application of chemistry to industry and agriculture, steam-navigation, railways, electric

telegraphs, clearing of whole continents for cultivation, canalization of rivers, whole populations conjured out of the ground – what earlier century had even a presentiment that such productive forces slumbered in the lap of social labor?" Marx and Engels 2010[1848], p.17.
60 Marx and Engels 2010[1848], p.18.
61 Menard 2014, p. 1038.
62 Welles in *F for Fake* (1973).
63 May 1981, p. 58.
64 May 1981, p. 191.

References

Benjamin, Walter (1940) 'On the Concept of History', www.efn.org/~dredmond/Theses_on_History.html.

Boyd, Frank (1938) 'Harlem Rent Parties', Library of Congress, https://memory.loc.gov/mss/wpalh2/21/2101/21011010/21011010.pdf.

Butsch, Richard (2000) *The Making of American Audiences: From Stage to Television, 1750–1990*, Cambridge: Cambridge University Press.

Daly, Steven (2008) 'Michel Gondry: The Mad Scientist of Cinema', *The Telegraph*, Jan. 27, https://www.telegraph.co.uk/culture/film/3670796/Michel-Gondry-the-mad-scientist-of-cinema.html.

Darley, John M. and Latané, Bibb (1968) 'Bystander Intervention in Emergencies: Diffusion of Responsibility', *Journal of Personality of Social Psychology*, 8(4): 377–383.

Ellison, Harlan (2001) 'The Whimper of Whipped Dogs', in Terry Dowling (ed.), *The Essential Ellison: A 50-Year Retrospective* (pp. 199–214), Beverly Hills, CA: Morpheus International.

French, Lawrence (2006) 'Orson Welles Introduces The Mercury Jazz Combo', wellesnet.com, www.wellesnet.com/orson-welles-introduces-the-mercury-jazz-combo.

Gioia, Ted (1998) *The History of Jazz*, Oxford: Oxford University Press.

Green, Daniel (2012) 'Film Review: *Extremely Loud & Incredibly Close*', https://cine-vue.com/2012/02/film-review-extremely-loud-incredibly-close.html.

BACM Research (n.d.) R. B. Hood, SAC, LA. 'Letter to Director, FBI October 17, 1947', www.paperlessarchives.com/FreeTitles/ArynRandFBIFiles.pdf.

Lemann, Nicholas (2014) 'A Call for Help', *The New Yorker*, Mar. 10, https://www.newyorker.com/magazine/2014/03/10/a-call-for-help.

Lester, Charlie (2012) 'The New Negro of Jazz: New Orleans, Chicago, New York, the First Great Migration, & the Harlem Renaissance, 1890–1930', Doctoral thesis, University of Cincinnati.

Lipsitz, George (1986) 'The Meaning of Memory: Family, Class, and Ethnicity in Early Network Television Programs', *Cultural Anthropology*, 1(4): 355–387.

Marx, Karl 1982([1867]) *Capital: A Critique of Political Economy, Volume I*, Harmondsworth: Penguin Books.

Marx, Karl and Fredrick Engels (1988[1848]) *Economic and Philosophic Manuscripts of 1844 and The Communist Manifesto*, New York: Prometheus Books.

Marx, Karl and Fredrick Engels (1998[1846]) *The German Ideology*, New York: Prometheus Books.

Marx, Karl and Engels, Fredrick (2010[1848]) *Manifesto of the Communist Party*, Marxist Internet Archive.

May, Rollo (1981) *Freedom and Destiny*, New York: A Delta Book.

May, Rollo (2007) *Love & Will*, New York: W. W. Norton & Company.

Menard, Andrew (2014) 'Robert Smithson's Toxic Tour of Passaic, New Jersey', *Journal of American Studies*, 48(4): 1019–1040.

Myers, William Starr (ed.) (2000) *Prominent Families of New Jersey, Volume 1*, Baltimore, MD: Clearfield.

Phipps, Keith (2008) 'Michel Gondry', *AV FILM*, https://film.avclub.com/michel-gon dry-1798213327.

Rand, Ayn (2014[1947]) 'Screen Guide for Americans'," in Scott MacKenzie (ed.), *Film Manifestos and Global Cinema Cultures: A Critical Anthology* (pp. 422–431), Berkeley: University of California Press.

Rosenthal, Abraham M. (1999) *Thirty-Eight Witnesses: The Kitty Genovese Case*, Berkeley: University of California Press.

Smithson, Robert (1967) 'The Monuments of Passaic: Has Passaic Replaced Rome as the Eternal City?', *Artform*, 6(4), https://www.artforum.com/features/the-monume nts-of-passaic-211237.

Spigel, Lynn (1992) *Television and the Family Ideal in Postwar America*, Chicago: The University of Chicago Press.

Stable, Nancy Mehrkens (1987) 'Helping Behavior in Rural and Urban Environments: A Meta-Analysis', *Psychological Bulletin*, 2(3): 346–356.

Sullivan, Joseph F. (1975) '"Birthplace of TV" to Hail Dumont', *New York Times*, Sept. 21, https://www.nytimes.com/1975/09/21/archives/birthplace-of-tv-to-fail-dumont-passaic-honoring-dumont.html.

Tichi, Cecelia (1991) *Electronic Hearth: Creating an American Television Culture*, New York: Oxford University Press.

Wall, Tim (2012) 'Duke Ellington, Radio Remotes, and the Mediation of Big City Nightlife, 1927 to 1933', *Jazz Perspectives*, 6(1–2): 197–222.

APPENDIX

Films/Television Programs Analyzed

Screen Media Text	Year Initially Released
9 to 5	1980
12 Years a Slave	2013
21 Jump Street	2012
22 Jump Street	2014
28 Days Later	2002
100, The (season 1)	2014
101 Dalmatians	1996
1917	2019
Absolute Power	1997
Accidental Love	2015
Accountant, The	2016
Ace Venture 2: When Nature Calls	1995
Admission	2013
Air	2023
Aladdin	2019
Alex, Inc (season 1)	2018
Allegiant	2016
All the Money in the World	2017
All the King's Men	2006

Appendix **227**

(Continued)

Screen Media Text	Year Initially Released
Amazing Grace	2006
American Beauty	1999
American Dreamz	2006
American Gangster	2007
American History X	1998
American Made	2017
Americans, The (season 1)	2013
Americans, The (season 2)	2014
Americans, The (season 3)	2015
Americans, The (season 4)	2016
Americans, The (season 5)	2017
Americans, The (season 6)	2018
Amistad	1997
Amsterdam	2022
Anarchist Cookbook, The	2002
Antitrust	2001
Ant-Man	2015
Archer (season 1)	2009
Archer (season 2)	2011
Archer (season 3)	2011
Archer (season 4)	2013
Archer (season 5)	2014
Archer (season 6)	2015
Arrested Development (season 1)	2003
Arrested Development (season 2)	2004
Arrested Development (season 3)	2005
Arrested Development (season 4)	2013
Arrested Development (season 5)	2018
As Good as it Gets	1997
Assassination of Richard Nixon, The	2004

(*Continued*)

228 Appendix

(Continued)

Screen Media Text	Year Initially Released
Avatar	2009
Avatar: The Way of Water	2022
Back to the Future	1985
Bad Boys	1995
Bad Lieutenant	1992
Battle in Seattle	2007
Be Kind Rewind	2008
Belle	2013
Better Off Ted (season 1)	2009
Better Off Ted (season 2)	2010
Big Short, The	2015
Billions (season 1)	2016
Billions (season 2)	2017
Billions (season 3)	2018
Billions (season 4)	2019
Billions (season 5)	2020
Billions (season 6)	2022
Billions (season 7)	2023
Birth of a Nation, The	2016
Black-ish (season 4)	2016
Black-ish (season 5)	2017
BlacKkKlansman	2018
Black Mirror (season 4, episode 1)	2017
Black Panther	2018
Black Panther: Wakanda Forever	2022
Black Sheep	1996
Blood Diamond	2006
Blow Out	1981
Boat That Rocked, The	2009
Bombshell	2019

(Continued)

(Continued)

Screen Media Text	Year Initially Released
Book of Eli, The	2010
Boondocks, The (season 1)	2005
Boss Baby, The	2017
Bourne Identity, The	2002
Bourne Legacy, The	2012
Bourne Supremacy, The	2004
Bourne Ultimatum, The	2007
Boys, The (season 1)	2019
Boys, The (season 2)	2020
Boys, The (season 3)	2022
BrainDead (season 1)	2016
Branded	2012
Breach	2007
Bright	2017
Broad City (season 1)	2014
Broad City (season 2)	2015
Broad City (season 3)	2016
Broad City (season 4)	2017
Broad City (season 5)	2018
Broken City	2013
Brooklyn Nine-Nine (season 1)	2013
Brooklyn Nine-Nine (season 2)	2014
Brooklyn Nine-Nine (season 3)	2015
Brooklyn Nine-Nine (season 4)	2016
Brooklyn Nine-Nine (season 5)	2017
Brooklyn Nine-Nine (season 6)	2019
Brooklyn Nine-Nine (season 7)	2020
Brooklyn Nine-Nine (season 8)	2021
Buffalo Soldiers	2001
Bug's Life, A	1998

(Continued)

230 Appendix

(Continued)

Screen Media Text	Year Initially Released
Bulworth	1998
Butler, The	2013
Campaign, The	2012
Casino Jack	2010
Catch a Fire	2006
Cesar Chavez	2014
Chamber, The	1996
Chappaquiddick	2017
Chernobyl	2019
Children of Men	2006
City of Hope	1991
Civil Action, A	1998
Class Action	1991
Cloud Atlas	2012
Company Men, The	2010
Conspiracy Theory	1997
Constant Gardener, The	2005
Contender, The	2000
Contract, The	2006
Cop Land	1997
Corporate (season 1)	2018
Corporate (season 2)	2019
Corporate (season 3)	2020
Cosmopolis	2012
Crisis	2021
Crucible, The	1996
Cry Freedom	1987
Crying Game, The	1992
CSI: Crime Scene Investigation (season 1)	2000
Dallas Buyers Club	2013

(*Continued*)

Appendix **231**

(Continued)

Screen Media Text	Year Initially Released
Dances with Wolves	1990
Dark Phoenix	2019
Dark Waters	2019
Dave	1993
Day After Tomorrow, The	2004
Deepwater Horizon	2016
Demolition Man	1993
Departed, The	2006
Detroit	2017
Dick	1999
Dictator, The	2012
Distinguished Gentleman, The	1992
District 9	2009
Don't Look Up	2021
Django Unchained	2012
Eagle Eye	2008
Easy A	2010
Elysium	2013
Emancipation	2022
End of Watch	2012
Enemy of the State	1998
Eraser	1996
Erin Brockovich	2000
Escape from LA	1997
Escape from Pretoria	2020
Evan Almighty	2007
Expanse, The (season 1)	2015
Expanse, The (season 2)	2017
Expanse, The (season 3)	2018
Expanse, The (season 4)	2019

(Continued)

232 Appendix

(Continued)

Screen Media Text	Year Initially Released
Expanse, The (season 5)	2020
Extremely Loud and Incredibly Close	2011
Eye in the Sky	2015
Fair Game	2010
Ford v Ferrari	2019
Forrest Gump	1994
Founder, The	2016
Freedomland	2006
Free Guy	2021
Free State of Jones	2016
Frost/Nixon	2008
Fun with Dick and Jane	2005
Game of Thrones (Season 1)	2011
Game of Thrones (Season 2)	2012
Game of Thrones (Season 3)	2013
Game of Thrones (Season 4)	2014
Game of Thrones (Season 5)	2015
Game of Thrones (Season 6)	2016
Game of Thrones (Season 7)	2017
Game of Thrones (Season 8)	2019
Gandhi	1982
Gangs of New York	2002
Gangster Squad	2013
Gaslit	2022
Ghost Writer, The	2010
Giver, The	2014
Glass Onion	2022
Glengarry Glen Ross	1992
Glory	1989
Gold	2016

(Continued)

(Continued)

Screen Media Text	Year Initially Released
Golden Compass, The	2007
Goliath (season 1)	2016
Good Kill	2014
Good Lord Bird, The	2010
Good Night and Good Luck	2005
Good Shepherd, The	2006
Grandma	2015
Gray Man, The	2022
Green Book, The	2018
Gringo	2018
Gunman, The	2015
Happyish (season 1)	2015
Harold and Kumar Escape from Guantanamo Bay	2008
Hate U Give, The	2018
Head of State	2003
Homicide	1991
Hook	1991
Horrible Bosses	2011
Hotel Rwanda	2004
Hot Shots!	1991
House of Cards (season 1)	2013
House of Cards (season 2)	2014
House, The	2017
Hunger Games: Catching Fire, The	2013
Hunger Games: Mockingjay – Part 1, The	2014
Hunger Games: Mockingjay – Part 2, The	2015
Hunger Games, The	2012
Hunting Party, The	2007
I Am Legend	2007

(Continued)

234 Appendix

(Continued)

Screen Media Text	Year Initially Released
I'm a Virgo (season 1)	2023
Imitation Game, The	2014
Inception	2010
Incorporated (season 1)	2016
Independence Day	1996
In Dubious Battle	2016
Infiltrator, The	2016
Informant!, The	2009
Insider, The	1999
Insurgent	2015
Internal Affairs	1990
International, The	2009
In the Electric Mist	2009
In Time	2011
Invictus	2009
Jason Bourne	2016
JFK	1991
John Q	2002
Jojo Rabbit	2019
Joker	2019
Judge Dredd	1995
Jupiter Ascending	2015
Jurassic Park	1993
Just Mercy	2019
Killing Them Softly	2012
Kill the Messenger	2014
Kimi	2022
Kingdom, The	2007
Kingsman: The Golden Circle	2017
LA Confidential	1997

(Continued)

(Continued)

Screen Media Text	Year Initially Released
Larry the Cable Guy: Health Inspector	2006
Lars and the Real Girl	2007
Last Duel, The	2021
Last of Us, The (season 1)	2023
Laundromat, The	2019
Leave the World Behind	2023
LEGO Movie, The	2014
Lincoln	2012
Looming Tower, The	2018
Lord of the Rings: The Fellowship of the Ring, The	2001
Lord of the Rings: The Return of the King, The	2003
Lord of the Rings: The Two Towers, The	2002
Lost World: Jurassic Park, The	1997
Luke Cage (season 1)	2016
Mad City	1997
Mad Max: Fury Road	2015
Malcolm X	1992
Manchurian Candidate, The	2004
Man of the Year	2006
Margin Call	2011
Matrix Reloaded, The	2003
Matrix Revolutions, The	2003
Matrix, The	1999
Mauritanian, The	2021
Medical Police (season 1)	2020
Men	2022
Menu, The	2022
Michael Clayton	2007

(Continued)

236 Appendix

(Continued)

Screen Media Text	Year Initially Released
Milk	2008
Minority Report	2002
Mission: Impossible	1996
Mission: Impossible II	2000
Mission: Impossible III	2006
Mission: Impossible – Fallout	2018
Mission: Impossible – Rogue Nation	2015
Mission, The	1986
Miss Sloane	2016
Money Monster	2016
Morning Show, The (season 1)	2019
Morning Show, The (season 3)	2023
Motherless Brooklyn	2019
Murder at 1600	1997
My Fellow Americans	1996
Negotiator, The	1998
Net, The	1995
Newsies	1992
New World, The	2005
Nice Guys, The	2016
Nick of Time	1995
Nixon	1995
No Sudden Move	2021
No Way Out	1987
Office Space	1999
Office, The (US – season 1)	2005
Office, The (US – season 2)	2005
Office, The (US – season 3)	2006
Office, The (US – season 4)	2007
Office, The (US – season 5)	2008

(Continued)

(Continued)

Screen Media Text	Year Initially Released
Office, The (US – season 6)	2009
Office, The (US – season 7)	2010
Office, The (US – season 8)	2011
Office, The (US – season 9)	2012
Official Secrets	2019
Oppenheimer	2023
Other Guys, The	2010
Our Brand Is Crisis	2015
Outbreak	1995
Outsourced	2006
Outsourced (TV series – season 1)	2010
Pain Hustlers	2023
Painkiller	2023
Patriot (season 1)	2015
Pelican Brief, The	1993
Peripheral, The (season 1)	2022
Peterloo	2018
Philadelphia	1993
Pleasantville	1998
Pokémon Detective Pikachu	2019
Portlandia (season 1)	2011
Portlandia (season 2)	2012
Portlandia (season 3)	2012
Portlandia (season 4)	2014
Portlandia (season 5)	2015
Portlandia (season 6)	2016
Portlandia (season 7)	2017
Portlandia (season 8)	2018
Pride and Glory	2008
Primary Colors	1998

(Continued)

238 Appendix

(Continued)

Screen Media Text	Year Initially Released
Promised Land	2012
Promise, The	2016
Promising Young Woman	2020
Quantum of Solace	2008
Rainmaker, The	1997
Rampart	2011
Ready Player One	2018
Rendition	2007
Report, The	2019
Richard Jewell	2019
Richie Rich	1994
Road, The	2009
Robocop	1987
Robocop	2014
RoboCop 2	1990
Roots	2016
Rosewater	2014
Runaway Jury	2003
Runner Runner	2013
Scarface	1983
Schindler's List	1993
Scrooged	1988
Selma	2014
Sentinel, The	2006
Severance (season 1)	2022
Shawshank Redemption, The	1994
Shock and Awe	2017
Shooter	2007
Sicario	2015
Siege, The	1998

(Continued)

Appendix **239**

(Continued)

Screen Media Text	Year Initially Released
Silkwood	1983
Silver City	2004
Snowden	2016
Snowpiercer	2013
Sorry to Bother You	2018
Spartacus (TV series – season 1)	2010
Speed Racer	2008
Starship Troopers	1997
Star Wars: Episode I	1999
Star Wars: Episode II	2002
Star Wars: Episode III	2005
Star Wars: Episode VIII –The Last Jedi	2017
Stranger Things (season 2)	2016
Stranger Things (season 3)	2017
Stranger Things (season 4)	2019
Stranger Things (season 5)	2022
Superstore (season 1)	2015
Superstore (season 2)	2016
Superstore (season 3)	2017
Superstore (season 4)	2018
Superstore (season 5)	2019
Superstore (season 6)	2020
Syriana	2005
Terminator 2: Judgement Day	1991
Terminator 3: Rise of the Machines	2003
Tetris	2023
Thank You for Smoking	2005
Thirteen Days	2000
Tinker Tailor Soldier Spy	2011
Titanic	1997

(*Continued*)

240 Appendix

(Continued)

Screen Media Text	Year Initially Released
Tomorrowland	2015
Tomorrow Never Dies	1997
Too Big to Fail	2011
Total Recall	2012
Training Day	2001
Traitor	2008
Treme (season 1)	2010
Treme (season 2)	2011
Treme (season 3)	2012
Treme (season 4)	2013
Trumbo	2015
Truth	2015
Tulip Fever	2017
Underground (season 1)	2016
Underground (season 2)	2017
Up in the Air	2009
V for Vandetta	2005
Veep (season 1)	2012
Veep (season 2)	2013
Veep (season 3)	2014
Veep (season 4)	2015
Veep (season 5)	2016
Veep (season 6)	2017
Veep (season 7)	2019
Vice	2018
Videodrome	1983
W.	2008
Wag the Dog	1997
Waiting for the Barbarians	2019
Wall-E	2008

(*Continued*)

(Continued)

Screen Media Text	Year Initially Released
Wall Street	1987
Wall Street: Money Never Sleeps	2010
Wanderlust	2012
War Dogs	2016
War, Inc.	2008
West Wing, The (season 1).	1999
White Lotus, The (season 1)	2021
Widows	2018
Wire, The (season 1)	2002
Wire, The (season 2)	2003
Wire, The (season 3)	2004
Wire, The (season 4)	2006
Wire, The (season 5)	2008
Wolf of Wall Street, The	2013
Working Girl	1988
World War Z	2013
xXx: State of the Union	2005
Years and Years	2019
Zoolander	2001

INDEX

Note: Page numbers in **bold** refers to Tables.

100, The (2014–2020)
101 Dalmatians (1996) 80–1
12 Years a Slave (2013) 131
1917 (2019) **56**
21 Jump Street (2012) 71n11
22 Jump Street (2014) 71n11
28 Days Later (2002) 31n35, **60**
9 to 5 (1980) **56**

abolition: of the police 167; prison 76;
  slavery 16
Abramoff, Jack 93–4
Absolute Power (1997) 96n19
Accidental Love (2015) **56, 59**
Accountant, The (2016) **56, 58**
Ace Venture 2: When Nature Calls
  (1995) 132
action (genre) 18, 60, 75
activism xii, 1, 62, 78–9, 105, 128,
  169n9, 181, 183–5, 209, 210;
  see also movements; activist habitus
activist habitus 183–184, 185, 186,
  191
actors 1, 2–3, 5, 23, 92, 218, 220–1
Admission (2013) **63**, 151–3, 154–5
adolescence *see* childhood
Adorno, Theodor 6, 24–5, 29,
  170n25, 214
advertising 19, 98n56, 111, 115, 117,
  118, 119, 124–5, 134, 136–7, 138–9,

140–1, 145n55, 163, 164, 166–7,
  179, 190, 211; *see also* marketing
aesthetics 22–3, 29, 53, 140, 163, 212
Africa 20, 55, 59, 70n7, 131, 168,
  190–1, 200, 212
agency, individual 80–1
Air (2023) **56**
Aladdin (2019) 165
Alex, Inc (2018) 169n8
alienation 4, 7, 113–15, 120, 209–10
All the King's Men (2006)
  96n19, 97n30
All the Money in the World (2017) **56**
Allegiant (2016) 79, 97n26, 192n10
allegory 42, 178–9, 183, 188, 189–90
alternatives 22, 26, 30, 48, 64, 69–70n7,
  106, 139, 146n57, 173, 186;
  alternative relationships 8, 38,
  148–54, 155–8; alternative
  representations 1, 5, 6, 25, 38–9,
  131, 139, 154, 162, 220; ; alternative
  societies 4, 24, 38; to capitalism
  18, 19, 38, 132–3, 162; economic
  24, 49–50n20, 167–8, 169n8;
  neoliberal 15; political 6, 24, 167–8;
  positive 5, 7, 38–9, 106, 151,
  162, 210; radical 1, 5, 22,
  150, 221; to the state 21, 153;
  see also ideology; lifestyles; There is
  No Alternative (TINA); vision

Index **243**

Amazing Grace (2006) 131
Amazon.com 2, 5, 113, 129
American Beauty (1999) **56**
American dream 83, 85, 156
American Dreamz (2006) 56
American Gangster (2007) **56**, 57
American History X (1998) 86
American Made (2017) 129
Americans, The (2013) 55, **56**
Amistad (1997) 131
Amsterdam (2022) **58**, 129
anarchic breeze 179–80
anarchism 30n9, 80, 86, 127,
    170n28, 193n46
Anarchist Cookbook, The (2002)
    86, 169n8
Andresen, Mark 163–4
Anonymous 78–80
Anthropocene 197, 200, 209
anthropology 74–5, 78, 81, 86, 88–9,
    93, 95–6, 193n46
anti-capitalism *see* capitalism
antihero 83–6, 89–90, 93–4
anti-racist 92, 165
antisemitism 59, 71n16
Antitrust (2001) **66**
anti-war *see* war, anti-war
Ant-Man (2015) **56**
Antonioni, Michelangelo 162–3
apocalypse 18–19, 60, 119, 176, 180–1,
    196–200, 210; post-apocalypse 19,
    22, 31n35, 60
Archer (2009–2015) 140, 146n58
Aristophanes 175
army *see* military
Aronofsky, Darren 107
Arrested Development (2003–2019)
    56, 145n55
art 22–3, 24, 25, 29, 32n54, 68,
    95–6, 165, 166, 170n28, 212–13;
    art cinema 3
As Good as It Gets (1997) 28, 42, 46
Assange, Julian 128
assassination 71n16, 80, 128
Assassination of Richard Nixon, The
    (2004) **56**
Atlantic (1929) 31n17
audience research 27
austerity 67
auteur theory 41–42
authenticity 24, 162–4, 214
authoritarianism 77, 79, 106,
    197

Avatar (2009) 31n24, 131
Avatar: The Way of Water (2022) 131

Back to the Future (1985) 96n8
Bad Boys (1995) 71n11
Bad Lieutenant (1992) 98n55
Badiou, Alain 20, 31–2n36
banks 16, 47, 77, 125–7, 133–4, 166,
    201–2; *see also* state, bailout
Bari, Judi 128
Barthes, Roland 26, 94–5, 102–3, 107
Batman 67, 71–2n18, 76–7, 97n22
Battle in Seattle (2007) 132
Baudrillard, Jean 124, 135–6,
    137, 145n45
Be Kind Rewind (2008) 215–18, 220
Belle (2013) 131
Benjamin, Walter 218
Berger, John 95–6
Berkman, Alexander 80
Better Off Ted (2009–2010)
    111, 116–20
Beyond a Reasonable Doubt
    (2009) 96n19
Big Short, The (2015) 125, 126, 127
Billions (2016–2023) 57, 82–3,
    97n36, 164–5
Birth of a Nation, The (1915) 41, 90–2
Birth of a Nation, The (2016) **64**
Black Mirror (2011–) 43, **58**,
    72n22, 97n30
Black Panther (2018) 55, 131, 144n25
Black Panther Party 132–3, 169n9
Black Panther: Wakanda Forever
    (2022) 131
Black Sheep (1996) **59**
Black-ish (2014–2022) 131
BlacKkKlansman (2018) 71n11, 71n14
Blood Diamond (2006) **58**, **59**
Blow Out (1981) 97n30
Boat That Rocked, The (2009) **64**
Bob Roberts (1992) 96–7n19
Bombshell (2019) **56**
Bono 20
Book of Eli, The (2010) 31n35, **60**
Boondocks, The (2005–2014) 121n40
Boss Baby, The (2017) **56**, **60**, 86
bosses 116–17
Bourdieu, Pierre 32n46, 183
bourgeoisie 11–12, 94–5, 102, 109,
    127, 223–4n59
Bourne Identity, The (2002) 55–7,
    71n10, 129

244 Index

Bourne Legacy, The (2012) 55–7, 58, 59, 71n10
Bourne Supremacy, The (2004) 55–7, 71n10, 129
Bourne Ultimatum, The (2007) 55–7, 58, 59, 71n10
Boys, The (2019–) 121n39
BrainDead (2016) 71n11, 72n19
Branded (2012) 139, 140–1
Breach (2007) 71n10
Brecht, Bertolt 25, 98n54
Bright (2017) 71n11
British National Criminal Intelligence Service 98n56
Broad City (2014–2018) 159–162, 164
Broken City (2013) 58
Brooklyn Nine-Nine (2013–2021) 59, 71n11
Buffalo Soldiers (2001) **56**
Bug's Life, A (1998) **63**
Bulletin of the Atomic Scientists 31n27, 180
Bulworth (1998) 127–8
Bush, George H.W. 65, 71–72n18, 166, 170n24
Bush, George W. 27, 65, 71n16
Butler, Smedley 128–9
Butler, The (2013) **56**
bystander effect 204–5

Campaign, The (2012) 59, 71n11
capital: accumulation of, 112, 118, 125; flight 19, 215; *see also* capitalism; market; Marx, Karl
capitalism: anti-capitalism 44, 89, 155, 167, 170n28; critiques of 3, 5, 6, 20, 38, 44, 46, 48, 54, 62, 64, 65, 67–8, 74, 96, 106; Darwinian 121n35; end of 18, 19, 22, 24, 53, 165, 196, 200; financialized capitalism 13, 87, 89; global circuit of 53; Hollywood capitalism 220; ideology of 8, 69, 133, 166; late capitalism 25; problems with 2, 7, 12–13, 19, 20, 21, 24–5, 38, 77, 81, 103–4, 113, 115–18, 120, 137, 159, 191, 204; welfare 67; *see also* anti-capitalism; alternatives to capitalism; capitalist class; capitalists; hidden abode, the; interests, of capitalism; Keynesianism; magical capitalism; neoliberalism; profit; racial capitalism; values, capitalist

capitalist class 11, 82, 89, 112, 117, 126, 127, 128, 129, 132, 150, 164–5
capitalists 2, 5, 11, 47, 55, 83, 84–6, 109, 110–11, 112, 116, 128, 135, 167, 190, 192n15, 194n50; *see also* banks
Capra, Frank 201–3, 207, 215
Carroll, Lewis 69–70n7
Casablanca (1942) 63
Casino (1995) 84
Casino Jack (2010) 93–94, 144n5
Catch a Fire (2006) 131
celebrity 169n9, 170n24, 214
censorship 6, 48, 103, 189
Central Intelligence Agency (CIA) 57, 65, 71n16, 129, 132, 146n58
Cesar Chavez (2014) 144n11
Chamber, The (1996) 56, 97n30
Chaplin, Charlie 102–3
Chappaquiddick (2017) 97n30
Chernobyl (2019) **60**
childhood 27, 177–9
Children of Men (2006) 4, 106, 174
China 18, 20, 21, 30, 132
Chomsky, Noam 1, 72n24, 96n17, 105, 126, 127, 137, 180–1
Churchill, Winston 20, 211
Citizen Kane (1941) 145n37
citizens 152–3
citizenship 141–2, 152
city *see* country/city
City of Hope (1991) 56, 144n10
Civil Action, A (1998) 58
civil liberties 25, 71–2n18, 144n11
civilization 19, 69, 149
class 13, 38, 47, 95, 126–7, 141, 211; contradictions 103; classlessness 168; creative class 158, 159, 170n25; hierarchy 168; inequalities 19; intellectual class 193n46; interests 38; lower class 13, 31n17; mercantile 124, 134; middle class 20, 113, 141, 151, 154, 159, 183; ruling class 68–9, 102, 209, 210, 220; suicide 168; upper class 17, 202, 214; working class 17, 23, 117–18, 121n36, 127, 141, 168, 183, 186, 189, 193n46; *see also* capitalist class
Class Action (1991) 118
climate change 2, 8n1, 13–14, 18, 19, 180–1, 193n34, 196, 197–8
Clinton, Bill 27, 71n16, 94

Index **245**

Clinton, Hillary 144
Cloud Atlas (2012) **58**, 72n23, 113
co-creation 220–2
codes 29, 90–3, 136, 137, 150, 158;
  see also transcoding
cognitive map 52–3, 67, 72n24
Cold War 65, 93, 129
collectivism 76–7, 202–3, 205–7, 215,
  218, 221–2
colonialism 32n50, 69–70n7, 105, 120,
  124, 124, 132, 142, 148–9, 150;
  colonizers 74, 131, 173; cultural
  neocolonialism 40; neocolonialism
  7, 40, 131–2, 133; representations
  of 60–1, 125, 129, 131, 150, 168;
  see also Dutch colonialism
Columbus, Christopher 172
comedy (genre) 18, 19, 41, 59, 104,
  112–3, 113–14, 119–20, 145n55,
  151–8, 159–62, 215
commercials *see* advertising
commodification 25, 142, 150, 163
commodities 108–9, 111–12, 124, 130,
  132–3, 143
commodity fetishism 7, 115, 134–9, 163
communalism 8, 204
commune 154
communism 41, 70n9, 77, 103, 106,
  107, 113, 140, 145n56, 173–4,
  194n50, 197, 202–3, 222n5; anti-
  communism 106
community 69n4, 78, 88, 133,
  149, 213, 218, 221; intentional
  community 154, 201; representations
  of 8, 132, 154, 201–2, 203–4, 205,
  206, 207, 208, 217, 218
Company Men, The (2010) 41, **56**
competition 12, 82–3, 112, 119–20,
  127, 132, 139, 140, 145n55,
  145–6n56, 191
computers 142, 179, 193n41, 209–10
consciousness 14, 15, 21, 22, 25, 29,
  53, 68, 70n7, 136, 142, 150, 151,
  200, 205, 222
conservatism 7, 8, 20, 27, 28, 49, 53,
  66–7, 76–8, 79, 94, 95, 97n38,
  120n16, 160, 165, 204, 205, 207,
  215, 222n13
Conservative Party 11; *see also*
  Thatcher, Margaret
conspiracy 31n23, 64–5, 71n16, 72n24,
  81, 188, 217
Conspiracy Theory (1997) 64–5

Constant Gardener, The (2005) **58**
consumer culture 13, 24–25, 81, 109–10,
  120, 124–5, 132–3, 135–9, 140–1,
  145–6n56, 156–7, 163–4, 166–7,
  177, 178, 181, 209, 211
Contender, The (2000) 71n11
content 3, 4–5, 8, 22, 25–6, 27, 29, 38,
  40–2, 43–4, 46, 49–50n20, 61, 96,
  98n56, 107, 110, 167–8, 179, 187–8,
  190, 210, *see also* political content
Contract, The (2006) **56**
Cop Land (1997) 71n11
Corbyn, Jeremy 67, 221
Corporate (2018) 19, 119–20,
  121n40, 145n54
corporations 46, 47, 55, 61, 111, 128,
  132, 163, 211; corporate division
  of labor 21; corporate subsidies 16;
  representations of 19, 57–8, 70n9,
  72n24, 84, 111, 112, 114, 115,
  117–20, 121n40, 138–9, 152, 154,
  164–5, 174, 181, 185, 188–9, 190–
  1, 193n49
corruption 48, 53, 57, 77, 78, 83, 94,
  158, 190, 191, 203
Cosmopolis (2012) 98n55
counterbalanced critique 7, 57, **58**
counterculture 165
counternormativity 8, 157, 160, 163,
  165, 166
country/city 205–8, 209, 211–12
coup 70n9, 129, 132, 142, 144n16
COVID pandemic 15, 16, 18, 49n17
Crassus, Marcus Licinius 104, 105, 106
creativity 108, 170n25, 178–9, 182–3,
  184, 186, 187, 197, 200, 220, 222
crime 27, 67, 77, 82–3, 84, 90, 98n86,
  154, 164–5, 166, 170n24, 172, 209;
  insider trading 83, 84–5
organized 84, 98n86; urban 209; war
  crime 166; white-collar 77, 82–3, 90,
  154, 164–5
crises 14, 15–17, 25; *see also* climate
  change; economic crisis; Tulip Mania
Crisis (2021) **58**
critique: of critique 48; feminist 157–8;
  progressive 28; radical 4, 5–6, 7, 8,
  22, 46, 48, 94, 95, 102–20, 124–40,
  144, 146n58, 181, 188, 190, 191,
  193n46, 210; *see also* capitalism,
  critiques of; limited critiques
Cronenberg, David 188
Crossley, Nick 183–4

246 Index

Crucible, The (1996) 41
Cruise, Tom 78–9
Cry Freedom (1987) 131
Crying Game, The (1992) 169n14
CSI: Crime Scene Investigation
  (2000) 71n11
cultivation theory 28
cultural studies 23, 26
cultural consumption 7, 21, 29, 177
culture 25–6, 29, 74, 105, 148,
  163, 165, 169n11, 174, 181,
  220, 221, 222; authentic culture
  25, 214; of capitalism 94–5;
  cultural struggle 21; mass 52,
  191, 214; popular 2–3, 4, 5–6,
  189–90, 201; subculture 163; *see also*
  counterculture; colonialism, cultural
  neocolonialism; production, cultural
culture industry 6, 25, 214, 221

Dallas Buyers Club (2013) 169n14
Dances with Wolves (1990) 131
Dark Phoenix (2019) **60**
Dark Waters (2019) 121n39
Dave (1993) 71n11
Day after Tomorrow, The (2004) 19,
  60, 200
de Sica, Vittorio 43, 206, 207
Dead Prez 167–8
death of the author 26
decoding 7, 26–7, 28–9, 150, 158
Deepwater Horizon (2016) 121n39
DeGeneres, Ellen 162, 166
dehumanization 209, 212
democracy 20, 55, 59–60, 88, 92,
  105, 128, 129, 140, 165, 180, 189;
  representative 140, 165; social 57,
  128, 221; workplace 169n8
Democratic Party 41, 164
Demolition Man (1993) 173
Departed, The (2006) 71n11,
  72n19
Detroit (2017) 53, 71n11
DiCaprio, Leonardo 17, 85, 87, 90
Dick (1999) 97n30
Dictator, The (2012) 59
dictatorship 20, 48, 59, 106
Die Rote Fahne (The Red Flag)
  103–4
Dietrich, William 190
director 5, 42, 53, 84, 90, 92, 98n56,
  107, 113, 120n15, 143, 162, 178,
  207, 212, 215

discourses 67–8, 81, 103, 106, 109,
  142–4, 149–50, 151, 155, 157, 158,
  165, 197
discursive plane 52, 66
Disney 19, 80, 221
Distinguished Gentleman, The
  (1992) **56, 59**
District 9 (2009) 131
Divergent (2014) 79, 97n26, 192n10
diversity 165–6, 167
documentaries 40, 144n26, 158,
  205, 218
Don't Look Up (2021) 19, 121n39,
  140
Doomsday Clock 180–1, 198
*Dr Strangelove or: How I Learned to
  Stop Worrying and Love the Bomb*
  (1964) 18
drama (genre) 21, 27, 57
Drescher, Fran 1, 2–3
drugs 85, 87, 129, 142, 169n9
DuMont Laboratories 210–11, 215
Dutch colonialism 124, 130–1, 134,
  148–9 *see also* East Indies
Dutch Indies *see* East Indies
dystopia 1, 79, 173–4, 175, 178, 180,
  196, 200, 209, 210, 219

Eagle Eye (2008) **59**
East Indies 124, 130–1, 148
Easy A (2010) 96
Eco, Umberto 26, 28–9
economic crisis 14, 21, 66–7, 120, 124–5,
  126, 127, 142–3, 154, 211; bubbles,
  economic 13; economic crashes
  124–5, 143; Great Depression 62;
  Great Recession 13, 16, 20, 125–6,
  150; housing bubble 15, 126; Long
  Depression 18; recession 20, 125;
  see also Tulip Mania
economic growth 20, 88, 136–7, 211;
  booms 7, 13, 15
economics 4, 5, 12–13, 14, 15, 24,
  26, 40, 41, 62, 87, 109–10, 165,
  189, 198; economic content 42,
  49–50n20; economic decline 12,
  16, 140, 218; economic inequality/
  equality 2, 25, 88; economic
  institutions 8, 159, 165–6; economic
  system 1, 4, 5, 6, 15, 22, 48,
  116, 129, 131–2, 162, 164, 191,
  198, 215; economic reforms 71n16;
  economic status 17; economists

12, 13, 121n35, 136, 137; *see also* alternatives, economic; economic crisis, economic growth; magical capitalism
ego 17, 203
Election (1999) 96–7n19
elections 12, 32n40, 40, 55, 68, 93–4, 127–8, 129, 145n30; rigged 59, 92
elites 13, 31n17, 59, 78, 80, 88, 102, 121n35, 128, 134, 136, 158–9, 161, 166, 168; institutions 152, 155
Ellen (1994–1998) 162
Ellen DeGeneres Show, The (2003–2022) 166
Ellington, Duke 213–14
Ellison, Harlan 205–6, 208
Elysium (2013) 133, 140, 141–2, 154
Emancipation (2022) 131
embodied cognition 46–7
embodiment 29, 44, 69–70n7, 78–81, 102, 151, 178, 219; embodied recognition 180; of evil 7, 78–81, 184, 187, 193n39; *see also* embodied cognition
empire 17, 55, 69–70n7, 93, 103–4, 106, 130–3, 134, 186, 187; counter-Empire 187
employees *see* workers
employer *see* capitalist
employment *see* jobs
empowerment *see* power
encoding 7, 26–7, 90, 92, 142
End of Watch (2012) 71n11
Enemy of the State (1998) **58**, **59**
Engels, Fredrick 12, 17, 67–8, 121n24, 127, 168, 206, 219–220; *see also* Marx, Karl
Enlightenment 105
entertainment 23, 53, 89, 96, 140, 212, 214, 217
entrepreneur *see* capitalist
environmental harms 5, 13–4, 27, 44, 119, 133, 181, 196, 197, 219
environmentalism 4, 14, 119, 165
episodic series 43, 44, 72n22
equality 17, 25, 31n17, 74, 104, 108–9, 125, 141; equal rights 97n38; *see also* inequality
Eraser (1996) 71n10, 121n42
Erin Brockovich (2000) **58**, 121n39
Escape from LA (1997) **56**
Escape from Pretoria (2020) 131

escapism 110, 120n18
ethics 25, 57, 93, 119, 129, 148, 156–8; *see also* morality
ethnicity 186, 211; *see also* race, racism
ethnography 94–5
Evan Almighty (2007) **58**
evil 20, 31–32n36, 76, 78, 92, 94–5, 106, 107, 119, 172, 200, 218; embodying evil 80–82; representations of 7, 75–6, 78, 79, 80–2, 207
exchange value 24–5, 135; *see also* symbolic exchange value
Expanse, The (2015–2020) **58**
exploitation 1, 2–3, 17, 55, 62, 82, 88, 112–3, 115, 131, 132, 144n11, 155, 165, 167, 187, 209; super-exploitation 132–3, 190
extinction 2, 19, 24, 180; *see also* apocalypse, post-apocalypse
Extremely Loud and Incredibly Close (2011) 207–8
Eye in the Sky (2015) **56**

Fair Game (2010) 71n10
fantasy (genre) 5, 60, 173
fascism 3, 48, 92–3, 129
fashion 24, 163, 165, 167, 183–4, 203
Fast, Howard 106
Fawkes, Guy 79
Federal Bureau of Investigation (FBI) 57, 65, 85, 86, 202–3, 222n5
feminism 151, 155, 157–8, 160, 184; anti-feminism 157, 158; liberal 165
fetishization 135, 136; *see also* commodity fetishism
filmmakers 31n17, 70n9, 84, 151, 188, 212
First World War 30n14, 69, 103, 105
flak machines 96n17
Ford v Ferrari (2019) **56**
Forrest Gump (1994) 169n9
Founder, The (2016) **56**
Fountainhead, The 202–3
Free Guy (2021) **56**
free market 125–7; free trade 132
Free State of Jones (2016) **64**, 131
freedom 23, 74, 80, 84, 104, 105, 107, 108, 109, 110, 144n11, 165, 168, 173, 175, 179, 201, 212, 213; and destiny 221–2; internet freedom 78–9
Freedomland (2006) 71n11
Freud, Sigmund 136, 151

248 Index

Frick, Henry Clay 80
Frost/Nixon (2008) **56**
Fun with Dick and Jane (2005) **56**,
121n40, 133

Game of Thrones (2011–2019) **61**, 75,
82, 192n8
Gandhi (1982) 131
Gangs of New York (2002) **64**
Gangster Squad (2013) 71n11
Gaslit (2022) **63**
gender 2, 30n1, 142, 157, 159, 160,
164, 169n10, 186
Genovese, Kitty 204–5, 208, 209, 210
gentrification 215–6
geography 69–70n7, 132–3, 141, 205
Germany 24, 48, 68, 103–4
Ghost Writer, The (2010) **56**
Gibson, Dorothy 23–4
Gibson, Mel 71n16
Gitlin, Todd 22
Giver, The (2014) 173
gladiators 104, 107
Glass Onion (2022) **56**
Glazer, Ilana 159–60
Glengarry Glen Ross (1992) 112
Global North 21, 59–60, 116, 128, 132,
133, 136, 141
Global South 132, 141
Glory (1989) 131
Glover, Danny 131, 216
Goebbels, Joseph 48
Gold (2016) 57
Golden Compass, The (2007) **61**
Goldgar, Anne 130
Goliath (2016–2021) **58**
Gondry, Michel 207, 215, 217, 218
Good Kill (2014) 129
Good Lord Bird, The (2010) 131
Good Night and Good Luck
(2005) **58**, **59**
Good Shepherd, The (2006) 71n10
good, the bad, and the ugly critique
7, 55–7
government *see* state
Graeber, David 193n46
Gramsci, Antonio 21
Grandma (2015) 169
Gray Man, The (2022) 71n10
Great Depression *see* economic crisis
Great Recession see economic crisis
greed 84, 90, 190, 197, 204, 210

Green Book, The (2018) **64**
Griffith, D.W. 41, 90–1
Gringo (2018) **58**, 97n30
grunge music 163–4, 166, 167
Guevara, Che 167
Gulf War 27
Gunman, The (2015) **58**, 121n40

Haag, Pamela 105, 120n14
habitus *see* activist habitus
Haitian Revolution 105, 131
Hall, Stuart 6, 26, 28–9, 109, 149
Hantise, La (1912) 24
Happyish (2015) 113–15, 119,
137–9, 146n57
Hardt, Michael 186–7
*Harold and Kumar Escape from
Guantanamo Bay* (2008) **59**
Hate U Give, The (2018) **63**
HBO 127, 154
Head of State (2003) 144n12
Health Maintenance Organizations
(HMOs) 28, 46, 47
healthcare 28, 42, 46, 57, 59, 66, 112,
142, 177; universal 133, 141
Hearst, Patty 133
Hearst, William Randolph 112,
133, 145n37
Heath, Joseph 165
hegemony 6, 14, 105, 109, 151,
155, 163, 164, 174; counter-
hegemony 67, 69
Heine, Heinrich 180
Herman, Edward S. 137
hero *see* protagonist
hidden abode, the 109–10, 117,
125, 139
hierarchy 2, 66, 76, 116, 117, 168
hip hop 167–8
hippies 154, 162–3, 166, 169n9
historicized critique 7, 64
history 1, 4, 11, 18, 30, 68, 69–70n7,
74, 95–6, 104–5, 1, 127, 131, 142,
152, 174, 177, 180, 187, 216;
ahistorical 53; cinema history
76, 81, 84; end of 25, 30, 174;
historian 22–3, 104, 135, 149, 173;
historical accuracy 90–2, 143;
historical context 67, 173; of jazz
212–14; of television 210–11;
see also historicized critique; Martyr
d'Anghera, Peter; Jacoby, Russell

Index **249**

Hitler, Adolf 139
Hollywood 2, 3, 4, 21, 29, 30, 41, 68,
77, 84, 85, 139, 143, 170n25, 192,
200, 202, 203, 217, 218; studios
23, 38, 42, 92, 188, 200, 202, 212,
217–18, 221; *see also* capitalism,
Hollywood; culture industry
Homicide (1991) **58**
Hook (1991) 121n34
Hoover, Edgar 222n5
horizons 52, 54, 211, 221;
see also vision
Horkheimer, Max 177
Horrible Bosses (2011) **56**
horror (genre) 18, 41
Hot Shots! (1991) **58**
Hotel Rwanda (2004) 131
House, The (2017) 97n30
House of Cards (2013) **66**, 78, 82
House of Un-American Activities
Committee (HUAC) 68, 106,
202, 222n5
Hubbard, Elbert 30n9
human rights 141, 180
Hunger Games, The (2012) 79, 97n25,
145, 173–4
Hunger Games: Catching Fire, The
(2013) 79, 97n25, 173–4
Hunger Games: Mockingjay – Part 1,
The (2014) 79, 97n25, 173–4
Hunger Games: Mockingjay – Part 2,
The (2015) 79, 97n25, 173–4
Hunting Party, The (2007) 129
Huxley, Aldous 180, 196
hypermasculinity 108
hypocrisy 59, 93–4, 129
hypodermic needle theory 26

I Am Legend (2007) 31n35, **60**
iceberg effect 12–3, 17
identities 2, 61, 78, 79, 163, 165, 166;
consumer 163, 211; cultural 163;
queer 160, 167, 186, 211
ideology 3, 5–6, 15, 18, 20, 21–2,
25, 28, 29–30, 43, 52, 63, 66,
69, 69–70n7, 72n19, 78, 82, 92,
109, 126, 158, 159, 173, 196,
200, 208; counter-hegemonic 15,
25, 68, 69, 106, 144, 151, 190;
hegemonic 4, 5–6, 8, 68, 88, 94,
105, 109, 132–3, 138, 163, 166,
181, 210; ideological abuse 94–5;

ideological content 5, 107, 110, 167,
177–8, 179; ideological filters 38;
ideological mask 8, 13, 172, 173;
ideological shift 15–16; ideological
superstructure 67; negative ideology
109, 134; political 40, 53, 151;
production of 96; Western ideology
149; *see also* magical capitalism;
neoliberalism; There is No
Alternative (TINA)
I'm a Virgo (2023) 113
imagination 24, 30, 105, 138, 162, 173,
177–9, 182, 184, 189, 222; political
2, 4, 67; radical 24, 162, 167, 179;
sociological 159; utopian 173, 220;
Western 177
Imitation Game, The (2014) **58**
immigration 79, 126, 193n34
imperialism *see* colonialism, empire
In Dubious Battle (2016) **60**, 61–64
In Nacht und Eis (In Night and Ice)
(1912) 24
In the Electric Mist (2009) **56**
In the Loop (2009) 96–7n19
In Time (2011) 115–6, 133–4
Inception (2010) 15, **59**
Incorporated (2016) 118,
145n35, 192n10
Independence Day (1996) **58**, **60**
India 20, 106, 131, 132
indigenous peoples 132, 148–9, 169n11,
172–3, 192n3
individualism 63–4, 107, 164, 202–3,
204, 205, 215; rugged 83, 105, 151
individualization 4, 25, 26, 82, 88,
139
inequality 2, 19, 88, 116
Infiltrator, The (2016) **58**
Informant!, The (2009) 57
Insider, The (1999) **58**, 121n39
Insurgent (2015) 79, 97n26, 192n10
Internal Affairs (1990) 71n11
International Monetary Fund (IMF) 65,
78, 132
International, The (2009) 57
internationalism 186–7, 189
Invictus (2009) 131
Iran 129, 144n16
Iraq 74, 120, 166, 170n24
Iraq War 120, 170n24
Irishman, The (2019) 84
Ismay, Bruce 48, 50n26

250 Index

Italy 106, 129, 206
It's a Wonderful Life (1946) 201–3, 204, 205, 206, 207, 215

J.P. Morgan 16, 31n23
Jack Nicholson effect 28
Jacobson, Abbi 159–60
Jacoby, Russell 66, 173, 174, 175, 177–8, 179–80, 190, 192n23
Jameson, Fredric 4, 6, 32n51, 52–3, 72n24, 97n33, 98n54, 166, 173, 174, 188–9
Jason Bourne (2016) 71n10, 129
jazz 212–15, 216, 217, 220
Jews 94, 160, 179–80, 221
JFK (1991) 65, **66**
John Q (2002) **59**
Jojo Rabbit (2019) **64**
Joker (2019) 86
Judge Dredd (1995) 71n11
Junkspace City 53, 54–5, 65–6, 67, 69
Jupiter Ascending (2015) **63**, 97n30
Jurassic Park (1993) 121n39
Just Mercy (2019) **58**
justice 55, 57, 58, 67, 80, 82, 95, 107, 108, 155, 167, 168, 170n24, 201, 207; collective 203, 206; injustice 62, 86; radical 77, 206
justice system 58, 86, 94; courts 40, 57–8, 77; lawsuits 78–9, 118; lawyers 41, 57, 86, 118 *see also* law

Kelley, Beverly Merrill 3
Kellner, Douglas 71–2n18, 142–4, 150
Keynesianism 12
Kill the Messenger (2014) 128, 129
Killing Them Softly (2012) **61**
Kimi (2022) **56**
Kingdom, The (2007) 55
Kingsman: The Golden Circle (2017) **56**
knowledge 27, 29, 65, 84, 89, 103, 149, 187, 216; political knowledge 74
Koolhaas, Rem 53
Kropotkin, Peter 127
Kubrick, Stanley 105, 120n15
Kumar, Krishan 23n47, 173

LA Confidential (1997) 53, 71n11
labor 1, 2–3, 45, 64, 109, 110–13, 115, 133, 134–5, 140, 186, 220, 223–4n59; division of 21, 132, 220; forced 113, 116; labor-power 108, 109, 111–112, 116, 145n45; labor

supply 113; living/dead labor 187; manual labor 32, 189, *see also* class, working; class, laboring; jobs; Marx, Karl, *Capital, Volume I*
Labour Party 20
Lake House, The (2006) 32n42
Larry the Cable Guy: Health Inspector (2006) 71n11
Lars and the Real Girl (2007) 203–4, 205, 207, 208–9
Lasswell, Harold 26
Last Duel, The (2021) 71n14
Last Man on Earth, The (2015–2018) 31n35
Last of Us, The (2023) **61**
Latin America 20, 55, 70n9, 75, 106, 129, 131, 132, 145n30
Laundromat, The (2019) 99n66, 144n5
law 67, 79, 108, 128, 141, 142, 172, 181, 183; breaking of 67, 83, 208; laws of capital 24–5, 53, 112; natural 12, 105; *see also* justice system
leaderless 154
leaders 14, 32n40, 59, 80, 104, 129, 189
least-worst system critique 7, 60
Leave the World Behind (2023) 71n13
legitimacy 57, 76, 88, 98n56, 136, 142, 211
Lego Movie, The (2014) 8, 174–7, 178–9, 181–8, 189–90, 191–2, 201
Lenin, Vladimir 5, 65, 127, 145–6n56, 190, 194n50
Levien, Devid 165
Leyva, Rodolfo 33n74
liberalism 4, 53, 54, 89, 105, 111, 156, 165, 191; *see also* feminism, liberal; neoliberalism
liberation 106, 133; *see also* freedom
Liebknecht, Karl 104
lifestyle 60, 84, 85, 115, 148–9, 183–4, 185; alternative 5–6, 7, 8, 49n20, 150–8, 159–66, 167, 169n9, 190; individualistic 63–4
limited critiques 6–7, 54–65, 66, 67, 106, 120, 190, 193n39; *see also* counterbalanced critique; good, the bad, and the ugly critique; historicized critique; least-worst system critique; obscured critique; overlooked critique; overreaching critique; reformable critique
Lincoln (2012) 131

Index **251**

Lipsitz, George 211
lobbying 14, 93–4, 126, 139; lobbyists 57, 77, 93–4, 128
Looming Tower, The (2018) 57
Lord of the Rings: The Fellowship of the Ring, The (2001) **61**, 192n8
Lord of the Rings: The Return of the King, The (2003) **61**, 192n8
Lord of the Rings: The Two Towers, The (2002) **61**, 192n8
Lord, Phil 178, 188, 189, 190, 192n13
Lost World: Jurassic Park, The (1997) 121n39
Lukács, György 6, 24
Luke Cage (2016) 67, 97n30
Luxemburg, Rosa 104
Lykidis, Alex 3, 98n54

Mad City (1997) **56**
Mad Max (1979) 200
Mad Max: Fury Road (2015) 31n35, **60**
magic bullet theories 26
magical capitalism 87–9
Malcolm X (1992) **64**
Malinowski, Bronisław 88
Man of the Year (2006) **58**
managerialism 117, 139–40
Manchurian Candidate, The (2004) **58**, 71n11, 96n19
Mankiewicz, Joseph L. 102
Mann, Anthony 120n15
Marcuse, Herbert 25–6
Margin Call (2011) 125–6
market 5, 12, 14, 15, 16, 24, 81, 108–10, 124, 130, 132–3, 135, 144n3, 145–6n56, 155; adaptation 218; black market 208; capitalization 16; commodity markets 143; crashes *see* economic crisis; international markets 40, 132; interventionism 12, 16, 17; *see also* capitalism; free market; stock market
market research 137, 216
marketing 20, 119, 127, 137, 139, 140–1, 145–6n56, 177; *see also* advertising
Martyr d'Anghera, Peter 149, 172–3
Marx, Karl 47, 71n16, 104, 113, 121n24, 121n35, 135–6, 140, 164, 220; *Capital, Volume I* 7, 108–11, 112, 115, 116, 124, 134; *German Ideology, The* 67–8, 210; *Manifesto of the Communist Party,*

The 12, 127, 206, 219–20, 223–224n59; *see also* hidden abode, the
Marxism 71n16, 222n13; Soviet 174
Marxists 13, 21, 24, 25, 52, 70, 186
masculinity 95, 151; hypermasculinity 108
Matrix, The (1999) 2, 18, 31n31, **61**, 174
Matrix Reloaded, The (2003) 18, 31n31, **61**, 174
Matrix Revolutions, The (2003) 18, 31n31, **61**, 174
Mauritanian, The (2021) **59**
Mauss, Marcel 88, 98n45
May, Rollo 208–10, 212, 221–2
McCain, John 93–4
McCarthy Era 42, 68, 106
McCracken, Grant 169n11
media consumption 4, 7–8, 21–2, 23, 24–30, 33n62, 81–2, 85, 98n54, 109–10, 179, 220–1
media effects 26–7, 33n62, 33n74
media studies 27
Medical Police (2020) **56**
Men (2022) **61**
mental health 27, 76, 169n14
Menu, The (2022) **56**
metaphor 14, 17, 23, 46–7, 52–3, 143, 188, 190–1, 221
Michael Clayton (2007) **58**, 121n39, 128
Middle East 77, 120; *see also* Iran, Iraq
migration 53, 141; *see also* immigration
Miliband, Ed 20
military 40, 74, 93, 103, 104, 118, 129, 170n24, 194n50; army 77, 104, 119, 190; representations of 57, 60–1, 65, 79–80, 81, 173, 190; *see also* security forces
Milk (2008) 71n11, 72n19
Mill, John Stuart 180, 193n30
Miller, Arthur 41
Miller, Chris 178, 188, 189–90, 192n13
Mills, C. Wright 159
Milton, John 86, 97n38
mini-series 43, 144n26, 212
Minority Report (2002) 97n30, 167
Miss Sloane (2016) **56**, 57, **59**
Mission, The (1986) 131
Mission: Impossible (1996) **56**, 71n10, 78, 79
Mission: Impossible II (2000) **56**, 71n10, 78, 79

252 Index

Mission: Impossible III (2006) **56,** 71n10, 72n19, 78, 79
Mission: Impossible – Fallout (2018) **56,** 72n19, 78, 79, 166–7
Mission: Impossible – Rogue Nation (2015) **56,** 71n10, 78, 79
Moggach, Deborah 143
money 5, 31–2n36, 32n50, 38, 42, 69, 77, 81, 110, 112, 124, 130, 191, 202, 212, 216; laundering 85; representations of 31n17, 82–3, 84, 85, 87, 90, 93–4, 112, 115, 117, 125, 126, 133, 150, 152, 190, 201, 202, 217–8; saving 57, 112; *see also* moneybags
Money Monster (2016) **56, 58**
moneybags 102, 104, 109, 121n24
Monitor 198–9, 200, 209–10, 212, 213, 214, 219, 220, 221
moral panics 139
morality 3, 53, 78, 83, 92, 93, 119, 169, 190, 203, 211; immoral 48, 205; moral ambiguity 83; *see also* ethics
More, Thomas 32n47, 54
mores 207, 215
Morning Show (2019–2023) **56,** 97n30
Motherless Brooklyn (2019) 97n30
Motion Picture Alliance for the Preservation of American Ideals 203
movements 28; movements, black power 132–3; hippie 162–3; revolutionary 222n13; *see also* activism; Anonymous; Occupy Wall Street; rebellion
movie stars *see* celebrities
multitude 8, 186–7, 200
Murder at 1600 (1997) **58,** 78
music xiii, 44, 90, 140, 154, 161, 163, 165, 174, 176; *see also* grunge music, jazz; hip hop, punk music
My Fellow Americans (1996) 72n19
myths 17, 69, 77, 83, 94–5, 96, 105, 107, 108, 121n35, 142, 174, 175

Nader, Laura 74, 93
Nameless Heroes (*Namenlose Helden*) (1925) 103–4
Narayan, John 132–3
nation-states *see* state
Nazism 48, 77, 86, 92–3, 119, 174
Negotiator, The (1998) 71n11
Negri, Antonio 186–7
neocolonialism *see* colonialism

neoliberalism 6, 11–13, 14–6, 17–8, 19, 38–9, 40, 53, 67, 106, 107, 141, 201
neo-Nazis *see* Nazism
Net, The (1995) 58
Netflix 5
New World, The (2005) 131
New York 17, 23–4, 128
New York City 67, 87, 112, 154, 156, 159–61, 164, 204, 205–6, 207, 208, 213–14, 216, 218; Gotham 71–2n18, 76–7; Manhattan 85, 87, 89
news media 20–1, 22, 40, 72n24, 78, 79, 127, 152, 181, 205; representations of 181, 197, 199; newspapers 213–14; *see also Die Rote Fahne* (*The Red Flag*); Hearst, William Randolph; *Newsies* (1992)
Newsies (1992) 57, 112
Newton, Huey P. 132–3
Nice Guys, The (2016) 58
Nick of Time (1995) 56
Nirvana 163; *see also* grunge music
Nixon (1995) 71n11
No Way Out (1987) 97n30
Nolan, Christopher 15, 76–7
normalcy 54, 76, 108, 151, 152, 153, 155, 156, 159, 160–1, 162, 182, 184–5, 191–2, 208; *see also* counternormativity
norms 183, 185, 208; social norms 17, 161
Nubicuculia *see* utopia, Cloud Cuckoo Land
nuclear weapons 18–19, 166, 180, 196

Obama, Barak 77
obscured critique 7, 60–1
Ocasio-Cortez, Alexandria 221
Occupy Wall Street 15, 18, 21, 76, 77, 95
Office Space (1999) 117, 139
Office, The (US) (2005–2012) **56,** 116
Official Secrets (2019) 58
oligopoly 16
Olivier, Laurence 11
Oppenheimer (2023) 18, 180
oppression 1, 2, 18, 76–7, 80, 105, 108, 142, 152, 163, 191, 207, 220; systemic oppression 2, 21, 80, 189, 206; *see also* racism, sexism, capitalism
Other Guys, The (2010) **63,** 144n5
Our Brand is Crisis (2015) 132

Index **253**

Outbreak (1995) **56**
Outsourced (film) (2006) 132, 140
Outsourced (TV series) (2010)
132, 145n33
overlooked critique 7, 61–4
overreaching critique 7, 64, 65,
66, 193n39

Pain Hustlers (2023) **56, 58**
Painkiller (2023) **56**
Parallax View, The (1974) 72n24
parliament 32n40
Passaic, New Jersey 210–11, 215,
217, 218–19
Patriot (2015) 129, 144n18
peace 1, 76, 82, 145n56, 150,
163, 169n9
Peele, Jordan 41
Pelican Brief, The (1993) **66**
perceptions 20, 24, 27, 29, 46–7, 76,
88, 141, 162, 207
Peripheral, The (2022) **61**
Peterloo (2018) **64**
Philadelphia (1993) **56, 58**
philanthropy 83, 133
Pietz, William 135
pinkwashing 165
planned obsolescence 137
Pleasantville (1998) 173
poetry 22–3, 32n49, 130, 170n28
Pokémon Detective Pikachu (2019) **56**
police 40, 57, 66–7, 71n11, 127, 79,
81, 84, 85, 86, 98n56, 112, 133,
140, 141–2, 145n56, 167, 175,
177, 184, 192n15, 193n41, 202,
205, 206, 210; brutality 144n18,
168, 190; corruption 53; police
state 79
policy 4, 12, 46, 55, 59, 117,
127, 128, 131–2, 169n8, 211;
liberal 105; neoliberal 12; socialist 68;
welfare 128
policymakers 11, 20, 40, 47, 55, 71n16,
77–8, 104, 128, 198; representations
of 57, 66–7, 71n11, 82–3, 96–7n19,
112, 164, 199
political consciousness 14, 15, 21, 22,
25, 29, 53, 68, 69–70n7, 150
political content 3, 4, 5, 40–2, 43,
61, 190
political economy 4, 121n35, 135
political ideology *see* ideology
political intent 40–1, 42
political participation 27, 79, 140

pollution *see* environmental harms
Portland, Oregon 157–8
Portlandia (2011–2018) 156–8, 159,
160, 161, 169n11
post-apocalypse *see* apocalypse
post-industrialization 215
poverty 1, 2, 13, 16, 20, 74, 103, 167,
213, 215; representations of 60, 67,
82–3, 103, 115–16, 117–18, 126,
127, 132, 133–4, 150, 168, 190
power 2, 14, 22–3; class power 126,
128, 169n8; empowerment 160;
of ideology 26, 29, 67, 88, 137,
149, 163, 165, 181; and individuals
67, 71n16, 77, 79–81, 96–7n19,
105, 172; representations of 55,
64–5, 75, 76, 77, 78, 79–81, 82–3,
90, 96–7n19, 112, 118, 151, 174,
175, 190; state power 14, 25, 74,
82–3, 104, 129, 180; systems of
1, 31–2n36, 72n24, 88, 126, 135,
187, 209
Pride and Glory (2008) 71n11
Primary Colors (1998) 71n11
prison 59, 76–7, 79, 82, 85–6, 94, 106,
126, 129, 130, 133, 175–6, 187, 201,
206–7, 218
production 2, 13, 14, 38, 62, 109, 110,
111, 112, 115, 125, 132, 134, 135,
136, 137, 140, 145–6n56, 198, 209,
220, 223–4n59; cultural 4, 22, 29,
40, 105, 162, 166, 190, 222; mass
13, 177; material 210; means of 21;
mental 68, 210; productivity 111,
116–17, 137; *see also* production,
film and television; hidden abode, the
production, film and television 3, 4, 5,
25, 26, 30, 110, 143, 188, 189, 203,
218, 220; producers 38, 42, 90, 143,
165, 200; 214; *see also* Hollywood;
Weinstein, Harvey
profit 2, 4, 25, 55, 62, 109, 111–12,
125, 135, 167, 187, 192n13,
198, 209; incentive 48; maximization
137, 214; motive 7, 57–8, 117–20;
over people 12; profitability 16, 130,
167, 216; -seeking 12, 13; *see also*
capitalism, problems with
proletariat *see* workers
Promise, The (2016) **64**
Promised Land (2012) 121n39
Promising Young Woman (2020) 97n30
propaganda 48, 80, 92, 181,
203, 222n5

propaganda of the deed 80
property 96, 104, 108–9, 191;
    collectivization of 76–7, 172;
    rights 97n29
protagonist 2, 44, 48, 57, 76, 78, 79,
    81, 84, 89, 90, 92, 117, 127–8, 130,
    133–4, 139, 145n30, 151–2, 176,
    178, 182, 189, 190, 201, 210; hero
    1, 8, 18, 55, 63, 75–6, 83, 85, 86, 89,
    90, 92–3, 94, 97n38, 104, 105, 107,
    109, 141, 142, 176, 184, 186, 191,
    198, 201, 203; see also antihero
protest see movements
psychological thrillers (genre) 76
psychology 76, 90, 136, 158–9, 161,
    169n9, 204, 205, 208–9, 221–2;
    psychoanalysis 3, 23, 136; see also
    Freud, Sigmund; May, Rollo
public relations 57
Pulitzer, Joseph 112
punk music 163–4, 165, 167
purplewashing 165
Putin, Vladimir 95, 106

Quantum of Solace (2008) 55, **58**

race 2, 28, 95, 186
racial capitalism 133
racism 28, 41, 59, 90, 92, 124,
    142, 213; anti-racist 92, 165; ethno-
    nationalism 48, 106; see also Griffith,
    D.W.; racial capitalism; white savior
radical habitus see activist habitus
radio 158–9, 181, 208, 211, 212–
    14, 219–20
Raging Bull (1980) 84
Rainmaker, The (1997) 57
Rampart (2011) 71n11
Rand, Ayn 82, 164, 202–3, 222n5
Ready Player One (2018) 56, **58**,
    113
Reagan, Ronald 12, 71n16
rebellion 80, 104–5, 106, 129, 180, 189;
    slave 104–5, 106, 131; see also
    movements
reception 26, 89; see also decoding
recession see economic crisis
reformable critique 7, 57–8, **59**, 127–8
reforms 2, 54, 55, 59, 126, 128;
    non-reformist xii; see also reformable
    critique
regulations 14, 21, 30n14, 41, 48, 64,
    82, 126, 143, 216; deregulation 16;
    unregulated capitalism 105

religion 19, 78, 86, 192n3, 213; see also
    Scientology
Rendition (2007) **59**
rent parties 213, 214–15, 216, 217
Report, The (2019) 129
repression 127, 191; see also police;
    security forces
Republicans Party 41, 71–2n18, 94,
    128, 158
re-transcoding 143–4, 150, 158;
    see also transcoding; transferable
    re-transcoding
revolution 21, 52, 69–70n7, 79, 103,
    104, 105, 106, 131, 140, 163,
    168, 173, 185, 186, 189, 209, 222,
    222n13, see also Haitian Revolution
revolutionary 23, 52, 76, 79, 104, 105,
    107, 142, 180; consciousness 21;
    subject 201, 205, 220–2
Richard Jewell (2019) **58**
Richie Rich (1994) 56, **58**
right wing 65, 71n16, 80, 97n29,
    106, 202
rights 62, 111, 141, 142; rights of man
    105, 108, 180; equal 97n38; gay 166;
    women's 27; see also human rights;
    property, rights
Riley, Boots 113
riots 139, 141, 198, 209
rituals 69–70n7, 75, 78, 87, 88, 89,
    93, 212; interpretive 92–3
Road, The (2009) 19
Robocop (1987) **58**, 93
Robocop (2014) **56**
RoboCop 2 (1990) **58, 60**
romance (genre) 21, 28, 41, 42
Rome, ancient 102, 104–6, 107
Roosevelt, Franklin D. 64, 129
Roots (1977) 144n26
Roots (2016) 131
Rope of Sand (1949) 190–1
Rosewater (2014) 129, 144n16
Ruffalo, Mark 170n24
ruling class see class, ruling
Runaway Jury (2003) 56, **58**
Runner Runner (2013) **56**
Russia 15, 23, 95, 106, 139, 140
Ryan, Michael 142, 143, 150

Said, Edward 67
sampling method 38, 39–40, 42–3, 44,
    49–50n20
Sanders, Bernie 67, 164, 221
Saved from the Titanic (1912) 24, 49

Scales Jr., Robert H. 74
Scarface (1983) 86
Scheper-Hughes, Nancy 93
Schindler's List (1993) **64**
Schoenberg, Arnold 170n25
Scholem, Gershom 179–80
science fiction (genre) 5, 18, 21, 30, 32n43, 59, 92, 115–16, 173, 177, 197
Scientology 78–9
Scorsese, Martin 84, 85, 89–90
screen media texts 3, 45
screenplay 42, 106, 143, 187, 188, 189, 192n13, 193n40
Scrooged (1988) **56**
security forces 55–6, 61, 80; *see also* military; repression
Selma (2014) **64**
semiotics 26, 102–3
Sentinel, The (2006) 71n10
Severance (2022) **56, 61**
sex 2, 89, 90, 116–17, 151, 153, 159
sexuality 97n38, 136, 157, 160–1, 162–3, 164, 169n9, 186
sexism 28, 59
sex-love 17, 168
sexual harassment 169n5
Shawshank Redemption, The (1994) **58**
Shock and Awe (2017) 144n17
Shooter (2007) **63**, 81, 97n28, 128, 131
Sicario (2015) 55
Sidney, Philip 6, 22–3, 32n49, 32n50, 32n51, 179
Siege, The (1998) **58**
Siegel, Don 42
signs 29, 102–2, 106, 107, 136, 163; iconic 29
silent film (genre) 23, 90, 102
Silkwood (1983) 128
Silver City (2004) 121n39, 144n10
sitcom (genre) 27, 111, 116, 158, 159, 162
sketch comedy (genre) 145n55, 156–8
slavery 16, 31n22, 104–5, 131, 173, 212, 214; representations of 105, 106, 107, 113, 131, 182; *see also* slave revolts, *see* rebellion
Smith, Adam 88, 105
Smithson, Robert 218–20
Snowden (2016) **59**
Snowpiercer (2013) 19, **60**, 192n10
social movements *see* movements
social order 20, 83, 94, 106, 163, 174–5, 178, 187, 190–1; cultural order 29; economic order 129

social psychology *see* psychology
social realism 24
social reproduction 220
social status 17, 81, 90, 124, 136, 168
socialism 16, 21, 32n40, 68, 103, 106, 128, 132–3, 140, 207; libertarian 105; socialists 17, 77, 132, 164
Soderbergh, Steven 57
solidarity 1, 90, 145n30, 205, 206–7, 208, 212, 215, 222n13
Sorry to Bother You (2018) 112–3, 127, 133, 144n11
South Africa 131, 190
South America *see* Latin America
Soviet Union 32n54, 77, 106, 173, 174, 180; representations of the 107, 129, 145–6n56; *see also* Marxism, Soviet; Stalinism
Spadoni, Robert 46
Spartacus 103–7
Spartacus (film) (1960) 105–6
Spartacus (TV series) (2010) 106–7
Spartacus League 104
specialness 158, 182–6, 193n41
Speed Racer (2008) **56**
Stalinism 20
standardized process 25
Starship Troopers (1997) **61**, 92–3
Star Wars: Episode I – The Phantom Menace (1999) **61**, 76
Star Wars: Episode II – Attack of the Clones (2002) **61**, 76
Star Wars: Episode III – Revenge of the Sith (2005) **61**, 76
Star Wars: Episode VI – Return of the Jedi (1983) 76
Star Wars: Episode VIII – The Last Jedi (2017) 121n42
state xii, xiii, 2, 20, 21, 24, 48, 67, 74, 88, 211, 220; alternatives to 21, 150–1, 162, 167, 172, 176, 200, 210; authoritarian 79; bailout 16, 126, 12; censorship 18, 21, 32n43; critique of 3, 5, 6, 7, 20, 32n43, 38, 48, 54, 67, 68, 72, 95, 96, 106, 110, 125, 127–34, 144, 150, 181, 197–8, 205, 206, 211, 220, 221; end of 66, 165, 167–8; formation 69–70n7; ideologies 4; interests 128–31, 208, 210; intervention 12–13, 14, 15, 16, 126, 127, 198; neoliberal 12, 15, 16, 19, 57, 67; ownership 12, 71n12; police state 79; powers 25, 209;

256 Index

propaganda 68; regulatory 21, 64, 143; relationship with capitalism 11–21, 126–7, 130–1, 137, 143, 174, 193n46; representations of 3, 7–8, 18–9, 21, 39, 43–4, 46–7, 48, 55, 57, 60–1, 64–5, 69, 70, 72n19, 75, 77, 80, 81, 82–3, 86, 93, 96n11, 118–20, 127–8, 131–4, 139–41, 146n58, 150, 159, 174, 177, 184, 186, 187–8, 200, 204, 206; state planning 12; welfare 12, 13, 66, 71n12, 128; *see also* totalitarianism
status quo 5, 20, 76, 153, 157–8, 159, 161, 163–4, 166
Sticchi, Francesco 23, 121n30
stock market 13, 15, 83; New York Stock Exchange 87; S&P500 89; Wall Street 15, 76, 83, 87, 89, 165; *see also* Occupy Wall Street; *Wall Street* (1987); *Wall Street: Money Never Sleeps* (2010); *Wolf of Wall Street, The* (2013)
Stone, Oliver 65, 84
Stranger Things (2016–2022) **56**
Streetcar Named Desire (1951) 96n11
structural critiques 4, 38, 102, 108–20
studios *see* Hollywood
suburb 67, 85, 153, 183, 218–19
superhero 55, 67, 71–2n18, 76, 182; MasterBuilders 175–7, 178–9, 182–7, 189
Superstore (2015–2021) **59**
surplus-value 7, 110–12, 120
Sweedler, Milo 4, 98n60
Symbionese Liberation Army (SLA) 133
symbolic exchange value 124–5, 135–7
Syriana (2005) **56**

Tarantino, Quintan 43
Tarkovsky, Andrei 19
Taxi Driver (1976) 84
technologies 13, 65, 74, 78, 118, 132, 211, 219–20; technological innovation 141, 142, 197, 211, 219, 220; *see also* computers; history, of television; radio
television *see* history, of television; production, film and television
Terminator (1984) 18, 31, 173
Terminator 2: Judgement Day (1991) 18, 31, **60**
Terminator 3: Rise of the Machines (2003) 18, 31, 59
Tetris (2023) **56**

Thank You for Smoking (2005) 98n55, 121n40
Thatcher, Margaret 6, 11, 12–4, 67, 68–9
The World's End (2013) 18
There is No Alternative (TINA) 6, 12–16, 19, 26, 39, 53–4, 67, 106–7, 142, 197, 200
Third World 44–5, 106, 132–3
Thirteen Days (2000) **64**
This is the End (2013) 18
thriller (genre) 42, 76
Thunberg, Greta 1
TikTok 191, 212, 220
TINA *see* There is No Alternative
Tinker Tailor Soldier Spy (2011) 71n10, 97n30
Titanic (1943) 47–8
Titanic (1997) 16–17, 31n24, 168, 191, 191
Titanic effect 12–14, 68
Titanic, RMS 6, 12–14, 16–17, 23–4, 30, 30n9, 30n14, 31n17, 31n22, 31n23, 47–8, 50n26, 199
Tomorrow Never Dies (1997) 58
Tomorrowland (2015) 8, 196–21, 210, 219
Too Big to Fail (2011) 125, 127, 144n5
torture 20, 59, 129, 170n24, 175, 190
Total Recall (2012) 56, 60–1, **66**
totalitarianism 80, 174, 175
totality 24–5, 53, 69–70n7, 72n24
Training Day (2001) 71n11
Traitor (2008) 55, **58**
transcoding 142–3, 149, 150, 164; *see also* re-transcoding; transferable re-transcoding
transferable re-transcoding 8, 150, 162
transgender 169n14
transphobia *see* transgender
Treme (2010–2013) 127
Trotsky, Leon 23, 32n54
Trumbo (2015) **64**, 106, 120n16
Trumbo, Dalton 106
Truth (2015) **56**
Tulip Fever (2017) 124, 130, 136, 142–3, 148, 149, 150, 169n5
Tulip Mania 124, 130–1, 134–6, 143, 148–9

Ukraine 15
Underground (2016–2017) 131
unemployment *see* employment

Index **257**

unions 1, 2, 14, 62–4, 112;
  membership 65; organizers 62–4, 128;
  organizing 2; unionization 127
United Kingdom 6, 11, 12, 14, 16,
  68, 90–1; UK Parliament 40, 47,
  79–80, 193n30
universities 20–1, 155, 213
Up in the Air (2009) 133, 140
urban 8, 93, 124, 200, 204–7, 208–9,
  210, 213, 215, 218–19; *see also*
  country/city
utopia 23, 43, 52, 60, 66, 75, 106, 109,
  133, 139, 142, 149, 161, 168, 172–4,
  175, 176–8, 180, 188, 189, 190,
  193n30, 197, 200, 203, 205, 211,
  215, 219; allegoric 187; blueprint
  utopia 175, 180; classless 168;
  Cloud Cuckoo Land 175, 176–7,
  183, 184, 187, 189; iconoclastic
  utopia 180, 210; literary
  utopias 32n49, 32n50, 54, 176;
  prefiguring 8; pseudo-utopias 54–5;
  and totalitarianism 174, 175; utopian
  communities 8 *see also* imagination,
  utopian; More, Thomas

V for Vendetta (2005) 63, 79–80,
  106, 192n10
values 23, 29, 66, 97n38, 152,
  156, 211; capitalist 168; family 1;
  national 223n28; progressive 27
Veblen, Thorstein 136–7
Veep (2012–2019) 41, 96n19, 140
Verhoeven, Paul 92–3
Vice (2018) 56
Videodrome (1983) 188–9
villains 7, 12, 18, 44, 55, 57, 70n9,
  71–2n18, 74–8, 79–82, 83, 84, 85,
  92, 95, 96n11, 96n19, 104, 127,
  166, 187, 192n13, 199
violence 1, 27, 75, 80, 103, 113, 175,
  205, 208
vision xii, 6, 7, 21–3, 32n50, 76–7,
  139, 140–1, 142, 164, 167,
  175, 185, 189, 199, 205, 221;
  dystopian 198; utopian 174–5, 198;
  see also dystopia; utopia
Voltaire 104
voting 41, 47, 88, 92, 93–4, 128, 164,
  174, 193n49

W. (2008) 71n10
Wacquant, Loïc 107
Wag the Dog (1997) **66**, 96–7n19

Waiting for the Barbarians (2019)
  131
Wall Street *see* stock market
Wall Street (1987) 84–5, 97n68
Wall Street: Money Never Sleeps
  (2010) **56**
Wall-E (2008) 19, 174
Waller, Fats 213, 215–16, 217, 218
Wanderlust (2012) 151, 154, 156
war 1, 2, 4, 18, 19, 27, 40, 59, 60, 104,
  129, 180, 211; anti-war 103; crimes
  of 166; on drugs 129; postwar 211;
  representations of 60, 65, 90, 92,
  103–4, 106, 119–20, 131; *see also*
  Cold War; First World War; Gulf
  War; Iraq War; military
War Dogs (2016) **56**, 57
War, Inc (2008) 129, 144n10, 145n31
Washington, Irving 67
wealth 2, 11, 13, 16, 17, 59, 88, 90, 96,
  103, 123, 124, 131, 133, 134, 136,
  148, 150, 168, 190, 191; affluence
  74, 161, 177; amassing of 76, 82,
  85, 104; creation 11, 89, 112, 117;
  distribution 13; extraction 131;
  redistribution 133; wealthy people
  16, 17, 54, 59, 65, 77, 80–1, 84, 86,
  89, 102, 104, 117, 118, 121n35,
  128, 133–4, 148, 161, 168, 172, 174;
  Webb, Gary 128
Weinstein, Harvey 143, 169n5
Welles, Orson 212–13, 214, 217,
  220, 221
Wenders, Wim 53
West Wing, The (1999–2006) 27,
  71n11
western (genre) 114
White House 40, 47, 77
White Lotus, The (2021) 131
white savior 131
Widows (2018) 144n10
Wilson, Tony 89
Wire, The (2002–2008) 43, 127, 139
Wolf of Wall Street, The (2013) 85,
  89–90, *91*, 94, 97n30, 98n60
Wolff, Robert Paul 121n24
work 27, 64, 83, 84, 85, 90–1, 110–12,
  113–17, 118, 120, 121n36, 132, 133,
  135, 138–40, 141, 159, 181, 192n15,
  209, 212–13, 220; representations
  of 62, 82, 84, 87, 90, 116, 132,
  134, 137, 138, 139–40, 144n18,
  145n30, 159, 192n15, 203;
  unemployment 110–11, 154, 159,

197; underemployment 215; work/life balance 46, 159; *see also* labor
workers *see* class, working; class, laboring
Working Girl (1988) 56
World Bank, The 132
World Climate Conference 14
World Trade Organization (WTO) 132
World War I *see* First World War
World War Z (2013) 31n35, **60**
wrestling 95, 103, 107–8, 120n18

xXx: State of the Union (2005) **56, 58**

Years and Years (2019) 78, 106
Yesterday, Today and Tomorrow (1963) 206–7, 208, 215

Zamyatin, Yevgeny 177
Žižek, Slavoj 6, 15, 16, 17, 18, 19, 20, 21, 53, 162–3
Zombieland (2009) 18, 31n30, 31n35
Zoolander (2001) 144n13
Zuccotti Park *see* Occupy Wall Street